JOHN WYCLIF

GREAT MEDIEVAL THINKERS

Series Editor
Brian Davies
Fordham University

DUNS SCOTUS
Richard Cross

BERNARD OF CLAIRVAUX
Gillian R. Evans

JOHN SCOTTUS ERIUGENA
Deirdre Carabine

ROBERT GROSSETESTE
James McEvoy

BOETHIUS
John Marenbon

PETER LOMBARD
Philipp W. Rosemann

BONAVENTURE
Christopher M. Cullen

AL-KINDĪ
Peter Adamson

JOHN BURIDAN
Gyula Klima

ANSELM
Sandra Visser and Thomas Williams

ABELARD AND HELOISE
Constance J. Mews

JOHN WYCLIF
Stephen E. Lahey

JOHN WYCLIF

Stephen E. Lahey

OXFORD
UNIVERSITY PRESS
2009

OXFORD
UNIVERSITY PRESS

Oxford University Press, Inc., publishes works that further
Oxford University's objective of excellence
in research, scholarship, and education.

Oxford   New York
Auckland   Cape Town   Dar es Salaam   Hong Kong   Karachi
Kuala Lumpur   Madrid   Melbourne   Mexico City   Nairobi
New Delhi   Shanghai   Taipei   Toronto

With offices in
Argentina   Austria   Brazil   Chile   Czech Republic   France   Greece
Guatemala   Hungary   Italy   Japan   Poland   Portugal   Singapore
South Korea   Switzerland   Thailand   Turkey   Ukraine   Vietnam

Published by Oxford University Press, Inc.
198 Madison Avenue, New York, New York 10016

www.oup.com

Oxford is a registered trademark of Oxford University Press

Library of Congress Cataloging-in-Publication Data

Lahey, Stephen E.
John Wyclif / by Stephen E. Lahey.
p.   cm. — (Great medieval thinkers)
Includes bibliographical references (p.   ) and index.
ISBN 978-0-19-518331-3; 978-0-19-518332-0 (pbk.)
1. Wycliffe, John, d. 1384. I. Title.
BX4905.L34 2008
270.5092—dc22   2008013774

1   3   5   7   9   8   6   4   2
Printed in the United States of America
on acid-free paper

SERIES FOREWORD

Many people would be surprised to be told that there *were* any great medieval thinkers. If a *great* thinker is one from whom we can learn today, and if "medieval" serves as an adjective for describing anything which existed from (roughly) AD 600 to 1500, then, so it is often supposed, medieval thinkers cannot be called "great."

Why not? One answer often given appeals to ways in which medieval authors with a taste for argument and speculation tend to invoke authorities, especially religious ones. Such invocations of authority are not the stuff of which great thought is made—so it is often said today. It is also frequently said that greatness is not to be found in the thinking of those who lived before the rise of modern science, modern philosophy, and theology. Students of science are nowadays hardly ever referred to literature earlier than the seventeenth century. Students of philosophy in the twentieth century were often taught nothing about the history of ideas between Aristotle (384–322 BC) and Descartes (1596–1650). Modern students of theology have often been frequently encouraged to believe that significant theological thinking is a product of the nineteenth century.

Yet the origins of modern science lie in the conviction that the world is open to rational investigation and is orderly rather than chaotic—a conviction which came fully to birth, and was systematically explored and developed, during the Middle Ages. And it is in medieval thinking that we find some of the most sophisticated and rigorous discussions in the areas of philosophy and theology ever offered for human consumption—not surprising, perhaps, if we note that medieval philosophers and theologians, like their contemporary counterparts, were mostly university teachers who participated in ongoing worldwide debates and were not (like many seventeenth-, eighteenth-, and even nineteenth-century philosophers and theologians) people working in relative isolation from a large community of teachers and students with whom they were regularly involved. As for the question of appeal to authority: it is certainly true that many medieval thinkers believed in authority (especially religious authority) as a serious court of appeal; and it is true that most people today would say that they cannot do this. But, as many contemporary philosophers are increasingly reminding us, authority is as much an ingredient in our thinking as it was for medieval thinkers (although, because of differences between thinkers, one might reasonably say that there is no such thing as "medieval thought"). Most of what we take ourselves to know derives from the trust we have in our various teachers, colleagues, friends, and general contacts. When it comes to reliance on authority, the main difference between us and medieval thinkers lies in the fact that their reliance on authority (insofar as they had it) was often more focused and explicitly acknowledged than is ours. It does not lie in the fact that it was uncritical and naive in a way that our reliance on authority is not.

In recent years, such truths have come to be increasingly recognized at what we might call the academic level. No longer disposed to think of the Middle Ages as "dark" (meaning, lacking in intellectual richness), many university departments (and many publishers of books and journals) now devote a lot of their energy to the study of medieval thinking. And they do so not simply on the assumption that it is historically significant but also in the light of the increasingly developing insight that it is full of things with which to dialogue and from which to learn. Following a long period in which medieval thinking was thought to be of only antiquarian interest, we are now witnessing its revival as a contemporary voice—one with which to converse, one from which we might learn.

The Great Medieval Thinkers series reflects and is part of this exciting revival. Written by a distinguished team of experts, the volumes in the series aim to provide substantial introductions to a range of medieval authors.

And they do so on the assumption that these authors are as worth reading today as they were when they wrote. Students of medieval literature (e.g., the writings of Chaucer) are currently well supplied (if not oversupplied) with secondary works to aid them when reading the objects of their concern. But those with an interest in medieval philosophy and theology are by no means so fortunate when it comes to reliable and accessible volumes to help them. The Great Medieval Thinkers series therefore aspires to remedy that deficiency by concentrating on medieval philosophers and theologians and by offering solid overviews of their lives and thought coupled with contemporary reflections on what they had to say. Taken individually, volumes in the series provide valuable treatments of single thinkers, many of whom are not currently covered by any comparable books. Taken together, they constitute a rich and distinguished history and discussion of medieval philosophy and theology considered as a whole. With an eye on college and university students, and with an eye on the general reader, authors of volumes in the series strive to write in a clear and accessible manner so that each of the thinkers can be investigated by those who have no previous knowledge about them. But each contributor to the series also intends to inform, engage, and generally entertain even those with specialist knowledge when it comes to medieval thinking. So, as well as surveying and introducing, the volumes in the series seek to advance the state of medieval studies at both the historical and the speculative levels.

The subject of the present volume belongs to the period of late scholasticism. Wyclif was the most prominent English philosopher of the second half of the fourteenth century. He wrote voluminously on topics such as logic, language, epistemology, and politics. Yet he was also a very distinguished theologian. He had things to say about, for example, God's existence and nature, the Bible, grace, the sacraments, and ecclesiology.

Condemned as a heretic after his death, Wyclif stressed the authority of scripture, attacked the notion of transubstantiation, and was a vigorous critic of several aspects of the church as he took it to be in his lifetime. So he has often been regarded as a forerunner (or the major forerunner) of sixteenth-century Reformation thinkers. But was Wyclif really that? To answer this question, we need to know how his philosophical and theological conclusions compare and contrast with those of his predecessors, and this is something that Stephen Lahey explains in some detail. In addition, Professor Lahey provides us with a comprehensive introduction to

Wyclif's thinking as a whole, one which will help readers to understand it in its own terms and even without reference to the work of other authors. Wyclif wrote in both English and Latin, but many of his Latin works have yet to be translated into English. So he is somewhat hard to get to know. Professor Lahey's volume will help to make him accessible to those who do want to get to know him.

—Brian Davies

PREFACE

The study of medieval thinkers can be hampered by the compartmentaliza-
tion of contemporary academic disciplines, which demand that an individual be examined through the lens of one specific approach. The result is a
host of generally brilliant portraits of fragments of the work of a thinker for
whom the subject-based differentiation of twenty-first-century scholarly
pursuits would be utterly foreign. That a thinker was actively engaged in
ongoing theological and political conflicts is easily overlooked by a scholar
intent on fishing out a particular argument or a commentary on a specific
text. This is certainly the case for John Wyclif. For historians, he is important as the instigator of the popular lay piety movement known as Lollardy,
or as the inspiration for the Hussite rebellion in Bohemia. For some church
historians, he is remembered as the antipapal and antifraternal heresiarch
responsible for the resurrection of Donatism and the denial of transubstantiation. For others, his evangelically motivated translation of the Vulgate
Bible into Middle English and his arguments for the royal divestment of
church property earn him status as the morning star of the Reformation.
For students of English literature, the influence of his sermons and biblical
hermeneutics on Lollardy nurtured vernacular religious dialogue among
the lower and middle classes, contributing a new theological edge to prose
and poetry. For philosophers, he was an ontological realist memorable for
his attempts to oppose Ockhamist conceptualism with a fourteenth-century

ix

version of the Augustinian Platonism of Grosseteste and Anselm. For historians of political thought, he was an advocate of a royalist version of the theory of grace-founded dominion, previously employed only by papalists like Giles of Rome and Richard Fitzralph. Historians of logic remember him for his influence on the *Logica Magna* of Paul of Venice, and historians of science study his spatiotemporal atomism, as well as his use of Vitello's optics in his metaphysics.

The 600-year anniversary of his death in 1984 saw an international flowering of scholarship on many aspects of Wyclif's life, thought, and age, the culmination of a century of scholarly effort. Toward the end of the nineteenth century, the Wyclif Society had begun to edit and publish Wyclif's Latin works, hoping to establish his reputation as England's most significant contribution to the Protestant Reformation. While the Wyclif Society editions continue to serve as they make the transition from crumbling volumes on library shelves to digitized texts on the Internet, the interest has shifted away from Wyclif the proto-Protestant to Wyclif the fourteenth-century thinker. Sir Anthony Kenny's 1986 *Wyclif* in Oxford's Past Masters series describes Wyclif the professional philosopher and theologian, for whom his contemporary cognomen, doctor evangelicus, was far more fitting than the anachronistic tag of "proto-Reformer." In the years since, scholars have contributed to our understanding of Wyclif the metaphysician and semanticist, Wyclif the scriptural exegete and hermeneuticist, and Wyclif the preacher and polemicist. In what follows, I will piece together a portrait of Wyclif by relying on the scholarship that has flourished in the past few decades. As scholars have researched Oxford in the fourteenth century, it has become increasingly obvious that those, like Wyclif, who were active there in the years following the Black Death in 1349 continued a dialogue that had begun in the early years of the century. As a consequence, the reader will learn of the arguments and ideas of Wyclif's Oxford predecessors, from William Ockham and Walter Burley in the first decade through to Bradwardine, Fitzralph, Holcot, and Wodeham in the years just before Wyclif entered the university. The guiding idea behind this survey of Wyclif's thought is that he cannot be understood without an appreciation for the philosophers and theologians who preceded him; in several chapters in this volume, Wyclif's predecessors get as much attention as Wyclif himself does. Because of the extra space devoted to establishing the intellectual atmosphere in which Wyclif's thought developed, I have had to reduce the amount of attention to the relatively large body of writings that

Wyclif devoted to attacking the papacy and the friars. Those with a taste for Wyclif's antipapal and antifraternal polemics should turn to the studies I list in the notes for chapter 6. Likewise, I have made no more than passing reference to the phenomena of Lollardy and the Hussites. In the first case, readers are advised to look to the relative wealth of studies of Lollardy that have followed on the groundbreaking work of Anne Hudson. In the second, readers unfamiliar with Czech have considerably fewer alternatives beyond the pioneering work of Thomas A. Fudge, Howard Kaminsky, and Matthew Spinka. The best bibliographic resource is at http://lollard society.org.

I am indebted to Lesley Ann Dyer for making available to me her discovery of the Wyclif Society's handwritten manuscripts of *De Ydeis* and *De Tempore*, which had been left in a drawer in Trinity College library. Similarly, I am indebted to Michael Dunne, Rega Wood, Aidan Breen, Dallas Denery, Laurent Cesalli, Christina van Nolcken, Michael Treschow, and Paul Streveler, each of whom have made their scholarship available to me as I researched this book. I am particularly grateful to the late Norman Kretzman, who kindly gave me his collected notes on and translations of Wyclif's atomism, and wished me luck in studying a heretic in a field in which such a thing still matters. I am also grateful to Stella Wilks who, with the help of Diana Wood, made the collected papers of the late Michael Wilks available to me. Ian Levy, Ruth Nisse, and Anne Hudson have read and commented on sections of this book, and Brian Davies, Merryl Sloan, Patrick Hornbeck, Fiona Somerset, and Julia McQuillan have read the whole of it; to each, I am very grateful for saving me from having made unfortunate mistakes. Those that remain are my own. Ian Levy has helped immeasurably in many conversations and e-mail exchanges, and his scholarship has contributed much to what follows. Finally, I am particularly grateful to A. S. "Steve" McGrade, my dissertation advisor and mentor, who, when I said I thought that Wyclif might be a good candidate for Oxford's Great Medieval Thinkers series, heartily encouraged me. I hope this book will serve as a token of thanks for the friendly guidance he has provided me over the years.

CONTENTS

JOHN WYCLIF

WYCLIF'S LIFE AND WORK

William James commented that, while there is no special affinity between crankiness as such and superior intellect, the cranky person's extraordinary emotional susceptibility, combined with a superior intellect, shows the "best possible condition for the kind of effective genius that gets into the biographical dictionaries." The cranky are not content to sit comfortably, cultivating a rich understanding of things. Instead, they are possessed by their ideas, and "they inflict them, for better or worse, upon their companions or their age."[1] James's comments apply readily to the life and thought of John Wyclif, who began as an Oxford philosopher and theologian, but ended in tumultuous conflict, an enemy of the church hierarchy and a frustration to the Crown. Certainly, the Wyclif of popular imagination is the angry old controversialist, a John Brown figure prophesying the eventual storm of the Reformation. It is not easy to connect this vituperative critic of the papacy, the friars, and the fourteenth-century ecclesiastical status quo with the abstractions of scholasticism. Yet Wyclif's later public life is incomprehensible without an understanding of his Oxford years. Thanks to the vigor with which Wyclif was opposed by his contemporaries, we have a wealth of biographical information for him from the final dozen years of his life, but records for his first four decades are almost nonexistent.

There is no clear evidence for either the year or the place of Wyclif's birth. In earlier biographies, the Yorkshire towns of Hipswell and Wycliff-on-Tees

3

are suggested as his birthplace, and historians generally recognize the latter as most likely.[2] This tiny village is not far from Richmond castle, a northern stronghold in a time when Bannockburn and Scots raiders haunted living memory. J. M. W. Turner's romantic depictions of Richmond castle and Wycliffe near Rokeby show a thickly wooded landscape of towering hills and secluded glens. While appealing to us, in Wyclif's time, this was frontier territory, the beauty of which may have been lost on its inhabitants. We know that Wyclif's family was of lesser nobility and that his parents were married in 1319. Many priests of the age were younger sons deprived by primogeniture of landholding, so it is probable that Wyclif, likely a younger son, was born sometime in the 1320s; the accepted date is 1328. Of his early life, nothing is known, save that his first teacher was one John de Clervaux, the rector of Wycliffe Church until his death in 1362. Extant records suggest that Wyclif became lord of the manor around 1360, thereby assuming responsibility for supplying Wycliffe Church with its rector. This office was occupied by William Wyclif, a cousin of John and a fellow student at Oxford, and later by other members of his family. More important, the small landholding's overlord was the Duke of Lancaster, John of Gaunt, which may account for the genesis of Wyclif's later political affiliation.

While we know little about the actual appearance of many medieval figures, we have an idea of Wyclif's physical presence. A contemporary source describes him as having a distinctly charismatic aura and a frail, perhaps birdlike physique, while an illumination in a 1410 Prague manuscript depicts a bearded, faintly scowling scholar. Certainly, Wyclif's writings give evidence of a contentious, acerbic personality who evolved from a philosopher with a quicksilver wit to a churchman unswervingly dedicated to the pastoral responsibilities of preaching and writing. Also, we can be sure that Wyclif's native tongue was what we now call Middle English, the version of English most often encountered by students reading Chaucer's *Canterbury Tales*. Despite the historically widespread belief that Wyclif wrote voluminously in English for the spiritual edification of the laity, there is no extant text that can be attributed to him with certainty. That Wyclif spoke, probably wrote, and very likely thought in his native tongue is relevant to understanding his Latin works, though. Wyclif's Latin is difficult to understand at its best, and sensitivity to the speech patterns and vocabulary of Middle English can help to clarify at least some of the difficult areas in it.

Wyclif likely began studying at Queen's College, Oxford, in the 1340s, perhaps with an eye on a career in the law, and we know that he graduated and became a fellow at Merton College in 1356. If he began his studies in his late teens, he was at Oxford during the Black Death in 1349, and would have heard Bradwardine preach at St. Paul's in London before the latter was made archbishop of Canterbury and then died in August of that year. Wyclif's early years at Oxford correspond to the heyday of the Mertonian calculators and to the years in which the logicians Richard Brinkley, Richard Kilvington, and William Heytesbury were active. Walter Burley and Richard Fitzralph had left Oxford by the time Wyclif arrived. Wyclif entered Oxford about the same time as the logician Ralph Strode, who would later become friendly with Chaucer.

Wyclif's life was given significant direction when he was ordained as a subdeacon at St. Mary's in Yorkshire on 12 March 1351, as a deacon on 18 April, and then as a priest on 24 September of the same year, by Archbishop William de la Zouche at York Minster. Shortly thereafter, the archbishopric of York was given to John Thoresby, a Yorkshireman who had been bishop of St. David's and then of Worcester. In 1357, Thoresby wrote a catechism for the instruction of the laity, which he had translated into English verse by John Gaytrick, a Benedictine of St. Mary's, the church in which Wyclif had served. This catechism explained the elements of belief, the sacraments, the seven deadly sins, and the virtues, and quickly became well known throughout the archdiocese. Thoresby's Lay-Folk's Catechism was an attempt to realize the reformative ideals of the Fourth Lateran Council (1215–1216) as implemented in England by Archbishop John Peckham in the Lambeth Constitutions of 1281. Arguing that priestly ignorance foments popular error, Peckham's goal was to enlighten both the lower clergy and the laity, and throughout the fourteenth century, manuals for priests inspired by Peckham were common throughout England. Thoresby's catechism inspired Archbishop Islip of Canterbury to publish a similar catechism in 1361. Given his university training, Wyclif could have been involved in Thoresby's project. It is conceivable that the young priest's association with Thoresby brought him to the attention of Archbishop Islip, who would later attempt to appoint him as warden of the newly founded Canterbury College. On the other hand, it is hard to imagine Wyclif's later followers not taking advantage of the fact, had he been associated with Thoresby; indeed, the Lay-Folk's Catechism was converted into a Lollard catechism, and no mention is made of Wyclif's relation to Thoresby.[3]

Wyclif's first accomplishment at Oxford was to graduate as a bachelor in the Faculty of Arts in 1356, the year he became a probationary fellow at

Merton College. He spent the next four years pursuing a master's degree at Balliol College, during which period he was also elected to be Balliol's third master. In gaining this distinction, Wyclif had to receive the concurrence of numerous other officials at Oxford, notably Uthred of Boldon, a Benedictine scholar who was to become one of his first intellectual opponents. Upon receiving his master of arts degree, Wyclif was installed as a parish priest in Fillingham, Lincolnshire, on 14 May 1361. The next year, he formally asked the pope for a canonry in Yorkshire, somewhat closer to home, but instead was granted another parish in Bristol, Aust at Westbury-on-Trym, which he held in addition to the one in Fillingham. Wyclif was at best an infrequent figure at Westbury. Instead, he requested permission to return to Oxford, which was granted on 29 August 1363. Holding several livings in different parishes was quite common, and had Wyclif been any other scholarly priest, this pluralism would have been unremarkable. Given Wyclif's later vehement excoriation of the practice, it is difficult to understand why he engaged in it throughout his Oxford career.

In the autumn of 1363, Wyclif began his theological training, which would involve four years of lectures and several more years of experience in formal disputation. Following this demanding curriculum, the theologian in training was required to begin studying and constructing a commentary on Peter Lombard's *Sentences*. Should he finish this, he would receive a doctorate in theology.[4] All the while, Wyclif was expected to remain responsible for his parish in Fillingham and his prebend at Aust, although he exchanged Fillingham for Ludgershall, Buckinghamshire, in November 1368. Wyclif achieved a bachelor's of theology in March 1369, and a doctorate in late 1372; the three-year period between the two was full of significance for his later career.

Archbishop Simon Islip of Canterbury had founded Canterbury College at Oxford in 1361 and, perhaps remembering the promising young cleric from Thoresby's diocese, selected Wyclif to be its warden in December 1365. The college was founded to include a mixture of monks and secular, nonmonastic students, which in those times could be a volatile combination. Quarreling between the two factions had driven out the first warden, a monk named Woodhull, and the monks had little interest in the supervision of a secular priest like Wyclif. Islip supported Wyclif for a year in the face of this tension, but died and was succeeded by John Langham, who had been a Benedictine abbot before becoming archbishop of Canterbury. Langham immediately ordered Wyclif from Canterbury's wardenship, but

Wyclif would not submit to this sort of politics and appealed the case to Pope Urban V at Avignon. Urban had little love for Langham, who had earlier thwarted Avignon's attempts to exact tribute from England. Five uncomfortable years passed at Canterbury College before Urban finally decided against Wyclif. During that period, Wyclif occasionally ran afoul of the "regulars," the scholars who as monks and friars had sworn to live according to a rule.

Wyclif's Oxford Works to 1372

To understand Wyclif's academic disputes, it is important to become familiar with the body of writing he produced during the years leading up to his association with the Duke of Lancaster. What led to his reputation as the greatest secular philosophical theologian in the Oxford of his day, and why did he get involved in so many high-profile arguments with other scholars? In one sense, being involved in many noteworthy disputations was a function of being an eminent scholar. As in academia today, most noteworthy philosophers and theologians in the Middle Ages were known for their frequent and lively disputes with one another. What is significant about Wyclif's reputation is the controversy his ideas seemed to stir up among his fellows, and the impact those ideas had on academic discourse in Oxford and elsewhere over the next century. While he never shook a fireplace poker in the face of a rival, as Wittgenstein is rumored to have done, his reputation as something of a hothead flourished at Oxford.[5]

A caveat is necessary before describing Wyclif's writings in the context of his biography. We have no certainty regarding the dates of his works, beyond those few in which he makes note of a particular event, like the Earthquake Council, when positions associated with Wyclif were condemned at Blackfriars in 1382, or the Peasants' Revolt of 1381, or of a specific date. Further, it is entirely likely that Wyclif reworked the contents of all of his writings during the last years of his life in Lutterworth. The extent to which he revised individual treatises may have been minimal, for example, simple rewriting or cross-referencing, or it may have been considerable, perhaps recasting sections from his lost *Sentences* commentary into individual treatises. It is tempting to rely on cross-referencing within the works themselves for a date before which a given treatise would not have been written. If, for example, we find in *De Ecclesia*, which includes discussion of a specific incident occurring in 1378, a reference to *De Incarnacione*, it is logical to conclude that Wyclif wrote the former after the latter. But our reasoning must be inductive, and our conclusion merely probable. It is entirely possible that a later copyist inserted the reference, using the first person, and even more likely that Wyclif himself put the reference in after both had been written. The majority of cross-references are in a neutral, third person, *ut dicitur* or *ut patet est* ("as it is said in," or "as it is clear in"), which suggests scribal insertion. We cannot be certain, however, in large part because we have no manuscripts we can identify with certainty to have been written by Wyclif himself. The editions published by the Wyclif Society a century ago give the appearance of static finality to treatises that Wyclif may have begun writing early in his career and continued revising until his death. Michael Wilks noted, for example, references in *De Logica, Tractatus Tercius*, a work associated with Wyclif's early days, to ideas about the Eucharist that only arose later in his life. All of this means that an intellectual biography of Wyclif must be provisional at best. I have argued elsewhere against the assumption among scholars that Wyclif had cast aside philosophical concerns for political and reformative ones after entering the service of John of Gaunt. Wyclif's continued philosophical interest is clear from the content of the treatises he wrote in royal service, and from treatises we can date with certainty to the period in Lutterworth. The ambiguity regarding certain dating of most of Wyclif's works need not keep us from an inductively consistent intellectual biography. At the very least, evidence of Wyclif's having engaged in revision of his philosophical works later in his life supports the idea that he never abandoned his earlier logical and metaphysical interests.[6] On the other hand, evidence suggesting antipathy toward the pope or the friars in the earlier works cannot be taken to mean that Wyclif had thought out his reformative ideas while still a young scholar, given that his rather jaundiced eye may well have revised these earlier writings much later in his life. In this narrative, all dates for Wyclif's works will be understood to be approximate, unless otherwise noted.

The earliest of Wyclif's works about which we know are his logic treatises. The first, *De Logica* (1360), is an exploration of the fundamentals of scholastic logic, intended to acquaint the beginning student with the complexities of formal reasoning. By the fourteenth century, logic had become highly specialized, complicated by attention to the relations holding between written and conceptual terms within propositions. It had subsumed what we today would call philosophy of language, along with the more recognizably formal science of syllogistic reasoning, and had built up such a rich vocabulary of specialized terms over two centuries as to require a handbook for easy reference.[7] Wyclif's treatise is interesting both for its frequent forays into ontological topics not usually found in introductory logic texts and for its stated purpose.

> Certain people who love God's law have persuaded me to compose a reliable treatise aimed at making plain the logic of Holy Scripture. For in view of the fact that many people go into logic having imagined that they would thereby come to know God's law better, and then, because of the tasteless concoction of pagan terms in every analysis or proof of propositions, because of the emptiness of the enterprise, they abandon it, I propose to sharpen the minds of the faithful by introducing analyses and proofs of propositions that are to be drawn from the Scriptures.[8]

Numerous similarly structured introductory logic texts survive from the later Middle Ages, but few are so explicitly aimed at elucidating the truths of scripture. The famous logician Paul of Venice composed a *Logica Parva* in 1393, which while similarly structured, is more fully developed while lacking the many references to scriptural examples that characterize Wyclif's text. Two logical treatises follow this handbook in the collection published as *Tractatus de Logica*, namely, *Logice continuacio* and *De Logica, Tractatus Tercius* (written prior to 1363), but they do not bear a strong resemblance to other scholastic logic texts, perhaps because Wyclif appears to have been unable to keep himself from wandering into ontological issues suggested by the logical and linguistic subjects at hand. More likely is the possibility that Wyclif substantially revised these works later in his life, using his early logico-semantic thought as a basis for the analysis of attendant philosophical problems. Another logical treatise is devoted wholly to *insolubilia* (1365), one of the subgenres of late medieval logic. Insolubles are paradoxical sentences or antinomies like "this sentence is false." Do such sentences say nothing at all, or do they say something simultaneously both false and true? Wyclif's approach, which we will discuss briefly in the next chapter, would interest logicians over the next century.

Two other early works address Aristotelian physics and psychology. Wyclif's commentary on the eight books of Aristotle's *Physics* has not yet been edited, nor even established with certainty to be his. His examination of how acts of the understanding relate to acts of sensation within the soul has, and indicates his conviction that philosophical realism is not inconsistent with Aristotelian thought. In *De Actibus Anime*, Wyclif examines mental acts. Are they really distinct from the mind, or are they only qualities of the mind? Or is it better to define them in terms of the genus "action" without putting all of the weight of explanation on their relation to the mind?

The first opinion suggests a propositional realism in which meaning-bearing mental acts have a reality of their own as disembodied, substanceless qualities. Initially, this seems odd, but given the linguistic philosopher's tendency to focus on propositional thoughts as having characteristics of their own, as being able to be thought simultaneously by several minds, and as being divisible into identifiable parts, it might be natural to assume that meaning-bearing mental acts have a reality apart from the mind. This is not the same as the objective being (*esse objectiva*) that Ockham briefly considered as the kind of being that concepts have, because objective being was meant to account for the existence of the intentional objects of the thoughts—what the thoughts are about—and not the being of the thought itself. Ockham never considered the possibility that thoughts could have existence apart from any minds thinking them.[9] Mental acts might also be qualities of the mind that produces them. On the analogy of substances having properties in themselves accidental to the being of the substances, the mind could have properties that convey intentionality that change over time. That is, just as red hair turns to grey, from one property to another, without a change in the underlying substantial being of the hair in which the properties inhere, so a sad mental act might become an angry one without changing the being of the mind itself.

Wyclif argues against both positions, first as ultimately incapable of explaining how the mind can produce, understand, or reflect on mental acts. Second, both positions involve metaphysical problems that raise more questions than they resolve. How can there be a substanceless quality, and in what sense is an act a quality? Both fly in the face of Aristotelian ontology. Wyclif continues his analysis by distinguishing means by which acts are individuable and how acts can have qualities or modal notions like contingency and necessity predicable of them. Both physical and mental acts, he argues, can only be defined by the common genus "act," which is itself given reality by the primary necessary truth of God's being. This primary act is the foundation of all created acts, the means by which created actions themselves have both their formal and their material being. The significance of *De Actibus Anime* is in its illustrating how Wyclif's metaphysics avoids Platonism, which supposes there to be a realm in which entities like "whiteness" or "circularity" have being apart from any substance, divine or created. This treatise also prepares the way for Wyclif's later description of the nature of universals, the existence of which relies on the ideas in God's mind, the divine mental acts by which created beings have their reality. Understanding mental acts per se prepares us for understanding the relation between divine thought and created being, even given the vast differences between the divine and human minds.

We have already paid closer attention to the earliest of Wyclif's writings than might be expected in a survey of his extant works because they illustrate two features typical of them. First, the analytic rigor with which Wyclif approaches any problem, whether it be the nature of a mental act, a universal, a sacrament, the church, or scripture, is relentless. To readers unaccustomed to fourteenth-century philosophy, including many of the nineteenth-century editors of Wyclif's Latin works, this seems to be academic nitpicking. To others, particularly philosophers trained in the second half of the twentieth century, Wyclif's zest for analysis embodies a precision comparable to contemporary philosophical debate. Second, Wyclif cannot keep himself from digressing. In his philosophical works, his hobby horse is ontology. For example, in his logical treatises, he typically begins by examining a fine point of philosophical logic, and inevitably wanders into talk of universals and particulars. He states his reason for this in *De Universalibus*: "Beyond all doubt, intellectual and emotional error about universals is the cause of all sin that reigns in the world."[10] In his later works, it is the failure of prelates, friars, bishops, and popes to live up to their ideals. His treatises on heresy, for example, begin as disquisitions on blasphemy, simony, and apostasy, but quickly turn into indictments of his fellow clergy. In each body of work, his analytic rigor and his tendency to return to specific issues suggest a mind determined to resolve error by using remorseless reason.

Thirteen of the remaining seventeen treatises that Wyclif wrote at Oxford before formally entering royal service comprise his *Summa de Ente*, a masterpiece of fourteenth-century Augustinianism. His second *summa*, the *Summa Theologie*, contains treatises he produced while associated with John of Gaunt, which we will discuss below. The *Summa de Ente* is divisible into two books, one of philosophical subjects that address our understanding of created reality, which contains seven treatises, and one of theological issues that concern the divine reality, which is made up of six treatises. Of these, the first book most fully depicts Wyclif's realist ontology and is indispensable for understanding how his philosophical theology differs from Ockhamism, Thomism, or Scotism. The second book consists of less philosophically controversial, more conventional Augustinian theology, and is likely evidence for Wyclif's commentary on the *Sentences* of Peter Lombard, the standard work required for an advanced theological degree.[11]

Summa de Ente

I.1. De Ente in Communi
I.2. De Ente Primo in Communi
I.3. Purgans Errores circa Veritates in Communi
I.4. Purgans Errores circa Universalia in Communi
I.5. De Universalibus
I.6. De Tempore
I.7. De Ente Predicamentali

II.1. De Intellectione Dei
II.2. De Sciencia Dei
II.3. De Volucione Dei
II.4. De Trinitate
II.5. De Ydeis
II.6. De Potencia Productiva Dei ad extra

Wyclif's conviction is that universals have a reality prior to and causally directive of their particulars, the significance of which we will discuss in chapter 3. He develops this ontological position throughout the first book of his first *Summa*, perhaps most fully in *De Universalibus*, which for dense argument and complexity rivals the writings of Scotus. In order to understand how the elements of *De Universalibus* fit together, one must turn back to the earlier four treatises, each of which explains aspects of Wyclif's realism leading directly to *De Universalibus*.

From our created viewpoint, explaining how things are related in the world, whether they are as fundamental as the relation of genera and species to individuals, or more complex, as in *dominium* relations, must involve reference to the universal-particular relation. The most fundamental thing understandable is being itself. Once we see how being differentiates into more specific universals, and thence into particulars, we are on the way to accurate metaphysics. Theology is directly connected to this progression. When Wyclif considers God's attributes, he explains that some are intrinsic to the divine nature, such as eternity, omniscience, and omnipotence.

Others are predicable of both divine and created nature, though only analogously. These are goodness, knowing, power, understanding, and volition. Wyclif begins with these in the second book of the *Summa de Ente*, devoting individual treatises to God's knowing, understanding, and willing. The contents of God's knowledge, the divine ideas, are the subject of *De Ydeis*, while *De Trinitate* addresses the relation of the three persons of the Trinity. We will consider these in our summary of Wyclif's conception of God's nature in chapter 3.

Wyclif's expressly philosophical works also include a discussion of Aristotelian hylomorphism in light of his realism, *De Materia et Forma*, and an exploration of the relation of body to soul in human beings, *De Composicione Hominis*. These treatises, while not part of the *Summa de Ente*, are important to Wyclif's later philosophy because the relation of soul to body, he explains, causally prefigures the relation of lord to master, which he views as the fundamental human relation in creation.[12] This is also a significant element of *De Benedicta Incarnacione*, Wyclif's analysis of the relation of divine and human natures in the incarnation. Here, he emphasizes that Christ's life as described in scripture embodies the intertwined relation of servanthood and lordship that holds between Christ's divinity and humanity. As with his conception of God's nature and the Trinity, his Christology is characterized by emphasis on the primary causative reality of the divine ideas and universals.

Throughout this book, reference will be made to "the *moderni*," a term frequently interpreted as synonymous with followers of Ockham. While this may be acceptable in contemporary historical studies, it is not accurate for fourteenth-century Oxford usage. In Wyclif's day, the term was generally used to refer to anybody active from the time of Aquinas onward. Wyclif himself uses the term with profligacy, sometimes referring to theologians like Henry of Ghent or Thomas Bradwardine, with whom he generally agrees. More often, his reference has a derisory tone, as when he charges the *moderni* with ignoring the universal "humanity's" place in Christ's assumption of created substantial form, which he holds as tantamount to closing one's eyes to the incarnation's majesty. This antagonism toward the Ockhamist rejection of realism runs throughout these early works, as does a concurrent frustration with Thomist and Scotist attempts at moderating Augustine's realism. It would be inaccurate to hold that Wyclif rejects Ockhamism as a whole, just as it would be shortsighted to ignore the influence of the Aristotelian syntheses of Thomas and Scotus on his work.[13] Throughout these expressly philosophical works, though, Wyclif's determination to emphasize the formal and efficient causal primacy of universals is never far from the subject at hand. As we will see in his later works, he did not abandon this realism. The term "modern" only came to be closely associated with Ockhamism after Wyclif's condemnation in 1415.

During the 1360s and '70s, Oxford was a battlefield on which several factions regularly met in combative disputation. As in universities today, tensions between professors in disparate disciplines regularly erupted into disputes over curriculum, university governance, and so forth. The four faculties of Oxford, and of many later medieval universities, were arts, theology, medicine, and the law. Of these, the Faculty of Arts had the most influence; each student had to master the seven liberal arts before proceeding on to the study of theology or one of the applied sciences, and Oxford's constitution ensured that the arts faculty was immune to encroachment by law or theology. This did not prevent the law faculty from attempting to draw arts students to the study of law, though, causing a marked rivalry between the two branches. Further complicating matters was the rivalry between "seculars" and "regulars," that is, between arts and theology professors who were priests associated with the hierarchy of the English church, and those who were priests or brothers associated with one of several fraternal orders of friars or monks.[14] We have already noted an instance of this tension in Wyclif's ill-fated appointment at the Benedictine-dominated Canterbury Hall. Another earlier, more notable instance is the tempest caused by Archbishop Richard Fitzralph's *De Pauperie Salvatoris*, his indictment of the Franciscan claims to apostolic poverty. Fitzralph presented the substance of his criticisms of the friars in several sermons at St. Paul's Cross in London from December 1356 through March 1357, returning to Avignon thereafter. His arguments became the subject of relentless debate at Oxford, and several of the foremost scholars during Wyclif's early days were friars determined to refute Fitzralph's arguments.

Although his later years were defined by a savage antifraternalism, Wyclif, a secular scholar, got on well with the friars at first. His early years were leavened by Fitzralph's discourse about grace, lordship, and poverty, which we will see led to his own distinctive theories of *dominium*. Among Wyclif's early fellow scholars were Thomas Winterton, an Augustinian ("Austyn") friar, and William Woodford, a Franciscan, both of whom showed sincere respect for their secular comrade's abilities.

Another friar, the Carmelite John Kenningham, argued vigorously against Wyclif's realist metaphysics, attacking it for being incommensurable with a full theological comprehension of scripture. Kenningham's arguments are important as evidence of early recognition that Wyclif's thought could lead to doctrinal error. Further, they suggest that Wyclif's personal style of argument was even more aggressive than was normal. "He says that my arguments are nothing but childish quibbles," Kenningham complained. "And that I am one of those wordy sophists who cannot distinguish between sign and signified. It is amazing that a man of such virtue allows himself such words."[15] Kenningham attacked Wyclif's theory of signification, which he held prevented a complex interpretation of scriptural commands, as well as his theory of how universals are part of the divine nature, holding that Wyclif's realism compromised correct understanding of God's unified perfection. These attacks appear in the compendium of documents attributed to another Carmelite, Thomas Netter, called *Fasciculi Zizianorum* (*The Bundle of Tares*). This is a rich source of contemporary documentation of the growth and persecution of Wyclif's ideas and provides a valuable record of his progression from Oxford don to liegeman of John of Gaunt.[16]

Wyclif's Royal Service

By November 1372, Wyclif had entered into the service of John of Gaunt, the Duke of Lancaster. Gaunt was the most powerful, and the most unpopular, individual in England in the 1370s. The third surviving son of Edward III was also the only member of the king's immediate family with a future, such as it was. The aging Edward suffered from dementia, while the heir apparent, Edward the Black Prince, was slowly dying of an infection contracted while campaigning on the Continent. The Black Prince had arranged that his younger brother John should have sufficient power to protect the dynastic line for his own son Richard, but had sowed discord among other nobles and prelates against his brother to keep John from making an attempt on the crown for himself. So John of Gaunt had custody of royal power, but no sovereignty. He had need of academic minds in his retinue, and his selection of Wyclif is not surprising. Wyclif had an agile mind, was a younger son of the lesser nobility, and was familiar with ecclesiastical politics. That the Duke of Lancaster was engaged in conflict with powerful bishops likely had nothing to do the invitation, for

Wyclif had not yet manifested the anticlericalism that would identify his later works.

One of Wyclif's first responsibilities, after receiving the living associated with the parish of Lutterworth in Lincolnshire, was to serve at a meeting between representatives of the Crown and the pope at Bruges in July 1374. The conference was ostensibly an attempt to iron out past differences on the subject of papal provisions, but in fact was meant to facilitate the flow of funds from the English church to the Crown. Wyclif's presence was unnecessary, and he returned to England that September. In the late summer, he had begun to develop his theory of *dominium*, explaining that "it is time to devote my energies as much to practical as to theoretical affairs, for as much time as God has given me."[17] His *dominium* treatises, in which he explains the relation of God's creation and subsequent lordship over creation to all instances of human lordship and servitude, mark a significant turning point in Wyclif's writing career. While he would refer regularly to metaphysical subjects in his writings, he would only address them in something resembling a sustained fashion once more, in *Trialogus*, a *summa summe*, in 1383. Now his attention was directed to producing the *Summa Theologie*, a collection of treatises on the foundation of all human law in God's law and its implications for secular politics, ecclesiology, scriptural interpretation, and crimes against God's commands. Just before beginning the work that would become his second *Summa*, Wyclif wrote *De Dominio Divino* (1373), a treatise in three books that examines the nature of God's lordship over creation. Given Wyclif's metaphysical realism, it is difficult to avoid concluding that he viewed God's lordship relation as having a primary causal bearing on human lordship relations, in the manner of a universal to particulars.[18]

The opening treatises of the *Summa Theologie* were the cause of Wyclif's first significant clashes with the church hierarchy. On the face of it, treatises on the foundation of just human law in the Ten Commandments (*De Mandatis Divinis*, 1375) and the ideal human state in Eden (*De Statu Innocencie*, 1376) seem innocent enough. In the former, there is already evidence for Wyclif's suspicion of the church's inordinate concern for temporalia, but Wyclif's contention that property ownership follows from original sin, which is outlined in these treatises, is consonant with Augustinian theology. The treatise on civil lordship that was to follow changed everything. *De Civili Dominio* (1376–1377) argued for a total royal divestment of all ecclesiastical property on this Augustinian foundation. Wyclif's argument included claims about the evils of property ownership that had been made by radical Franciscans during the poverty controversy, arguments for clerical submission to secular justice, the renunciation of papal authority, and the assertions that the damned are no part of the church and that no one in mortal sin can function as a priest. As we will see, these positions follow logically from his earlier treatises, but their effect, given Wyclif's prominence in the service of the noble most at odds with Canterbury and the papacy, was dramatic.

On 19 February 1377, Wyclif answered a summons to appear before Archbishop Sudbury, Bishop William Courtenay of London, and several other notables at St. Paul's to account for his heretical ideas. He did not appear alone, though; John of Gaunt, his associate Henry Percy, and various other nobles of the duke's retinue accompanied him to the arraignment, much to the interest of the gathering crowd of Londoners. The proceedings resembled a stereotypical press conference before a championship bout. John of Gaunt's appearance guaranteed that little of substance would occur, given his well-known energetic antipathy for England's ecclesiastical establishment, and little did occur beyond some name calling, grumbled threats, and acrimonious posturing. Upon hearing the duke threaten to drag Courtenay out of the chapel by his hair, the crowd erupted in clamorous rage against the nobles, and the arraignment dissolved into confusion. Had it not been for the duke's soldiers, a full-scale riot would have followed. As it was, Wyclif and his protectors escaped to safety elsewhere, while the mob spent the next day tearing London apart in search for the hated duke.

It is unlikely that the duke had paid much attention to the substance of Wyclif's arguments. The arraignment at St. Paul's had been an opportunity for him to humiliate his enemies, and the angry Londoners had interceded too quickly for his purposes. John would bide his time and wait for a new chance to attack the bishops. Wyclif, perhaps sensing that he had been used by his patron, attempted to address criticisms of *De Civili Dominio* made by his Franciscan colleague William Woodford, hoping that his many arguments taken from canon law, patristic authority, and especially from scripture would help to win over his erring fellow clerics. The result, the second and third books of the treatise, introduces many of the topics that would later occupy Wyclif's full attention, including the church's need for pastoral reform, the problems inherent in devoting one's life to a monastic or fraternal rule, the nature of heresy, and the place of scripture in a life of faith.[19]

The English bishops were not the only church authorities alarmed by *De Civili Dominio*. The pope, who had until very recently been based in Avignon, had moved to Rome. Unaware of the theatrics at St. Paul's, Gregory XI issued a series of five bulls on 22 May 1377, demanding that Sudbury and Courtenay address the problem by extracting a confession from Wyclif and imprisoning him to await judgment from Rome. Should Wyclif go into hiding, Gregory continued, he should be ferreted out. Judgment from Rome would have been contingent on the Crown's reaction to Wyclif's seizure. Gregory had been trying to reconcile England with France, and may have had Wyclif's disposition in mind as a means of persuading Edward to reconsider his antipathy toward the French. Certainly, the language Gregory used made it clear that he expected Edward to recognize the danger that Wyclif posed to England's well-being:

> Recently, with great bitterness of heart we have learned from the report of many trustworthy persons that John of Wiclyffe, rector of the church of Lutterworth, of the diocese of Lincoln, a professor of holy writ—would that he were not a master of error!—has burst forth in such execrable and abominable folly, that he does not fear to maintain dogmatically in said kingdom and publicly to preach, or rather to vomit forth from the poisonous confines of his own breast, some propositions and conclusions . . . which threaten to subvert and weaken the condition of the entire church.[20]

Gregory appended a list of nineteen errors of which Wyclif was accused, should Edward miss the significance of the problem. These catalog Wyclif's accusations of the church's supposed abuse of its authority, including papal excommunication, the validity of its claims on property willed to it by civil lords, and the church's refusal to recognize secular authority over its temporal goods. Were the Crown not to act on such accusations, the implication was that the progress that had been made in England's relations with the papacy would be jeopardized. Even had Edward been lucid, Gregory's timing was unfortunate; his bulls did not reach England until December, by which time Edward had died, and John of Gaunt was made the young Richard's protector. The pope's luck held, however, in that the new government's reaction to Wyclif's approach was less than enthusiastic.

Arnald Garnier, a papal agent assigned to collect funds, had begun pressing the Crown for a substantial sum of money. The child king's council requested that Wyclif provide a written assessment of whether or not the kingdom of England could lawfully withhold these funds, which he provided in his *Responsio* of 1377. Here, he attacked the papal presumption of worldly pomp, just as he had in *De Civili Dominio*. The council's reaction to Wyclif's rousing argument supporting its request was enigmatic; it ordered him to cease his attacks on the church and proceeded to give Garnier what he had requested. Had Wyclif been an influential advisor to the duke, it is hard to imagine that he would have been treated this way. Appearances suggest that the government had wind of Gregory's bulls, and acted with their general sentiments in mind, to give Gregory the impression that his concerns were being taken seriously. When the bulls were published shortly before Christmas, Wyclif was in residence in Oxford. The vice chancellor ordered him held in Black Hall, presumably believing himself to be obeying papal command, but friends soon released Wyclif, who was likely spluttering with rage. Archbishop Sudbury and Bishop Courtenay acted quickly and ordered Wyclif to appear at Lambeth palace for a formal trial no later than 27 March 1378.

This time, the duke could not afford to shout down the bishops, which would have been a direct affront to the papacy, something the young Richard's court could ill afford. So it looked as if Wyclif might have to answer for his opinions about widespread clerical negligence to the authority that had the most to lose from his version of reform. The prelates were rumored to be set on destroying him, whatever the shape of his arguments, ensuring a humiliating trip to Rome, imprisonment, and possibly torture and death. On the scheduled day of the trial, though, someone in the royal family undercut the bishops. As the trial began, Sir Lewis Clifford, a haughty knight in the royal retinue, announced to the assembled bishops that Joan, the queen mother and widow of the Black Prince, would not allow any ecclesiastical court to presume to pass judgment on Wyclif, who had acted in royal service. No doubt very relieved, Wyclif proceeded to explain that he had not explicitly said that the church was presently in the state that he had been excoriating; such judgments were the province of political authorities, not priests. While showing his blindness to the bishops' indignation that his arguments implied that they ought not to claim autonomy from secular authority, this explanation accords with the argument of *De Civili Dominio*. Thomas Walsingham, the contemporary chronicler of the Lambeth trial, fumes that Wyclif dissembled, when in fact he likely honestly believed that his explanation would mollify the prelates. It is impossible to know whether Joan herself interceded for Wyclif, or whether

her younger brother-in-law John of Gaunt employed her revered name for his purposes. Given the royal council's earlier orders that Wyclif desist his troublemaking, though, it appears that the duke was beginning to weary of his servant's zeal. The zealous and cultured Sir Lewis Clifford would later be among the seven highly placed knights accused of having Lollard sympathies in the early days of the movement.

Wyclif's usefulness to the duke ended later that year. Two English soldiers, Robert Hauley and John Shakyl, had captured a Spanish nobleman while on campaign with the Black Prince eleven years previously, and had been holding him for ransom, as was common in medieval warfare. In 1377, the Crown had decided that it would profit more from holding the nobleman directly and ordered the two soldiers to surrender their hostage. They refused and were thrown into prison. The next summer, they managed to escape and received sanctuary at Westminster Abbey. On 11 August, the duke's soldiers broke into the abbey during mass and tricked Shakyl into fleeing to the steeple, which did not count as sanctuary. Meanwhile, Hauley had run to hide at the altar, where he was caught and butchered by the soldiers, who also murdered one of the priests celebrating the Eucharist. Walsingham reports that the soldiers took Hauley's corpse by the ankles and heaved it outside, "bespattering everything with his blood and brains."

Canterbury's reaction was outrage, although the cautious Archbishop Sudbury waited three days before formally excommunicating the soldiers involved. That October, when Parliament met at Gloucester, the archbishop made formal demands that those responsible, namely, John of Gaunt, be held accountable for polluting Westminster and violating sanctuary. Wyclif had been asked to represent the duke, who presumably expected his servant to have learned about diplomacy from the Lambeth incident. His arguments showed that he had learned little: sanctuary was in no wise permissible when the royal authority was so flagrantly threatened, he argued, and while the violence was regrettable, it had been brought on by Hauley's aggressive behavior. Parliament tabled discussion of the incident, but Wyclif's unsuitability as a public spokesman for the Crown was by now painfully obvious to the duke.[21]

Royal service must have been disagreeably confusing to Wyclif, who had been used to the intellectual duels of Oxford. Why would his lord ask him for arguments, which he could craft with such incisive skill and theological purity, only to back away from them as being too likely to upset his opponents? Was that not the whole point? He had been engaged for some years in running debate with the eminent lawyer and Mertonian logician Ralph Strode, who disagreed forcefully with Wyclif's determinism and its implications for a church of the predestinate. Strode argued that Wyclif's ideas led to a dozen distinct problems linked to predestination and presented a host of objections about the dangers of total church reform.[22] A lawyer of some renown, Strode had not quailed before Wyclif's intellectual onslaught; he had responded in kind. On the other hand, the prelates responsible for the church's welfare hid behind the questionable authority of their office and of the power of the pope of Rome. Could the duke not see that this gave evidence of their own guilt?

When Gregory XI died in March 1378, Bartolomeo Prignano, well known for his probity and devotion to the ideal of apostolic poverty, became Pope Urban VI. Hoping that this election signaled a new beginning for an ailing church, and suspecting that Gregory had harbored personal animus against him, Wyclif wrote to Urban to explain the orthodoxy of his thought. He never lost hope that Urban would live up to his judicious reputation, as is clear from an extant 1384 letter to that pope.[23] Unfortunately, Urban rarely gave evidence of his earlier sagacity. Shortly after his election, he displayed a pugnacity that contributed to the French cardinals' decision to elect Robert of Geneva to the papacy instead. With the election of Clement VII, the Western schism had begun, and prospects for serious, sober dialogue with the papacy on reform had vanished.

During these years, Wyclif wrote many of the treatises for which he is now best known, including *De Veritate Sacrae Scripturae* (1377–1378), *De Ecclesia* (1378–1379), *De Officio Regis, De Officio Pastoralis,* and *De Potestate Pape* (all 1379). In addition, throughout the 1370s, Wyclif maintained a heavy schedule of preaching and biblical scholarship, producing several hundred sermons and commentaries on the Bible, including *Postilla super totam Bibliam* and *Opus Evangelicum.* As we consider the arguments of the works of the late 1370s in later chapters, we should remember that their author made weekly appearances in London to preach and was probably involved in pastoral responsibilities at Oxford. When he left Oxford in the summer of 1381, he went to serve as the parish priest for the Leicestershire village of Lutterworth, where he continued his scholarly projects as he cared for the needs of the villagers. While reading his polemical outbursts against the abuses he perceived throughout England and his sustained arguments for a renewed church, it is easy to forget that Wyclif was all along actively engaged in *cura animarum*, the care of souls.

The Bible, Rebellion, and Earthquake

Wyclif's last year in Oxford was one of controversy, in which ongoing arguments that he and his disciples had with various opponents escalated into
hostile conflict. His followers were primarily younger, secular scholars eager
to defend their master's views against their more conservative opponents,
who tended to be monks or friars. Among these followers, three stand out
because of their later roles in the genesis of Lollardy: Philip Repingdon,
Nicholas Hereford, and John Purvey. Repingdon was held in high regard
among his fellows at Oxford, and his extant writings give evidence of a
broad, seasoned theological mind. His sensitivity to theological error led
him to disavow his Wycliffite leanings early on, shortly after Wyclif himself left Oxford, forever vilifying himself to his former associates and their
Lollard disciples.[24] Repingdon went on to become the bishop of Lincoln
and personal confessor to Henry IV. He would even receive a cardinal's
hat, but from Gregory XII, whose papal authority would ultimately be nul-
lified. Despite almost joining the princes of the church, though, Repingdon
never abandoned his belief in the need for clerical reform; however, unlike
the Wycliffites, he believed such reform to be possible from within the hierarchy of the church.[25]

Hereford and Purvey remained within the Wycliffite fold longer, one
at least until shortly after his master's death and the other for the rest of his
life. Hereford, a zealous preacher, was condemned along with Repingdon
by Archbishop Courtenay in May 1382. Rather than bow to local ecclesiastical authority, as Repingdon would do, Hereford chose to travel to Rome to
appeal personally to Urban VI. He was immediately imprisoned, but managed to escape somehow and return to England. There, he continued leading Lollards until 1391, when he was forced to recant in Nottingham. Ever
the zealot, he became a vigorous prosecutor of Wycliffism and continued
for the rest of his days to serve his new masters as enthusiastically as he had
Wyclif. Purvey, known as the librarian of Lollardy, was made to recant in
1401 and was given a benefice near Archbishop Arundel's castle, where he
struggled to restrain himself from heresy for three years. Finally, he could
stand no more and returned to Lollardy for the rest of his life.[26]

The debates at Oxford shifted from intellectual duels to theological
combat following Wyclif's volte-face regarding the Eucharist. As we will
see in a later chapter, Wyclif's position evolved from orthodoxy to heresy.
In 1376, he had embraced transubstantiation, in which the bread and wine

become the true body and blood of Christ in substance while retaining the physical properties of bread and wine, but he would come to reject this as metaphysically impossible several years later. William Berton, a secular scholar from Merton College and the new chancellor of Oxford, sensed a shift in the political wind when the Crown attempted to mollify the church after the Hauley-Shakyl incident. Likely hoping that this signaled the end of Wyclif's political protection, he summoned a formal council of twelve scholars—eight regular and four secular—to weigh the orthodoxy of Wyclif's views on the Eucharist. Given Berton's leeway in selecting the members of the council, it is surprising that any of its members were disposed to entertain the prospect of Wyclif's innocence, but four eventually concluded that he was orthodox. The remaining eight (one apparently abstained) were convinced that he was a heretic, and they published a list of twelve conclusions that included the demand that Wyclif's teaching be banned at Oxford. This document was formally promulgated by a public reading, at which Wyclif was present. Having had no knowledge of the chancellor's actions, Wyclif was thunderstruck and responded, "Neither the chancellor, nor any of his accomplices, can cast aspersions on what I say!"[27]

Rather than register an appeal in the approved academic courts, Wyclif immediately asked John of Gaunt for help. Mindful of his responsibility, the duke complied, advising his charge to be silent henceforth. Wyclif was incapable of this and published a formal response on 10 May 1381, his *Confessio* (see appendix). Here, he declaims his fidelity to the spirit of the church fathers and doctors and accuses his opponents of sliding into innovations that sully the sacrament and the church itself: "Woe to this generation of adulterers, who puts more belief in the testimony of an Innocent or a Raymond than the sense of the gospel . . . who moulds the later church in ways contrary to the earlier!"[28] Blistering responses came from the Franciscan John Tissington, the Augustinian Thomas Winterton, and several Benedictines, but Wyclif seems to have ignored them. There is an anecdote from this period that could account for this. Wyclif, sick to the point of death, is lying in bed, surrounded by friars intent on rescuing him from his heresy. Wyclif rallies, rising up and crying, "I shall not die, but shall live and declare the works of the Lord!"[29] Whatever the state of Wyclif's health, this was his last season at Oxford; he left for Lutterworth in the fateful summer of 1381, when rebellion was in the air.

During this period, Wyclif was involved in the project for which posterity remembers him best, the translation of the Bible from the Vulgate

Latin into English. By the fourteenth century, scripture was still largely beyond the reach of English folk unable to read Latin. Several much earlier Old English translations existed, ascribed to Alfred the Great, Bede, and Aelfric, and there were French versions as well, one completed as recently as 1355. Richard Rolle, the Yorkshire mystic, had translated the Psalms into English earlier in the fourteenth century, and there were other translated books and sections available in scattered locations, but no complete vernacular scripture existed. As a young priest, Wyclif had likely been inspired by Archbishop Thoresby's translation of the catechism; by now, it had become clear to him that this was not enough. The church's present state demanded a wide-scale return to the truths most clearly expressed in scripture itself, and Wyclif determined that a translation project was the best means of achieving that end.

It is easy to confuse this with what was to follow in the Reformation, but Wyclif was not intent on a *scriptura sola* theology. As we shall see in a later chapter, Wyclif's theology of scripture did not involve the idea that the reader needed nothing but faith to read the Bible. Nor, in fact, was Wyclif himself actively engaged in the actual translation. Scholarship indicates that work on the Old and New Testaments was undertaken by John Purvey, among others, at first in Oxford, then in Lutterworth and elsewhere, into the 1390s. There are 250 manuscripts of the Wycliffite Bible that survive, of which 21 contain the entirety of both testaments. This is the largest number of copies known for any medieval English text; in comparison, only 64 copies of Chaucer's *Canterbury Tales* exist, none complete. Of these Bibles, there appear to be two versions, one stiffly literal, the other more natural and less Latinate. Tradition holds that Hereford was responsible for most of the literal version, and Purvey for most of the latter, with Wyclif serving as the inspiration and guide for one, if not both. More recent scholarship suggests otherwise; the scope of this project and the variation in translation styles suggests a host of anonymous hands at work, thereby forestalling attempts to trace individual personalities behind the translations.[30]

The summer of 1381 was a tumultuous one throughout southern England. Early June saw a popular rising against taxes in Essex, which spread within a fortnight through Kent, Middlesex, Hertfordshire, Cambridgeshire, Norfolk, and Suffolk to London. Its leaders, Wat Tyler and a vagrant priest named John Ball, rallied a huge mob against injustices they perceived in both secular and sacred rule, and for a brief period, both church and Crown were in serious danger. Riots and burning in London and its outskirts led to the capture and murder of Archbishop Simon Sudbury, among other notables. While the mob also burned John of Gaunt's Savoy palace, the duke himself was in Scotland, where he remained for a time. The weekend of 15–17 June saw similar violence throughout southern England, with crowds hurling documents that provided legal structure to the feudal machinery into bonfires. The young Richard II, in what would turn out to be the highpoint of his reign, managed to quell the rebellion outside London by sheer force of his youthful character, and Tyler and Ball were hastily executed. Thereafter, the revolt fizzled out, although its clamor echoed in the minds of ecclesiastical and royal authorities for the next quarter-century. That so much rage had been directed against the church, and that it had come to a head so quickly, led many among the clergy to connect Wyclif's preaching and writings to the uprising. Had Wyclif restricted his activities to Oxford, these accusations would be easily dismissed, but his disciples were active in the world outside of academe.

Wyclif's disdain for the friars was founded on his anger that their orders were defined by manmade sets of rules, but not on their dedication to a life of apostolic purity. If we live the apostle's life as imitators of the rule that Jesus the man exemplified, he reasoned, we are but "Jesusans," followers of a man. If grace inspires us to a life in faithful service to God, which is likely to result in a life of apostolic poverty, we are "Christians," followers of the Christ.[31] To outward appearances, the results are the same, but Wyclif was convinced that it was the mediation of another man's interpretation of scriptural truth that made monks or friars prone to error. Why rely on the teaching of Francis, or Benedict, or Dominic when one can learn to read scripture for oneself? The result was that Wyclif's disciples took on the cast of a mendicant order of preachers whose mission was to bring scripture's truth to everyone. Preaching this truth involved exposing the present evils of political ambition and greed afflicting the church hierarchy, which illustrated the divergence between scripture's ideal and ecclesiastical reality.

Contemporary chronicles describe Wyclif's "poor preachers" wandering the countryside in russet robes, enthusiastically fomenting discord in an already disaffected populace. One chronicler, Thomas Walsingham, is unequivocal in connecting these preachers with the revolt of June 1381, decrying Wyclif's teachings as the cause of the fire and death of rebellion. Scholars today are less likely to equate the two phenomena of Wyclif's preachers and the rebellion, although many agree that some crossover was likely. John Ball, the vagrant priest and rebel, claimed Wycliffite sympathies, but his connection to Wyclif's movement is doubtful. Interestingly, Wyclif's condemnation of the rebellion is tepid, considering his allegiance to the unpopular duke. While the violence and loss of life are lamentable, he wrote, the common people "acted a little beyond the law." Had secular authority acted to divest the church of its ill-gotten political station, such unpleasantness could have been avoided.[32] While it is hard to believe that Wyclif actually delighted in the murder of Sudbury, it is equally difficult to overlook the *schadenfreude* in his comments.[33]

The new archbishop of Canterbury wasted no time in connecting Wyclif with the revolt. William Courtenay, the bishop of London and a long-time opponent of Wyclif, was elevated to the See of Canterbury in January 1382. He was only able to begin his duties, though, upon receiving the pallium from Urban VI, which he did on 6 May. Determined to stamp out Wycliffism at Oxford, the source of its respectability for the middle and upper classes, Courtenay summoned seven other bishops, sixteen masters of theology, fourteen doctors of civil and canon law, and six bachelors of theology to council in the chapter house of the Dominicans (known as Blackfriars) on 17 May 1382. For several days, the council deliberated on the orthodoxy of at least twenty-four separate propositions that Courtenay had culled from Wyclif's writings, each member testing each proposition for the taint of heresy. Four days later, the council reconvened and began formal discussion. That day, London was shaken by a rare and violent earthquake, which terrified several council members. Could God be on Wyclif's side? Courtenay would brook no such sentiment:

> For as there are held in the bowels of the earth the air and spirit of infection, and which escape by means of some earthquake, by means of which the earth is purified not without great violence, so there were previously buried in the hearts of the reprobate many heresies of which the realm has been cleansed after their condemnation, but not without travail and great effort.[34]

The sense of the propositions in question suggests a shift away from the comparatively innocent propositions that Gregory XI had condemned in 1377. Now, Wyclif was guilty of denying the efficacy of the mass, denying transubstantiation, denying papal authority, and worst of all, denying a priest's capacity to carry out his office should he not be in a state of grace. This last proposition is the Donatist heresy against which Augustine himself struggled. Can Wyclif have knowingly countenanced so anti-Augustinian a position? As we will see in a later chapter, this is not as easily answered as Courtenay's council believed. Wyclif did indeed deny that a cleric in a state of sin has just authority to execute his office, but he did not believe this to be Donatism. While Wyclif dismissed the Blackfriars council as friars and bishops in conclave to condemn England and Christ himself as heretical, Courtenay succeeded in having a royal proclamation against false and heretical preaching promulgated throughout the realm on the force of the Earthquake Council's conclusions. Within the month, the new archbishop was free to begin a vigorous, nationwide prosecution of Wycliffism.

The first instance of Courtenay's success was at Oxford. While Wyclif had been in rural isolation for almost a year, Courtenay saw the university as swarming with his disciples. Foremost was Philip Repingdon, who actively preached Wycliffism and recruited more "poor preachers." Oxford's chancellor, Robert Rigg, would have none of Courtenay's attempted interference and reacted angrily to the archbishop's pressure. Rigg was called to a second Blackfriars council, and on 12 June 1382 was forced to give in to ecclesiastical power. Repingdon and his associate John Aston were immediately called to Blackfriars to recant, which they refused to do. The council excommunicated them, and the die was cast. Refusal to recant Wycliffite beliefs meant excommunication and opprobrium, virtual suicide for any medieval scholar. To avoid this, scholars had to formally disassociate themselves from Wyclif's thought, and Wycliffism soon gave up the ghost at Oxford.

Wyclif spent his last few years as a parish priest at Lutterworth but did not enjoy a peaceful retirement there. During those three years, he wrote a truly voluminous body of treatises directed against the problems that plagued the church, its priests, and Christendom as a whole. Many were relatively short pieces with titles like "On Christ and His Adversary Antichrist," "On False Commands and Other Subtleties of the Antichrist," "On the Devil and His Parts," "The Empty Religions of the Monks," and "On the Loosing of Satan," which were polemical diatribes against the papacy and the friars. Others were explicit commentaries on the Gospel of Matthew, which were filled with references to the present sorry state of the church. Several were directed at one contemporary event that especially infuriated Wyclif. Henry Despenser, the bishop of Norwich, undertook a crusade against the French in Picardy, ostensibly to fight supporters of Clement VII, the French pope, but primarily to shore up English interests in Flanders. Despenser led an army of professional soldiers, mercenaries, and thugs from Calais to Dunkirk to Ypres in the summer of 1383 in an improvised *chevauche* of looting, burning, and killing. As soon as the French army was in position to destroy Despenser, the campaign dissolved in confusion, and the bellicose bishop returned to England in disgrace. Wyclif vented his rage against a purported servant of Christ who indulged in the obscenity of warfare and plunder in tracts like "On the Torment (Against War of the Clerics)."

The last significant work that Wyclif completed was *Trialogus*, an overview of all that had occupied his mind from his early Oxford days through to 1383. Approachable summaries of his ontology, philosophical theology, and conception of human nature flow naturally into discussions on the nature of the incarnation, the founding and purpose of the church, the sacraments, scripture, and explorations of virtues, vice, penance, and salvation. Any suspicion that his earlier interest in metaphysics had waned is dispelled in this *summa summe*, which is framed in the form of a three-way conversation among Alithia (Wyclif's version of pure philosophy), Phronesis (Wyclif himself), and Pseustis (the infidel). Unlike his earlier, academic works, Wyclif apparently meant this to be read by a non-academic, educated upper class. It is refreshingly free of the apparatus of formal argument, and moves at what, for Wyclif, must have been a very brisk pace. Absence of mention of Despenser's crusade suggests that it was completed before the summer of 1383. Perhaps most notable is that Wyclif had suffered a stroke in November 1382, but apparently did not allow this to interfere with the work's composition.[35]

Wyclif's final work is *Opus Evangelicum*, an exegetical analysis of Matthew 5–7 and 23–25, and John 13–17. Unlike his other exegetical works and sermons, the *Opus Evangelicum* ranges from biblical commentary, to philosophical theology, to antifraternal and antipapal polemics. The last two volumes are entitled "Of the Antichrist" and contain some of Wyclif's most vehement indictments of the misuse of clerical office. He does not hesitate to identify the pope, or popes, with Antichrist here, although it would be a mistake to interpret this as later antipapalists who made similar claims were to do. It is not clear that Wyclif's Antichrist is the harbinger of apocalypse, for he says, "Any person, whether an individual or a group, who is perceptibly against Christ according to the sense of Scripture, is Antichrist."[36]

In addition to these treatises, Wyclif continued to compose and preach sermons to the very last. It is interesting to speculate what his South

Leicestershire parishioners made of their fiery pastor and his entourage of preachers and hangers-on. While it is tempting to assume that most paid little attention to the finer points of Wyclif's program of stipulating the universal applicability of the law of the Gospels, this would follow the Enlightenment canard that medieval commoners were superstitious illiterates. Twentieth-century scholarship suggests that literacy, and hence appreciation for the nuances present in Wyclif's sermons and treatises, was more widespread than previously believed.[37] That Wyclif made his ideas available in English is certain; he writes that he has translated some of his antifraternal writings into the common tongue in *Trialogus*.[38] Unfortunately, none of the Middle English writings attributed to Wyclif by earlier editors can be ascribed to him with certainty, as Anne Hudson and Margaret Aston have amply established.[39]

In the midst of his work on the *Opus Evangelicum*, Wyclif was no doubt aware that the end was near. In 1381, he had written that death would be a gift, "the freeing from the prison of the body that our soul like an eagle may soar on high."[40] It is likely that Wyclif had become physically incapacitated by his first stroke and that many of his duties had been shouldered by John Horn, his curate at Lutterworth. Horn writes that Wyclif had been attending mass, and that, at the elevation of the host, he had fallen down paralyzed and speechless by a second stroke. He lingered for three days and died on 31 December 1384.

Wyclif's story does not end without a macabre coda. His writings and teachings were formally condemned at the Council of Constance in 1415, the same event at which the Bohemian priest Jan Hus, who had been influenced by Wyclif, was burned for heresy. While he had never been excommunicated, Wyclif was declared to be a heresiarch, the founder of a new heresy, and on 4 May 1415, the council ordered that he be exhumed and burned. These orders were not carried out for some time, possibly because Philip Repingdon, the bishop of Lincoln and thereby the one responsible for this act, could not bring himself to do it. It was not until the spring of 1428 that a party of churchmen exhumed Wyclif's bones and burned them. Later Wyclif hagiographers took grisly delight in depictions of the event; Fox's *Book of Martyrs* includes a lithograph of grimacing clerics engaged in opening the coffin, disarticulating the skeleton, roasting the bones, and throwing the ashes into the river Swift.

The story of Wyclif's posthumous reputation is complex, and this survey cannot do more than make the briefest reference to it. Two movements

grew out of Wyclif's ideas in the fifteenth century. In England, the phenomenon of Lollardy, which evolved into a vehicle for vernacular theology and
political ideology, would come to be equated with treason during the reign
of Henry IV and would be the cause for the introduction of burning at the
stake into England in 1401. Despite this dire punishment, Lollardy lasted
into the sixteenth century in some quarters, although its ties to Protestant
Reform in England are tenuous at best. In Bohemia, Wycliffism catalyzed
the Czech nationalist movement and quickly became the framework on
which Hus and Jerome of Prague constructed their own reform movement.
Wycliffism came to Prague through academic connections that had arisen
from Richard II's marriage to Anne of Bohemia, and the force of its philosophical realism appealed to Czechs resentful of the *moderni* Germans who
exercised control at Charles University. Wycliffism soon became an ideology for revolution and led to open conflict with the Holy Roman Empire.
Jan Hus, the gifted preacher and leader of the movement, explicitly denied
following Wyclif into any of his heretical positions regarding the Eucharist
or Donatism, but was nonetheless made to suffer and die at the Council of
Constance in 1415. The war that broke out shortly after Hus's martyrdom
would tear apart Central Europe for decades to come. Wyclif's ideas were
known through early publication of *Trialogus* in 1525, but played no significant role in Reformation thought. His place in history grew in import
as scholarship began to view the medieval as worthy of serious study in the
nineteenth century, with a series of nineteenth-century biographies endorsing a view of Wyclif as the "morning star of the Reformation."

The work of the Wyclif Society, which flourished from the 1880s to
the 1920s, made Wyclif's Latin works available in then state-of-the-art
editions to libraries throughout the Anglophone world. His reputation
evolved during the twentieth century from a proto-Reformer to a philosopher and theologian of his age as contemporary academics learned how to
read fourteenth-century thought. Recently, the earlier view of Wyclif as
an Augustinian "ultrarealist" braving a forlorn hope against the forces of
Ockhamism has been replaced by a nuanced understanding of philosophical theology in fourteenth-century Oxford. The great growth of interest
in late medieval English literature, both of Lollards and of more orthodox writers, has sparked real interest in Wyclif's ideas as indicative of the
fourteenth-century English theological milieu, and Wyclif now seems able
to be understood as something more than heretic, or proto-Reformer, or
lone intellectual holdout facing the Ockhamist tide of change. Hume's

assessment of Wyclif as "a man of parts and learning, [having] the honor of being the first person in Europe that publically [*sic*] called in question those principles which had universally passed for certain and undisputed during so many ages," while suitable for justifying scholarly interest in the evangelical doctor over the past two centuries, no longer carries the day. Now, Wyclif is interesting not as presaging the future, nor as a reactionary throwback to earlier theological ideals, but as one of the great voices of fourteenth-century England.[41]

2

THE OXFORD CONTEXT
OF WYCLIF'S THOUGHT

In late August 1909, Charles Doolittle Walcott was prospecting for fossils
on the Burgess ridge in what is now Yoho National Park, in the Canadian
Rockies of British Columbia. He found a section of rock embedded in the
mountainside that contained the richest and strangest collection of fossils
ever discovered, which today we call the Burgess shale. Walcott struggled
to classify these tiny animals from the Middle Cambrian period, 530 million
years ago, because they just didn't fit the expectations of early twentieth-
century paleontology. So he described them as he felt they should have been,
interpreting the fossil evidence to fit into the accepted scientific expectations
of what lived in the warm sea beds of the early Paleozoic era. In the 1970s,
when paleontologists at Cambridge recognized Walcott's error, they began
to explore the fascinating possibilities of almost twenty unknown phyla.
Today, there are some thirty-two distinct phyla in the animal kingdom; the
Burgess shale shows us almost twenty directions that evolution *could* have
taken, but didn't, thus giving paleontologists and evolutionary biologists a
tremendous opportunity to explore possibilities that would otherwise never
have been imagined.

Our understanding of the period in which Wyclif developed as a theologian has changed in the same way that our understanding of the Burgess
shale has changed. What looked like a degenerate, inbred version of high
medieval theology to scholars as recently as the mid-twentieth century now

seems a century rich in innovation, particularly important for understanding the theological arguments that raged during the Reformation and the philosophical and scientific ideas of early modernity. This is thanks to scholars committed to state-of-the-art editions of texts, to historians of thought tracing the development of ideas, and to philosophers who have been influenced by the analytic approach of the twentieth century. What appeared to one editor at the Wyclif Society as philosophy of "a spuriously technical type . . . [lacking] the true philosophical spirit which, in spite of its over-refinement, impresses one with admiration in Duns Scotus" has since come to be recognized as evocative of the interests and methodology of philosophers today.[1]

To understand the positions that Wyclif adopted during his years at Oxford, from the early 1350s through the 1370s, a familiarity with the issues that were in the forefront of intellectual debate at the time is necessary. It was understandable for scholars a century ago to have seen Wyclif as a proto-Reformer emerging from the sterile debate of the schools, imbued with a vision of the needs the church would face in the coming centuries. Given the conviction that theologians spent their days parsing logical phrases and splitting ontological hairs, what else but a vision of the Reformation to come could explain the volumes demanding ecclesiastical reform, a rebirth of scriptural hermeneutics, criticism of the sacraments, and indictment of the friars that came from the evangelical doctor's pen? But much of what Wyclif would later write had already been debated in the early decades of the fourteenth century, and in many instances, his seemingly forward-looking ideas had been in the works at the Oxford schools for years before he was born.

Theology in the thirteenth century was characterized by grand, all-encompassing systematizing, but in the fourteenth century, it evolved into a more epistemologically oriented project, preoccupied with questions as to the possibility of understanding theology to be a science. The most important figure in this evolution was William Ockham (1287–1347), whose logical and linguistic investigations catalyzed a new approach, both at Paris and Oxford.[2] Indeed, the period beginning with Ockham's presence at Oxford and extending to 1349, when the plague hit England, has been described as a golden age of theology for the university. Ockham was born in Surrey and was probably in London before 1300. He began formal theological training in 1310, and given the general requirement of seven years' training in the trivium and quadrivium of the arts curriculum prior to the study of theology, he was likely studying at Oxford by 1304. At that point, Henry Harclay, a secular trained in Paris, was chancellor of the university. Harclay and Richard Campsall, who was affiliated with Merton College, were Oxford's most eminent figures at the time, and both were skeptical of the Scotist approach then dominant at Paris. Campsall in particular was interested in the use of terminist analysis, the increasingly influential logicosemantical approach, for ferreting out the metaphysical phantoms that clouded theological problems. During his period in Oxford, Ockham wrote the influential *Summa Logicae*, an exposition of the relation of things to words and concepts, which embodied his philosophical approach. He also wrote commentaries on Aristotle's logic, works on physics, and a treatise on future contingents grounded in Aristotle's *On Interpretation*. In addition, his quodlibetal disputations, *Sentences* commentaries, and treatises on the Eucharist also date from this period.

His innovations led to questions both within his provincial chapter of friars and at Avignon, and Ockham departed for the Franciscan convent at the papal see in 1324. There, he met Michael of Cesena and other influential continental Franciscans, and in the midst of increasingly hostile criticism of his thought, he fled to Munich with his like-minded fellows on 26 May 1328. His flight was not from cowardice, but from a conviction that the pope, John XXII, was incapable of objectivity. Ockham had identified himself with the Franciscans committed to St. Francis's ideal of apostolic poverty, and John had famously condemned their theological arguments against the legitimacy of property ownership in 1323. This papal condemnation put a formal end to the "poverty controversy," to be discussed in chapter 7. Ockham's arguments for the "spiritual" Franciscans date from this period in Germany, and include detailed examination of lordship, the ownership and use of property, legal and natural rights, and the authority of the papacy both within the church and in the secular realm.

Ockham's metaphysics and epistemology did not have a causal philosophical bearing on these latter works, but Ockham (or more likely, someone close to him) explains in *Tractatus de Principiis Theologiae* that his overall approach is based on two fundamental principles, namely, the principle of parsimony and the principle of absolute divine power. The former, known popularly as "Ockham's razor" is usually formulated "plurality is never to be posited without necessity," or "it is foolish to do with more what can be done with fewer," an Aristotelian maxim well known throughout the medieval period. Ockham's philosophical approach involved using the principle

to avoid positing metaphysical entities beyond what was absolutely necessary. The classic example of this is with the ten Aristotelian predicables. In
Categories, Aristotle lists ten things that can be said of an object: substance,
quality, quantity, relation, place, time, position, state, action, and passion.
Ockham argued that philosophers were too quick to allow abstract reasoning about these categories to lead to supposing that there were such things
as relations or points in time or space existing apart from related things.
His position was to restrict the number of kinds of things to two: substances
and qualities. Everything else, including relations, places, times, motions,
instants, are not real beings, but the products of our thinking and speaking about the world. Why did Ockham allow qualities to remain? Most
of his contemporaries believed that the doctrine of transubstantiation, the
theological account of what takes place at Eucharist, lies at the heart of
Ockham's belief that qualities are real beings, as we will discuss in chapter 4
on Wyclif's eucharistic theology.

The principle that "God can produce anything the production of which
does not involve a contradiction" is a succinct statement of God's absolute
power. In discussing God's omnipotence, theologians since Peter Damian
(d. 1072) had found it useful to distinguish between what God in fact wills
and does in creation, and what God could do, all things being equal. That
is, God has ordained that creation proceed according to fundamental laws,
and what God wills and does within creation is in accord with those laws.
But God *could* have willed that different laws be in effect, or that fewer
laws apply, or more, which would have made for a different structure to
creation. In 1290, the conflict between the mendicant orders and papal
authority involved Nicholas IV moving to rescind the privileges granted to
the friars in *Ad fructus uberes* (1281) by his predecessor, Martin IV. Nicholas
relied on Henry of Ghent, who saw *potentia absoluta* as involving change in
the created structure laid out according to *potentia ordinata*, allowing muta-
bility in divine law. Henry argued that popes could conceivably change rul-
ings of their predecessors on the strength of papal power's analogy to divine
power, but was loath to admit that God would actually make such changes.
By the end of the thirteenth century, the distinction had come to suggest the
possibility of God altering the created order of things. Further complicating
matters, Scotus continued to use it in the traditional manner, despite having
acknowledged this mutation in the distinction's applicability.[3] This opened
the door to his followers' using the distinction to generate possible divine
courses of action within creation outside the purview of *potentia ordinata*.

In 1315, regent masters of theology at Oxford condemned several theologians for making use of the distinction in generating counterfactuals. While not condemning use of the distinction, this effectively limited the scope of possible scenarios that theologians might generate.

The distinction figured again in 1324–1328, during the Avignon commission's investigation and ultimate condemnation of Ockham. Included among the positions condemned were some that Ockham had adopted from Scotus on the possibility of God, through *potentia absoluta*, being able to accept someone lacking the created habit of grace among those predestined for salvation. Ockham's argument in *Quodlibet* VI.1 was a response to those who conceived of the two kinds of divine power as license to speculate about God doing things in creation that might depart from the divinely ordained plan. The distinction should not be understood to mean "that God is able to do certain things ordinately and certain things absolutely and not ordinately, for God cannot do anything inordinately."[4] Here, Ockham argued that, by *potentia absoluta,* God could conceivably save an unbaptized person, but that he would not do it against his will. John XXII, Ockham's papal nemesis, argued that the distinction was theologically useless, holding that since God's eternal knowledge is immutable, and since all things can only happen as God knows them, then all things must happen of necessity. Since scriptures are unequivocal about baptism now being necessary for salvation, nobody can possibly argue that God would ever countenance the unbaptized being saved, through whatever kind of trumped-up distinction in the divine power one might cook up. Ockham angrily responded from Munich, in his *Opus Nonaginta Dierum*, that the pope completely missed the point of the distinction, denying all freedom, divine and human; this was the sort of nonsense one might expect from heretics, laymen, and old women.[5] It would be easy to dismiss this as political bickering under the guise of theological controversy, but the argument set the stage for much that would comprise fourteenth-century Oxford's debates, particularly about the relation of theology to the other sciences.

But before we survey Oxford's theological golden age, it is important to bear in mind that the theological positions that evolved over the next three decades were not simply members of one camp championing their founder's position against the paladins of another theologian's school. It would be very convenient if the Dominicans were uniformly Thomists, the Franciscans were either Scotist or Ockhamist, the Augustinians disciples of Giles of Rome, and the seculars generally adherents of the approach of

Grosseteste. But this was not the case; among Ockham's most active opponents at Oxford was Walter Chatton (d. 1343), a fellow Franciscan, while Henry Harclay, Oxford's chancellor during the latter part of Ockham's stay there, whose ontology was quite similar to Ockham's, was a secular. Despite the great impact that Scotus had in Paris, Scotism at Oxford was a paltry thing, and Thomism was not the authoritative approach among Oxford Dominicans that it might have been. The emphasis on science and logic that characterized Oxford thought led away from broad, all-encompassing metaphysical approaches and tended to foster a more individualistic, analytic brand of theology than the phrase "school of thought" might allow.

Adam Wodeham (d. 1358), Ockham's student and friend, attacked the arguments of his fellow Franciscan Walter Chatton with notable vigor. Chatton had argued, as Wyclif would, that a return to the safety of theological tradition and scriptural foundation would best serve the needs of the day.[6] Wodeham argued against using natural reasoning to broaden our understanding of the divine, rejecting Chatton's attempts at natural theology to emphasize this impossibility. While one scientific conclusion may seem applicable in another field, it would be foolhardy to assume that this holds across all science. We may presume that two diverse lines of argument lead to the same conclusion, as in the famous five ways that Aquinas uses to demonstrate God's existence, but "diverse sciences do not prove formally the same conclusion through the same medium, unless by mendacity."[7] Scientific reasoning's ability, for example, to construct arguments demonstrating the existence of an infinite being may entice one to suppose that it can demonstrate God's existence, but the God it constructs is ultimately nothing in comparison to the God of theology. There is no possibility of reason establishing the falsity of the apparently valid syllogism "this thing is the Father; this same thing is the Son; therefore the Father is the same as the Son," for by Aristotle's rules, the conclusion follows neatly from the premises. "And thus unless through our faith it were known that one thing is three things, we would believe firmly the aforesaid sophism to have been well argued."[8]

Bradwardine and the Calculators

Further emphasizing the problems that come with trying to fit these theologians into neatly defined groups is the thought of the calculators, a group of

secular scholars at Oxford's Merton College. Like Ockham and his followers, the calculators were philosophers with a keen interest in logical disputation and the complexities of mathematics and theoretical physics to which
they could lead. Being a calculator was certainly not the same as being an
Ockhamist. One of the foremost calculators, Thomas Bradwardine, vigorously opposed Ockhamist theology. Disputations *de sophismatibus* were the
standard genre of argument in which undergraduate students learned to
engage one another in intellectual dispute in medieval universities. The
students used ambiguously worded sentences like "Socrates twice sees every
man besides Plato" to analyze how terms functioned within propositions.
In most cases, the analysis focused on syncategorematic terms, which lack
independent signification outside of their use in sentences. In the example,
the term "besides" has an ambiguous reference, and resolving the ambiguity would involve addressing the larger question of how exceptive terms
function in the distribution of meaning within a proposition. While, at first
sight, *sophismata* may appear to be a recondite academic exercise, the purpose of the genre was to sensitize students to the relation of language use
and reasoning by exploring the problems that come from assuming things
about meaning that have not been established. As is the case now with
courses in logic or programming, formulating texts whereby the rules for
this level of analysis could be established was a very specialized affair, and
the logicians at Merton College were tasked with this responsibility.

Merton College had been founded in 1264 and was reserved for those
studying for higher degrees. Both Scotus and Ockham had studied there,
and many of the foremost figures in fourteenth-century Oxford were associated with the college. Here, a movement arose among the logical theorists
intent on regulating *sophismata* in which physics and theoretical mathematics began to figure importantly. Take a proposition like "Socrates is
whiter than Plato begins to be white." This *sophisma*, the first in Richard
Kilvington's collection from the 1320s, tests the extent to which we can
understand a degree of a quality, whiteness, and its ratio to a lesser degree of
whiteness.[9] Kilvington's sentences, with their problems involving degrees
of quantity or quality, or traversing distances, find their resolution in logical
analyses of the terms, but as the genre developed, mathematical and physical
speculation became increasingly complex. Walter Burley, a Mertonian from
1305 to 1309, had investigated the physics of a substance beginning to be and
ceasing nonexistence in his quodlibetal question *De primo et ultimo instanti*,
and he introduced analyses of problems of natural philosophy into the

genre. Bradwardine's interest was in the mathematics of ratios and how it applied to theoretical understanding of force, resistance, and velocity, and his *De Proportionibus* (1328) would revolutionize the physics of motion.

Thomas Bradwardine (c. 1300–1349) began his career as a theologian and natural philosopher at Merton College in the 1320s, and had entered the service of Edward III in 1339 as royal chaplain. In the king's service, Bradwardine was witness to the battle of Crécy in 1346, served as a negotiator for peace with France, and delivered a famous sermon on the occasion of victory over the Scots at Neville's Cross. He was elected archbishop of Canterbury in August 1348, but because the election had bypassed Edward's permission, he had to stand aside and allow John Ufford to occupy the See at Canterbury. When Ufford died later that year, Bradwardine was elected again, and Edward appears to have allowed his chaplain to become archbishop in July 1349. The Black Death had been devastating English society for several months, and it claimed Bradwardine only thirty-eight days after his accession. Despite the fact that he likely had left Oxford toward the end of the 1330s, the effects of his presence were felt well into the 1360s and '70s, when Wyclif was active. Not only had he been foremost among the calculators of Merton College, but he had formulated a theological response to Ockhamism during the 1340s that was influential into the sixteenth century. Historians of science remember him for advances in kinematics and mathematical theory, while students of the Reformation turn to his *De Causa Dei contra Pelagium* to understand the debates that raged in the universities when Luther and Melancthon studied. Each of these venues figure importantly in Wyclif's writings, in which Bradwardine—alone among all the figures of Oxford's golden age—is frequently mentioned with respect and reverence.

"Mathematics," Bradwardine wrote, "is the revelatrix of truth, has brought to life every hidden secret, and carries the key to all subtle letters." An example of Bradwardine's mathematical thought can be found in his assessment of how to explain the relation of variation in the velocities of a moving thing to variation in the forces and resistances that affect velocity. The traditional understanding in Aristotelian physics relied on the axiom that motion occurs only when the motive force is greater than the resistance offered, so that velocity is explained as proportionate to the ratio of force to resistance. Bradwardine reasoned that, if we begin with a rate of motion in which the force is greater than the resistance, and if we continually double the rate of resistance while holding the rate of force constant, at some point the rate of resistance will be greater than the rate of force. The problem lies in the axiom of velocity being proportionate to the ratio of force to resistance; as the rate of velocity decreases in proportion to the increase of resistance, there will still be a rate of velocity assignable at the point that resistance is greater than force. This would mean that there is a measurable, albeit tiny, rate of velocity assignable to a stationary object. Better, Bradwardine argued, to recognize that velocities vary arithmetically, while the ratios of force to resistance vary geometrically.[10]

In the two decades that followed, the calculator tradition at Oxford would flourish. Foremost among the calculators was William Heytesbury, who would become chancellor of the university in 1370. Heytesbury's interest was in infinite divisibility and the nature of continua, and he was a pioneer in analyzing the logic of quantitative statements about heat and color. His *Regulae Solvendi Sophismata*, one of the textbooks for undergraduates that was the initial aim of the calculators, illustrates the reciprocity of logic and mathematical physics that characterized the movement. In it, problems of physics and mathematics are examined as logical constructs, with the application of physical and mathematical principles mixed into the semantical analysis. Another important figure, Richard Swineshead (pronounced Swinnis-et), elevated the abstraction in the mathematical analysis of physical propositions to new levels of intricacy. His *Liber calculationum* considers how to parse propositions concerning the measurement of the intensity or absence of qualities. Does one understand a quality's intensity by proximity to the highest degree of a quality, or by distance from the absolute absence of the quality? Further, is it possible to analyze the distribution of intensities of a quality across a given substance? What of the intensity of light? And building on Bradwardine's understanding of motion, if we consider an object falling through the center of the earth, does the part of the object that has already passed the center resist the descent of the parts that have yet to reach the center? The practical, physical applicability of these questions is beside the point. Swineshead, like all of the calculators, was more interested in the complexity of mathematical analysis that the logically formulable problems demand.[11] Leibniz would later praise Swineshead as the individual who introduced mathematics into philosophy, and Robert Burton, author of the encyclopedic *Anatomy of Melancholy,* described him as exceeding the bounds of human genius, but later humanists would generally reject the calculator tradition as typifying the subtleties that had complicated scholasticism to the point of irrelevance. From the standpoint of the history of science, the Oxford calculators introduced mathematics into speculations about problems in physics, illustrating the need for advanced mathematical operations, but their interest was primarily in using science as a heuristic device for logical analysis. For the purposes of our survey of fourteenth-century Oxford, though, this calculator tradition shows the level of the analytic nature of philosophical discourse in Wyclif's day.

Skepticism and Certitude

The meticulous logical analysis of propositions was not, despite appearances, an end in itself. The calculators were motivated by a strong desire to unravel theological problems that had long plagued Christian thinkers, a prime example of which was the problem of predestination and human freedom. Bradwardine's *De Causa Dei contra Pelagium* is the most important fourteenth-century articulation of a traditional, Augustinian approach to this problem. Ockham had formulated a position that Bradwardine thought to be suspiciously evocative of Pelagianism. This position, first articulated by Pelagius in the fourth century, entails a radical voluntarism, in which God's causal power has no purchase on human willing. In effect, Pelagius's position allowed human beings to merit salvation through their own good works, without God's cooperation through grace. We will discuss Bradwardine's association with the circle of Bishop Richard de Bury of Durham in chapter 3; it was during these years that he composed *De Causa Dei*, a work that was to have a significant impact on Wyclif's understanding of divine knowledge and of the nature of the church. Because tracing out Bradwardine's argument would take us too far astray from the topic of theology and epistemology, we will save that for chapter 6, on Wyclif's ecclesiology.

If the reaction to Ockham at Oxford had just been an old-fashioned Augustinian hostility toward Pelagianism, we could classify this as a largely in-house theological debate and move on. But there was more at stake than the right approach to the hoary problem of God's foreknowledge and human freedom. The arguments consequent on Ockham's approach suggested that theology might not fit the standard of scientific reasoning. Given the possibility of God causing our perception of nonexistent entities, it was even plausible that all human knowledge might be, at best, only probable. If it is possible that God can cause us to perceive things that are not present, or to believe things to be true that are not true, then all that seems evident to human reason runs the risk of being dubitable. When discussing the history of skepticism in Western thought, the usual course is to proceed from the academics of ancient Greece and Rome to the use of systematic doubt as the basis for modern thought in Descartes' *Meditations*, on the assumption that Christian dogmatism forbade its use in scholastic thought, or that Aristotelian thought provided sufficient material to stave off skeptical tendencies. The great figures in skepticism include Pyrrho, Carneades, and Sextus Empiricus in antiquity, and Descartes, Bayle, and Hume in early modernity. Augustine had rejected skepticism as a useful philosophical method in *Contra Academicos* (386 CE) and had argued in *De Utiliate Credendi* (392 CE) that, since few men were sufficiently wise as to understand the truth, it is better to believe and avoid sin than to doubt and risk damnation. And until the fourteenth century, skepticism had a bad reputation; to accuse one's opponent of having a position that led to skepticism, as Scotus did to Henry of Ghent, was as good as rendering it untenable.[12] Etienne Gilson set the terms for twentieth-century consideration of skepticism in scholastic thought by identifying it with Ockhamism, describing Ockham's thought as an apprentice sorcerer unleashing forces that would overturn the classical scholasticism of the thirteenth century. Because Ockham was ontologically a "nominalist," it became the norm to equate Ockham's ontological approach with a skeptical distrust of natural theology and a correspondent fideism.[13] But the reality of later medieval skepticism is much more complex. Not every fourteenth-century theologian with a healthy respect for the limits of human reasoning was a skeptic. Still, burgeoning interest in the absolute power of God and its relation to human knowledge, an important aspect of Ockham's thought, led many to explore the philosophical uses of epistemic skepticism.

For centuries, scholastic thinkers had Aristotelian reasoning as their firm foundation, and by the end of the thirteenth century, theologians had used syllogistic reasoning to articulate ideas of great subtlety about the divine nature. In his *Summa Logica* III, 16, Ockham argued that great care should be taken with the terms in an expository syllogism, the building block of scholastic reasoning. It could not have as its subject a term that is ambiguous in number. For instance, "homo est Socrates, homo est Plato, ergo Socrates est Plato" may be true, and it may be false, depending on how the term "man" refers. If the term stands for a singular thing, a man, then the syllogism would prove that Socrates and Plato are two names for the same person. This is either the truth, or it is not. If the term stands for a plural, then the conclusion would be impossible if Socrates and Plato are two different people. So the ambiguity of the term "man" means that the syllogism doesn't really tell us anything. The subject of a syllogism must be either recognizably singular or recognizably plural to prevent the syllogism from being useless. The problem for theology arises in discussing God's triune nature. "This essence is the Father, this essence is the Son, therefore the Son is the Father" is useless as an expository syllogism because of the ambiguity of the term "essence" when describing God. Does it refer to one thing or to more than one? If essence describes one thing, then the syllogism is saying something about the identity of the persons of the Son and the Father within the essence. If it describes several things, then its meaning is confusing: do the different persons themselves have essences? Or is the syllogism just falsely conceived, since the faith holds that there can only be one essence and several persons? The syllogism is not wrong in itself; in *Quodlibet* III, q.3, Ockham explains that if we could enjoy the vision that those in heaven have of God, the ambiguity of the term would vanish and the syllogism would clearly and unequivocally describe the reality we perceive. But the unbeliever, for whom the term "God" refers to a fictional entity, will not recognize the truth of any syllogism in which there is reasoning about the divine nature as something real. Ought we then to conclude that philosophy is of no help whatever to theology? In *Quodlibet* V, q.1, Ockham explains that delineating the way that terms in statements refer, whereby he has established that a theological truth cannot be proven scientifically, is itself a philosophical activity. Hence, philosophy is of tremendous utility for the theological project. The result of this general line of reasoning, though, is that theology is distinct from other sciences, and philosophy, theology's erstwhile handmaiden, becomes the de facto queen of the sciences.

Peter Aureol (1280–1322), a contemporary of Ockham's in Paris, had warned strenuously against assuming that "whatever appears, exists" in his analysis of human cognition, indicating that the appearances of things perceived serve as the basis for our knowledge of things in the world. In the next generation of Parisian theologians, Nicholas of Autrecourt (c. 1295–1369) stunned his colleagues by arguing that, aside from the certainties of faith, all that we have to rely on in our reasoning is the principle of noncontradiction. This means that basic principles of cause and effect, and metaphysical fundamentals like "accidents require substances for their existence" are ruled out as the bases for knowledge, because doubting them does not entail a contradiction. While we may never have experienced an accident without a substance, or smoke without fire, it would not involve a contradiction of terms to imagine them, in the way that one imagines a square circle or a married bachelor. This seriously endangers the certainties of science, broadly understood to include all descriptions about the world around us. Nicholas was famously censured at Avignon in 1346. Although his skeptical tendencies do not amount to classical skepticism, they are indicative of a tendency toward skeptical reasoning in fourteenth-century theology that was quite active in Oxford.[14]

Some Oxford theologians were willing to question the tenets of causality to test the extent to which we are capable of certain empirical knowledge, even if only to sharpen their students' wits. One, a Benedictine known only as Monachus Niger, or the Black Monk, who wrote between 1337 and 1341, suggested that we cannot know substances by natural knowledge:

> [B]ecause then it could be known in the Sacrament of the Altar [i.e., the Eucharist] when it would be bread there, and when not. From this it follows that it is not pure philosophy to hold a substance to exist in the nature of things. I prove this because nothing holds naturally unless the knowing of it naturally comes, and the knowledge of substance cannot come naturally, as demonstrated with the Sacrament of the Altar . . . so there can be no experience had of a substance.

We seem to have knowledge of a substance underlying accidents, because something remains underneath even as the accidents change. Just because something seems to remain constant as a ball of wax melts from a solid lump to a liquid mass, it does not follow that there *is* something underneath.[15]

Richard Fitzralph was another prominent member of Richard de Bury's Durham circle, and we will describe the relation of his thought to Wyclif's in our discussion of *dominium* in chapter 7. Later in his career, he would become the archbishop of Armagh, earning the nickname "Armachanus," and proved to be an influential figure at Avignon during negotiations with the Orthodox church in the late 1330s and early 1340s. His *Summa de Quaestionibus Armenorum*, a dialogue in nineteen books outlining papal primacy in the face of Greek and Armenian theological objections, is a storehouse of classical arguments for papal authority and was used extensively in Reformation and Counter-Reformation debates. Included in this work is an autobiographical prayer, from which we can get a sense of his feelings about his time at Oxford:

> Before, I supposed myself profound through Aristotelian dogmas and argumentation with men of limitless shallowness, when You touched me at my core with Your heavenly truth, dazzling me with Your scripture, scattering the clouds of my error, showing me how I was croaking with the frogs and toads in the swamps.[16]

One manuscript of Fitzralph's *Sentences* commentary contains a question in which the author argues that one cannot know whether there is any material substance aside from oneself. The sensations experienced of one's own body are not sufficient for knowing the body, though; we need some sort of dialectical argument to establish that we have a body, which would provide the certainty that we cannot attain with sense experience alone. Does this make him a skeptic? Fitzralph knew that Henry of Ghent had answered a similar question by advocating an epistemology reliant upon divine illumination, in keeping with traditional Augustinian thought. In his *De Magistro,* Augustine had argued that we attain understanding of any truth only through God's illumination of our minds: "Regarding each of the things we understand, however, we don't consult a speaker who makes sounds outside of us, but the Truth that presides within over the mind itself."[17] If God provides human understanding of truth, then this argument would only show that, without divine illumination, we are helpless. Aquinas, Scotus, and Ockham rejected illumination theory, but it was by no means lacking proponents in fourteenth-century Oxford; Wyclif would be an advocate. Fitzralph devotes considerable attention to epistemology in his *Sentences* commentary, distinguishing between what is present to our understanding as a result of perception and what the act of understanding what is present involves. Further, he continued throughout his academic career to revise his thoughts on the unity of the soul and on the issue of how correctly to delineate the process of understanding, complicating any attempt to categorize Fitzralph's epistemic program. Gordon Leff argues that Fitzralph was a proponent of illumination theory, but more work needs to be done before we can understand the place of this question in his overall epistemology.[18]

A somewhat later figure, also suggesting the skeptical approach of Nicholas of Autrecourt, instead uses the uncertainty of human knowledge to underscore a determinism suggestive of Bradwardine. Nicholas Aston, a post–Black Death theologian slightly older than Wyclif, was chancellor of Oxford from 1359 to 1361. He argued that only God is necessary; the past is contingent, as is the present, and God can make it to have been different, although he does not. Any truth we have about created being might easily dissolve into falsehood without our understanding the reason. This does not mean that the created order is so fluid as to bring about that change. God is necessarily perfect and is reliable as the necessary foundation for created order. The problem lies in our understanding, which is based in dubitable sense perception and is thus possibly illusory. Even something as apparently certain as "nothing can be in two places at the same time" is up for questioning: "God can make it that the same man would be in differ-ent places, [and] a man could meet himself and not know that it was him, and cut off his [own] head without knowing."[19] Causality is likewise open to doubt, because if some particular effect has to follow from some cause, as our thinking suggests, then God's being would not be the only neces-sary thing in creation. Likewise, logical inference is jeopardized, because a given conclusion need not follow from premises that appear necessarily to lead to it.

Interestingly, Aston's extreme position is more in keeping with Brad-wardine than with Ockham or others. First, Aston believes that only God's being is necessary and that propositionally structured truth exists indepen-dently of the sentences we construct. While our understanding of causality, and hence of the causal order, is so imperfect as to be incapable of demon-strating God's existence in the way that Aquinas or Scotus suggested, it is still possible to use logic to show the necessity of God's being. Aston notes that his opponents, the *moderni*, hold that the statement "God does not exist" is not formally contradictory, despite the fact that all created being is contingent on God's existence. Consider a proposition and the state of affairs it describes. If the state of affairs changes, so does the truth value of the proposition. But if the proposition contains a contradiction, it is always false, even if the proposition also accurately describes the state of affairs. If God exists, then a proposition p asserting that God does not exist would contain a contradiction, namely, that a necessary being does not exist. It's being made false by God's existence would not be the cause of its inherent falsity; that it contains a contradiction is the cause of its inherent falsity. Now, Aston continues, if God's existence were contingent, like the mod-erns say it is, then it could begin to be and cease to be. The proposition would still contain a contradiction, though, so it cannot be that a necessary being does not exist. This is what Aston calls his "Achilles argument," and it is obviously based on an assumed real relation holding between true statements and things. A skeptic holding that true statements only accidentally reflect reality would never agree to this variation on Anselm's famous argument from *Proslogion* 2–4, and a follower of Ockham, for whom the reference of terms within propositions is dependent upon the concepts we derive from what we perceive, would reject Aston's semantic realism. Further, since God is the only necessary being, any true answer to the question "why is this the way things are?" must find its basis in God's being. This includes every case of human willing, whether good or evil, although Aston shies away from what he sees as an excessive determinism in Bradwardine. Because his approach is semantically oriented, grounded in a propositional realism in which true statements are made true by their correspondence to a propositionally structured truth in God's being, it would be a mistake to call Aston a skeptic. It is difficult to avoid the powerful skeptical overtones in his description of the contingency of human understanding, though.

The case is similar for Robert Holcot (d. 1349), whose arguments are easily interpreted as skeptical but are better understood in their theological context. Holcot was a Dominican known both for his incisive logical mind and his remarkable gifts as a preacher. He was active at Oxford from 1330, but by 1337 may have left to join Richard de Bury in Durham, where we will see him in our discussion of the de Bury circle in chapter 3, on Wyclif's realism. By 1342, he was active as a pastor in Salisbury, and later in Northampton, where he died of plague. He was best known during the centuries after his death for his remarkable *Commentary on Wisdom*, an encyclopedic scripture commentary on the apocryphal Book of Wisdom, which contains pastoral advice about the path of one's life, just political rule, married life, and many social issues. At present, this fascinating work is all but forgotten; those few familiar with his thought today recognize him as an important, original response to Ockham. In his *Sentences* commentary, Holcot addressed the incompatibility of Aristotelian logic and the nature of the Trinity typified by this syllogism: "the divine essence is the Father, the divine essence is the Son, therefore the Father is the Son," the premises of which are true, which lead to a valid but false conclusion. While earlier theologians had addressed this by qualifying how the divine essence "is" the person, Holcot denied the validity of using a distinction to avoid the doctrinally problematic conclusion. This led him to decide that the demands of the faith so contrasted with the rules of logic that there must be two systems of logic: the Aristotelian one, applicable to the natural order of creation, and a higher logic in which supernatural truths are comprehensible.

It is likely that Wyclif formulated his own position on the relation of faith to reasoning in response to Holcot, who held that what is evident as scientific knowledge is born from demonstrative arguments; no faith is involved in the process. Theology could only be considered a science if it conformed to one of the three senses in which the term *scientia* is understood. In the broadest sense, it is firm adherence to the truth, and in this sense theology is a science. But what is the basis for this adherence? If the assent is based in evident knowledge of empirical data, or in necessary first principles, then one cannot include theology among the sciences, for no viator can claim either empirical knowledge or intuitive comprehension of supernatural truths as necessary first principles.[20] Holcot would change his position somewhat in his *Quodlibeta*, where he agrees with Ockham about the ambiguity in the reference of terms about God impeding syllogistic function. One simply cannot form syllogisms about God that suggest that we are reasoning about him. This allows Aristotelian logic to remain universal, because its principles do not include reasoning about such a being as God. Thus, truths of faith, which are essential for salvation, must be held on the doctrinal authority of the church. Attempting to demonstrate such truths by using reason is a waste of time, for the light of reason simply cannot shine brightly enough and needs the help of Catholic teachings. Logic does have an important role to play for theology, however; one can—and in some cases must—use it to investigate theological statements and arguments. With heretics, it is best to stick to analyses of the forms of the arguments they use and to leave the divergence in content to ecclesiastic authority. Theologians must be well versed in logic, since sophistic arguments frequently arise that require careful parsing.[21] Later, in his *Wisdom* commentary, he explains that true seekers can count on God to reveal himself, despite the limits of reason:

> It has not been proven by any reason up to now that God exists, or that God is the creator of the world, but to all who bear themselves innocently in God's sight and use their natural reason to enquire, putting no obstacle in the way of divine grace, God will communicate sufficient knowledge of himself in such a way as to suffice for their salvation. . . . the man who uses his natural reason blamelessly will never lack real knowledge of God.[22]

This is not fideism, for Holcot does not evoke an individual faith, but the security and stability of ecclesiastical authority. Those entrusted with this authority must hold more truths of the faith through belief than those without it, because their duty is to understand and teach the faith. This does not mean that a separate faith exists for the clergy—every statement held true by scripture or the church must be conceded by every Catholic— but that some of the relations of the truths of the faith are the concern of the magisterium alone.

We are left, then, with a sampling of theologians who were writing when the cohesive theological systematizing of figures like Thomas Aquinas and Scotus was no longer an option. While theological problems like the determinism–human freedom issue commanded great interest, the shift of attention from primarily ontological issues to problems involving language and logic made epistemology the field in which theological innovation was necessary. Bradwardine's *De Causa Dei* contains little that addresses the difficult questions of how we gain understanding and how we use it as a basis for theological certainty. Those thinkers who do face down this problem are haunted by the specter of skepticism, and, for Wyclif, their results seemed inadequate to address theology's needs. So his approach was to engage in questions like "what is knowing?" "what is mind?" and "what is the basis for theological science?" to shore up Bradwardine's approach with reliable, philosophical underpinnings.

Wyclif's Epistemology:
The Mind and the Eye

At this point, it would be very helpful for us to turn to Wyclif's *Sentences* commentary, as we can do with figures like Wodeham, Holcot, and Crathorn, to find his developed positions on the questions that defined fourteenth-century Oxford epistemology. While he certainly would have had to construct a *Sentences* commentary during his theological studies, we have no record of it. The only evidence we have for one are the treatises *De Composicione Hominis, De Trinitate,* and *De Incarnacione*, which clearly address questions connected to the commentary tradition.[23] The first third of *De Trinitate* addresses whether theology is a science, but its argument is comprehensible only with familiarity with the fundamental questions then current, about knowledge, certainty, and what is involved in understanding.

A glance at a catalog of his Latin works suggests that he had little interest in the problems. The titles of his treatises preceding the *Summa de Ente* appear to focus on logic, with only the brief *De Actibus Anime* addressing the problem at hand. And *De Actibus Anime*, it turns out, does little more than argue that mental acts are indeed properties of the mind and not entities distinct from it. The key lies in seeing through the deceptive title of the collection of treatises known as *Tractatus de Logica*. Scholars of medieval logic have noted that Wyclif does relatively little formal logic in these early works. While the first treatise, entitled *De Logica,* is a primer-level introduction to Aristotelian logic, it is not comparable to Paul of Venice's somewhat later *Logica Parva* in scope or depth. The remaining treatises, entitled *Logice continuacio* and *Tractatus Tercius*, are filled with chapters that begin with formal logical issues, but quickly seem to bog down in frustratingly detailed semantic minutiae. *Logice continuacio* appears to be two treatises, the first dealing with simple, categorical propositions, while the second deals with propositions involving exceptive terms like "but" or "except." *Tractatus Tercius*, by far the most extensive, is devoted to hypothetical propositions. The chapter containing Wyclif's account of how our vision functions and how it serves as a heuristic device by which to explain our understanding begins with the formidable question of how kinds of terms function within comparative hypothetical sentences. This approach is confusing and obscure for readers used to the more clearly defined structure of a standard *Sentences* commentary, but patience yields evidence that Wyclif was engaged in the ongoing epistemological dialogue that characterized much of fourteenth-century Oxford thought.

Vision and understanding, which are frequently connected in epistemological theories, had an important relationship for thirteenth- and fourteenth-century philosophers. Roger Bacon had advocated an understanding of the sciences of optics, psychology, epistemology, and logic under the uniting idea that objects generate iterative similitudes, or "species" of themselves into the media that contain them. Just as light moves through the air, from the sun to our eyes, so too does every appearance perceptible move through every medium and into our perception and understanding. This seems both bizarre and not very explicative. How can an individual object emit iterative similitudes of itself, which fly about in the air until they are caught in the organ of sense perception? And how does positing perceptible similitudes emitted by objects explain anything about the accuracy of what we perceive? Is this the same as saying that digestion occurs through the stomach secreting a digestive enzyme onto a digestible characteristic in the thing eaten? While a considerable number of thinkers accepted the existence of species to explain perception, Ockham would have none of it. For him, the act of intuitive cognition in which the perceiving mind apprehends an object of perception involved no phantom intermediaries. When I see a tree, I do not see the species of the tree that the tree emits into the atmosphere; I directly see the tree in all its glory. Twenty-first-century epistemologists look wistfully at Ockham's approach, called "direct perception," as touchingly naive in its simplicity. Most of his contemporaries regarded it as shortsighted, not least because it did not accurately take into account the optical phenomena of lenses, which anyone could see was the basis for the functioning of the eye.

Vision, Wyclif explains, is the most subtle of our senses, capable of perceiving the greatest diversity, and since it is closest in complexity to the way our understanding works, it is the ideal means of explaining intellection.[24] So the best way to explain our understanding is to explain the mechanics of vision. In both sensitive and intellective vision, the vision might be distinct or confused. In both, there are three kinds: direct, when seeing the object directly; refractive, or seeing through a medium; and reflexive vision, as in seeing through a mirror. Our eyes cannot see the finite points of which a thing is made, no matter how distinct the visual act, but our intellective powers are capable of isolating these points, as we will see in Wyclif's assessment of the Eucharist. Aside from the reference to atomism, Wyclif is not saying anything revolutionary here, although he is simplifying matters considerably. Peter Aureol had taken Scotus's distinction between intuitive and abstractive cognition and converted it into one between ocular and imaginary cognition, between exterior and interior acts of perception. The latter is not the vision of the understanding that Wyclif describes, but only the imaginative faculty, whereby we call to mind things not immediately evident to the external senses. Wyclif's predecessors, from Ockham and Scotus onward, intended the distinction between intuitive and abstractive cognition to explain acts of perception, but they allowed the distinction to play at the level of the intellect as well. Indeed, philosophers devoted great care to explicating the relation of interior to exterior acts of perception, and to the analogy of perception and its objects to the understanding and its conceptual objects. In asserting that both species of vision involve degrees of clarity and are divisible into direct, reflective, and refractive subspecies, Wyclif is deliberately papering over some very complex issues.[25]

In his discussion of how human intellectual faculties are deducible from analyses of intuitive and abstractive cognition, John Rodington, O.F.M. (d. 1348) had expressed an interest in the functioning of the eye, especially in whether the visual power is located on the eye's surface, as Bacon had suggested, or inside the eye, in the optic nerve, as Scotus had thought. Rodington pursued the matter carefully, comprehensively analyzing the theories of vision available to fourteenth-century science. Wyclif's brief account of the anatomy of the eye, describing the aqueous and vitreous humors, the path of the optic nerves, the dura and pia mater protecting the brain, and the connective web of veins and arteries that "bear life and spirit from the heart, and nutrition from the liver" suggests familiarity with Rodington's interest in the connection of anatomy and perception. Medieval scientists were not certain that the eye actively sends out rays of perception (as Aristotle had suggested) that meet up with the species being emitted by perceptible objects. Rodington struggled with this question. Alhazen (Ibn al-Haitham c. 965–1039), the Persian scientist whose *Kitâb al-Manâzir,* known to medievals as *De Aspectibus* or *Perspectiva*, was the primary source for optics, thought that "extramission" was nonsense, as would the influential thirteenth-century Polish scientist Witelo, whose *Liber Perspectivae* would be an important text for fourteenth-century Mertonians. Bacon and Pecham advocated a combination of extramission and intromission, as did Rodington. Wyclif, too, suggests that vision involves both the eye sending something out to contact the object perceived and the eye's reception of species emitted by the perceived object.[26]

In Wyclif's *Trialogus,* a later work written for the instruction of the educated laity, he argues that an understanding of brain anatomy reveals the different areas in which sense perception is interpreted into thought. In the first ventricle, at the front of the brain, the *sensus communis* flourishes, where sense data from all of the sense organs are sorted and interpreted into a common sensory language that is interpreted by the higher powers. Here also is where imagination is based, where we construct the illusory stuff of dreams. The estimative and fantastic powers occupy the middle ventricle, where we make judgments about the physical world and, like other animals, "syllogize about particulars," as when a fox stalks its prey. In the rear ventricle, memory and locomotive power are located, "through nerves in junctures in the back of the spine it is diverted to the other parts of the body."[27] Defects in the eye, such as cataracts or trauma to the eye or optic nerve, cause distortion in the objects as they are perceived. Changes in the media through which perception occurs bring about changes in perception itself, as when a torch, when waved in a rapid circular motion at night, appears to be a ring of fire. Wyclif's gross anatomy of the brain is in keeping with the understanding of his contemporaries; William Crathorn, whose unique epistemology particularly incensed Wyclif, gives a similar account in his *Sentences* commentary I, q.2, conclusion 4, although he uses *cellula* where Wyclif uses *ventricula.*

Why does Wyclif wander into an anatomical explanation of the eye in explaining knowledge? Wyclif's approach is to follow the lead of a Polish theologian and scientist, Erazmo Witelo (c. 1230–c. 1300), whose thought provides a ready source of heuristic devices throughout Wyclif's Latin works. Witelo's *Perspectivae* is a ten-volume analysis of the science of optics as applied mathematics, and its impact on Western scientific thought was remarkable. For centuries, scientific theorists would make considerable use of Witelo's approach in their own attempts to mathematize the understanding of physical phenomena. Wyclif's Parisian contemporary Nicole Oresme (1323–1382) made considerable use of it in his own scientific thought, as did later theorists from Regiomontanus and da Vinci, Galileo and Tycho Brahe, to Descartes. Kepler's work *Ad Vitellionem paralipomena* (1604) marks the end of Witelo's tenure as a scientific authority. More recently, Witelo has been interpreted as being an advocate of the theological light metaphysics best articulated by Grosseteste in *De Luce*, but this is an overstatement; his interest was in systematizing Alhazen, the great Persian optic theorist, along the lines of Euclidean demonstration.[28] Witelo was not a great mathematician, although he was the first to introduce ideas of Eutochius and Apollonius of Pergia into European thought, thanks to the translating work of his contemporary William of Moerbeke. His importance rests in his systematic presentation and application of theory to applied mathematics; *Perspectivae* appears to have been a particularly important text for Mertonian instruction. Wyclif's description of the eye in *Logica Continuacio* is a precis of Witelo's *Perspectivae,* book 3. His account of how the species follows a perpendicular line from the object to a point in the core of the eye is that of Witelo, who describes very carefully the function of the aqueous and vitreous humors in the act of perception. Hence, for Wyclif as for other Oxford theorists, optics provided a useful means of modeling and analyzing our understanding of ideas. But what is involved in knowing ideas?

Using Logic to Resolve Confusion I:
Mental Acts as Qualities of the Mind

Early in his career, Wyclif addressed the nature of the mental act of know-ing in *De Actibus Anime*. He devotes a large portion of the treatise to refut-ing the position of an unnamed predecessor who believed that mental acts are absolute things capable of per se existence, the way bodies are. Instead, Wyclif argues that the acts of the mind are accidents of the genus action, and not beings distinct from the mind that forms them. The usual assumption that Wyclif is addressing Ockham or his followers is groundless, because neither Ockham nor most of the philosophers who wrote in response to him thought of mental acts as really different from the mind.

Ockham's innovation was to dismiss the need for species in the act of understanding. Earlier epistemic models, like that of Aquinas, held that we arrive at judgments about extramental objects through an involved process. First, our senses take in the perceptible appearance of some object that is transmitted from the object through the air and received in the senses as "sensible species." Next, another part of the cognitive apparatus takes these raw sensible species and turns them into mentally encoded "phantasms," which become the mental image of the object perceived when cognized by the mind. The mind does not yet recognize the object of which it has a mental image, though; the understanding is simultaneously abstracting from the raw sensible species a higher, more comprehensive form of the object perceived by the senses, which Aquinas calls the "intelligible spe-cies." This intelligible species is what Aquinas believes to be the univer-sal, which is converted into a concept, and it is this concept that is used to interpret the mental image. None of these beings by which we comprehend extramental objects, these species or phantasms, can exist on their own; each is an act of the mind the purpose of which is to facilitate understanding. Ockham rejected the existence of species in our act of understanding some-thing extramental, in part because of doubts he had about the reliability of the species' representation of their object. Instead, we directly perceive the object through "intuitive cognition," from which the understanding abstracts in a distinct action called "abstractive cognition."

At an early point in his career, Ockham was willing to concede that the product of abstractive cognition, namely, a concept, might have a kind of being of its own. This being, which he called "objective being" and which today's philosophers might call "intentional being," is but a ghost in comparison to the being that substances and accidents have. Ultimately, he rejected this objective reality as superfluous, having been convinced by Walter Chatton's arguments that concepts are merely acts of the mind, with no more being of their own than any other action.[29] Very simply, when one runs, there are not two things, the runner and the running, but only one, the runner. When one thinks, there are not two things, the thinker and the thinking, but only one, the thinker.

Ockham's trimmed-down epistemology was not terribly popular at Oxford. Chatton argued that, in eliminating species, Ockham had destroyed the means by which we distinguish between the acts of the senses and the qualitative contents of those acts. During the 1320s and '30s, most agreed with Chatton, endorsing the importance of species in the mind's cognitive processes and differing only in the species' relation to the mind's acts of sensing and judgment. The important thinkers, particularly John Rodington, Richard Fitzralph, Adam Wodeham, and Robert Holcot, each argued against Ockham's reduction of our epistemic machinery. Only William Crathorn, whose epistemology had prompted Holcot to comment that one should only read Crathorn's *Sentences Commentary* for laughs, seems a likely candidate for Wyclif's opponent. While Crathorn, like the others, agreed that species should not be eliminated from the process, he advocated the elimination of mental acts. This leaves only the mind and species, which amounts to a unique epistemology. The mind receives the species, which are reflective of the qualities of the object to which they are connected, and so in cognizing the object, the mind takes on the qualities of the species. "When something is such accidentally, through another, then that other is essentially and through itself."[30] If the species is that through which the mind knows its object, then the species must exist per se. So, when I recognize a white cat before me, the species that contains the qualities of felineness, white, furry, quadrupedal, and so forth, is a real being distinct from my mind, but in my mind, meaning that my idea of the white cat is, in fact, white, furry, quadrupedal, and feline.[31]

Wyclif describes a mental act as likely to be one of three things: it is either nothing but the mind itself, or it is a quality of the mind, accidental and reliant upon it, or it is a thing separate from the mind. He devotes the first half of *De Actibus Anime* to constructing six arguments against the third possibility, and turns to a discussion of the nature of our ideas about the past in the treatise's second half. He never addresses arguments against the first possibility, namely, that a mental act is nothing but the mind itself, a position which could be a reference to Ockham's argument that concepts are merely acts of the mind, with no more being of their own than any other action. That Wyclif declines to pursue this suggests that his efforts are indirectly aimed at Crathorn. Crathorn argued that there are no mental acts, only the mind and species, and Wyclif is arguing vigorously for mental acts as qualities of the mind by rejecting the possibility that our ideas are distinct from our minds. If we assume that Wyclif recognizes that there are species distinct from our mental acts, then arguing against the third possibility is sufficient for dismissing the first as well.

Wyclif begins *De Actibus Anime* by explaining that all of the soul's actions, its powers, intentions, and habits, are best approached through understanding its acts, which are best known and the ideal medium through which to know the others:

> Few or none would disagree that there are acts of the soul. Nobody doubts that at some time [the soul] can sense, understand, wish or eschew, and other particular acts. And it is impossible thus to have one's self, unless there were a being indicating itself to be in this way; therefore such a being is recognized as such.[32]

After a little unpacking of the language, the sense of the last sentence should be familiar. Even if one doubts that there are acts of the soul, one cannot doubt that there is something there doing the doubting. This truth, generally connected with the *Meditations* of Descartes, was well known by the scholastics and had been mentioned by Augustine in *De Civitate Dei* 11.26 and *De Trinitate* XI. Scotus and Henry of Ghent made reference to it in arguing against skepticism, while Nicholas of Autrecourt argued that it did not provide sufficient epistemic certainty. In the 1330s, Fitzralph referred to it as reliable evidence that some things can be known with certainty, and Crathorn did as well: "If someone doubts a proposition like this one, 'I exist,' it follows that he exists, because this follows: 'I doubt that I exist; therefore, I exist.' For anyone who does not exist does not doubt. Therefore no one can doubt this proposition: 'I exist.'"[33]

Wyclif includes another approach among his arguments for mental acts as qualities. Acts of the mind, he begins, have attributes that no thing existing on its own could have, which means that they would have to be accidents, beings reliant on the existence of another. Imagine assuming that the statement "every man understands himself to be a non-understanding being" is true. Call the statement A. It is possible to imagine assuming this, because we immediately recognize that it is impossible that A is true. "And it is clear that A, when it is understood, does not name its subject [i.e., a member of the set 'every man'] to be not-understanding, but to be understanding." If A did designate a man to be not-understanding, it would designate every man to be not-understanding and would be contradicted by the fact that there is somebody who is understanding A. Now, if ideas are things distinct from the mind and per se substantial beings, then some would exist as true and some as false. It would be impossible for one to exist where both its affirmation and its denial leads to a contradiction. But A, if true, would be contradictory, because it would require an understanding man to recognize its truth. If A is false, then there would be some man who does not understand himself to be a non-understanding being. Then that man would be able truly to say "I am not understanding." But if he were truly saying this, he must have *some* understanding, at least of what is involved in understanding something, which would be a contradiction. Hence, Wyclif argues that he can imagine a statement the truth and the falsity of which lead to a contradiction, and since no per se substantial being can do this, then this kind of idea, at least, must be reliant on the existence of the mind that comprehends it.

The argument rests on the ontological status of a class of statements that fascinated medieval thinkers, *insolubilia*, which they used to probe the relations among spoken, written, and mental language. These statements can be understood as a class by thinking of the famous liar paradox, in which the speaker says, "I am lying." Is the statement true or false? If true, then it is false, and if false, then it is true. Thomas Bradwardine suggested that such sentences signify that they are at once true and false, and Burley responded that all sentences imply that they are the truth. Following Burley's reasoning, such insoluble sentences are true only if they are both true and false at the same time. Since this is impossible, then all insoluble sentences are simply false. Richard Swineshead had suggested that such sentences are useful in helping us to distinguish between a sentence's truth and its correspondence to reality. Consider the pair of sentences "this sentence is false" and its contradiction, "this sentence is not false." The first is itself false, because what it is asserting is the truth. But it does correspond to reality. But the second sentence, its contradiction, does not correspond to reality, so it really is a false sentence, which also makes the contradiction false. Wyclif's interest in these sentences was so great that he wrote an entire treatise on them, apparently during the same time that he wrote *De Actibus Anime*.[34]

Using Logic to Resolve Confusion II:
Knowing and Belief

In the questions of what knowledge involves, and what the act of knowing is, Wyclif's approach is to turn to logic to clear up problems that threaten to swamp the project of theology. Wyclif's conception of what knowledge involves will influence his argument that theology, which involves faith, counts as a science. His discussion in *Logice Continuacio* is part of a larger analysis of the kinds of terms that need special treatment when parsing the meaning of propositions. The assertion of knowing, or of doubt, within a proposition points to the nature of knowledge itself. If we have knowledge, we have something present to us the certainty of which can be measured. If what we know is certain because anytime we test it, it turns out to be the truth, we have knowledge of a universally holding statement. Knowing that "every fire is hot" is an example of this kind of knowing. Knowing a first principle is even more certain. Once every part of such a statement is understood, the truth of the statement is given. Knowing that "nothing at once is and is not" is like this, since its truth is evident from the very nature of the terms. Finally, knowing a deductively clear truth is the best sort of knowing, Wyclif argues, because such a truth tells us more about the world than the first two. Such a truth, which arises from the conjoining of two simpler statements in syllogistic reasoning, is the basis for deductive science. Here, Wyclif has deductive systems like Euclidean geometry in mind.

But there are more kinds of knowledge than these. Acts of knowing either proceed from these habitually present things known, or they proceed from what is evident to the senses, or from evidence of what *could* be perceived, if the knower were locally or temporally situated. That is, I might recognize a triangle that I happen upon in architecture or in a painting as being a right triangle, and so know both from what is evident to my senses and from what I have in my head about right triangles. Or I might know that Paris is a beautiful city, even though I've never been there. Actual knowing, Wyclif explains, is ultimately belief in the truth of something, without fear of the contrary being true. My actual knowing might be either of a universal, as in knowing what "humanity" is, or it might be of a particular person. Knowing the universal allows me to recognize the particular. Knowing that this recognition is a dependable result, in that I will usually recognize people to be human beings, given my knowledge of humanity, allows me to know with a general certainty that when I meet the next person, I'll recognize her as being a person. But an element of doubt has crept in. There is always the possibility that I might not recognize the next person I meet as a human being, so I can't say with certainty that I know that I will recognize her.

Actual knowing, which always includes belief, functions on a par with habitual knowing, the term Wyclif uses for the first kind of more certain knowing. If yesterday I saw the pope standing before me, I knew him to be alive at that time, but because I do not now see him, my knowledge of him being alive involves belief that nothing has since happened to him. Strictly speaking, my knowledge about him now is not really knowing: it is believing that counts as knowing. Now, when I saw him standing before me yesterday, there was certainly a degree of belief involved. I believed my senses, and I believed that the man before me was indeed the person he presented himself as being. But now, belief is more of an issue, because while certainty that the pope still lives is high, it is not absolute.

Ordinarily, people don't make this kind of distinction. We don't usually measure what we know based on the percentage of slippage caused by the possibility of doubt: "So the laity, who do not doubt or argue about the media that verify the thing believed, frequently know, while the literate, and especially the philosophers, are ignorant."[35] Philosophers can easily let this need for belief lead to problems with skepticism. The right approach to measuring knowing, Wyclif argues, is not to wander in skeptical speculation, but to focus attention on how the language we use about knowing shows what is present to our minds. At a very basic level, a proposition Fx either signifies (a) that you know that there is a given proposition, Fx, or (b) that you know that the proposition Fx signifies a state of affairs about x and F, or (c) that the proposed state of affairs Fx is the truth. Without specifying which way of signifying we have in mind, Fx is something that can be both known and not known at the same time. We can know Fx in the first and the second senses, without knowing whether Fx is really true, in the third sense.

Imagine that you are told that you know a sentence A. Sentence A could be one of two sentences: "God exists" or "a man is an ass." Now we know at the outset that the first is necessarily true, while the second is impossible. Still, you must admit to the truth of knowing the sentence A, with A's content being indeterminate. If by indeterminate, we mean "either of the two" (*altera istorum*), all is well. Even if A *most likely* stands for the impossible proposition, there is always the chance, since "either of the two" admits of both, that the other, necessary sentence is what A stands for. But if by indeterminate, we mean "only one of the two" (*alterum istorum*), then of course there will be a problem, because the leeway that "either of the two" provides is gone. You commit yourself to either knowing that something is necessarily true, or knowing something that you cannot know. "Either of the two" provides a middle ground, while "only one of the two" does not. The point of this example is to show that how we conceive of the names of the things that are given in a proposition that we claim to know has everything to do with whether we really know what we think we know.

Wyclif's Arguments for Theology as Science in *De Trinitate*

By now, the grounds for Wyclif's argument that theology should indeed be counted among the sciences are clear. He has argued that all knowledge outside of the limited sphere of habitual knowledge of indubitable truths, first principles, and deductively certain conclusions involves an element of belief. Given that belief is the foundation for theological reasoning as well, it follows that theology is a science like any other. Wyclif makes the case for this in *De Trinitate*, a treatise included in the *Summa de Ente,* which he appears to have written around 1370. Despite its title, which suggests Augustine's magisterial work on the Trinity, *De Trinitate* focuses on several particular problems that had become set pieces for theologians in the mid-fourteenth century. The complexity of the reasoning that had evolved from theologians' commentaries on book I of Peter Lombard's *Sentences* had become breathtaking.

If God the Father (G[f]) generates God the Son (G[s]), meaning that God generates God, God would have to be distinct from God insofar as the Son and the Father differ. Otherwise, insofar as G(f) is not the same as G(s), then God is not God. One way of interpreting this would be to say that "God is different from God." This could mean that God is not the same as G(f), G(s), and G(hg), which would mean that the Trinity is other than God. Or if G(f) is not the same as G(s), then God the Trinity differs from G(insert a person here). If God is not the same as God, then the difference either lies in number within God, or somehow outside of God, with a distinct God. The former, that there is a difference in number within God, cannot be held by reason of the indiscernibility of identicals. But the latter leads to a difference between God as God and God (a person).

Wyclif's approach to resolving puzzles like this should not be a surprise at this point. Paying attention to how language is used in reasoning about the Trinity, and how that language use pinpoints our ontological commitments, is the key to finding a way out of problems like this one. He had laid the groundwork for his approach to understanding the relation of the persons in the Trinity earlier, between 1366 and 1368, in *Purgans Errores circa Universalia in Communi*:

> In predication according to essence the singular and its universal are distinct, since the singular is one, as the universal another individual. It does not follow, "these are distinct things, so to these we assign number" because through most general and most singular demonstrating of its supposit, any things distinct are these, yet they are not held numerable, since one of them remains. Thus they are distinct formally, but not formally distinct things. Nor are they formally "these two" [indicating this universal and this singular] but they are *this*, and so the differences are to this sense, that these differ, but not through numerical difference; because only by difference formally or according to reason are they "these."[36]

The details of Wyclif's use of Scotus's formal distinction in his own approach to resolving issues like this are manifold, incorporating ontological questions of how God might function as a universal of which the divine persons are particulars, as well as semantic problems as deeply rooted as how to use analogy in talking about God. While these details illustrate Wyclif's conviction that his metaphysical realism is the ideal approach to the complex questions that had developed in the previous decades, our interest here lies in his more general arguments for recognizing theology as foremost among the sciences. Augustine had famously argued that we can come to appreciate the triune nature of God by using our reason to recognize the trinities in nature, most particularly the threefold nature of the human mind: reason, memory, and willing. This use of human reason to reach truth about divinity was among the many called into question by fourteenth-century theologians. Wyclif was not the first to argue that Augustine's approach was valid; Richard Fitzralph argued that the human mind is an imperfect image of the Trinity in his *Sentences Commentary*.[37] Before addressing this issue, the more general question of whether, given the skeptical tendencies that affected fourteenth-century philosophy, we can even use our reason for such a problem needs to be answered.

Wyclif was not the first to raise the banner for theology as a science in response to the *moderni*. We have seen that Bradwardine's thought in *De Causa Dei* presupposes some kind of connection, although he did not articulate it. Further, Aston had shown that we can use logic to demonstrate the necessity of God's being, even if we cannot actually argue from created being to the divine as Aquinas and Scotus had thought. Finally, Richard Brinkley, O.F.M. (f1. 1355–1375) appears to have blazed the path for Wyclif in arguing that man can, by evident reason, infer that human life is itself ordered to another life than the present. Sadly, we do not have Brinkley's *Sentences* commentary, and all that remains appears to be an *abbrevatio* prepared by Etienne Gaudet, a Parisian scholar in the 1360s.[38] Further work on Brinkley will likely yield evidence of his influence on Wyclif.

Wyclif believed that when human reason establishes God's existence, it also establishes the triune nature of the divine essence, even if the demonstrator is unaware of this feat. His interest in relating our rational recognition of God's existence is limited. Elsewhere, he asserts that it is part of our fallen nature that we do not know created beings as they are in their universals, but come to knowledge of universals from their particulars. That is, we come to know the universal X by knowing individual x's. Yet within us, he argues, is the possibility of knowing divine things: "Any such created nature has an innate concrete knowledge by which it knows things as they are in their natural order, and thus the soul has innate comprehensions which it does not receive from the things of sense."[39] Apparently, then, we know innately of God's existence and have no need of a demonstrative proof. In *Trialogus*, Wyclif's character Phronesis, the wise theologian, says, "God's existence is the first thing following from any truth, such that a formal contradiction would arise when holding something to be, or something to be in some way, without first recognizing God to exist."[40] In our discussion of the first treatises of *Summa de Ente* in the next chapter, it will turn out that anyone with a clear understanding of being will recognize that God's existence is necessary for the being of, and our knowing of, anything in creation.

Authorities like Anselm, Augustine, the Victorines, and Grosseteste all argue that the Trinity is evident through recognition of trinities in creatures, natural signs by which we can deduce syllogistically the divine Trinity. Augustine's arguments show that reason allows us to recognize the divine truths woven into creation, but in each case the faith must serve as foundation. "This is generally said," Wyclif continues, "that no one can assent to this deduction [of the threefold divine nature from perceived created trinities] without faith, and so it is not merely natural, and is not demonstrated in the natural light."[41] But if faith is the foundation, is demonstration through natural reasoning impossible? All reasoning demands some sort of nonrational assent, Wyclif argues, either before or outside of the reasoning process, to conditions that serve as evidence for the reasoning to take place. Learning to read or to speak requires a degree of faith in the teacher. The absence of the light of faith infused in the mind allows one to give assent to many ideas, but in each case, the mind craves evidence of some kind. The testimony of authority counts as such even in matters otherwise neutral, so assent can be given in these matters from the authority of scripture or teaching that will be, in light of divine reality, rationally clear to all.

Later in his life, Wyclif made a similar argument in *Trialogus*, where his foil, Pseustis, argues a simplified version of the Ockhamist position. His champion, Phronesis, responds:

> It is impossible for the faithful or the heretic to know something, unless they know it fundamentally through faith; because just as nobody knows letters—that one is A, the next B, and so of other—unless they believe, so nobody by their senses know[s] anything sensible, unless first truth speaks and teaches that, that a thing is sensible in one way or in another.[42]

Faith is not judged to be better relative to the wealth of evidence available; the faith of a rich man with a Bible is not superior to that of a poor man without one. Not all acts of faith result in immediate understanding. Sometimes, we believe something, yet never understand it, while at other times, we come to an understanding immediately on giving assent to it, and at still others, what is believed is only understood after thought. This shows that not all faiths are of a kind.

But are they always present in any act of knowledge? And if so, and if faith is a virtuous qualitative *habitus*, which all theologians recognize to be a theological virtue, can we know anything without the assistance of grace, which is necessary for any theological virtue? Wyclif is not clear on the place of illumination in knowledge in *De Trinitate*, although he does argue that grace is necessary for any virtuous act in *De Dominio Divino* III. We must deduce his allegiance to Augustine, Grosseteste, and Bonaventure.

Their position was that every act of understanding entails the divine illumination of the mind, a participation in the light of Truth every time we apprehend the truth. Aquinas and Scotus limited the need for this illumination to the sphere of revelation, arguing that the unassisted human reason is capable of accurately perceiving the truth about things in this world without the need of divine assistance. Faith factors into this question when truths understood by pagans such as Aristotle must be explained; Aristotle lacked the Christian faith, yet reasoned out the truth of things in the world. This led Aquinas to conclude that one could not have faith and knowledge about the same thing. Faith requires assent without evidence, while knowledge entails having that evidence. Henry of Ghent (d. 1293) is the last widely studied philosopher to have argued the need for divine illumination before Nicholas of Cusa in the fifteenth century. By the shape of Wyclif's arguments here, it is difficult to avoid concluding that he followed Henry, Bonaventure, and Grosseteste in arguing the need for divine illumination. "For it is impossible for a creature to know anything unless it knows it through grounding from the authority of God teaching and moving to assent."[43]

All that we understand, then, requires some faithful assent of the human mind, some acquiescence to evidence that might be doubted. In the case of understanding objects we perceive, our intuition of sense data entails faith, which kindles the growth of knowledge as our experiences increase and leads to acts of judgment about the world. Faith has a natural place in all of our acts of understanding, great and small, and if we can claim to have an accurate explanation for even the least act of understanding the simplest thing, we should also admit to the possibility that great truths of faith, like the Trinity, may be explored and understood by human reason. If the articles of faith were demonstrable scientifically, philosophers would already have done so, without the need for revelation. But the articles of faith are subtle, hidden from natural light. The merit that comes from faith consists in voluntarily and humbly submitting the sensibility to the authority of the Catholic church and the articles of faith, against which rebellion is a sin. So to view faith and reason as incompatible is premature. Faith is at once an act of believing, a habit, an assent to a truth; since what is known is believed as well, faith and knowing are not really incompatible.

WYCLIF IN OXFORD

Logic, Metaphysics

Grosseteste, Ockham, and
Schools of Thought

Two English thinkers define later medieval Oxford philosophy and theology: Robert Grosseteste (1170–1273) and William Ockham (1287–1347).
Each attracted students who would further their intellectual vision and
profoundly influenced thought in fourteenth-century Oxford. It would
be premature to view their differing approaches as inherently antithetical to one another, though. Both were willing to countenance Aristotelian
thought as the basis for understanding the created universe, and both have
been described as philosophical mathematizers, in reference to their interest in taking an analytical approach to problems. The differences between
them lie more in how they thought Aristotle's philosophy could articulate
the traditional Augustinian Christian ideal.[1]

A handy means of distinguishing them is their answer to the question
of what there is in the universe. Do individual members of a species have
their special identities through their relations to an unchanging universal,
or are individuals of a species related to one another without reference to
an additional universal? That is, is there a universal "dog" by virtue of
which all animals that have a canine nature are defined, or are all canine
animals members of the species dog without reference to some immutable,

eternal dog-ness? Grosseteste argued for the existence of universals *ante res*, following the traditional Boethian version of the *Categories* in which a Neoplatonist reading of Aristotle's ontology determined much of twelfth-century philosophy. This does not mean that Grosseteste conceived of a realm of universals having existence between God and creation, a Platonic world of forms. Universals do not exist apart from their particulars, but are ontologically distinct from the particulars in which they inhere. This distinction is most fully realized in our mind's understanding of them, but it does not depend upon our recognition for its reality. The subordinate relationship of species universals to genus universals, for example, is not dependent upon our recognition of that relation, but is a real relation based in the directive creative force of the divine ideas, God's definitive understanding of creation. Grosseteste's position appears to have been the ideal formulation of a Christian Aristotelian ontology for Wyclif, and it will help our understanding to discuss it briefly.

Grosseteste's realism arises in his *Commentary* on Aristotle's *Posterior Analytics*, where he explains how the objects of demonstration in scientific knowledge are incorruptible. Aristotle argues in *Posterior Analytics* I.8 (75b22–36) that, if the premises in a syllogism are universally true, the conclusion must also be universally true, or eternal. If you formulate a proof for a universal truth like "all dogs are mammals," and you rely on existing dogs as your only verification, Aristotle appears to be saying, the truth is not universal and eternally true, but reliant on the contingent being of individual dogs. For Grosseteste, this led to an exploration of the kinds of universal truths that our minds can encounter. First, we are capable of recognizing that God's mind contains uncreated reasons, the eternal ideas that are the archetypes for all of the kinds of creatures. Second, angelic minds, or intelligences, have a complete knowledge of creation, which they derive from their contemplation of the divine ideas. The universal truths as understood by the intelligences can be communicated to human minds through divine illumination, and these are the bases for human understanding of incorruptible truth. Third, we can recognize with our unaided reason that the heavenly bodies have the power to cause acts in the world, to bring about events without themselves experiencing change or diminution. Fourth, we are capable of recognizing forms in created substances that can be classified according to genera and species.

Ockham is famous for having interpreted Aristotle as having eliminated universals from ontology altogether, rejecting talk of "natures" as philosophical constructs grounded in a misunderstanding of what there is in the world. A being is either really distinct from all other beings, as Snoopy is distinct from all other dogs, or is only distinct from them by virtue of our thinking them so. There are no real universal natures, only conceptual constructs that human beings have put together from experience with beings in the world. Thus, Grosseteste is more of a Platonist, and Ockham much less of one, denying the existence of universals *ante res* altogether.[2] These two positions represent comparative extremes in the debate about universals. Between them are arrayed a host of more refined, "moderate" positions, most of which recognize the existence of universal natures, but only insofar as individual members of a species have common natures that we, in cognizing them, recognize to be universal. The positions of Aquinas, Scotus, Henry of Ghent, and others fit into this middle ground, as do many of the thinkers we will discuss later in this chapter. The most extreme realist position, like that of Burley or, later, Wyclif, would hold that a universal exists whole and complete in each of its particulars and is not affected by changes in the number of these particulars. Their conceptualist opponents, like Henry Harclay and, later, Adam Wodeham, rejected the idea that a thing can exist unchanging and undivided in two distinct particulars. So when Wyclif championed the existence of universals *ante res*, citing Grosseteste as his authority and the "doctors of signs" as the agents of deception, he was not arguing for the existence of universals apart from their particulars, as Plato did, but for the priority of the existence of universals in the being of their particulars. This appears to have been the consensus of those who followed in the footsteps of Grosseteste at Oxford, particularly at Merton College.

The Circle of Richard de Bury

Of the many important thinkers who figured in the theological and scientific debates at Oxford between 1315 and 1349, several tower over the rest. Not by coincidence, these theologians also play an important role in Wyclif's thought. Walter Burley, Thomas Bradwardine, and Richard Fitzralph are each mentioned by Wyclif as authoritative in the arguments that underlie his own theological vision: Burley in metaphysics, Bradwardine in formal theology, and Fitzralph in his theory of dominion. Robert Holcot's name, on the other hand, does not appear in Wyclif's works, but his presence looms nonetheless, because Holcot embodied much of what Wyclif detested, both as a philosopher and as a preacher. These four figures were included in a remarkable unofficial affiliation of theologians at Durham, a circle of comrades associated with the highly placed Bishop Richard de Bury (1287–1345), whose love of the world of ideas had led him to gather a select group of scholars and clerics into his household. Bury had studied at Oxford in the first decade of the fourteenth century and then moved on to royal service, where he occupied a trusted position with the young Edward III. During the mid-1330s, he served Edward as treasurer of the exchequer, chancellor of the realm, and diplomatic envoy to the French, the pope, and the Scots.

Bury was an enthusiastic bibliophile, amassing a remarkable library of theological and philosophical works. He also wrote the *Philobiblon*, which begins as an encomium to the book's status as a permanent repository of human wisdom, worthy of infinite respect and care. It moves into an indictment of contemporary attitudes toward the liberal arts, castigating scholars for plagiarism, monks for indifference to the treasures in their libraries, and friars for turning from their founders' ideals. Soon, Bury is expressing his anguish that scholars have turned from the depth and profundity of the masters of antiquity to the flashy seductions of modern novelties. At the universities, young scholars confuse general familiarity with the liberal arts for wisdom:

> While still beardless boys they gabble with childish stammering the Categorics and the Peri Hermeneias. . . . Passing through these faculties with baneful haste and a harmful diploma, they lay violent hands upon Moses, and sprinkling about their faces dark waters and thick clouds of the skies, they offer their heads, unhonoured by the snows of age, for the mitre of the pontificate.

Paris is particularly infected with this tendency to wrap shabby doctrine in unskilled discourse; its scholars are weak in logic and devoid of the depth of true wisdom. Only in England's scholars is wisdom served:

> Admirable Minerva seems to bend her course to all the nations of the earth. . . . she has already visited the Indians, the Babylonians, the Egyptians and Greeks, the Arabs and Romans. Now she has passed by Paris, and has happily come to Britain, the most noble of islands, nay, rather a microcosm in itself, that she may show herself a debtor both to the Greeks and to the Barbarians.[3]

Bury's words suggest that Oxford scholars saw their university as the new Athens, where the rich heritage of classical antiquity, notably the works of Aristotle, could enrich Christian doctrine and discourse. The members of Bury's circle of scholars included most of the important Oxonians of the middle decades of the fourteenth century: in addition to Burley, Bradwardine, Fitzralph, and Holcot, Bury included a number of other scientists and theologians, including Richard Kilvington and Walter Chatton, in his entourage. Scholars continue to suspect that the long-standing view that Holcot helped in the writing of *Philobiblon* is the truth, suggesting a general understanding among the theology faculty that Oxford had established itself as a worthy successor to the academic mantle that Paris claimed. The ideal of recovering the riches of classical antiquity for the benefits of contemporary society, which is usually associated with Renaissance humanism, is very much in evidence in the writings of Bury's circle, suggesting that only the horrors of the plague staved off a humanist florescence at Oxford.[4]

Walter Burley and Universals

Walter Burley was renowned at both Oxford and Paris as a logician, philosopher, and theologian, and in his early years at Merton College, he was likely to have been a student of Scotus and a contemporary of Ockham. When Burley had moved to Paris to lecture on the *Sentences* in 1318, Ockham was teaching his austere ontology at Oxford. The two seem to have been well acquainted by this point. Burley energetically opposed Ockham's logic and metaphysics, and Ockham made use of Burley's thought both to formulate his own philosophy and to respond to Burley's challenges. The cliché that Ockham's logical and semantic analytic approach necessarily entails a rejection of metaphysical realism is undone with a reading of Burley's philosophy. He was an important innovator in several logical genres, including the theory of the logical disputations called *obligationes*, the theory of reference called supposition theory, and other questions in the semantic analysis of the language of written terms and concepts. While his ontology rates as the most realist regarding the existence of universals, his understanding of the importance of linguistic and logical analysis of how terms function in arguments rivals Ockham's. The realists who were to follow at Oxford throughout the fourteenth century were heavily indebted to Burley's thought, and even thinkers more disposed to Ockham's meta-physics, like Adam Wodeham, recognized his importance.

Burley left Paris in 1327 and served Edward III as a diplomat to Avignon, along with John Thoresby, later archbishop of York and patron to the young Wyclif. He returned to England to stay with Bury in 1334, and there he produced most of his philosophical works. By now in his six-ties, he left in 1341 for southern France and Italy, where he engaged in a *Commentary* on Aristotle's *Politics* in honor of his comrade from his days at Paris, now Clement VI. He returned to England several years later to serve as rector at Kent, where he likely died.[5] Scholarship has recently begun to reflect the many facets of Burley's philosophical corpus, but our attention will focus only on his realist metaphysics because of its bearing on Wyclif's thought. Burley was not the only thinker to formulate a real-ist metaphysics in response to Ockhamist conceptualism. Walter Chatton, O.F.M., the Carmelite Robert Walsingham (d. 1313), and the secular Richard Kilvington number among those who argued that while the terms we use, like "human" and "animal," do signify concepts that we have formulated in our minds, the concepts naturally signify extramental, real, universal beings the existence of which is mind-independent. While there were certainly conceptualists to oppose them, the proponents of realism seem to have been widespread in Oxford in the first half of the fourteenth century.

Burley's realism evolved. Before 1324, his ontology was similar to the "moderate" approach of Henry of Ghent, in which a universal is not some-thing really distinct from its particulars. In this stage of his thought, universals have being outside of our minds in the individual things they define, and they have being as concepts within our minds. Beyond our minds, these universals are capable of being in many things at once, and they have a part to play in the concepts we form of them, but they do not have any real being beyond the things in which they inhere and the concepts that we form of them. Further, they are constitutive parts of the things in which they inhere and lack any individuality of their own. This approach differs from Aquinas's in that Aquinas believed that universals exist in potentiality only in things and are brought into real being by our understanding of them, while Burley believed that universals do not require our understanding for their being. All they require, in this early view, is the being of particulars. For example, humanity does not require our understanding of it to exist as a universal; it requires only the existence of individual people. The change came about when he began responding to Ockham's criticisms of the moderate realist ontology in general. Ockham's attacks had validity, Burley responded, insofar as universals are believed not to be really distinct from their particulars, and so rather than discard them altogether, it would be better to recognize that universals are really distinct from, and indeed superior to, their particulars.[6]

Burley, like many medievals, did not understand Aristotle to have ruled out the existence of universals altogether. One of the texts most commonly used as access to Aristotle's *Categories*, where Aristotle explores the relation between words and things, was the *Isagoge* of Porphyry, a student of Plotinus. This text gives a Neoplatonic approach to Aristotle's understanding of ontology and language. Porphyry leads the reader along a line of reasoning that lends itself to realism. He explains that, in examining the relation of universals to singulars, one must first ask whether universals exist, and if so, whether they have being as concepts only or as extraconceptual beings, and if the latter, whether they exist corporeally or incorporeally, and if incorporeally, whether they exist apart from perceptible objects or not. In his later commentary on Porphyry, Burley began on the assumption, for which he had argued in his 1310 analysis of the *Categories*, that there is an important link between how we compound sentences or propositions out of terms, and how things are arranged in the world into facts.

Take a person like Socrates. He is a being existing in the world, and we can recognize the fact that he is (or was) a human being. We describe this state of affairs with the proposition "Socrates is a human." Burley's reasoning was that "is a human" describes a truth about Socrates, so being human must be something distinct somehow from being Socrates. We can formulate the proposition "Socrates is not a human," and it makes enough sense for us to recognize that it is not the truth. Duns Scotus had argued earlier that being human is indeed distinct from being Socrates, but that the distinction is formal. This means that we can separate out being human from being Socrates in our minds, allowing us to recognize a common human nature in Socrates distinct from the particularized being peculiar to Socrates alone ("haecceity" is Scotus's term for this), and this recognition mirrors a reality within Socrates. But because Scotus thought it impossible for the haecceity of Socrates to be really separated from his common human nature, the two are only distinct formally. Burley thought that the common human nature would have to be really distinct from the being of the individual person, in part because Ockham pointed out that attributing reality to the common human nature within Socrates would lead to some uncomfortable consequences. For example, if the common human nature in Socrates is a constitutive part of Socrates, and if it is a constitutive part of Plato as well, then if Plato is sitting and Socrates is not, the real human nature must be both sitting and not sitting. If the universal humanity is not a part of Socrates, then, and if it is not merely a concept, as Ockham thought, it must be something real and mind-independent existing in Socrates. It is not in Socrates like a swallowed cherry pit, though, because the swallowed cherry pit does not contribute to the metaphysical makeup of Socrates, while humanity does. Nor is it in Socrates like an accident, like being six feet tall or weighing 150 pounds, because a substance can exist without a particular accident (Socrates could gain weight, or grow), but a singular would not exist without the universal defining it.

The time-honored response to this is called the Third Man argument, which was first formulated by Plato in *Parmenides* (132A1–B2; 132D1–133A3) and wielded by Aristotle in his refutation of Platonism in *Metaphysics* 1.9. If every agreement between two things is an agreement in something they share, and the universal humanity exists in Socrates, and if these two agree because both share a nature, then there must be some common nature that is the ground for which the universal humanity and Socrates are in agreement. Call this H1. In what, then, do the universal humanity, Socrates, and H1 agree? This leads to an infinite regress, which suggests an infinite number of men in Socrates, who is himself a finite substance. The problem with this reasoning, Burley explains, lies in the signification mechanism we use to differentiate the universal humanity and the singular Socrates. These two names, "humanity" and "Socrates," are used as signs for individuals, but they are different kinds of individuals: humanity is a universal, and Socrates is a singular, and there are no grounds for comparing the two in the same way that one would compare two individuals.

Burley explicitly rules out Platonism, the position that universals exist separately from individuals in an ideal realm. Scientific knowledge is of sensible things, but not of individual things. If a universal, like humanity, were separate from the individual people to whom it gives definition, it would be an individual thing, and we could not have scientific knowledge of it.[7] Universals exist in individual substances, which are composed of matter and form. Burley's realism addresses the problem of the unity of form by recognizing that there is one primary substantial form that gives identity to the matter of an individual, but this does not rule out the existence of secondary substantial forms that give identity to parts. For example, in Socrates, there is one substantial form, namely, his intellective soul, which gives Socrates his individual identity, but since there are differences in his various parts, in that his bones are different from his muscles, there must be forms by which parts of the matter of Socrates are differentiated into muscle and other parts into bone. Thus far, Burley's account is similar to that of Aquinas described above, in that one substantial form gives identity to a substance, while lesser forms coexist within it. Burley's departure lies in his assertion that there are other general forms or natures in a given substance that can be shared with other substances, forms like humanity and animality, substantiality and rationality. Earlier, he had argued that these are component parts of a substance, but his later position was to rule out these general forms being constitutive of an individual. This does not mean that humanity is not part of the makeup of Socrates. When we cognize Socrates, our intellective soul actualizes the potential of the universal humanity that is naturally present to it as an organizing force, which makes the universal essential to Socrates, but not actively constitutive of his being. The intellective soul relies on these universals, making them quidditative parts, but this reliance does not make them component parts of Socrates.

These universals do not exist apart from the individuals to which they give identity, but their identity is not the same kind as the identity that they give. "This name 'man' signifies a thing outside the soul yet this thing is not one in number, but one according to species, nor is every thing outside the soul one thing in number."[8] Burley calls the identity of a universal "specific or generic identity," while the identity of a substance is "numerical identity." Beings with specific or generic identity are not limited by the rule that a thing cannot be two places at the same time, simply because they do not have the numerical identity that would make this rule apply. Burley is not simply using an invented identity distinction to define universals into existence. He is following Aristotle's division of the categories of being, where a secondary substance is described as being different from a primary substance. A *primary* substance is something that can exist on its own, with its own essence, capable of accidents or properties, while a *secondary* substance is dependent on individual primary substances for their own existence. Burley understands Aristotle as describing secondary substances as universal types, of which primary substances are the individual tokens. The identity of the individual depends on the universal, but the being of the type rests on the being of the tokens.

This is the strongest sort of realism about universals that there was in fourteenth-century Aristotelian metaphysics, but Burley appears to have emerged as the benchmark for realism only in the 1360s. Most in Oxford recognized Adam Wodeham as the chief exponent of Ockhamism, and it would be logical to expect him to have argued energetically against Burley. But Wodeham rarely mentions him, leading William Courtenay to suspect that Walter Chatton's realism was more widely discussed at the time.[9] Chatton was vigorously attacked by Wodeham for espousing an ontology similar to Burley's around 1330, long after Burley had left Oxford. By the time Burley was in Bury's circle in Durham, he would likely have been familiar with Wodeham's arguments. It was during this period that he wrote the *Commentaries* on Porphyry and Aristotle that express most fully his belief that universals have real being apart from particulars. In the meantime, Chatton was in the company of Walsingham, Ralph Pigaz, and Kilvington, although none of these were to present as forceful and extended an argument for realism as Burley did. By the 1340s, Richard Kilvington had joined Bury in Durham, Walter Chatton had moved to Avignon, and we have no evidence for Ralph Pigaz beyond 1329.

William Crathorn

William Crathorn, O.P., formulated a conceptualist viewpoint worth considering, partially because its ontology accurately reflects Ockham's own and partially because his conceptualism serves only as a basis for his chief concern, which is about how we know things. In this, Crathorn is very much like many of his colleagues, for whom epistemic questions were more important than ontological ones. While Crathorn's account of how we understand was certainly not typical of fourteenth-century theorists of knowledge, his ontology is sufficiently representative of the pared-down Ockhamist position against which Burley had argued. We know little about Crathorn save that he was present at Oxford in the 1330s and that, despite being a fellow Dominican, he was the target of Holcot's determined opposition. While his position appears related to the position against which Wyclif argued in *De Actibus Anime*, he is especially worth our attention here because his discussion of how universal terms signify figures significantly in Wyclif's *De Universalibus*.

The topic of Crathorn's discussion in the second question of his *Sentences* commentary is not ontology, but epistemology. How we form mental propositions and how we reason with them occupies center stage, but the subject matter demands being clear about what singular and universal terms are. Aristotle had said in *Physics* that universals are the place where we begin with our understanding of things in the world. Crathorn explains that there are five ways that a universal term may be understood. First, the term may refer to something having causal power over all or many things, as God has over creation, or as a heavenly body has over beings inferior to it. Another way something is said to be universal is through its perfection, as God is perfect in anything that can be said of him, and each thing that can be said is equivalent to all the rest within the unity of God's perfection. Then again, universality can be predicated of something similar to many other things. A fourth way is when something represents other things either naturally, as with smoke signifying combustion, or artificially, as when a given word, like "dog," stands for anything canine. Finally, Crathorn concludes by saying that something could be universal according to essence or existence, "in the way that Aristotle explains about what Plato believed to be universal."

In this brief catalog of the uses of the term "universal," Crathorn displays a decidedly Ockhamist position: there are no real, extramental, universal entities listed, nor is there room for the introduction of concepts that naturally signify natures or essences having universal identity. Things are similar to one another, and words stand for concepts and things by human convention. A thing may naturally stand for another thing all of the time, as with the relation of smoke and fire, but by no means are we to think that there is some supervening universal relation involved. His final comment about what Aristotle attributes to Plato intimates that he understands Aristotle effectively to have refuted Plato's ontology. In short, the only thing that is universal is a term, which may be mental or written. It is important to ask where Crathorn came up with his list of variant uses of the term universal, though; his arrangement is by no means novel. His listing suggests familiarity with the kinds of universal truths that Grosseteste lists in his *Commentary on the Posterior Analytics*. Wyclif may have had Crathorn's list in mind in his recounting of Grosseteste's list in *De Universalibus* 2, since he comments that all of the respectable authors he can recall having read understand Aristotle only to have argued against the divine ideas being included among the universals.

Crathorn figured in the previous chapter as having advocated the odd position that, since there are no mental acts, when we know something like a white cat, we have a white feline-ness in our minds. In eliminating mental acts and formulating the outlandish idea that our minds take on the qualities of the species of the perceived objects, he seems to be approaching the idea that our knowing involves more than just knowing a proposition only, and more than just knowing the thing that the proposition is about. While he followed Ockham in rejecting universals, he departed from Ockham epistemologically by holding that even the most basic elements of knowing are propositional. Given that there are no universals, it follows that there are only individual things in the world about which we make propositions. But knowing these individual things always involves complexity: "To be white, or not to be white, is not something simple [*incomplexum*] but complex."[10] So, for any given proposition we formulate, there must be something complex, and distinct from the proposition, that the proposition is about. Holcot regarded this position with disdain, arguing that, if this were true, there would have to be two classes of things signified: simples and complexes. A proposition like "Socrates exists" would signify the simple Socrates, while "Socrates is white" signifies the complex Socrates and his whiteness. But a proposition like "man is not an ass" signifies neither man nor ass; are we to conclude that there is a third class that propositions can signify, namely, the class of nothing?[11] Holcot's rejection of Crathorn's belief that the objects of science are more than just propositions, while consonant with Ockham, did not convince Wodeham, who developed a more philosophically tenable version of what Crathorn was moving toward, without the attendant epistemological peculiarity.

Adam Wodeham contra Walter Chatton

Fourteenth-century thinkers concentrated on the relation between how things are in the world and how we know them. All talk of universals, whether in favor or against, boils down to the relation between how extramental reality is structured, and how our understanding of it is structured by how thought itself is structured. One does not simply assert that there are no universals in things outside the mind without accounting for how those things relate to the universal concepts that our minds construct and use to explain extramental reality. Likewise, one does not argue for the existence of universals without explaining how the concepts that our minds use are related to the extramental universal realities they describe. The argument about universals has, thus far, been described in deceptively simple terms. Some thinkers, like Grosseteste and Burley, have been portrayed as arguing for universals outside the mind, with attention to the propositional structure of language, while others, like Ockham, have been described as rejecting extramental universals as extraneous to a more simplified ontology of things and accidents. In both cases, the positions represent ontological extremes without much attention to the logical and epistemological complexity that was the hallmark of fourteenth-century philosophical debate. Some attention to that complexity will help us to understand why Wyclif took the position that he did.

Adam Wodeham's *Sentences* commentary provides a convenient starting point for our exploration of the relation of logic and epistemology to ontology. Wodeham enjoyed great prominence at Oxford as Ockham's foremost disciple, and was active there from 1322 to his death in 1358, except for a short stay in Norwich in the mid-1320s and a trip to Basel in 1339. Lombard's *Sentences* begins with Augustine's dictum that all teaching is either of things, or of signs.[12] Wodeham takes this opportunity to contrast the approaches of two of his senior colleagues, Walter Chatton and William Ockham. Chatton, he explains, had argued that the objects of scientific knowledge are things outside the mind, which are mind-independent realities that we translate into the terms that make up mental propositions. Ockham, on the other hand, held that the object of knowing is the mental proposition we formulate about the things we perceive. Both views are admissible, Wodeham admits, but taken separately, each falls short.

On the face of it, Chatton and Ockham may not appear to be in too much disagreement. Chatton holds that we understand things outside the mind, make judgments about them, and translate that understanding into mental propositions, while Ockham argues that we perceive things outside the mind and immediately translate those perceptions into mental propositions, which are what we understand and about which we make judgments. Either way, our understanding tracks directly onto extramental reality and is naturally structured in our minds according to the propositional structure of subjects and predicates. But Chatton's position dispenses with the mediation of propositions, while Ockham's emphasizes this. Chatton argued:

> Assent to a proposition itself necessarily presupposes assent to the thing signified by the proposition, because I assent that "thus it is in reality as is signified by the proposition" before I assent that the proposition is true. Hence the first assent which the intellect has in forming the proposition does not have the proposition itself for an object but [instead] the thing or things signified by means of [the proposition].[13]

Ockham, on the other hand, argued that the first assent our intellect gives in an act of knowledge is to a proposition naturally formed about what we perceive:

> The intellect apprehending a singular thing performs within itself a cognition of this singular only. This cognition is called a state of mind, and it is capable of standing for this singular thing by its very nature. . . . The mind's own intellectual acts are called states of mind. By their nature they stand for the actual things outside the mind or for other things in the mind, just as spoken words stand for them by convention.[14]

Chatton's was only one voice among the many critics of Ockham's approach in fourteenth-century Oxford, but his was a critical one because it led to Wodeham's idea that, in making judgments about things in the world, we take more into consideration than the bare particulars under discussion. Wodeham agreed with Chatton that we make judgments about the perceived thing, and not about the mental proposition we form about it. Science is not about sentences, after all, but about things. But scientific knowledge involves time-relative truths that are glossed over by Chatton's approach. If all that is needed is a thing to serve as a statement's reference, then so long as there is an angel, the statements "there was an angel" or "there will be an angel" are not just true, but functionally identical. This seems wrong. Hence, Wodeham argued that our knowledge is not just about bare particulars, things in themselves, but about how things are in the world. Wodeham calls this thing known *quoddam significabile per complexum*, something signifiable through a complex (proposition), or a complexly significable. What Wodeham believes that we understand and make judgments about is how things are in the world when the world conforms to the mode of signifying that is characteristic of the proposition formed by the mind. That is, Wodeham's complexly significable theory propositionalizes the world. Put another way, complexly significables are "modes of things rather than things, answers to questions about how things are rather than what they are."[15]

In 1918, Bertrand Russell gave a series of lectures entitled "The Philosophy of Logical Atomism" in which he argued that true statements describe facts, but that facts are not particular things in the world. While facts are a part of the natural world, they are not real things apart from, or in addition to, the objects to which they refer. They arise from objects in the world as we make statements about the world. We use symbols, words, numbers, and so on to refer to the elements of these facts. He sternly warned against philosophers, and other scientists, presuming that the symbols they use to describe the world map directly onto things in the world: "Unless you are fairly self-conscious about symbols, . . . aware of the relation of the symbol to what it symbolizes, you will find yourself attributing to the thing properties which only belong to the symbol."[16] Wodeham's ontology is in no real way complicated by his compromise between Chatton and Ockham, because he does not believe that this logical means of distinguishing the complexity of what is known entails the separate existence of a corresponding complexity in being. Likewise, Crathorn, who seems to have adopted the complexly signifiable for his own uses in the account just given of his conception of universals, did nothing with the idea to suggest ontological complexity. Russell would have approved. But the idea of a complexly significable lent itself to trouble. Nicholas of Autrecourt was charged with holding that the complexly significable expressed by this statement, "God and creatures are distinct," is nothing, and Gregory of Rimini (c. 1300–1358) appears to have used the idea to enrich his ontology considerably. Autrecourt's condemned teaching suggests that scholars were soon debating the ontological status of an idea that Wodeham had used to mediate the disagreement about the object of scientific knowledge. Wyclif used the idea to explain the relation of propositions about things to things themselves in a way that would have appalled Wodeham and infuriated Russell.

Wyclif's Propositional Realism

Wyclif's conception of the relation of propositions to things has been usefully characterized as "pan-propositionalism": at its core, Wyclif's theory is that whatever is, is a proposition.[17] "A proposition, broadly speaking, is 'a being signifying in a complex way'; and so, because everything that is signifies in a complex way that it exists, everything that is can well enough be said to be a proposition."[18] The problems that arise from this vie noisily with one another for our attention. One might ask immediately how, assuming every proposition to have a truth value, there could be false propositions like "nobody exists." How can this verbal construct, which signifies an absence of everybody, including somebody to put these words together as they have been, have being? How can there be any false propositions at all? And what about propositions of indeterminate or future contingent truth value? Another problem would be, how can a thing "say itself" if it has no language, or no mouth? Another problem would be, what is the relation between the being of a thing and the being of the proposition that it "says"? Are they the same? How can there be anything "propositional" in the being of a stone lying on the ground? There may be a propositional structure to my recognition of the stone lying on the ground, but why should that suggest anything about the being of the stone?

Wyclif begins explaining this seemingly bizarre assertion by distinguishing between natural and artificial signification:

> The primary signification of a natural proposition is that mediating by which proposing it naturally signifies itself. The primary signification of an artificial [proposition] is that mediating by which proposing it signifies from idiomatic imposition the truth as it is, or as it is not; but this proposition, "God is" primarily signifies from imposition this truth, namely, "God's being"; and this proposition, "man is" primarily from imposition signifies "man's being," and this proposition, "there is no God" signifies primarily from imposition such as is not, nor is possible to be.[19]

By "idiomatic imposition," Wyclif means attaching words, which are human inventions, to the reality they function to describe. Combining the noun "God" with the verb "to be" conjugated in the third-person singular makes an artificially signifying proposition that refers to the extra-verbal truth that there is a God. His theory of the reference of terms is not anything new for fourteenth-century thinkers, who, following Ockham, understood that terms naturally signify concepts, which naturally represent things in the world. The remarkable thing is that Wyclif made the leap to suppose that reality is structured in exactly the way that the sentences we form in our minds, and with our words, suggest. He explains that there are five kinds of propositions: mental, vocal, and written ones, real ones, and true ones. Leaving aside the complex relations among the first three, our chief concern should be the latter two.

A "real proposition" would be the individuated reality of a creature, such as a man or a stone. In it, Wyclif explains, there is a subject and a predicate. Take Socrates; in him, there is this person, an individuated particular of the human species, which functions as the subject. In him, there is also a human nature, which is essentially present in the subject as a predicate. Uniting the subject, Socrates, and the predicate, a human nature, is his essence, which functions as the actualization of the union of the two, making the real proposition "Socrates (subject) is (essential actualization) a human being (predicate)." A "true proposition" is a truth that is significant apart from the thing. This truth, "to be a man," is a complex truth, because it reflects the truth of a number of real propositions considered in itself. That is, the existence of all of the male subjects having human being as a predicate essentially actualized in them must be a reality formulable into a more general proposition, "to be a man." So there are real propositions existing as individuals in creation, and true propositions existing as describing, and likely organizing, the individuals.

At the base of Wyclif's ontology, then, is an isomorphism between language and reality. Just as a linguistic proposition has a subject and a predicate, so too, every being, of whatever kind, has a predicative structure. This makes his account of predication particularly important not just for his philosophy of language, but for his entire metaphysical scheme, and he presents three kinds of predication in the opening chapter of *De Universalibus* that encompass every aspect of the being of a particular thing. *Real formal predication* expresses the existence of a form in a subject. The proposition "Peter is a man" describes the state of affairs of the form humanity existing in Peter, while "Peter is musical" describes the state of affairs of a formal quality in Peter whereby he is musical. In each case, the proposition maps directly onto the being of the object it describes, with the subject of the proposition referring directly to the being itself and the predicate referring directly to the quidditative or qualitative formal aspect of the being.

Real essential predication involves an identity between subject and predicate that is absolutely indissoluble, although we can rationally distinguish between the definition of the subject and the definition of the predicate. We have used the proposition "Peter is a man" to describe real formal predication, in which the form humanity exists in Peter, as Peter's particular "to be a man." What of the proposition "humanity is in Peter"? While the two propositions appear to tell us the same thing, the first says something about the natural form of Peter, while the second suggests something beyond Peter but, in Peter's case, inseparable from him. Humanity is something that is formally distinct from Peter, in that we can distill an idea of humanity from our experience of Peter, but we could never take humanity from Peter. Likewise, we could never take any of the individuals in which there is humanity from humanity. The same essence, Peter, is both subject and predicate, while the notion of the subject differs from the notion of the predicate.

To explain real formal predication, Wyclif gives the puzzling example of "the universal is particular." It appears to be a contradiction to say that something that is universal is particular as well. How can the same thing be common and not common at the same time? He means for us to think of things this way: "In the same essence, there inheres both being a man, and being this man. And being a man is common to every man, and thus is formally universal, while being this man is restricted individually to this essence."[20] This predication describes the union of two formally distinct entities, like humanity and Socrates, in the same essential substratum and, in Wyclif's metaphysics, provides the definition for his philosophical reasoning about the relation of universals and particulars.

The third kind of real predication is *relational*, in which some kind of change takes place with a subject, although the subject itself does not change. Say that the father of Peter is bigger than Peter when Peter is a child, but smaller than Peter when Peter is an adult. Peter's father has not changed at all, but with relation to Peter, there has been a change that one can quite correctly predicate of Peter's father. There is no formal or essential reality within the subject of real relational predication. Paul Spade notes that this kind of predication suggests the "Cambridge changes" of twentieth-century analytic philosophy. Taken together, the three kinds of real predication encompass the essential and qualitative characteristics within a being, the real ties between a particular being and a universal one, and the accidental ties between a being and other beings.[21]

Philosophy of Being

Wyclif's *Summa de Ente*, which he wrote between 1365 and 1372, contains many of the treatises that articulate his metaphysics. Our understanding of fourteenth-century philosophy can easily be colored by the interests of past historians of thought. The primacy of universals over particulars in Wyclif's thought has led to extended focus on his realism, and the relatively recent (1985) edition and translation of the *Tractatus de Universalibus* has kept scholarly attention squarely on the role that universals play in his philosophical program. But even though he rashly exclaims that error about universals is at the base of all that is wrong in society, realism about universals is only one aspect of his metaphysics.[22] The *Summa de Ente* is made up of two books, the first (I) with seven treatises about being and how it relates to man, and the second (II) with six concerning formal theology (the divine nature, its attributes, divine ideas, and the Trinity). The fifth treatises in each of the two books (I.5 and II.5) appear to relate to one another from the standpoint of the other. In the first book, concerning being and how we can understand it, I.5 is *De Universalibus*, while in the second, concerning the divine being, II.5 is *De Ydeis*, which explores the philosophical possibilities of how God's ideas relate to one another and to things in creation. Taken together, I.5 and II.5 might provide a useful means of moving back and forth between the metaphysics of created being and the metaphysics of divine being. Given the depth and breadth of the subject matter of the *Summa de Ente*, what follows will do little more than suggest the philosophical richness of Wyclif's metaphysics, which deserves much further study.

Aristotle begins *Physics* by explaining that scientific knowledge about anything involves, first, gaining acquaintance with the more general, and then moving in analysis toward the particular. When considering any class of beings, we begin by asking whether the principle or element that ultimately constitutes it is one or many. Since everything that we might consider would fall under the category "being," Aristotle explores whether Parmenides was right to hold that it is one or more than one, and points out the many problems consequent for the scientist involved in taking Parmenides seriously. Wyclif comments that Aristotle has made "being" and "what is" interchangeable in this, and concludes that it would be contradictory, then, for someone "actually or habitudinally to know something to be, unless he cognizes proportionately Being to be."[23]

In one sense, this is consonant with the linguistic approach that has defined twentieth-century Anglo-American philosophy. When we say something about a subject, like "the apple is red," we are really saying two things: first, there is such a thing as the apple, and, second, it is red. There is an "existential predication," or an existence claim, inherent in any statement we make about something, whether true, false, or ambiguous.[24] But in another sense, to claim that there is a correlative "being," in which the subject that has been identified as existing participates, is something else entirely. Most philosophers, at least since Kant, reject the idea that existence is a property that a thing can or cannot have. Nor can it fairly be said that Aristotle himself believed there to be such a thing as "being" really or possibly distinct from individual beings.

Aquinas's description of the two possible concepts of being is a good place to begin. At a very basic cognitive level, he says, "what comes first to our apprehension is being, an understanding of which is included in anything else anyone apprehends." At the level of metaphysical inquiry, we discover by intellectual abstraction that the purest thing one can study is being as being. At this level, we consider things as abstracted, or freed, from their particularizing limits; substance, quality, being, potentiality, actuality, and such do not depend on matter to exist and to be understood, Aquinas explains, and of these, being as being is most removed from metaphysical boundaries. In discussing God's essence, Aquinas describes it as pure, subsisting being. When discussing created things or natures, he describes them as participating in existence in general (*esse commune*). When discussing individuals, he characterizes the act of being that is intrinsically within the existing creature. One's philosophical point of departure has everything to do with which of these senses of being as being is under discussion. If our project is theological, we begin with an attempt to understand the perfect, subsisting being of the divine essence. If our aim is to understand creation, we are likely to come upon the notion of existence in general before the individuated being of a particular creature. It is in this sense, our attempt to understand creation from general to particular, that Wyclif begins his *Summa de Ente*.[25]

On Being in Common

We cannot demonstrate deductively that being is; all that we can do is draw it out from our thinking about individual things. "Every thinking thing thinks such Being to be in common at the same time as it thinks of some other thing, and it can understand Being to be in common without thinking of some distinct other, that is less than it."[26] The reason that we are able to abstract being from our thinking of any given thing, Wyclif explains, is that there is an ontological connection between any true thought and Truth as such. As Aristotle explains in *Metaphysics* II, when we give an account of a given property of something, or a set of things, we must first know what the source of that property is. Anything that has heat gets it ultimately from fire, which is the hottest thing; likewise, "what is most true is the reason why other things are derivatively true. Hence the principles of eternal things are necessarily the most true, for they are true always . . . and there is nothing that explains their being what they are, since they are what explain the being of other things." If the first thing we think when we think about something is the being of that something, then when we recognize its being, we are mentally referring to the transcendental being, which is the reason for that individual being.

Here, Aquinas and Wyclif differ. Aquinas recognized an important distinction when considering being: "In one way, it is used apropos of what is divided into the ten genera; in another way, it is used to signify the truth of propositions. The difference between the two is that in the second way everything about which we can form an affirmative proposition can be called a being, even though it posits nothing in reality."[27] Aquinas recognized that there are substances and accidents in the extramental world, and he begins with them to catalog being in the first, ontological sense. He also recognized that we use the term "being" to make true affirmative statements about subjects, whether the subjects exist extramentally or not. If we can say "it is" in answer to the question "is it true that x is F?" we are using the term in the second, logical sense that Aquinas described. It is important not to mix the two senses together, not least because something may be true in the logical sense about a subject that lacks ontological reality, as in the statement "blindness exists." The subject of this kind of truth is a being of reason in Aquinas's system, and not something in the world. Aquinas equates being with truth in his "fourth way" to demonstrate God's existence, from degrees of perfection, in *Summa Theologica* Ia, q.2, a.3.

Do we really think of the transcendental being when we think about the being of, say, a rabbit? Other animals, like foxes, think about rabbits without thinking about the transcendental being. Surprisingly, Wyclif suggests that other animals, too, think about being at some level. Following the lead of Roger Bacon, who had argued that nonhuman animals are capable of estimative judgment in *Opus Maius* II.4 a century earlier, Wyclif argues that beasts compose, divide, and indeed syllogize about individuals and common properties. The dog recognizes its master, so it must think at some level that its master is. Hence, it must cognize being to be.

> Just as men discourse by compounding through interior senses about a sensible thing, so beasts having [an] interior sense of the same species are equally vivid, as a dog knows by experience that blows and other punishments are harmful, it cognizes through estimation that the man calling sensibly intends it with his words, just as do birds, and other animals. Thus it concludes fleeing to exist, as if it were arguing: everything harmful to me is to be fled, these blows are harmful to me, so they are to be fled. Many men think this way, just like beasts. . . . it is clear that the cat and other irrational things cognize movement.[28]

Wyclif does not really expect us to believe that nonhuman animals think about being. First, he admits that this would suggest that they might also love God, and so turn away from loving God and thus sin. Probably their idea of something general is nothing at all like our idea of the transcendent. After all, they don't have a language. But then, neither are the ideas of the *moderni* about general things anything like Wyclif's conception of the transcendent; they reject transcendentals and lay all their metaphysical explanations on individual things and terms about them. So, the doctors of signs would attribute to human beings no higher a level of comprehension of truth than is available to beasts. Here is the real point of Wyclif's introduction of nonhuman judgment: given that animals make decisions without understanding transcendental truths, and given that his opponents hold that there are no such truths available to metaphysicians, it follows in his eyes that his opponents make us into nothing more than animals that have a language. We would have no knowledge whatever of the eternal, if all of our knowledge was composed of terms about things in the world. If the first truth is the cause of knowing what is true, and if we are able to reason back to this, as Aristotle has suggested, it must be that we are able to use our words to refer to the transcendental reality of the existence of being.

We are able to sort how we perceive things from how things are by recognizing that our perceptions of individual, material things lead us to recognize universals, which have ontological priority to the things we perceive. It does not follow that, because our perceptions of things precedes our recognizing general truths, these general truths only have their bases in individual things. Our fallen nature keeps us from seeing things as they are in the natural order, causing a division between the order of knowing, which is ascending, and the order of being, which is descending. In our analysis of Wyclif's conception of the relation of God's knowledge of our actions and the freedom of our will, this will be particularly important. Here, everything rests on the distinction between the hypothetical necessity of God's knowledge and the freedom with which we will and act. It will appear that God's necessary knowledge of what we do is dependent upon our willing and acting, which preserves human freedom, but this is only the result of our inability to reconcile the order of knowing with the order of being. Wyclif's condemnation for a fatalistic determinism rested, in his view at least, on a confusion between the two orders. This will occupy our attention in chapter 6.

Those who would hold that Aristotle meant for us to suppose that a proposition like "man is an animal" is about terms that refer only to individual beings, men, need to reconsider to what the embedded proposition "man is" refers. Any singular man, the referent of this embedded proposition, is in fact a metaphysical proposition: wherever any man is, there is "man is." But we need to distinguish between "*this* man is" and "man is." Here, Wyclif suggests that we recognize that Aristotle distinguished between two types of substances in the *Categories*: a primary substance, which is articulated by "*this* man is," and a secondary substance, which is directly connected to the primary substance of this man, but is signified by "man is."

The doctors of signs who deny that "man is" signifies anything beyond individual men are guilty of more than misunderstanding Aristotle, though; they make understanding the ontology expressed in scripture impossible:

> Indeed I often wonder now how anyone could so churlishly explain the philosophical sense of a philosophical text. But even more, I wonder how an advanced theologian would dare this, because of the danger to the soul in interpreting the words of Scripture about universals to be only about signs.[29]

The Bible often refers to creatures according to their kinds; are we to think that these kinds have no referent? When we read in Genesis that God said, "Let the earth put forth vegetation: plants yielding seed, and fruit trees of every kind on earth that bear fruit with the seed in it," are we to suppose that the "excellent philosopher Moses brought from [his] clear vision of God on the mountain the sense that the earth would make seed according to a concept" that was extrapolated from mere particular things? When we read that God created man shortly afterward, what is the referent of "man" (*hominem*)? Just the individual Adam, "*this* man," or the entire kind, "man"? According to Aristotle, "For in definition, universals are prior, in relation to perception, individuals [are]." One might well mistake how we perceive things to be prior, Wyclif explains, but ontologically the kind is prior to the individual, meaning that, in the passage relating the creation of man, the term "man" means primarily the universal, and only secondarily the particular, Adam.[30]

Divine Ideas

Is being something different from God and individual creatures? Someone seems to have understood Wyclif as having meant this; *Summa de Ente* I.3, entitled *Purgans Errores circa Veritates in Communi*, begins by addressing the problem of whether there is some being distinct from the Creator and creation. The chief contenders seem to be the divine ideas, the eternal exemplars through which God creates; are these beings distinct from the Creator and creation? Answering this involves discussing Augustine's deduction that, while God is eternally the foundation of truth, his dominion over creation—and hence, God's lordship—began with the act of creation. "It appears to me that God eternally beforehand would be God of Truth, and in time, Lord of Truth."[31] But what about God's understanding of what he would create? These ideas are eternally "about" what God would create, and so could arguably be distinct from one another. If they are analogous to our own ideas, which are distinct from our essence, they must also be distinct in some way from the eternal knower, as well. Are they eternal beings distinct from God? Are God's ideas of being and truth, as they are directive of creation, things other than God himself?

In question 83 of *De Diversis Quaestionibus*, Augustine wrote:

> There are certain principal ideas of form, or stable and incommutable reasons of things, which themselves were not formed (and so, having themselves eternally and always in the same way), which are contained in the divine understanding; and since these neither come into being nor perish, everything that can come into being or perish, and everything that does, is said to be formed according to them.[32]

It might seem the height of intellectual arrogance for a theologian to presume to comment upon the nature of the contents of God's mind, particularly given the ongoing controversies regarding how the human understanding functions. Yet medieval thinkers from Eriugena to Anselm, and particularly from Aquinas onward, were keen to do just that, precisely because so much rests on what we are able to deduce from considering creation from God's perspective. In our discussion, if God has an idea of humanity, and God eternally knows who will be among the predestinate, something about the idea of humanity must be in some way connected to that knowledge. If God has an idea of the predestinate in humanity, and of the foreknown, are there two kinds of human beings?

Two problems in particular arose in these debates, notably the resolution of divine simplicity with the plurality of things divinely known, and the problem of whether God knows creatures through ideas, or directly in themselves. The first is a problem regarding our understanding of the divine nature, because the possibility of a multiplicity of ideas suggests a limit to the extent to which we are to understand the divine nature to be absolutely one and simple. We assume that because we perceive multiplicity through the discursive operation of our understanding, Wyclif responds, there must be a correlative multiplicity in the divine essence. The ideas are not things, though, but the reasons whereby creatures come into being. They are formally not reasons, but the divine essence, and so are neither essentially nor formally many. If we reason backward, from the human intellect to God's, we misconstrue the nature of the ideas as well as their being in God's understanding.[33]

The second problem allows us to contrast Wyclif's position with that of some of his predecessors. If it is true that God knows Peter, does he know Peter through an idea of Peter, or does he know Peter as he is in creation? If God knows humanity, does he know it through the immutable, eternal idea, through the universal that provides special form to all of the individual human beings, or does he know it through knowing all of the human beings that ever were, are, or will be as they are in themselves? And most worrisome, does God know the elect through an unchanging, uncreated idea, or does he know each of them individually, according to the choices they make in this life? The former possibility suggests a determinism that rules out human free will's relevance to salvation, while the latter suggests that God's knowledge is caused by a created act.

Aquinas had argued that the divine ideas are identical to God's essence, yet different through a distinction of reason. They exist because God considers his essence as imitatable by something he creates, allowing Aquinas to posit standards against which created beings are measurable without compromising divine unity. When a creature comes into being, the idea becomes more than a divine consideration; it is an exemplar through which God creates. This is not to say that every creature has a correspondent, exemplary divine idea. The understanding of individuals that God has necessarily comes about from his perfect knowledge of their formal and material causes.[34]

In response to this, Henry of Ghent emphasized the primacy of God's attention to divine ideas. Henry's objection to what he conceived as Aquinas's attempt to generalize the focus of the divine understanding as broadly as possible sparked considerable debate in the early fourteenth century. Scotus objected to the emphasis in both Henry and Aquinas on God's knowledge of the ideas as mediated through a relation produced by the divine intellect, stressing instead their immediacy to God's understanding. Divine ideas do not arise from God's consideration of his essence as imitatable in creation, because if they did, they would be beings grounded in mental relation and, to that extent, independent beings. Better to think of the divine ideas as immediately known, not dependent on the primacy of God's self-knowledge. Peter Aureol agreed with Scotus that Aquinas's explanation tended to hypostasize the ideas, attributing independence that compromises the divine simplicity. But Scotus erred by upholding the distinction between God's essence and the ideas themselves, even if it is a formal distinction. Aureol denied any "mental being" of a creature in God's understanding whatsoever, whether as an individual or as a possible iteration of a species. For him, the divine ideas play no role in creation, because creation comes about from the act of the simple divine essence. It is the divine essence itself that is imitated by what follows from creation, by the creatures which are brought into being as a result of God knowing his own essence. The ideas arise denominatively, Aureol held, connotated by the divine essence.[35]

Aureol's critique of any position willing to admit any kind of reality to divine ideas suggests Ockham's, even if the two Franciscans had little in common philosophically save a repugnance for metaphysical realism. Like Aureol, Ockham reacted vigorously against Henry and Scotus, formulating a searing indictment of any reality to divine ideas. There can be no relative being mediating between the knowing God and the known creatures. If anything must serve as the idea by which God knows the creature, it is the creature itself. Adding something to the divine essence, even if it were only a "being of reason," formally distinct from the divine nature, compromises God's simplicity. There is no call for a known similitude of a created being, because a similitude is either real or rational: if real, divine simplicity is jeopardized, and if rational, it is redundant, since God's understanding already encompasses all of creation in his essence. God's understanding of species and genera arises from his perfect grasp of how our minds work, for these are concepts naturally signifying reality for us. A species, then, has its reality in the divine mind through its conceptual being in our own, while God immediately knows each individual. Ockham's point is to deny any sort of being whatsoever to anything corresponding to a class term. Positing any sort of being to a genus or a species opens the door to Platonism.[36]

Response to Ockham was hostile, and the dialogue ground to a halt for the first half of the fourteenth century. In 1326, the papal committee investigating his thought, spearheaded by John Lutterell, declared

Ockham's position to be an affront to orthodoxy. Lutterell's committee included Durandus de St. Pourcain, whose position was not far removed from Ockham's, so the official report did not venture an articulated orthodox position on the ontological status of ideas. *Sentences* commentaries in the decades immediately following followed suit. Holcot and Wodeham say little in their commentaries, and Bradwardine has relatively little to say in *De Causa Dei*:

> It seems to me that the divine essence might be like an intelligible mirror, absolutely clear and infinite, carrying nothing from its object, or reflecting, but active by its infinite clarity, distinctly not confusedly preferring the countenance and idea of every intelligible object; in which mirror of the divine eye of the intellect all things regarded are reflected.

Walter Chatton edges carefully around the issue, arguing against Ockham and Aureol without making any commitment to ontological reality in any way.[37]

Wyclif begins his analysis by bringing the problem back to the pre-Ockhamist approach: the very term "idea" signifies an eternal, rational exemplar by which God creates, a medium between the being of the creature and God's act of knowing. The host of problems accompanying the doctrine, which have led to so much erroneous speculation, arises from confusion about the nature and extent of the ideas. Assuming that they have reality, the questions become, how much reality, and how many of them can there be? Wyclif's attention lies with the latter problem first: can there be ideas for impossibles? What about unactualized possibles, or counterfactuals? These questions in themselves should suggest Wyclif's realism; they would not long interest someone thinking that the ideas arise out of the fact of creation. Thus, it is likely that Wyclif has a more developed picture than Aquinas, whom Scotus and Aureol had accused of hypostasizing. At the very outset, then, Wyclif is ready to argue for ideas of actual beings, if ideas for impossibles and counterfactuals are on the table.

Wyclif dismisses ideas for impossibles and counterfactuals quickly, if for no other reason than because scripture rules them out. "In Him are all things that were made" (John 1:3) is also evidence suitable for arguing in favor of ideas for all actualized creatures. Dionysius the Areopagite argued that the goodness of all things preexists in God's understanding, having their origin in his unity and their formal identity in the actuality of form, just as the human soul provides the basis for all of our organic powers, as well as our willing and understanding. While a Platonic realm of ideals would compromise divine simplicity, Wyclif argues for an Augustinian model similar to the one envisioned by Anselm and Grosseteste.

Further, the absence of an idea for a counterfactual or an impossible may help with the threat of skepticism that arose from the Ockhamist fascination with absolute power. Recall that Ockham had argued that God's absolute power is so complete as to allow God to cause us to perceive things that are not real. Thinking about this led to a widespread tendency to limit the certainty associated with sense perception. But if God only has ideas of the actual, how likely is it that God could cause intuition of a nonexistent in a perceiver? God would have to have an idea of the phantom object, which is impossible in Wyclif's model. Even if I perceive an actual object that is not present, there would have to be a counterfactuality associated with the object in God's idea of it for this to be possible. This is beyond pink elephants; say that I am in my office, and I perceive the Great Wall of China outside of my window, brought about by God's absolute power and not my own delusion. (My office is in Nebraska, nowhere near the Great Wall.) God would have to have associated with the divine idea of the Great Wall the possibility of it being in Nebraska, which it certainly lacks. Thus, the stipulation that God only has ideas of actuals defeats one of the great bugbears of the moderns, namely, the possibility that God might deceive us. The philosophical approach that Wyclif associates with the moderns, which puts great emphasis on what can be known with certainty through the senses, is blind to the kinds of subtlety possible for those who take ideas seriously, Wyclif continues. To suppose this approach suitable for comprehending scripture with the depth of understanding necessary to teach the sacred page surely strains credibility.

But it would also be foolish to attribute any sort of being distinct from the divine essence to these ideas. They are formally or essentially the divine essence only, and so not formally many. We must be very careful to avoid reasoning backward from multiplicity in creation to multiplicity in God. Aristotle's arguments against Plato's forms have some validity in this regard, but Wyclif cannot imagine that Plato would have envisioned the forms as distinct somehow from God. Wyclif decides that Aristotle probably misunderstands Plato. Since Augustine was sufficiently confident that ideas have reality in the divine mind, and since scripture asserts that all things have being in God, then it is likely that Aristotle's disagreement with Plato is predicated on a semantic or logical misunderstanding. Wyclif's habit is to assume that Aristotle implicitly assumed divine ideas, even if at times this is difficult to ascertain. To suppose otherwise would make scripture incomprehensible: "I preach to the laity that every creature was alive eternally in God, but because of my limits, I am subtle about it. Nor do I know how to express the sense of Scripture, if not in this way."[38]

Aquinas and Grosseteste suggest that an idea is best understood as a relation of reason, Wyclif continues, but this cannot be right. Any relation other than an identity relation must have *relata*, but what would be the second term of the relation, if not the creature understood? If it were the creature, the idea would presuppose itself, since God knows what comes into being through the ideas. Hence, Aquinas's belief that ideas fall out of God's creative relation to creation cannot be accurate, either:

> Thus I believe that an Idea is understood in this way: it is something known in the intellect from the beginning, which regarded, can in the same knowing produce *ad extra* something that, if ampliated to be to intelligible being with truth, would be a reasoning, specifically that a given creature according to its eternally being intelligible is an exemplar of itself according to the creature's existence.[39]

After unraveling the tortured syntax, we can see that the statement allows Wyclif to avoid hypostasizing the ideas as known by God. The "creature as understood by God" is the cause for the creature's production without having anything like substantial being. It is a "body through which," intelligible as actualized in creation, yet eternal and complete in God's mind. With this conception of ideas, we need not concern ourselves with ideas of ideas, or other problematic issues.

Universals

The extent of Wyclif's realism has been exaggerated, at least from the time of Thomas Netter, and certainly in contemporary scholarship. In J. A. Robson's *Wyclif and the Oxford Schools*, he is described as "ultrarealist" in an otherwise excellent treatment of his *Summa de Ente*. As we gain a more developed picture of fourteenth-century Oxford's metaphysics, it is clear that Wyclif's understanding of universals was much more moderate than was Burley's, whose position Wyclif had expressly hoped to modify.[40] Wyclif makes comments throughout the treatises of the *Summa de Ente* that lead one to believe that he thought there were any number of kinds of universals: "Here we must say that there are only five universals, and that there are only ten universals, and that there are any number of universals that you want; because numbers, as things counted, vary in accordance with the size of the units chosen."[41] It is easy to envision him smiling while making a comment like this in a lecture, as his students scratch their heads in frustration. In fact, he argued for only three: universals by causation, universals by community, and universals by signification. Both in *De Ente in Communi*, the first treatise of the first half of the *Summa*, and in *De Universalibus*, this is Wyclif's list. The differing medieval approaches to universals suggest his reasoning for this list. The traditional, ontologically oriented approach, founded in Boethius's second *Commentary* on Porphyry's *Isagoge*, understands a universal to be one something common to many, with each particular containing the whole universal in itself. Thus, the universal man is fully in Socrates, and in Plato, and in any other male human being as well. Further, the universal man "constitutes and forms the substance of the [men] to which it is common." Peter Abelard's approach was different. He explained universals by concentrating on predication, shifting the explanation from ontological to a more logically oriented account. Universals are predicated in many things, but what sorts of things are "capable of being predicated of many"? The statements "Socrates is a man" and "Plato is a man" use the predicate "is a man." These statements reflect how things are in the world, for their subjects are things in the world. So the question is whether "is a man" is also something in the world; if it is, what is it? Abelard's approach allowed philosophers to argue about whether predication could be a relation applied to nonlinguistic things, and while Wyclif is committed to the Boethian approach, he is also an enthusiastic advocate of framing metaphysical accounts in terms of predication. Both sorts of universals fit into his system.[42]

He is also very sensitive to Ockham's critique of realism and recognizes that we can easily suppose that something real lies behind linguistic signs or concepts, when frequently there is nothing there. When we say that the universal man is argued by one philosopher to be a real thing, part of every male animal with a human form, while it is explained away by another philosopher as but a puff of air, or marks on paper, or a concept used to stand for something similar in the nature of every male animal with human form, what is the status of the terms we use? Is there some universal term "man" that gives meaning to each use of the term in a sentence? And is there a membership relation holding between that and the universal term "animal" that is similar to the membership relation holding between the universal man and the universal animal? What would be the relation between the universal term "man" and the universal man? Wyclif's universals by representation are the terms we use to account for the other two kinds of universals, but he says that they are only equivocally universal, as when we see a picture of Abraham Lincoln and say, "That's Lincoln."[43]

Wyclif's universal by community, which he describes as a thing shared by many supposits, corresponds to the Boethian universal. General and specific natures, like animal and human, fit this bill. Albert the Great and Aquinas had thought that genus and species are the products of our intellects' actualization of potential commonalities of common forms, but Wyclif was frustrated with their denial of these universals having extramental reality. He understands them as being faced with a problem, namely, how can a universal man exist in several other, particular human beings, without being divided up between them? Their answer was to emphasize the commonality of the form of the human beings, which commonality is realized as a universal man in our understanding of the things. His answer was to distinguish between man's existence in God's mind and man's existence in creation, a distinction between first- and second-intention universals. A first-intention term is a concept we derive from a real thing: when I hold a red apple, I can consider the redness of that apple. That concept is a first-intention concept of the apple's redness. I can then reflect back on all of the other red apples I've encountered, and compare this apple's redness with them. This reflection back is itself a concept, derived from earlier concepts, and is a second-intention concept. Similarly, universals by community have existence as objects of God's mind, or divine ideas, and they also have existence in the being of things. When we encounter an individual apple, we recognize the universal "fruit" as it exists in the essential nature of the apple as a universal of the first intention. This gives us a foundation for understanding the universal's primary being, which is to have being as a second-intention idea in God's mind. Since the divine ideas are eternal, while universals are created, this means that second-intention universals have ontological primacy over first-intention universals.

This does not mean that God's knowledge is reliant on the being of creatures. Wyclif's use of first- and second-intention universals should not confuse us into thinking that the created order is the basis for divine reality. Logically, we consider universals from their particulars back to their correlates in the divine ideas, but metaphysically, the idea is the basis for the being of all the particulars. The being of man as a divine idea is the ground for the existence of all individual people. The being of man in Socrates is not different from the being of Socrates; it is only formally distinct from the being of Socrates. Put another way, the universal man is each of its particulars, but with differing supposits, or different individual referents. Still, it is nothing more than its particulars. In this way, Wyclif sees himself as avoiding Platonism, which he thinks Burley has not avoided, without sacrificing the reality of universals, as the Thomists, Scotists, and the Ockhamists have done.[44] In Wyclif's Christology, his conception of the universal man is central to the metaphysics of the incarnation. On becoming a man, Christ incorporated the universal man into the identity of the second person of the Trinity. Since the universal man is each of its particulars, by Wyclif's description, Christ became Everyman.

Universals by commonality, the familiar Boethian universals, are joined by universals by causality, because everything in creation that is, was, or will be exists in a certain way in its causes at the beginning of time. The most universal cause is God, and all secondary causes that act in creation have their structure and being from the divine nature. So when God made the first human being, all of his progeny, the entire human race, was within Adam. When Adam sinned, then all sinned. This is not part of the created human nature, though, because the universal man was created free of the stain of sin. Universals by commonality do not explain how we came to be the way we are, so the causal agency of the first human being's sin, which affects all subsequent human beings, functions as a universal in this sense. This universal by causality is the reason that I have been brought into being by my father, by Adam, and ultimately, by God's creation of man. Because the universal by causality has its primary being in God's creation, it follows that God's causal knowledge is the most primary kind of universal by causality. If this is so, God's causal knowledge of my coming into existence is the primary cause of my being, and my father's efficient causality is only a mediate cause, determined by God's knowing from eternity. In our discussion of determinism in a later chapter, it will be clear that this causal account is made more complex by understanding the reciprocity that holds between created action and divine knowledge.

Efficient causality is not the only kind of causal relation Wyclif has in mind for universals by causality. Every relation describable by Aristotle's categorical structure is founded in universals by causality because the categories themselves are based in God's understanding of the ontology of creation. That is, the general structure of substances and the various kinds of accidents of which substances are capable—qualities, quantities, relations, locations, acting upon, being acted upon, and so forth—has its primary being as a divine idea. So when we consider the fact of Socrates being black, we recognize that Socrates is the substance, and black is the qualitative accident that has its being in Socrates. The relation that defines every quality's dependence on some substance has its foundation in the primary divine idea of the relation of the categories, in this case, the category "quality" to the category "substance." In the case of the being of a quality and its dependent relation on a substance, the relation is, in effect, the expression of the black of Socrates. This relational realism, in which a state of affairs holding between two *relata* is asserted to have being apart from the two *relata*, has its basis in Wyclif's propositional realism. The predication of an accident of a subject is of less importance than the predication of a universal by commonality of a subject. The being of the subject expresses the being of the accident, and this expression *per accidens,* while a real thing distinct from the dependent being of the accident and the independent being of the substance, does not describe the essential nature of the substance. Recall that, in Socrates being a man, Wyclif understands Socrates to be "saying" his specific nature, the universal man by which he is speciated, in his very existence as a human being. The proposition "Socrates is a man" accurately reflects the reality of Socrates being a man, down to the very structure of being.

In explaining the metaphysics behind "Socrates is black," Wyclif does not need to explain anything beyond Socrates, but when he explains "Socrates is a man," more is involved. He needs not only to explain the secondary substance "man," which he does by positing universals by causality, but he needs to account for the relation of one substance (the primary substance, Socrates) to another formally distinct one (the secondary substance, or universal by commonality, man). This he does by pointing to the relation of formal causality that holds between man and Socrates. In Aristotle's metaphysics, four kinds of causality explain a substance: formal, efficient, material, and final. The efficient cause of Socrates is Socrates' parents, his material cause is physical matter, and his final cause is happiness. His formal cause is the universal by commonality man, and the cause of Socrates' essential nature lies in Adam, at the beginning of the species' causal chain. In Socrates expressing man in his being, he is instantiating the universal by causality of the being of his formal cause, which was first instantiated in Adam. Simply, while universals by commonality give the basis for *what* a thing is, universals by causality provide the reason for *how* that thing has come into being.

But it would be a mistake to interpret this as leading to the belief that universals by commonality simply account for essences, and universals by causality account for the actual being of the essential nature. The relation between essence and existence was a matter of some disagreement among the later scholastics. Aquinas and Giles of Rome had argued for a real distinction between essence and existence in the composition of a substantial being, which Ockham, Henry of Ghent, and Scotus rejected. Perhaps influenced by Henry of Ghent's attention to the different kinds of being of an essence, Wyclif insisted that there is no real distinction between being and essence, that the essence of a given substance does not precede its being in creation. He explains:

> [An essence is t]he matter, the form, and the union of these. There is no matter, unless [it is] able to exist or be informed by the absolute essence, and there is no form unless [it is] actually existing or informing the same essence, and there is no union of these unless the same essence is one from this: that formally it is this, that it is to its potency, and all this is the essence. From which it is clear that any essence exists perpetually, because it cannot be brought to an end, save through annihilation. But nothing can be annihilated. . . . For prime matter is not corrupted because of generations of different kinds of forms; but it remains constant underneath, with various forms at different times; therefore so with essence, which exists with this matter, since matter predicates, beyond the essence, a relation to form in common.[45]

This is confusing, in that it seems to say that essence is both limited to the duration of the union of a particular form with some particular matter, and unlimited in that it holds across all time in the relation of prime matter to form in common. There are, in fact, two kinds of essence. The individual being of a substance in time and space is defined by its singular essence, while the type that this individual instantiates is its universal essence. Being, too, is manifold: Wyclif describes creatures as having four kinds in the same discussion. First, there is the eternal mental being of ideas in God. From eternity, for example, God has understood the idea of a "rose." Next, there is the being that a creature has in its causes. This can either be being in a universal cause, like a species, or in a particular cause,

as with an efficient cause like a parent, or Adam. A particular rose growing in my yard has had its being in the universal by commonality rose
from the beginning of creation, and in its seed in its parent flower from the
time of pollination. In these first two kinds of being, the creature's substantial potential is not yet actualized, but the grounds for the actual existence
of the individual nature are sufficiently real as to compel us to recognize
a degree of particular being. The third kind is the familiar substantial
being of the individual in time; "this is the only being the modern doctors
accept."[46] Finally, the accidental being caused in a substance by the inherence of one predicable of the nine categories must count as a kind of being,
albeit dependent on the actuality of the substantial being of a creature. The
third kind would be the existence in time of the rose in my garden, and the
fourth might be the hue of red that inheres in its blooms, as distinct from
the shape of its petals.

Perhaps it is tempting to assign the universal essence to the first two
kinds of being and the particular essence to the third, as the basis for the
fourth. Here, Wyclif faces the fact that there must be some sort of distinction between being and essence, if one can speak of the essence of rose in a
universal sense when there are no roses in actual being. This reality suggests
some sort of distinction that remains to be drawn between the universal
essence of rose and the individual essence of a rose. If this is so, there must
be a distinction between the actual existence of a particular rose and the
universal essence of rose and, likewise, a distinction between the individual
essence of a rose and its particular existence. Each pair, he says, is defined
by a formal distinction. This is best understood by recognizing "essence" as
meaning not the essential quiddity of a thing, but as the kind of being that
proceeds from it:

> For just as a thing is an entity before it is any kind of thing, since the
> question "Is there such a thing?" presupposes the question "What kind
> of thing is it?," and a man is an entity before he is a substance, so too
> it seems that essence, the putting of the bare question "Is there such a
> thing?" precedes the quiddity which adds genus to being. In such cases
> therefore there is a mental distinction.[47]

This mental distinction, or *distinctio rationis*, allows him to assert the reality of universals by commonality and by causality without bringing free-
floating universals into the discussion, as Burley did, and without relegating
universals to being only creatures of the understanding, brought about by

our perception of natures as common, as the moderate realists like Aquinas argued.

Many of Wyclif's metaphysical works have been in modern editions for almost a century. But the philosophy of some of his predecessors, notably Ockham, Scotus, and Henry of Ghent, only began to be widely understood in the latter half of the twentieth century. Without a secure grasp of their ontological programs, Wyclif's positions could not hope for a fair hearing, and the result has been an undue attention to the question of universals, to the exclusion of his wider program of a metaphysics of being. While Wyclif's realism about universals is worth much more investigation, a more thorough understanding of his metaphysics might arise from a broader line of questioning. Desmond P. Henry has suggested mereology, the study of the relation of parts to a whole, as a useful means of understanding how Wyclif departs from standard medieval thought.[48] Wyclif's ontologically manifold understanding of reality as propositionally structured may not be Platonist, but it certainly is divergent from standard Aristotelian models. It is normal for us to say something like "the Union is preserved!" without presuming there to be something above and apart from the collection of things we call the Union. Wyclif's approach, on the other hand, allowed an aggregate with identifiable ontological reality to arise from any set of two substantial beings. What follows from this is that, for any set of three people, there are four aggregate beings: the three ordered pairs derived from the set, and the universal humanity defining the particularized humanity of each member. There cannot be more than this, he argues, for each aggregate being can only arise from substantially real beings.[49] Wyclif devotes considerable effort to refuting the predictable Third Man arguments that arise from his position throughout *De Universalibus*, and he uses the reality of aggregate beings in his descriptions of how "a certain man" in the parable of the Good Samaritan serves as an aggregate for all saved people, among other things. Still, Henry remains puzzled as to why Wyclif would have made such an ontological claim, suggesting that the grounds for such a baroque ontology have yet to be identified. Why, then, would he attribute reality to aggregate beings derivable from any set of two particular objects? Aren't universals enough of an ontological problem without including another class of being?

The beginnings of an answer may rest in Wyclif's handling of the nature of the Trinity, both in *De Universalibus* and *De Trinitate*. A century and a half earlier, Joachim of Fiore had criticized Peter Lombard's innovative analysis of how terms refer to the persons within the Trinity. The Calabrian claimed that Lombard's description of a Trinity that neither begets nor is begotten entailed a fourth entity in addition to the three divine persons. Lombard had emphasized the impossibility of attributing particular actions of the divine persons to the divine essence, and caused Joachim consternation by having used the term "essence" to mean something other than "person." Joachim was rebuked by the Fourth Lateran Council for conceiving of the divine unity as a collective, or group of individual persons.[50] He erred, Wyclif explains, by confusing the reference of terms predicated of the divine essence and terms predicated of persons. The absolute nature of the divine essence precludes generating or being generated, so the presence of this generating, which holds between Father and Son, cannot be essential to God. Yet to hold that the essence is something beyond the generating and the being generated of the persons seems to lead to positing a quaternity that includes a fourth divine being beyond the generating, the generated, and the spirated persons. The divine Trinity, he argues, is an aggregate of the three persons, Father, Son, and Spirit. While the Father begets, the Son is begotten, and the Spirit is spirated from the Father and Son together, the aggregate godhead neither begets nor is begotten. The Trinity is a universal, of which the divine persons are the instantiates. But this aggregate of the three persons is more than just a universal, because universals only give being to their particulars, while the godhead is both subsistent being and the source of being to all creatures. So this aggregate must have reality of some kind, beyond that of a universal. If Wyclif's trinitarian thought is the basis for his belief that any ordered pair of creatures gives rise to an aggregate third, apart from any universal the two might have in common in their natures, then it would seem that here his metaphysics is, at least in part, an outgrowth of theology. The same cannot be said for his understanding of the Eucharist. There, his conviction of the impossibility of annihilation, along with spatiotemporal atomism, leads to his argument that transubstantiation is impossible.

DENYING TRANSUBSTANTIATION

Physics, Eucharist, and Apostasy

When the mass of cardinals, archbishops, abbots, bishops, and other clergy met in ecclesiastical council at Constance in the fall of 1414, much needed to be done. Five years earlier, they had met in Pisa hoping to resolve the schism that had divided Western Christendom in 1378, when the election of Urban VI in Rome had prompted French cardinals to name Clement VII in Avignon. The result had been a third pope, John XXIII, who proved anything but unifying in his dealings with the other churchmen. Sigismund of Luxembourg had managed to force John to decree the council at Constance, and hopes were high among the conciliarists that a watershed in Christian history was at hand. The conciliarists, political theorists who advocated an Aristotelian polity rather than a papal monarchy within the church, were determined to use the crisis to eliminate the basis for any pope to exercise absolute power over the cardinals and bishops. The drama that would play out over the coming three years saw the ultimate triumph of the papacy and the conciliarists' defeat. But this was only after the drama of a decree declaring the pope's duty to obey the council, the resignation of Gregory XII (who had succeeded Innocent VII, Urban's successor), the deposing of Benedict XIII (Clement's successor), and the trial and deposing of the slippery John XXIII.

In the midst of all this, Bohemia was headed toward open rebellion against both the church and the empire. The conciliarists could ill afford to show weakness when quelling heresy, and they brought the full weight of their corrective power against Jan Hus and Jerome of Prague, both of whom had been inspired by Wyclif's theological vision. In the course of this, the council also formally condemned 45 propositions directly associated with Wyclif's thought, and 260 others more indirectly relevant. Of all of these, Wyclif's eucharistic errors topped the list, but among the propositions that drew the council's ire, several seem less predictably inflammatory: "It is impossible for two corporeal substances to be co-extensive, the one continuously at rest in a place and the other continuously penetrating the body of Christ at rest." Further, "[a]ny continuous mathematical line is composed of two, three or four contiguous points, or of only a simply finite number of points; and time is, was and will be composed of contiguous instants."[1] What these assertions about physics have to do with Wyclif's heresies is by no means immediately obvious, and it is difficult to imagine the beleaguered churchmen fulminating for very long about the assertion that time and space are composed of indivisible atoms. Yet, in Wyclif's analysis of the Thomist doctrine of transubstantiation, this innocuous position features prominently. In this dense section of *De Eucharistia,* Wyclif seems to suggest that error about the makeup of spatiotemporal continua leads to believing that transubstantiation somehow makes sense. This connection is by no means an easy one to make, but if it is tenable, it might help us to understand why Wyclif seemed driven to deny a doctrine that was central to the medieval world. Philosophers generally like to have alternatives ready when they disprove long-held beliefs, and one wants to read that a clever philosopher like Wyclif came up with some sort of tenable eucharistic theory to replace transubstantiation. Unfortunately, aside from insisting that Christ is really present in the consecrated host, Wyclif did not present a philosophically developed alternative to what he angrily dismissed as "accidents without a subject." In fairness to him, Wyclif might have replied that such an alternative was unnecessary; the words of scripture and the teachings of the fathers should be sufficient. A response like this would be consonant with the *Confessio,* which is translated as an appendix in this work. We will be forced to jump from sacramental theology to spatiotemporal physical theory in what follows, if we are to understand why Wyclif felt that the prevalent explanations of transubstantiation were insufficient. So, following a discussion of the development of eucharistic theology, we will explore Wyclif's theory of indivisible instants of time and space and his arguments against the possibility of annihilation.

The Doctrine of Transubstantiation:
Radbertus to Ockham

During the meal Jesus shared with his disciples on the evening before his arrest, the Gospels tell us that he took bread and said, "Take; this is my body." Next, he took a cup of wine and told them to drink from it, saying, "This is my blood of the covenant, which is poured out for many" (Mark 14:22–25; Matthew 26:26–29; Luke 22:19–21). Throughout the medieval period, the words Jesus used, called the words of "institution," were the basis for the central liturgical office of the faith, the Eucharist. Of the sacraments recognized to be outward signs of inward grace, the liturgical celebration of Eucharist in the Mass was regarded as the supreme sacrament, in which the entire salvation of the world is embodied. The attempt to understand exactly what occurs in the Eucharist was an important part of medieval theology from the ninth century onward. Extensive theological dialogue was devoted to understanding exactly what Jesus meant by "this is my body." After all, anyone could see that it was bread he was holding. Today, many Christians, particularly Protestants, are content to approach the Eucharist as a communal activity in which believers participate. Whether the elements undergo some sort of mystic change is of much less importance than the accompanying grace that moves within the participants. In antiquity, Augustine's interests were similarly directed, although it would be an overstatement to say that he had no interest in the reality of Christ's presence in the elements.[2]

The great rebirth of scientific interest in the ninth century was accompanied by serious efforts to shore up liturgical practice, and two monks from the French monastery of Corbie defined the beginning of medieval eucharistic thought. Paschasius Radbertus (c. 790–865) argued that the elements of bread and wine change into Christ's body and blood at the consecration. They may not change in appearance, but in a spiritual sense, they really do become parts of the risen Christ. Ratramnus (d. 868) agreed that Christ's spiritual presence in the elements is real, but objected to what he perceived to be a lack of sensitivity regarding the means through which the consecrated elements "are" the body and blood. He distinguished between "figure" and "reality" in the being of Christ in the elements. If Christ were "in reality" in the elements, he would be empirically present, but if he were there "in figure," he would not be perceptibly present but "proclaimed inwardly to the minds of the faithful." A very useful way of understanding

Ratramnus's position, particularly from Wyclif's linguistically oriented viewpoint, is to understand him as thinking of the Eucharist as an activity in the empirical world that is analogous to metaphor in the logical order.[3] For Radbertus, then, a theology of the Eucharist begins in the ontology of the perceptible world, while for Ratramnus, the starting point is hermeneutics, a recognition that the liturgical text of the sacrament signifies a division foreign to empirical analysis of things in the world. It is important to remember that the term "transubstantiation" was not coined until 1079, so to summarize their difference as based on affirming or denying the idea is anachronistic. While Radbertus would be remembered through the medieval period as the first great eucharistic theologian, Ratramnus was soon forgotten. When his works were discovered a century later, they were attributed to Eriugena.

The next important disagreement about the Eucharist began in 1047, when Berengar of Tours (999–1088), believing himself in agreement with Eriugena, argued that the substance of the bread and wine remained after the consecration. His position caused him great trouble, drawing official condemnation in 1050 and leading to his being forced to sign a retraction in 1059. This retraction was not carefully worded, and it allowed for the interpretation that the elements remained in some sense what they had been before consecration. As Berengar afterward pointed out, the retraction's semantics required one to recognize that there is something bread and something wine that is the true body and blood of Christ. In saying that "the bread of the altar is only the true body of Christ, one is not denying that the bread exists on the altar, but is instead confirming that the bread and the wine are present on the Lord's table."[4] Berengar's main opponent was Lanfranc of Bec (d. 1089), who took him to task for failing to pay sufficient attention to Christ's words of institution; Berengar appeared to refuse to follow the progressive logic of Christ's declaration that the bread he held in his hand had been substantially converted into his body. In stubbornly insisting that "this" refers to the same thing, bread, at the beginning and the completion of the utterance, Berengar completely overlooked the mystic transformation that the Gospels describe. But Berengar's position was not so simplistic. He distinguished between that which is visible, the physical elements, or *sacramentum*, and the invisible *res sacramenti*, Christ's body, as analogous to the sign and what is signified. Take a simple example (obviously not Berengar's): the handle on the left hand of the faucet is marked "hot," but it is likely the same temperature as the handle on the right. The label refers not to the handle, but to the water that comes from the faucet. In the same way, the visible sacrament is not Christ, but it signifies the invisible body of Christ one receives when eating it.

Lanfranc's criticism of Berengar was bolstered by his use of a more complex notion of substance than Berengar seems to have envisioned. He was the first to formulate the essential change of bread into body by using the framework of the *Categories*, which allows for the exchange of one substantial platform for another, without a change in the perceptible qualities resting upon them. The stage was set for the introduction of the concept of transubstantiation. This term was being used by 1140 to distinguish between the usual sort of change we see in bodies, when qualities or properties change, while the underlying nature remains constant, and the mystical change of the Eucharist, when the opposite occurs. Of the many theologians who addressed the metaphysics of the Eucharist in the late twelfth century, Lothario of Segni stands out. Lothario's approach was not novel, nor were his explanations that much more compelling than those of his fellows. He distilled the best of the explanations then prevalent in his own mind, and on becoming Innocent III, he convened the Fourth Lateran Council, where transubstantiation became the established term for explaining the real presence of Christ. Lateran IV's codification of transubstantiation was not the end of eucharistic speculation; three distinct means by which the miracle occurs attracted their own admirers, and each was judged to be a valid explanation. First, the substance of the bread might remain along with the substance of Christ's body, which is consubstantiation. Where once there was one thing, bread, now there are two, for the body of Christ is now in the same place. Second, the substance of the bread might be annihilated and replaced by the substance of Christ's body. Third, the substance of the bread itself might change, becoming the substance of Christ's body, without passing out of existence. Here, the substance itself converts, from "being bread" to "being body" without a change in the underlying subject.[5]

While the advent of commentary on Lombard's *Sentences* afforded some structure, it wasn't until 1234, with the publication of the *Decretales* by Gregory IX, that canon law provided firm boundaries to define late medieval eucharistic theology. While many theologians in the ensuing two centuries assayed explanations of the real presence, the limits of space in this volume prevent us from doing more than mentioning the three landmark theologians' approaches. For Aquinas, the Eucharist is "the summit of spiritual life, and all the sacraments are ordered to it." Its centrality to the

Christian life defines the individual's continued self-identification in the living body of Christ. Through it, we remember his sacrifice, we continue to live in the unity of the church, and we anticipate our enjoyment of God in heaven. As such, Aquinas felt that Christians ought to take Eucharist as often as possible. By the thirteenth century, it was common for only the priest to consume the consecrated elements, leaving the laity only the chance to commune by "receiving the species," i.e., looking at it. He insisted that the laity ought to consume it as well, given its centrality to the life of the church. Likewise, the theologian should guard carefully against misrepresenting the mystery with explanations of transubstantiation that could lead the believer into error. Of the three alternatives, his approach is nearest to the second, for he rejects both consubstantiation and the idea that there is an underlying substantial being that shifts in form from "being bread" to "being Christ." To suggest that the bread, or something else, remains would be to allow that one worships something created when rendering the consecrated host the adoration it is due as Christ. This rules out consubstantiation, which he declares to be heretical. Yet he does not advocate annihilation; the elements are changed substantially to become body and blood. But if this is so, how does one explain the consistency of the accidents after consecration? Does Christ's body go from not being round and white to being round and white? Aquinas explains that these accidents cease to inhere in any substance, since they cannot continue to be related to the bread, which has substantially changed to become body. Further, they do not inhere in Christ, for Christ's resurrected body is at rest in heaven, where it exists unchangeably: "We are left to conclude that the accidents in this sacrament do not inhere in any subject." What causes them to remain coherent is "dimensive quantity"; in effect, quantity steps in and serves as a surrogate platform for the substance of Christ's body.[6]

Scotus agreed with Aquinas that transubstantiation occurs through the conversion of substance, but he did not reject consubstantiation as heretical. God could, by absolute power, allow Christ to be present in the substance of the bread, two things being in one place, but the teaching office of the church has shown that this is not what occurs. Scotus disagreed with Aquinas regarding how Christ's body can begin to be present in the host. While both agreed that Christ does not physically move through space into the host, Scotus was frustrated with Aquinas's apparent willingness to allow the phenomenon of transubstantiation to be a sufficient explanation for how Christ can be both in heaven and on an altar. There must be some sense in which the conversion involves Christ being in two places at once, with one being in place remaining unchanging, and the other beginning to be at the moment of consecration. His approach is to look at what is involved in being in a place, and he thinks of it as relation based. That is, "being in a place" is like "having a relation." Just as someone can have one relation to one person, and another to another, so God could arrange it that Christ's body is in one place and that it can begin to be in another place at the same time. Hence, God can make Christ's body present in many separate locations without a change in Christ. But if Christ can begin to be on an altar, and be unchangeable in heaven, what about the being of the bread? Does it undergo a commensurate ceasing to be at the same time? Scotus seemed to envision the bread as losing its "being here" without losing its "being as such," avoiding annihilation, but only barely. In general, Scotus was willing to support conversion on the force of his adherence to church teachings, even if he could imagine that consubstantiation might fit more to the structure of our reasoning than does transubstantiation by conversion.[7]

Ockham's approach seems to be the last important variation before Wyclif's rejection of transubstantiation. Like Scotus, Ockham was willing to countenance consubstantiation as a reasonable possibility. If two bodies can exist in the same place, which is certainly within God's power to effect, then Christ's body can exist alongside the substance of the elements. Like Scotus again, Ockham addressed being in a place as central to explaining how Christ's body can be both in heaven and on a thousand altars across Christendom. While consubstantiation is a reasonable possibility, transubstantiation is the church's preferred approach, and Ockham abided by this in his eucharistic theology. Ockham's innovation was to distinguish between being in a place and being in part of a place. When a given substance is whole in one place and exists in part in a correspondent part of that place, this is *circumspective* place, the way that extended bodies normally exist in space. But a thing might exist whole in a given place, and whole in every part of the given place; this would be an indivisible being, and it would have *definitive* place. Our experience tells us that no material substance can occupy a place in this way, although Christ's body and blood exist in definitive place in the consecrated elements. So at least one material substance must have definitive place, for Christ's ascended body remains extended, material substance. And this is also the way the intellectual soul exists in the body: whole in the body and whole in each of its parts. But Ockham was not simply inventing a distinction to explain dogma. God could cause Christ's material body to be present on a thousand altars at once while whole in one place and in part in parts of a place. Given this, there is no need to posit the qualities of the host existing in the quantity of the bread; they can exist in the converted, and definitely present, body of Christ.

The substance of the bread, though, has been annihilated. Two kinds of annihilation are possible. In one, the substance is absolutely destroyed, so that nothing remains to be converted into something else. In the other, the substance is reduced to nothing, but not absolute nothingness. Instead, the annihilated substance reverts to the being it had as a potential substance in God's mind before creation. This second, "weaker" species of annihilation, Ockham asserted, is what occurs to the substance of the bread. Once this occurs, the whole Christ is present in the consecrated host under the species of the bread, transubstantiated into definitive place. Yet despite the apparent consistency of Ockham's account with the church's position, he was called to account by a council of theologians at Avignon in 1325. His erstwhile colleague John Lutterell, who had gone from being chancellor of Oxford to service at Avignon the previous year, had found over fifty propositions associated with Ockham's thought that he felt were sufficiently dangerous to warrant condemnation. Among these was Ockham's account of annihilation, which Lutterell felt was too excessive. After consideration, the panel of theologians decided that Ockham's eucharistic theology fell short of actual error. The same cannot be said for his political and ecclesiological thought, the condemnation of which led to his fleeing Avignon three years later. He remained in Munich for the remaining twenty years of his life.[8]

Eucharistic Theology at Oxford
after Ockham

Ockham's influence regarding the Eucharist at Oxford in the years following his departure from England in 1324 remains to be analyzed. During the following quarter-century, Franciscans, Dominicans, Carmelites, and secular doctors would all compose *Sentences* commentaries. The fourth book of Lombard's *Sentences* is primarily devoted to the sacraments, and given the philosophical variety of the period, it is difficult to imagine little being said about the metaphysics of transubstantiation. The problem, for now, lies in the relative absence of extant editions of commentaries on *Sententiae* IV. The only record we have of the range of Carmelite philosophical theology,

for example, remains Xiberta's 1931 *De Scriptoribus Scholasticis Saeculis XIV
ex Ordine Carmelitarum*. Here, we see that Robert Walsingham, who flourished in the decades just prior to Ockham's departure, stoutly defended the
eucharistic theology of Henry of Ghent. Further, John Baconthorpe, a student of Walsingham who was prominent at Oxford in the 1330s, explored
eucharistic theology in five questions in his *Commentary* on *Sententiae* IV.
Interestingly, he later rewrote his *Commentary* on book IV, calling his earlier questions "speculative" and his later ones "canonical." His eucharistic
questions fall in the former category. Osbert Pickenham, another Carmelite
who may have been known to the young Wyclif, rejected annihilation and
challenged the contention that the quantity of Christ's body was not immediately present in the consecrated host. My account of the contributions of
Adam Wodeham and Robert Holcot, then, will be very general, and possibly not indicative of the tenor of eucharistic theology of the period before
Wyclif. Still, both appear to have had a bearing of some sort on Wyclif's
eventual rejection of transubstantiation.[9]

Wodeham's foray into the territory of the Lord's Supper is primarily an argument about whether the quantity defining the bread is mind-
independent and really distinct from the bread's substance and qualities.
Ockham's position was that quantity is, from an ontological standpoint,
but another quality. This put him at odds with the Thomists, who believed
the bread's quantity to be really distinct from its other qualities, a kind
of substitute substance in which qualities like white, round, hard, and so
forth inhere. As Ockham's chief disciple at Oxford, it comes as no surprise that Wodeham takes up this cause. Perhaps in an attempt to elucidate
Ockham's position, he also argues against the possibility of interpreting
annihilation as an alternative to the orthodox position:

> I say that transubstantiation is not annihilation but the conversion of
> bread's substance into the body of Christ from the power of consecra-
> tion, so that in the instant of conversion the substance of bread and wine
> ceases to be under the species in which they existed before, and the
> body of Christ succeeds under the same by the sacramental power of
> consecration.[10]

Of special interest to understanding Wyclif's position are the references
Wodeham makes to spatiotemporal atomism throughout his energetic
arguments against quantity being anything more than another quality. As
we will see, Wodeham's commitment to refuting indivisiblists was resolute;

it appears that his opponents made arguments in which indivisible atoms were a live possibility. In one case, Wodeham tackles an argument designed to establish quantity's separability from substance and other qualities in which the hypothesis is that, if quantity is a separable part, it would be either an indivisible part or divisible. In another, he struggles with the possibility that substance is quantifiable and extended through something that is itself divisible, and again brushes up against the possibility that there is a smallest possible unit of quantity. In each case, he dismisses indivisiblism in substance as having been effectively refuted in his *Tractatus de Indivisibilibus*. He makes no reference to indivisibles in the temporal continuum, though; his attention is not on change over time, but on the change within the substance as it undergoes consecration. Had temporal atoms figured in his eucharistic theology, though, he would certainly have referred his reader to his earlier treatise, where he devotes attention to refuting the temporal arguments of Henry Harclay and Walter Chatton, the primary exponents of indivisibles.

Robert Holcot takes a very different approach, one that some have seen to be suggestive of Wyclif's overall frustration with the doctrine of transubstantiation.[11] He begins with a general discussion of whether the body of Christ truly and really exists under the appearance of bread. Either something of the bread remains after the conversion, he continues, or the bread is annihilated altogether. But discussing this troubles Holcot: "If such a conversion of one thing into another were possible, then either the thing into which it was converted would not increase, and it would follow that God could convert the entire machinery of the world into the body of a fly, or He could place any substance under the appearance of any other substance." In arguing the mechanics of conversion in transubstantiation, we are missing a much larger problem. Nothing we perceive could be what it seems: "If such transubstantiation of one thing into another were possible for God, it would follow that God could transubstantiate a man into a stone, and vice versa, and so every accident of the man would remain in the same place where there was a man, and now is a stone." His reasoning continues relentlessly, considering the possibility that, if a consecrated host contains one of Christ's eyes on one altar and another of his eyes on another, then Christ could see himself from one altar to the other, all the while presumably knowing himself to be bodily in heaven.

Another problem, in addition to the threat to human knowledge the doctrine presents, is what role the intention of the priest plays in the sacramental transformation. For our discussion, this possibility is of interest, not least because of its backhanded dismissal of indivisiblism:

> Again, I posit a certain priest who believes a continuum to be composed of indivisibles, and blesses the body of one host, which he believes to be composed of a certain specific number of indivisibles; and I want him to be thinking that he is consecrating only one of the indivisibles in the host today, and tomorrow the second, and the third on the third day, so that on the fifth day he wants the entire host to have been consecrated. With this posited, I ask whether he has consecrated it or not ... [given that] the host is not composed of indivisibles in the truth of things.

His arguments regarding the untenability of transubstantiation increase in seriousness as he proceeds, ultimately leading him to conclude that the faith asks us to believe that accidents remain without a subject and that, if the species were moved, during the elevation of the host, for example, motion would occur without a moveable subject. If there were a subject, it would be the body of Christ. If there were two priests at two conjoined altars, and one priest was a step ahead of the other in the Mass, then it would be accurate to say that, when the first priest was bringing the consecrated host down from elevation and the second was still in the process of elevating the host being consecrated, Christ is at one and the same time both ascending and descending. The problems that we are asked to accept along with this doctrine, Holcot concludes, are almost more than can be borne. But the faith requires it.

> God can do more than we are able to understand, and can cause things in the world that we cannot investigate. So it does not follow that, because man cannot sufficiently explain how Christ really exists under the species of bread and wine, that this is not how things are, and not what should be believed. For from this, we undoubtedly believe God is more able to do what we cannot, from our own natures, investigate. ... as far as transubstantiation or the conversion of one thing into another is concerned, it is not a greater insult to reason than the many transformations that not just the unlettered are held to believe.

For example, Augustine and Boethius both note the widespread acceptance of the story of Circe, who turned the comrades of Ulysses into beasts, and the story about the Arcadians, who swam across a pool and turned into wolves. Scripture itself tells us of Lot's wife being turned into a pillar of salt; the transubstantiation of bread into the body of Christ is not harder to believe than these examples are. As to Christ being in many places at once, Holcot continues, so it is with the intellects who direct the celestial spheres. Avicenna thought that all human beings share one intellect in common, which, while admittedly a misreading of Aristotle's *De Anima*, is no more difficult than believing that Christ can be in many places at once. In the end, reason will not be able to persuade those who reject the irrational aspects of transubstantiation, nor should we expect it to be able to do so. Holcot's argument here is markedly fideistic, suggesting that *moderni* reasoning has cordoned off yet another section of traditional scholastic theology as beyond rational analysis. Wyclif's rejection of this tendency throughout his writings should lead us to expect him to formulate a coherent, realist alternative to this species of argument. After all, he has championed universals as the metaphysical answer to the church's woes, so some explanation in which universals figure would be in keeping with his general program. Unfortunately, eucharistic theology seems to be one subject where his realism does not provide a ready answer. To begin understanding why this happened, it is important to remember that, for Wyclif, reality is structured propositionally. Universals, like humanity, animality, and so forth, follow logically from the need for an unchanging truth value for statements like "man is a rational animal." So, we cannot begin explanation of the Eucharist with recourse to universals of commonality, causality, or representation. This is a different kind of argument, about the relation of the scriptural words of institution to change over time and place, with the confusion over how the bread changes to Christ being only one aspect of the problem. Our discussion of Wyclif's eucharistic theology will have to begin with what we understand about the deep structure of physical objects and how linguistic statements correspond to changes in that structure.

Indivisibles

Wyclif's conviction that reality is propositionally structured and mathematically comprehensible led him to take on difficult questions about how to understand statements about change over time. *De Logica* contains nothing terribly innovative regarding the theory of syllogistic logic, but it does provide a rich source for readers interested in the semantic properties of different kinds of terms in propositions. And given his propositional realism, when he addresses terms like "begins to be" or "ceases to be," or "infinite" or "in a place," he cannot help but address complicated issues of physics. As mentioned earlier, the Mertonian calculators were famous for their meticulous analyses of propositions, patiently using logic to tease out truths about the physical world from the semantics of terms. *De Logica*, likely completed before 1364, is interesting because it gives evidence of Wyclif developing his philosophical method in the Mertonian tradition, using semantic analysis to uncover basic truths about nature.

The truth central to our discussion is the existence of atoms, indivisible particles of space and time, individual degrees of change and quality, and their relation to continuous objects—periods of time, extents of space, units of motion, physical objects—called *continua*. Not all medieval thinkers were willing to accept Aristotle's arguments in *Physics* VI.1 that indivisibles do not compose continua, although they largely denied that continua were entirely composed of indivisibles.[12] Ockham rejected indivisibles entirely, arguing that a "point" or an "instant" is not even a "something," but only a hypothetical construct used to explain geometric truths about lines or mathematical truths about duration. In 1323, Ockham presented a line of reasoning in *Tractatus de Quantitate* that began by denying the existence of spatiotemporal points, or indivisibles, and led to an analysis of change in the quantity and quality of the bread in the Eucharist. Here, Ockham argued against Aquinas, who believed that dimensive quantity could act as a subject for the other accidents of the bread, by arguing that quantity cannot be considered an absolute thing distinct from the substance in which it inheres. Beginning with points, Ockham argued that the points of a line cannot be considered as really distinct from the line, the lines making up a surface cannot be considered really distinct from the surface, and the surfaces of the body likewise cannot be considered really distinct from the body. In the same way, the quantity of a body cannot be considered really distinct from a body, and Aquinas's theory runs aground. Because points are hypothetical constructs, not really distinct from the lines or bodies they make up, the kind of division within a substance that Aquinas has in mind is impossible.

Aquinas, of course, would have agreed with Ockham about there not being indivisible atoms in the makeup of objects, or of any continua, hence the telling nature of Ockham's argument. But in Oxford, several of Ockham's contemporaries argued that continua were wholly composed of indivisibles; Henry Harclay, Walter Chatton, and William Crathorn are among the better known. Chatton opted for a finite number of indivisibles in a continuum, while Henry argued for an infinite number in every continuum. Henry understood Grosseteste as having been an advocate of indivisibles, because Lincolniensis had argued that any finite extended entity is composed of both an infinite number of divisible parts and an infinite number of indivisible parts. Crathorn agreed with Chatton, supporting a finite number of indivisibles in any given continua.

Crathorn seems to have been among the last at Oxford to advocate indivisiblism. Between them, Adam Wodeham and Thomas Bradwardine eliminated spatiotemporal atomism as a viable means of explaining quantity in continua. Wodeham, a student of Chatton, collected a mass of arguments against indivisibles, cataloging every possible philosophical problem that can arise from supporting the infinite divisibility of space and time. Indeed, Wodeham eagerly waded into the Zeno paradoxes familiar to philosophy students today, exploring the soundness of Aristotle's resolutions of these classic problems. The *Tractatus de Indivisibilibus*, perhaps among his earliest works, dating to the mid-1320s, addresses Henry and Chatton directly, but does not mention Crathorn, who would comment on the *Sentences* several years later, along with Wodeham. Bradwardine anatomized the indivisiblist position and its possible iterations in his *Tractatus de Continuo*:

> [T]here are five well known opinions among the old philosophers and the moderns about the composition of continua. Some hold, as Aristotle and Averroes and many moderns, that a continuum is not composed from atoms, but from parts divisible without end. Others say that it is composed from indivisibles variant in two ways, since Democritus holds a continuum to be composed from indivisible bodies. Others, though, from points, and these in two ways, because Pythagoras, father of this sect, and Plato, and Walter the Modern [Chatton], hold it to be composed from finite indivisibles. Others, though, from infinite[ly many], and these are in two groups, because some of them, as Henry the Modern [Harclay] says it is composed from infinitely many indivisibles immediately conjoined, and others, as Lincolniensis, from infinitely many alternately mediated.[13]

Given Wyclif's by-now familiar allegiance to Bradwardine and Grosseteste, it seems nothing short of astounding that he would join Crathorn in supporting spatiotemporal atomism. Norman Kretzman commented that, given the generally recognized impossibility of indivisiblism in Oxford in the 1350s and '60s, Wyclif's approach seems anachronistic at best. Certainly, it seems that Wyclif himself recognized the immense problems associated with the position that time and space are divisible into atomic units. At one point in his attempts to overcome the prevalent rejection of indivisiblism, he admits, "And I do not yet know how to disprove any of these three replies effectively."[14] Walter Burley had weighed in against indivisiblists, but he did not reject the possibility of the existence of indivisibles in continua. Not all parts of a given continuum actually exist, but God sees all the atoms on a continuum as potentially existing, and the intervals between them as well. Logic demands that there be indivisibles in time. Two contradictory sentences about a given time cannot both be true, but if they are about a unit of time that is divisible, like an hour or a minute, they could both be true, if one is about the first part and the other is about the second part. Of course, these would not be real contradictories; two truly contradictory sentences about a given unit of time would require that the unit be indivisible. Since there are such sets of contradictories, there must also, Burley reasoned, be indivisibles in time.[15]

It is possible that Wyclif's approach is related to Burley's reasoning as a consequence of his propositional realism. Kretzman describes Wyclif's indivisiblism in terms of his use of Mertonian methodology to disprove the calculators' rejection of indivisiblism. As described in chapter 2, the calculators were skilled in using the analysis of *sophismata* to reason out the physical laws of mechanics. Wyclif, a product of Merton College, was certainly adept at this method, and he appears to have developed one *sophisma* to show the untenability of the infinite divisibility of time. Unlike Zeno's paradox of complete divisibility, which Aristotle described as having compelled the ancient atomists to advocate indivisibles, this puzzle is meant solely to show a problem with how we understand the truth of a statement like "Socrates begins to move east." This puzzle, known as the "vacillating man," asks that we imagine a period of time, say, an hour, with a marked midpoint, and divided such that each half on either side of the midpoint is respectively divided in half, and then in half again, and so on. The number of divisions, according to the continuist, can be infinite. Consider one of the halves, say, the first half hour. It is divided in an infinitely diminishing number of halves, so that each division consists of half of the previous quantity and an infinitely divided other half. Give each half a number. Now, imagine Socrates moving in this period of time, so that he moves east during the odd-numbered periods of time, and west during the even-numbered periods. Never mind that, at a certain point, this will be physically impossible; the point is that, at the midpoint, Socrates would be both beginning to move and beginning to be at rest:

> And yet immediately after this, he will begin to move, and the same holds regarding rest. Indeed, now he is not moving, and immediately after this he will not be moving, and immediately before this he was not moving; and yet he begins to move, and he ceases not moving—just as immediately before this he ceased not moving, and immediately after this he will cease not moving.[16]

The result of this thought experiment is, for Wyclif, forcing the continuist to acknowledge that beginning to move is not instantaneous but successive, so that there will always be contradictories true of any given case of something beginning to move:

> But those who claim that a continuum is composed of indivisibles—e.g., Time composed of instants, a line composed of points, a surface composed of lines, a body composed of surfaces, a motion composed of *mutata esse*, and so on . . . say that it is impossible that any entity begin or cease to be except in virtue of the introduction of the present.

This means that any sentence involving "begin" or "cease" must involve a uniform unit of indivisible time.[17] Wyclif's indivisiblism is not enthusiastic, though; he recognizes that reason throws up as many arguments against spatiotemporal indivisibles as it presents supports:

> Leaving the deeper investigation of all these matters to the subtle logicians and natural philosophers, I ask those who read through this chapter not to condemn or deride the things that have been said here . . . for I know that these things are rejected by many authorities, and that they demolish the Calculators' arguments [along with] many doctrines and fanciful examples put forward by the moderns.[18]

Kretzman suggests that, seeing the inevitable difficulty of defending indivisiblism, Wyclif ultimately fell back on theological necessity as trumping the rational objections posed by continuists. This is understandable, given Wyclif's final comment on the matter in *Trialogus*: "I give this response along with Augustine and faith in Scripture, that just as God saw everything that He had made, so He understands distinctly every part of every continuum, so that there are not given more or other components of that continuum. And in that way the reasoning seems plainly to succeed."[19]

The problem with this, though, is that this reasoning in obedience to authority is what compelled Holcot to accept transubstantiation in the face of the welter of reasons to the contrary. One might well respond that Holcot's acceptance of transubstantiation on faith is something altogether different from Wyclif's acceptance of atomism on faith, were it not for the connection that had been established in Ockham's argument against Aquinas's version of transubstantiation.

Temporal Atomism

Wyclif's apparent dissatisfaction with his general discussion of spatiotemporal atomism in *De Logica* led him to compose *De Tempore* (1368), which explores the philosophical problems associated with time and is included as the sixth treatise of the first part of the *Summa de Ente*. This treatise, among the last from this *Summa* to be edited, has been rightly described as central to our understanding of Wyclif's realism. Just as *De Universalibus* explores the formal aspects of the being of universals, *De Tempore* analyzes their eternality and the nature of temporal succession in their created particulars.[20] Here, Wyclif's sensitivity to the questions that captivated the Mertonian calculators is most obvious, as he probes the nature of time's constancy and of the gradations of motion's acceleration and deceleration in relation to time. If time is an accident of the world, if there were several worlds, would there be different kinds of time, each relative to its world? Wyclif's response, predicated on possible worlds theorizing, will introduce us to his conception of how time is divided into indivisible instants.

Contemporary philosophers are familiar with possible worlds theories as useful means of exploring questions of modality or the nature of necessity and possibility. Asking questions about possible worlds was also a means whereby medieval thinkers struggled with modal metaphysics. Most notably, it has been argued that Scotus revolutionized the analysis of modal semantics with his use of possible worlds theorizing to explore questions of human free will and divine knowledge.[21] Wyclif's question about temporal continuity across worlds, or synchronic unity across possible worlds, points to the consistent relation of time to the world. In whatever world we choose, time is a property of the world's substantial nature. If we posit two worlds, in the first of which, A, there is consistent motion, and in the second of which, B, there is none, then there must be some sense in which, at a moment N on A, it would be true to say, "Now there is no movement on B." The temporal indicator "now" must refer to something on B that is at least like moment N on A, Wyclif reasons, suggesting grounds for cross-world temporal continuity. Some species of a unit of duration would have to be analogous between A and B, and because of this more general concept of duration ranging across worlds, in which the time N on A is analogous to some time on B, there must be some broader plane on which the two worlds share being: "And thus from the unity of time it appears plainly that it would be impossible for many worlds to exist unless they constitute one world."[22]

This one, overarching world that could contain all possible worlds must itself have a temporality that is a property of its substantial nature. This Wyclif calls "duration," which contains what we perceive as temporal succession, as well as the *aevitas* defining the angelic existence, and the eternal instant of divine being.[23] Aristotle had argued that time relies on movement to give it identity in *Physics* IV, but Scotus broke with tradition by arguing that there can be time without motion, even without the motion of the heavens.[24] Wyclif, true to his realism, follows Scotus, viewing time's independence from motion as essential to its place among the predicables. While our arrangement of time into hours, days, months, and years may be dependent upon how we perceive time, time itself has a nature, independent of our perception. Indeed, God understands any time "by its instant number," its individuating principle, which makes the members of the species time distinct from individuals in *aevitas* or the sole being in eternity.[25]

At the outset of his treatise, Wyclif asserts that time is individuated by temporal instants, and he begins arguing for their indivisibility. The magnitude of duration within the world, which he calls *diurnitas*, suggests that it is the smallest possible mass, an unextended point. If a body moves in some unit of duration, of whatever magnitude, or *diurnitas*, it remains the same substance continuously. An essence can retain its constancy even without the same body, as the same thing is first a caterpillar and then a butterfly. So much the more for a universal form, or a number; humanity remains a constant even as human beings come and go. A nonextended essence or number is prior before it is extended in act, as is the smallest possible unit of magnitude. *Diurnitas* is the principle of magnitude in the duration of time, and it is what makes up "lastingness," or duration, over temporal succession. If *diurnitas* is the form that precedes extension in act, it must be unified; so, too, must any of its instantiations in act be unified. Hence, time is measured by the indivisible mass, or point, that instantiates the magnitude of time. There is a one-to-one correspondence of body to instant, then, in which the body's continuity persists from instant to instant, because the body's form is anterior to its material extension. For moving bodies, the movement is itself composed of indivisible instants, and these correspond directly with temporal instants.[26]

What Wyclif has in mind is a picture of time structured in the way we watch movies. Each frame of the movie is in itself unified, a moment frozen in time. From one frame to the next, the subject portrayed seems to move, but in fact there is no movement distinct from the time in which it occurs, or the succession of frames. On this analogy, God is the great director, viewing all created being through the medium of time, knowing each occurrence and each individual through its placement in individual frames of the movie. This structure, Wyclif suggests, is more coherent than the one in which there is no one-to-one correspondence of body to instant, for there we are expected to believe that some accident of a substance might have a greater reality than the substance itself. Wyclif throws this comment off quickly, and moves back to the virtues of his own position, but this statement bears closer examination. In the context, Wyclif appears to be referring to an understanding of time and movement in which there are no indivisibles, and a body moves continuously through two infinitely divisible media. Here, the substance moving is finite, but it is moving across infinitely divisible time and space. In holding this, "I have denied substance to be equal to its duration and consequently some accident of a subject is great which does not have a subject equally great, but equally lasting." In itself, the criticism points to a disparity in the Aristotelian scheme wherein the accidents depend for their being on a substance. In a later chapter, Wyclif is discussing the nature of indivisibles, and the question of persons arises. Are persons indivisible? It does not lead to a contradiction to suppose that several natures might be contained in one person, he reasons, given that Christ had both a divine and a human nature, "but it is contradictory for the same to be communicated as [the] same nature to many supposits, as is clear elsewhere." By "the same," does Wyclif mean Christ? Thomson notes in his catalog of Wyclif's Latin works that Wyclif seems to have had the Eucharist on his mind in this work; these two comments can be construed as supporting his thesis.[27]

Annihilation

Wyclif's rejection of the possibility of annihilation is another constant in his thought, one he repeats tirelessly in his critiques of contemporary arguments for transubstantiation. If he formulated it in response to extant eucharistic theology, we would be justified in our suspicions that Wyclif had harbored a grudge against transubstantiation for extraphilosophical reasons. But the evidence suggests that he rejected annihilation as a possible physical option very early on. In the third part of *De Logica*, he considers annihilation as a repellent consequence of misunderstanding the semantics of "going to be" and "was being." If we imagine the reality of "the sun is going to rise" to be dependent upon time, and not upon the being of the sun, then as time progresses, all things would continue to be made new, and creation would be continual. This would mean that all substantial form would be continually dissolving and resolving, "but it is impossible for something to be recreated, and likewise it appears that nothing can be annihilated."[28]

But surely if God can bring a thing into being from nothing, he can likewise bring it back from being into the nothingness from which it came? This is the question in *De Potencia Productiva Dei ad Extra* 12.[29] It seems that denying God's ability to annihilate would limit omnipotence. But annihilation is different from creation, and equally difficult to conceive for a realist of Wyclif's bent. To undo creation, not by making a part of it simply pass out of being in the usual way, through substantial corruption, but by eradicating the substance so that both form and matter cease to be, has disastrous consequences for the being of the universals identified with the substantial form in question. If it were simply the elimination of one, isolated substantial composite of matter and form, it would be analogous to replacing one number in a series of numbers with a zero. This, it seems, is what Wyclif imagines his opponents to conceive. But because the substantial form of any given thing enjoys an identity relation with the universals it instantiates, dire consequences await the universals as well as the particular substance. For example, the substance of a plant instantiates the universal "rose" so that its form has identity with its universal. But the universal rose is a species of a larger genus, "plant," which is itself a species of "animal" (by Aristotelian biology), and so on up to "substance" itself. If the rose were annihilated, because of this identity, so would rose, plant, and substance itself be annihilated: "God cannot annihilate any substance unless He annihilate the whole created universe."[30] On our mathematical analogy, annihilation would be multiplying the sum of a complex equation by zero; not only do you turn the sum into zero, you also render to a nullity the complexity on the other side of the equals sign.

At this point, Wyclif takes up the Eucharist and considers the possibility of annihilation as a means of explaining transubstantiation. To imagine that the substance of the bread is annihilated in its entirety is madness, because the accidents are part of the substance, and they remain. So perhaps the form of the bread itself, apart from the accidents, is annihilated? But this cannot be, because then "bread" itself would cease to be, and so on up the chain to "substance." In fact, given that the universals have their being by virtue of instantiating the divine ideas, Wyclif continues, destroying universals would entail destroying the contents of the divine mind as well, and ultimately God himself: "A thing could not be annihilated unless God as well as its ideal reason would cease to be; because each of these is essentially the same as the remaining [subject annihilated], at least according to intelligible being."[31] An important piece of the puzzle remains to be considered: how can a change in the substantial form of a created being, even one so radical as to involve its ceasing to be, bring about change in the eternal divine ideas? Even given the conception of identity that Wyclif has in mind, which allows for annihilation up the chain of universals, which are created beings, how can he countenance such a radical jump from created to uncreated being? We will see in the chapter on determinism that Wyclif's conception of the reciprocal causality of divine knowing and creation provides the basis for arguing that God's understanding is, to a certain extent, caused by created being. It is likely that he had this in mind while he argued against annihilation. Any theory accounting for transubstantiation that depends upon it, as Ockham's does, will fail; this, indeed, is the conclusion that Wyclif would reach in *De Eucharistia* 3.

Wyclif's First Position: A Mathematical Object

Wyclif never really constructed the kind of philosophically complex, logically coherent position about the Eucharist that thinkers like Aquinas, Scotus, and Ockham did. Those topics that he felt he had fully grasped, like universals and dominion relations, he fully described in the treatises associated with them; his major treatise *De Eucharistia*, written in mid- to late 1380, does not so much articulate a Wycliffian eucharistic theology as it explores the problems plaguing the extant explanations of transubstantiation. The other works that feature his eucharistic thought, including the famed *Confessio*, either attest to the orthodoxy of his approach or, as in *De Eucharistia Conclusiones Duodecim* (1381), describe points of disagreement with his contemporaries. Had he arrived at a systematic understanding of the sacrament at some point in his life, we could expect to see it carefully espoused in *Trialogus*, but as we will see, his treatment of the subject there is murky. It is possible that his intellectual reach exceeded his grasp regarding the sacrament of the altar, and that while he imagined the possibility of a coherent metaphysics of the Eucharist that didn't involve transubstantiation, he simply didn't live to make the attempt.

Early in his career, Wyclif tackled questions about how the Aristotelian predicables function in sentences, and how this helps us to understand the nature of things in the world. As mentioned, his *De Logica* may not contain much of interest to the historian of logic, but as a resource for understanding his ontology, it is invaluable. When we say that a given thing is in a particular place, when we predicate a location of a subject, we are making certain claims about how things are related to their locations. For example, the simple truth "two things cannot be in the same place at the same time" seems clear enough. Something being in a particular place seems to involve there not being the possibility that something else is in that exact place in the same way. We might both be in a given field, for instance, but it's probably big enough for you to be in one particular part of it and me to be in another with room to spare. "For as the logicians say, every body of the world is in the same place, broadly construed, and all bodies are however much distinct in their particular places."[32] But what about the monumental problems attendant upon Christ being in the same place as the consecrated host, and about Christ being in a number of places at once? While advocates of transubstantiation may believe that the former problem is easily addressed by having Christ's substance occupy the same location as the bread's accidents, how can Christ be on all of those altars across Christendom? And what of Holcot's example of two masses being said in the same cathedral, with one priest a step behind the other?

Being in a place, Wyclif explains, can be understood in three ways. First, just as a king is in a kingdom where his power lies, so one can be in a place insofar as one's power extends there. Second, just as a king is said to be everywhere when present in his hall, by which he has actual knowing of everything going on in it and is present to every point in it, so one can be in a place insofar as one's presence is immediate. Third, when one is filling up a given place with one's physical being, one is essentially in a given place. We can be certain that Christ, insofar as he is the second person of the Trinity, is everywhere in all three senses. And it is likewise certain that he is present everywhere in the first two senses insofar as he is the incarnate word. But the corporeal quantity and quality corresponding to the incarnate Christ is not present in the Eucharist; it is in heaven, whence it ascended centuries ago. Those who would say that Christ is present in quantity and quality in the Eucharist, just as he is extended in bodily presence in heaven, open themselves to many complex problems, Wyclif notes. As for him, it is likely that every part correspondent to Christ is in the Eucharist, without specific position, figure, or quantity, just as the humanity of Christ is not concomitantly everywhere existing in the second person of the Trinity, although it is the same person. Still, the consecrated host does not cease to be bread:

> [B]ut it remains one body serving as subject to the accidents of the bread, which I call an abstract mathematical body. Just as a substance is first not a being more than it is a something, so the bread first in its nature is a body more than it is bread. . . . And thus the same being, which first is bread, remains a body under this degree of general quiddity, but it does not remain purely the body of Christ, nor pure bread, but the bread is converted into the body of Christ, because the bread remains the body of Christ sacramentally, existing under those accidents under which formally it was bread.[33]

What Wyclif means by "mathematical body" is not terribly clear. Perhaps he envisions the body in question as like a set containing even numbers. Set P could contain 2, 6, 10 at one point, and 4, 8, 12 at another point, and at both points be accurately described as "P, the set containing even numbers." Correspondingly, the body that started off as bread need not cease to be what it was, namely, a body, on being converted into the body of Christ. Wyclif knows that he has veered into dangerous waters and immediately follows with a disclaimer: "Because this matter is irrelevant here, I do not treat it further, but I expect a determination to treat of the special quiddity of this sacrament remaining to the senses. An accident is just as any creature is a substance, because otherwise it would be a sensory illusion."

Better to continue by talking about how two things *can* be in the same place at the same time; a thing that is at once corporeal and spiritual is said to be located equivocally. As Grosseteste said, the soul is more truly with that of which it is desirous than where it provides form, and in this way, Wyclif continues, we speak about visual abilities. When the sensible species of something appears in a medium that causes it to be multiplied throughout the medium, as when something appears in a mirror, and is reflected again in another mirror, the image of the thing reflected can be said to be present to the vision of one seeing the thing in the mirror. When I look at my back in a mirror in a clothing store, I do not see my back; I see an image of my back with clarity, and I see the color and shape of the mirror confusedly. Characteristically, Wyclif returns to the example that haunts him: "In this sensible way is the body of Christ in the Eucharist, but not extensively. And so it is not right that the same [body of Christ] be moved, but that it be multiplied, as it is here [in the mirror example]."

That Christ is present in the Eucharist as an image is in a mirror is as near to a positive assertion of how Wyclif understands the sacrament as we are likely to get. Heather Phillips has argued that we ought not underestimate this imagery from a philosopher given to enthusiastic use of the science of optics in his philosophical reasoning.[34] She points out that he gives exactly the same explanation several times throughout *De Eucharistia*, as here in chapter 5:

> [T]he pious philosopher says that a body has intentional being through a medium which receives its species, spiritual being in the soul through the consideration of the soul, without being moved there. Why can it not be thus of the sacramental being which the body of Christ has in the host by virtue imparted to the host, without being moved there locally?[35]

Indeed, in his *Postilla*, Wyclif says much the same thing in his comments on 1 Corinthians 10:

> It could be said, then, if it pleases the satraps, that the bread and wine remain, and every particle of the body of Christ is sacramentally multiplied to every one of their points. Nor is this inconvenient for God, because according to another perspective the sensible body is multiplied through every distance, where it is perceived, therefore the body of Christ has a certain being under the sacrament, but not a dimensional one, nor is it perceptibly there as a quantum or quality, nor is it there a non-quantum, but it is there a non-quantum there.[36]

This again appears in *Trialogus* IV.9, following which he explains again the need for care in predicating place:

> So the body of Christ is to every point of the world, since the power of this body perfects any part of the world more than a terrestrial king can perfect any part of his kingdom. Nevertheless it is believed, that the body of Christ is in another way largely in the consecrated host, since it would be habitudinally the same as the host, and by reason of [its] power and of virtual existence it is otherwise to any of its points. And it is clear that according to this two-fold reason the body of Christ is in the place of the consecrated host.[37]

One could be forgiven for supposing that Wyclif has formulated a clear philosophical explanation for the Eucharist to counter transubstantiation; after all, he uses this mirror analogy repeatedly throughout his career. But making an analogy is one thing, and constructing a philosophical account is quite another. One could as easily dismiss any thorny problem in Christian theology with a handy analogy. The real heavy lifting comes in explaining the analogy. If Christ is to bread as an image is to mirror, what is to stop us from freezing that image on the glass, as in a daguerreotype, and making the claim that just as Christ is really present in the bread, so Abraham Lincoln is really present in the picture I have of him on the wall? Of course, Wyclif recognized this, and while he continued to use the example until he died, he seems to have realized that he needed substantially more early on, at least by Easter Sunday 1378, when he preached on Mark 16:2.

Beginning from a discussion of the appearance of the risen Christ, he distinguishes between our perception of Christ in the host with our vision and with our mind, and asserts that the Christian perceives "by faith that the fullness of the body of Christ, and the blood and the soul, is from its integrity to every point of this sacrament." But how this takes place has given rise to erroneous theorizing, "some supposing that the bread is the body of Christ, some that the bread becomes and will be the body of Christ, some that the bread is converted into the body of Christ through the draining away of the bread in some of its parts." All of this should be swept away as useless theorizing: "It is enough that a Christian believe that the body of Christ is in some spiritual, sacramental way present to every point of the consecrated host." In the mirror of the world, Christ appears to every point as a full likeness, which one sees in one place, and another somewhere else: "If a created nature can make itself or its likeness to be multiplied, according to intentional being, to every point of a given medium or mirror, it is simple for uncreated nature to make a body of its supposit to be sacramentally throughout every part of the perceptible sacrament."[38]

Wyclif makes a final attempt to clarify the situation by using Lombard's threefold distinction involving the sacrament and "thing":

> [There is] the sacrament alone as the consecrated host, as theologians call the sacrament and not the "thing," second in this sacrament there is the body of the Lord, which is at once sacrament and "thing," and third in this sacrament there is grace as God gives through rightly taking this venerable sacrament, and this is the "thing" and not the sacrament; and so it is necessary to understand the sacrament and not the "thing" as consecrated host, sacrament and "thing" as the body of the Lord, and the "thing" and not-sacrament as grace.[39]

Wyclif is following Lombard's approach here, matching up sacrament-and-not-thing to the consecrated host (although, significantly, Lombard refers to it as "the visible appearance of the bread and wine"), sacrament-and-thing to the body of Christ ("Christ's proper flesh and blood" in Lombard), but he departs from the master by identifying thing-and-not-sacrament as the grace given by the sacrament, where Lombard describes this as "His mystical flesh." This is consonant with general practice, for Aquinas describes it similarly: "We can consider three things in this sacrament: namely, that which is sacrament only, and this is the bread and wine; that which is both reality and sacrament, to wit, Christ's true body; and lastly that which is reality only, namely, the effect of this sacrament."[40]

Wyclif seems not yet ready to turn from the scholastic model of the Eucharist. Henri de Lubac noted that Lombard drastically changed the conception of the church's relation to the Eucharist. In the patristic vision, the church is the "true body," while the Eucharist is the "mystical body," but by the eleventh century the emphasis had switched, and the Eucharist was the "real body" on the altar, present in the "mystical body" of the church. Lombard's use of "mystical body" to mean the church, de Lubac explains, made a "real Church" reliant upon a "real Eucharist," emphasizing the need for scientific exactitude regarding the ontology of the central sacrament.[41] Had Wyclif been ready to start a revolution, he would have identified sacrament-and-thing as Christ's mystical body, not as the generic "body of the Lord," which can be interpreted either way.

Denying Transubstantiation
by Process of Elimination

Wyclif's *De Eucharistia* is most notable for its critical analysis of the extant theories of transubstantiation of Scotus, Aquinas, and, in a different context, Ockham. His rejection of Ockham's position is based primarily in his refutation of the possibility of annihilation. Wyclif addresses Scotus by exploring how one says that the soul and the body of Christ are, at the same time, in many places at once. The Scotist approach, based as it is on the assertion that a thing can be whole in several places at once, would allow us to conclude that God could make it possible that someone other than Christ be multiplied across time and space. Importing God's absolute power into creation to allow for the multiplication of Christ effectively undercuts all laws of God's ordinate command, Wyclif argues, and can as easily be used to allow that two contraries coexist. Does the need for transubstantiation to be true go so far as to violate the idea that God's absolute power would not surpass the laws of logic? Further, multiplying any being, even a point of space, would eliminate the coherence of time and space, the dependability of the senses in accurately measuring the world, and the way we use terms to explain reality:

> Every man would be dizzy, not knowing how to discern sensible things—and all of this error was born in the lying story of the sacrament of the altar! . . . there are a thousand such instances disturbing the church, all of which are dependent upon, or are based in, the most impossible fantasy and occasion of heresy introduced by the sacrament of the Eucharist.[42]

The key here seems to lie in Wyclif's conception that all continua are composed of indivisibles, because if there are infinitely many possible places between any two given places, as Scotus would have asserted, there would be room for the insertion of something new without destroying the cohesion of time and space. Wyclif's atomism compels him to declare Scotus's theory of *conversio* guilty of the introduction of skepticism; but with infinitely divisible continua, there is room for change without the peril of illusion causing us to doubt our every step.

Aquinas's conception of transubstantiation requires an understanding of change over time, and seems to be the place where atomism plays the most important role in Wyclif's eucharistic thought. If time really is divided in discrete units, continuous motion seems impossible, while if our senses are correct, and continuous motion is real, time must also be similarly continuous, and infinitely divisible. But because time is naturally prior to motion, Wyclif reasons, there is no need to justify time to continuous motion by admitting it to be continuous. Wyclif is making use of an innovation of Scotus here; Scotus had argued for the priority of time to motion in a significant break with Aristotelian physics, likely reacting to the 1277 condemnation of the proposition "if heaven stood still, fire would not burn flax, because time would not exist." He is likewise in direct opposition to Ockham, for whom time and movement are directly related, such that movement is what allows us to define time. Wyclif reads Aquinas's *Sentences Commentary* IIa, d.3, q.25, as recognizing the possibility of indivisibles in time, thereby supporting a model of time made up of indivisibles in the midst of an otherwise infinitely divisible continuum, rather like pebbles caught in concrete. But why have both? "God could annihilate every continuum of this sensible world while preserving every one of its [indivisible] points . . . and it is clear that there would be a temporal continuum just as there is a permanent spatial continuum, yet time would be composed of instants."[43] Simply, if God could ensure motion across time defined by indivisibles, why hold onto the idea of an infinitely divisible temporal continuum? Wyclif concludes that Aquinas gave in to the laws of man here and bent his theory of time to suit the desires of his ecclesiastical superiors: "Who would believe this of such a man?" It looks very much as if Wyclif is hinting that Aquinas would have been more favorably inclined toward atomism than his followers had wanted him to be. Wyclif is probably goading later Thomists, whom he appears to have believed were using Aquinas for their own purposes.[44]

Piecing together Wyclif's temporal atomism and its relation to his rejection of the Thomistic version of transubstantiation will require a full understanding of the contents of *De Tempore*, which he wrote twelve years prior. The best we can do here is reason through the problem. Let us follow Aristotle in holding that the accidents we perceive depend on some underlying substantial being. Up to time 1, that substantial being is bread. At time 2, that substantial being is Christ. The use of "x" is a temporal placeholder, and contains no ontological assumptions beyond what is given.

1.A. Assume that, at time 1, x is bread at a point n on the altar; this is the last instant of the substance being bread.

1.B. At time 2, x is the body of Christ at point n on the altar; this is the first instant of the substance being Christ.

2. For any given substance to exist at a given time, it cannot both have and not have a given substantial nature. It cannot both be and not be bread.

2.A. For instantaneous change to occur, there must be an underlying subject of this change; it is not sufficient for instantaneous change that one thing cease to be in a given place and something else begin to be in the same place at the same time.

3. Either there is, or there is not, an intermediate time N, between time 1 and time 2.

Now, assume that time is composed of indivisibles.

3.A. If there is an intermediate time N, then either x is bread and not Christ, or x is Christ and not bread, or x is both bread and Christ, or x is neither bread nor Christ.

3.A.i. If at time N, x is bread and not Christ, then 1.A is false.

3.A.ii. If at time N, x is Christ and not bread, then 1.B is false.

3.A.iii. If at time N, x is both bread and Christ, then 2 is false.

3.A.iv. At time N, x must then be neither Christ nor bread. This would make accidents without a supporting substance, which is impossible.

3.B. If there is no intermediate time N, then the conversion of bread to substance is instantaneous.

Therefore, if you are an indivisiblist, you must hold that the change is instantaneous.

4. If time is infinitely divisible, then instantaneous change between time 1 and time 2 will permit the continuation of the accidents despite the conversion, because there will always be a possible time in which the first substance is ceasing to be and the second substance is beginning to be. This is the potentially gradual change model.

5. If time is composed of indivisible points, and if there is no time N, and the change is instantaneous, then,

5.A. there is no point at which x ceases to be bread and begins to be Christ, and nothing underlies the change. If x were substantial, this problem would not arise, given that "beginning to be" and "ceasing to be" are predicated of only one subject. But since x is only a temporal placeholder, there is nothing to serve as an underlying supporter of the change; "beginning to be" and "ceasing to be" cannot be predicated of a substanceless bundle of accidents.

Therefore, instantaneous change is only possible if there is an underlying substance to experience that change.

Conclusion: The change from bread to Christ is only possible on a model of time entailing its infinite divisibility. So given that (a) Wyclif had earlier established that time is composed of indivisible instants, and (b) Aquinas appears to have entertained the same idea as a live possibility, it follows, for Wyclif anyway, that Aquinas may have recognized the limits of his doctrine, even if his followers lack the capability.

Apostasy, Blasphemy, and Antichrist

Wyclif's denial of transubstantiation was to be the crucial factor in determining his relations with the friars, the bishops, and possibly the Duke of Lancaster for the remaining years of his life. His public assertion that the standing philosophical explanations for the doctrine were untenable in the treatise *De Eucharistia* in mid- to late 1380 cast the die. The sharpening in tone of his reformulation of his critiques is notable; he began with cordial academic dissatisfaction in *De Apostasia*, probably written just after *De Eucharistia*, and slid into bitter recrimination in *De Blasphemia*, likely written in the teeth of his colleagues' condemnation. This condemnation, the result of a committee of twelve theologians' analysis of his position, was the basis for his *Confessio*, Wyclif's public defense of his eucharistic position, which was delivered on 10 May 1381. He appears to have promised John of Gaunt that he would stop using the terms "substance of material bread and wine" outside of the classrooms around this time, possibly as the result of a visit the duke made to Oxford.[45] While he may have stuck to the letter of his promise by not using those specific words, Wyclif was by no means silent about the Eucharist. Transubstantiation's philosophical problems, and the errors of its defenders, appear frequently in his later works.

The tenth, eleventh, and twelfth books of his *Summa Theologie* make up a trilogy of sin, one for each of the three persons of the Trinity. *De Simonia*, written in early 1380, is ostensibly devoted to the selling of ecclesiastical office, which Wyclif describes as a sin against the Holy Spirit. *De Apostasia* concerns the turning away from religion, a sin against the Father, and *De Blasphemia* concerns the slander of God's power, a sin against the Son:

> And thus in this threefold way is the entire Trinity offended: by apostasy, God the Father, who binds the bride of Christ strongly to himself

with a pure and spotless religion; God the Son, who, since he is the virtue and wisdom of God, is daily blasphemed . . . God the Holy Spirit, who, although by his great benevolence he wisely establishes a peaceful order in his house, is thwarted by simoniacal corruption contrary to his plan.[46]

This catalog of sin, a project he had envisioned since finishing *De Veritate Sacrae Scripturae* two years earlier, encompasses the range of evils that Wyclif had come to see bedeviling the church: selling office, papal tyranny, episcopal negligence, clerical ignorance, and the lies and malpractice of the friars each receive their share of Wyclif's polemical ire. The doctrine of transubstantiation figures as a perfect example of the lies with which the hierarchy manipulates the good will of the faithful.

Transubstantiation is a sign of apostasy in that the fathers, including Jerome, Augustine, and John Damascene, refer to Christ's presence in the bread; if the bread is annihilated, how could he be in it? The great mistake, Wyclif explains, was made by Innocent III, when he asserted that the accidents of the bread remain without the bread's substance. Neither God nor man can make accidents without a subject, and no pope should be believed who does not speak with the guidance of the Holy Ghost, or foundation in scripture. Why would the Holy Ghost have waited more than a thousand years, for this pope's appearance, to make such an astounding revelation? After all, this is the same pope who levied a tax of 900 marks on England: are we to believe that all that Innocent did and said was de facto correct? In the first millennium, heretics abounded, but the great teachers of the church consistently uncovered their lies. Nowadays, lying seems to be increasingly acceptable: "A certain teacher, whose religion should, according to the truth, lie securely locked away, publicly dogmatized on behalf of the father of lies in the Oxford schools, [saying] that in many cases it is licit and meritorious to lie."[47] The line of reasoning illustrates the structure of Wyclif's argument in *De Apostasia* and in many of the works that would follow. In many cases, the argument trails off into vituperative digression and rant, until Wyclif comes to himself and returns to the subject at hand. In this case, the argument comes to rest on the impossibility of the multiplication of Christ's body. His arguments do not differ markedly from those given earlier, and while describing Christ's figurative perceptibility in the sacrament as being like seeing a coal burning without wondering whether it is stone or wood, he does not make the analogy between the host and a mirror reflecting Christ.

When he is not careful, Wyclif allows himself to slide from serious argument into ridicule, giving some sense of what it must have been like to
listen to him lecture when he was in high spirits. For example, later in
De Apostasia, while engaged in a catalog of theological authorities whose
thought would unweave the web of authority supporting transubstantiation, he wanders into a discussion of papal authority. Many popes are too
quick to allow themselves to use their power for their own ends, he complains, and they may even veer into madness:

> The pope could fall into such a madness as to believe that the entire rest
> of the world depends on his willing, in temporal as much as in spiritual
> things . . . so that the church cannot be governed without it, so that not
> only all sublunar corporeal bodies, but even all spiritual gifts, like grace
> and the virtues, depend on him. This is as blasphemous as to believe
> that the body of Christ is, in its nature, as imperfect as rat feces. The rat
> is a melancholic animal, and the madness of philosophers grows from
> melancholy; Magog is read in Genesis as having been the son of Joseph,
> whose generation is said to have occupied the western territory, where
> melancholy reigns.[48]

Comments like these certainly lead the reader to regard his continual avow-
als of willingness to be corrected by ecclesiastical authority with skepticism.

Given that the doctrine of transubstantiation is about Christ's presence
in created being, it would be natural to expect the book assigned to sins
against God the Son to be devoted to more of the same. *De Blasphemia*
has a wider scope than *De Apostasia*, though; blasphemy is a detraction
from the honor due to God, in particular, when we attribute honor to
creatures which are due to God alone. Adoring the host is one aspect of
blasphemy, but so is honoring a man as one ought to submit oneself to
God. All are part of too great an allegiance to temporal, mutable things and
too little thought given to the spiritual. The triumph of Satan has turned
men's minds from their spiritual welfare and toward fascination with the
mundane. His daughters, hypocrisy and tyranny, have enchanted men:
"And just as the thorny briar and the poisonous herb grows out of the earth
and perchance flourishes, despite many attempts to root them out, so it is
with the words of hypocrisy and tyranny."[49] The ecclesiastical hierarchy,
from pope down to verger, is as likely to be infected with this tendency as
any secular organization. And thus the treatise launches into the indictment of clerical corruption, the misuse of office, and the priestly neglect of

the spiritual needs of the people that characterizes many of Wyclif's later works. In *De Blasphemia*, foisting off bread as the body of the Savior is but one of the ploys that clergymen use in furthering their worldly aims, albeit one of the more pernicious ones.

Wyclif reiterated his eucharistic theology during the remaining six years of his life, attacking transubstantiation in *De Fide Sacramenti* (a portion of which was translated into English perhaps a year after its composition), in *Trialogus*, and finally in the section of *Opus Evangelicum* entitled *De Antichristo*.[50] The *Opus Evangelicum* is an extended commentary on three selections from the Gospels; the first, Matthew 5–7, on the Sermon on the Mount, is followed by *De Antichristo*, an exegesis on Matthew 23–25 and John 13–17. His criticism of transubstantiation here is a summary of his earlier arguments against the doctrine, interlarded with vituperative comments like "if these lying disciples of Antichrist would have us believe that they annihilate substance when they bless it, perhaps we should ask rather that they curse us at the benediction."[51] Still, he does not shy away from discussions of the need for distinctions in kinds of identity and predication in understanding the force of "this is my body," repeatedly reminding his reader of the arguments he made in *De Eucharistia* and *De Apostasia*.

Scholars have long argued about the relation of Wyclif's eucharistic theology and his metaphysics, some holding that there is an important tie between the two, others denying one. In arguing against this connection, Maurice Keen has suggested that Wyclif was angrier with the clerical abuse of a sacrament than with the ontological twisting the abuse involved, and that he was angriest of all about how the "followers of Antichrist" misused scripture to their own ends. In arguing for a connection, Gordon Leff has held that Wyclif's realist system was the beginning point for an unavoidable collision with the ontologies that admitted transubstantiation. While the intent of this chapter has been to show the tie between Wyclif's atomism and his eucharistic theology, his overall position on the subject involves scriptural hermeneutics as much as philosophy, and granting pride of place to either "theology" or "philosophy" misdirects the force of Wyclif's thought. Throughout his writings, he insisted that "the logic of Christ" is the proper instrument with which to read scripture and to understand any theological position. In this case of the Christ being asserted to be present in the elements of a sacrament, the eternal word's presence to those taking the sacrament is at issue, and in Christ there is no room for an either-or relation between theology and philosophy.[52]

THE LOGIC OF SCRIPTURE

Medieval thinkers who achieved the doctorate in theology had to have completed a sustained commentary on the *Sententiae* of Peter Lombard. In the course of that commentary, if his philosophical and theological position were sufficiently indicative of some species of *phronesis*, the theologian might eventually come to be known by a cognomen tailor-made for him. Henry of Ghent was known as doctor solemnis, Thomas Bradwardine as doctor profundus, Bonaventure was referred to as the seraphic doctor, Scotus was called, not surprisingly, the subtle doctor, and Aquinas was known both as angelic doctor and doctor communis. Wyclif's zeal to emphasize the centrality of scripture in his philosophy and theology led him to be known as doctor evangelicus—although "detestable heresiarch" also became common.[1]

This dichotomy, in which one man is known both for his enthusiasm for scripture in philosophical theology and for having been condemned as heretical in the eyes of the Catholic church, has led many to associate Wyclif's scriptural theology with the biblical emphasis of the early Protestants. The radically Protestant John Bale even coined the epithet "morning star of the Reformation" for Wyclif in 1548. This association has guaranteed Wyclif's place in a class with other figures anachronistically defined by events that took place decades, if not centuries, after their deaths. Wyclif's approach to scripture is typically medieval in hermeneutical approach, of a piece with the traditional Augustinian *quadriga*, or four-level reading of scripture. Here, the reader looks for four interrelated, yet distinct, senses within each scriptural proposition in an interpretive tradition stretching across Christian history. The four-level approach was endorsed in the earliest period of the church by Origen, formalized by Augustine in *De Doctrina Christiana* (397, 426 CE), and institutionalized in Western Christendom in the ninth century with the Carolingian revival.[2]

By the fourteenth century, Robert Holcot argued that natural reason and scripture were sufficiently disparate to warrant considering questions pertinent to unaided reason without reference to scripture. Wyclif's position, likely formulated in response to Holcot's influence, was to argue for the centrality of scripture to all human experience. His *De Veritate Sacrae Scripturae* (1377–1378) emphasizes the need for the reader to understand scripture's proper logic, or hermeneutical structure. Wyclif's well-known connection with the first English translation of the Bible, his earlier *Postilla* (1371–1376), a comprehensive summary of both Old and New Testaments meant to give students a sense of the order and structure of scripture, his later, extensive commentaries on Matthew and John in the *Opus Evangelicum* (1383–1384), and his many surviving Latin sermons all point to the centrality of scripture. With this kind of orientation, it is tempting to envision Wyclif as having foreseen Reformation ideals. Until recently, many of the vernacular sermons associated with the Lollard movement were assumed to be Wyclif's. Thomas Arnold published three volumes of vernacular writings entitled *The English Works of John Wyclif* (1869, 1871), and in 1902 F. D. Matthew revised his 1880 edition of *The English Works of Wyclif Hitherto Unprinted*, but by the 1970s Anne Hudson had established that none of these could be attributed to Wyclif with any certainty. By the time Hudson's argument had been promulgated, the scholarly wind had shifted, and Wyclif was no longer universally seen as a proto-Reformer. Heiko Oberman has argued that Holcot's approach to scripture, which emphasizes the need for faith to overcome the skepticism to which unassisted reason is prone, is important for understanding the development of Reformation thought.[3] As we will see, Wyclif's approach is, in comparison to Holcot's, much more thoroughly medieval.

But if we discard the Reformation lens through which some have examined Wyclif's extensive works on scripture, what should we use instead? Simply to describe a "theology of scripture" without reference to other elements of a thinker's philosophical theology is shortsighted. Who would venture to describe Aquinas's scriptural hermeneutic without relying on his formal theology? How could we understand Augustine's assertion in *De Doctrina Christiana* that all instruction is about either signs or things, without a grasp of his epistemology? It is the same with Wyclif. In *De Veritate Sacrae Scripturae* (*DVSS*), he describes the relation of the spoken and written word of the Bible in all its physical instantiations to its universal, the "Book of Life" of Revelation 20 and 21. This book, Wyclif explains, containing all uncreated truth, became incarnate in Jesus. Citing John 10:35–36, "and the Scripture cannot be destroyed, whom the Father sanctified and sent into the world," Wyclif reasons, "[f]rom these words he seems to imply that he is the truth itself, when Christ had been established and became a human being. . . . God the Father sent this book into the world in order to save the world."[4]

Wyclif begins *DVSS* by arguing against sophists who would subject scripture to logical analysis. They are sophomoric fools who would be so bold as to exclaim, "Look how you were proven to have contradicted yourself! Today I learned in the lecture halls to concede that there are contradictions found within the sacred page." He was one once, he says, but now knows that apparent contradictions in scripture should educate its readers in a more subtle revelation of truth than a literal reading affords: "One must learn a new grammar and a new logic when attempting to explicate or understand Holy Scripture."[5] Holcot had come to a similar conclusion thirty years earlier, in his *Sentences Commentary*, when he faced the incompatibility between Aristotelian logic and the persons of the Trinity. He concluded that there are really two logics: Aristotle's, which applies to the natural world, and a higher one, applicable to the supernatural order. As mentioned in chapter 2, Holcot's view developed and led him to concur, with Ockham, Wodeham, and others, that while God could not be the subject of an expository syllogism, Aristotle's logic was not thereby restricted to the natural order. Aristotle's logic and grammar are universally applicable, but where they appear to cause scripture to be untenable, they must be understood to be only human constructs. Still, Holcot's commitment was to the separation of theology from the other sciences. This was because its first principles are not things evident to any reasoning mind, as they are in the natural sciences, but things taken on faith.[6] Wyclif's argument seems a response to Holcot's position, which would have been well known in the

Oxford of his day. Philosophers, Wyclif responds, are devoted to what is true, and must reject the false:

> Now a philosopher is described as a lover of prudence, though it is evident that nobody is a philosopher inasmuch as he lapses into error. For then he is a fool who hates prudence or wisdom, the very opposites of falsehood. Therefore, the greatest philosopher is none other than Christ, Wisdom itself, our God. Consequently, it is by following and studying Him that we too become philosophers, while in learning various falsehoods we are straying from philosophy insofar as we drift away from the authentic understanding of the saints, who are the true philosophers.[7]

Even before engaging in the reasoning that Holcot used to separate out what is tenable to the human mind lacking faith from what is theologically grounded, Wyclif argues, one must proceed on the assumption that all of our reasoning has its basis in the authority of Christ. This is Augustine's approach, and Wyclif's admiration for it is as enthusiastic as is his antipathy toward those who would sidestep its dedication to scripture's centrality in all reasoning: "In every case I am in conformity with both the logic and the metaphysics of Augustine, which are all the more excellent for belonging to Holy Scripture, the very first rule of all human perfection."[8] Anselm, Hugh of St. Victor, Bernard, and Grosseteste are his authorities, and, he continues, they would certainly have agreed. Scripture is the source of every valid system of logic and the eternal source of truth in creation. To understand it, one must recognize that it has its own all-encompassing logic, and devote oneself to learning it. And if there is a real connection between Holy Scripture and the Christ himself, this logic of scripture must be tied to the nature of the incarnation somehow. So, in this chapter, we will pursue this connection between hermeneutics and incarnational theology.

The Law of Love

His *moderni* colleagues would have regarded Wyclif's identification of scripture with Christ as reactionary at best, if not ludicrous. For Holcot, the Bible is a text. It is the revealed holy text of salvation, but like the classical sources he delights in using to develop his commentary on the book of Wisdom, it remains a text. To identify it with the being of the second person of the Trinity in some ontological sense would be bibliolatrous. Why would Wyclif make such a case for equating Christ's nature with the Bible? By 1378, when he was at work on *DVSS*, he suggests that the case has been made: "I have often said that the entire Holy Scripture is the one word of God, and that every one of its parts should be condensed into the totality of that Word in whom the blessed in heaven see the multitude of truths spoken by God."[9] He had argued this way at least as early as 1372 in *De Benedicta Incarnacione*, when he considered the unlikelihood of a dissolution of the union of God and man in Christ. Following John 10:35–36 (as it appears in the Vulgate: "'Scripture,' He said, 'cannot be dissolved, which the Father blessed and sent into the world'"), Wyclif reasoned that Christ cannot mean the physical books themselves, because they can be destroyed just like anything else. What the Father has blessed and sent into the world is the incarnate word, and Christ's words are self-referential.[10] He carried this relation between Bibles and Christ further, explaining that Bibles are suggestive of a hypostatic union themselves. They are a union of the divine word and parchment, just as Christ was the word made flesh. This does not mean that we should worship Bibles, though. The material book is no more scripture than Jesus' body was the Christ when it lay dead in the tomb.

Robert Grosseteste's influence on Wyclif resonates in the idea that Christ's centrality to the very being of the Bible emerges as we trace the evolution of God's covenant with humanity. Grosseteste had written two treatises central to his formal theology in the 1230s. In *De Decem Mandatis*, Grosseteste gives a pastoral analysis of the Ten Commandments, with a central focus on the implicit command to love God and our neighbors. The accompanying, longer *De Cessatione Legalium* contains his account of the evolution of the divine law given to man, from the Mosaic code of ceremony and behavior to the law of Christ, through which salvation is possible. In both treatises, the development of law from commands given to subjects to a code of love depends on the incarnation, in particular the passion and resurrection. So, if scripture is the record containing this evolution of law, Christ occupies the foremost position. Grosseteste explains in *De Decem Mandatis* that love lies at the heart of all the teachings and laws of scripture, citing Matthew 7:12 ("All things therefore whatsoever you would that men should do to you, do you also to them. For this is the law and the prophets"): "In these brief words the Lord gave the law of love, from which alone hang all the laws and commands of the prophets."[11] In *De Cessatione*, Grosseteste describes Christ's primacy as lawgiver to all of humanity, as both the living word of God and the perfect exemplar of the law of love: "So then with all works of the good the Word is the eternal principle, just as was written [in the prologue to *De Decem Mandatis*]: the foundation of all works [is] the Word. For the life and the form of everything exterior to the Word that proceeds by ordained, loving cognition, is the eternal Word of the Father Jesus Christ."[12] Here, he distinguishes himself by arguing that the incarnation would have occurred even without sin. As he had explained in his *Hexamaeron*, his commentary on the creation, it was the necessary conclusion to creation, completing the Neoplatonic return of all being to God: "But when God became a human being, the God-man shared in a nature with the rational creature in a univocal way, and the making of the circle was perfect, and the circular return to God was joined up."[13] With this, Grosseteste shifts the Christological emphasis on redemption from sin to cosmological completion, allowing him to emphasize the "law of love" as what binds the elements of creation. This motif lies at the center of Wyclif's prolonged study of the law of scripture as the purpose for a revealed body of truth.

Wyclif wrote *De Mandatis Divinis*, a treatise grounded firmly in these two works of Grosseteste, in early 1376. Here, he takes this theme of Christ's loving command as the basis for all of the laws and teachings of scripture and develops it as the basis for understanding his relation of Christ to scripture. Contained within every word of scripture, Wyclif argues, is an underlying truth that was known before the Fall. Now, because of our damaged faculties, it must be written: love of God is our first and final duty, which when carried out, will unite all creatures in harmonious concord. The core of *De Mandatis Divinis* is five chapters that he calls "the more pleasant treatise on love," a development of Grosseteste's discussion of love in *De Decem Mandatis*. Wyclif argues that the command to love God with all your heart, soul, mind, and strength of Deuteronomy 6:5–9, echoed in Matthew 22:37–40, is the primary rule for all created being, the foundational precept for all human endeavor, and the chief scriptural truth. All of the virtues that Aristotle describes, as well as the theological virtues, have the command to love God as their necessary condition. Without this absolute submission of the self to God, a right ordering to the rest of created being is impossible. Our first urge, he explains, is to know that which we are created to love, so more than anything, we need knowledge of God. God may be comprehended, and so loved, in three ways. The blessed receive intuitive awareness in paradise, philosophers achieve a discursive awareness through philosophical reasoning, and the simple Christian gains God through simple faith. The infidel, who balks at elevating the mind to a love of that which surpasses empirical evidence, cannot hope to lead a properly ordered life. His virtuous behavior is accidental at best.

Naturally, Wyclif takes this opportunity for a riposte at the *moderni*, who reject the possibility of theological knowledge of God grounded in created being, and at the Thomists and Scotists, who reject *illuminatio* as the basis for understanding God. Regarding the latter, who think that theology is possible from the created order, Wyclif suggests that their way, taken in itself, has limited value:

> But since nothing is loved unless known, it is clear that the true order of knowing God leads the reason into His love, and although from creatures they take philosophically evident knowledge of God . . . the way is more compendious and more certain in which, following the exemplary reasons or the intelligible being of creatures, it ascends to God.[14]

Regarding the *moderni*, who imagine that knowledge of the sensible order of created being is grounded in empirical evidence, Wyclif is less forgiving. To gain knowledge of a thing simply for the sake of having knowledge of that thing is intellectual fornication, or using a means as an end unto itself. We are to know creatures as a means to know, and love, God. In words certainly meant to evoke Romans 13:13, and so the climactic moment of Augustine's *Confessions*, he equates *moderni* empiricism with wanton chambering: "Not in contemplating the tumultuous cares of the world, nor the subject spirit's collisions with fantasmata, to which the imagination is led hurriedly here and there, nor indeed to the passions of the body, but by quiet speculation is the highest good contemplated."[15]

We should begin our knowledge, and love, of God, in the way Anselm had suggested in *Proslogion* 5. Reasoning from the idea of a being greater than which cannot be conceived to recognition of its necessary existence outside the mind leads us to recognize God as the "most useful, most beautiful, and most delectable" being, the supreme good. Plunging from this pinnacle of being down to created being is madness. When we recognize the absolute nature of God, our first instinct should be to seek the reasons of things in the world in the divine. Rather than try to understand the contents of God's mind from things as they exist in the world, we should use our reason to touch the divine ideas, which are "so necessary [to created being] that without knowledge of them, no one would be wise, nor as a consequence, virtuous." Short of the divine ideas, our concern should be universals, the created exemplars by which particulars have their being in species. To work the other way around, to move toward God from individual creatures, is to risk constructing a palpable, sensible god for oneself, a hollow mockery of divine being.

If we have access to something so universal, so perfectly connected to the divine mind, as a written record of truth, we must surely use it if we are to love God in all that we do. This is the line of reasoning in *De Amore sive ad Quinque quaestiones*, a letter written in the last year of Wyclif's life. Here, as the title suggests, he addresses five questions on the love of God, of which the last is about the state of life in which the faithful can best love God. While some in this life can enjoy the ideal Christian state, that of virginity and/or priesthood, others must serve God as members of the military or peasant classes. Because servants of the devil constantly prowl in search of prey among all Christians:

> Many viators should carefully study the Gospel in that language in which the sentences of the evangelists are most clear, because from faith all the faithful should follow the lord Jesus Christ, and however many will have followed Him, that many and more love Him meritoriously. Since, then, the story of Christ is even more fully expressed than His doctrine, it is clear how carefully the faithful ought [to] study this book.[16]

The story of Christ's life, the center of scripture for medieval exegetes, is as important to the viator as are his teachings. Christ gave his law, the most perfect vehicle for loving God available to us, in the manner of his life as well as in his teachings. This gift does not dissolve the law of the Jews, Wyclif says, following Grosseteste's *De Cessatione*. It completes it. He gives two examples, one from the world of objects, and the other from the world of words. Imagine a house the foundation of which is the eternal truths of God's mind. The stones of its walls are the laws of Moses, and the mortar binding them together is love and grace. This is the law of Christ, he explains, a house that will stand for as long as time endure. Now consider the letter *i* (*iota*). In its form, it is the simplest of letters, without twist, bend, or break. In the same way, the chief commandment to love God is the most brief and direct, without possibility of misinterpretation. The dot on the letter, the simplest of all written marks, is equivalent to all letters figuratively, and so denotes all of the other laws of God in the figurative sense. One needs the industry of a bee to study scripture, and an understanding of all of its content, surpassing a simple historical understanding, to plumb its depths. Yet all of its content, all of its depth, all of its mystery is signified by the dot on the *i*, while the body of the letter is the law of love.[17] The example of the house shows how Wyclif has incorporated Grosseteste's understanding of the incarnation as completing creation. Christ's law is the house, and Christ is the architect; the law of Moses is as much a part of the revealed word as are Christ's own life and teachings. The example of the letter *i* underscores the centrality of the command to love God to all precepts, laws, and accounts of scripture. The word speaks the letter, and the letter on the page stands for more than one simple sound. It stands for all of the letters and words of the truth revealed by Christ.

Christ and Everyman

Clarity about the metaphysics of the incarnation is important. So far, Wyclif has argued that the word of God is at once the great legislator of all justice and the living Book of Life. Christ and scripture are somehow identical, and the incarnate word is contained within all scripture. The possibilities for confusion are legion. How can the Bible be at once Christ, and have the incarnate Christ as its chief figure, and also be spoken by Christ? Put in Aristotelian causal terms, scripture appears to have the second person of the Trinity as its formal, efficient, and material cause. What really is Christ? Since the great figures in medieval philosophy from the thirteenth century onward were theologians first and foremost, they frequently used this question as a showcase for their metaphysics, and no place was better suited to this than during the required commentary on Peter Lombard's *Sentences*, in which the third book is devoted to questions on the incarnation. Fourteenth-century Oxford theologians did not devote their attention to covering every distinction in the *Sentences*, preferring instead to analyze a few distinctions relevant to their own interests. In many cases, when theologians did have something to say about the metaphysics of the incarnation, it was consonant with a recognized luminary, like Aquinas, Scotus, or Ockham.

In general, the models for explaining the incarnation fall into two groups. In the first group, epitomized by Peter Abelard and Thomas Aquinas, divinity and humanity are described as parts that make up the whole Christ. Peter Lombard described three variations on this first approach in *Sententiae* III.6.

In the first, the word clothed himself with human nature as a man wears a cloak. This is the *habitus* theory, suggested by Augustine. In the second, a man composed of body and soul was assumed by the word so that he became identical with the word. This is the *assumptus homo* theory, endorsed by Hugh of St. Victor and Anselm. In the third, Christ begins to be composed of divinity, along with body and soul, in a subsistence relation. This appears to have been Lombard's approximation of the position of Gilbert of Poitiers.[18] Aquinas understood both the *habitus* and the *assumptus homo* position to have been condemned by Alexander III in 1170 and 1177, and he supposed that any theory in which Christ's humanity is described as accident was heretical. In the second general group, including Bonaventure, Giles of Rome, Henry of Ghent, and Scotus, the theologians used a substance-accident model, where Christ's humanity is related to the word as an accident or property is related to its substance. Ockham's ontology, where "humanity" is a concept naturally referring to a concrete individual or individuals, denies any further reality to what his predecessors called universals. In his pared-down ontology, Ockham rejected the existence of a common nature like humanity apart from individual people. But this easily leads to understanding him to have held that in Christ was an individual human person in addition to the divine nature, making up either a two-person person (that is, the human person Jesus and, with the added word, the person of the Christ), or a Christ in which a human person and the divine person of the word are not united by anything into a third composite. Both suggest the Nestorian heresy, and despite his arguments, many opponents of Ockham interpret him as a Nestorian.[19]

After Ockham, both Holcot and Adam Wodeham wrote on incarnational theology. Wodeham's *Oxford Lectures* of 1332 and several of Holcot's *Quodlibeta* suggest a sustained interest in Christology among the *moderni*. These works are not yet edited, and may prove to be a gold mine for post-Ockham incarnational theology at Oxford. Wyclif's contemporary Nicholas Aston, who was by no means Ockhamist in his theology, also lectured on Christological questions, but what survives of Aston's work in this vein is unedited as well. The major secular figures among Wyclif's predecessors, Walter Burley and Thomas Bradwardine, leave no record of contributing to the debate. Burley's *Sentences* commentary, if he produced one, has never been identified, while what remains of Bradwardine's does not touch significantly on the incarnation's metaphysics.[20] Of the Franciscans, Walter

Chatton, a determined opponent of Ockham whose *Sentences Commentary* has recently been published, would be a good resource in tracing the history of Christological controversy after Ockham.

In rejecting Ockham's austere ontology, Wyclif used the Scotist substance-accident model for his more full-bodied ontological articulation of humanity being assumed by the word. His treatise on the incarnation, *De Incarnacione*, also called *De Verbi Incarnacione*, written in 1372, evokes Anselm's similarly titled work in title, but in content it is more concerned with the metaphysics of the incarnation than with the doctrine of substitutionary atonement. He had written a treatise on the ontological makeup of human beings, *De Composicione Hominis*, almost immediately beforehand, and Wyclif's description of the incarnation relies heavily on his analysis of the relation of body and soul in that work. Scripture shows us that the human soul is a created spirit itself indivisible, able to be unified to a body. The resulting union is an integrated human being: soul, flesh, and the union of the two (body + soul), which aggregate Wyclif calls the integrated nature, ontologically commensurate to body and soul considered in themselves. If body and soul are distinct from one another, what provides the formal basis for accidents for a body without a soul? Wyclif posits a corporeal form in the body prior to ensoulment. This causes the problem of there being two possible ontological beings contained in one person. One being, a body with a corporeal form considered as such, is distinct from the ensouled integrated person. Yet the two are not really distinct, because these coextensive bodies communicate equally in the same material essence. The soul requires the preexistence of the body since its chief act is to animate a body, but not necessarily a temporal priority:

> It appears more likely that "this man" communicates more than "this body and this animal" for it communicates "this spirit," which remains [a] human spirit existing as such, even when it no longer remains a body or an animal. It is not the case that these two [spirit and body] are the same animal or the same body in number, for the prior corporeal nature is a body and yet is not thereby an animal. Since man is all three [body, soul, and integrated body + soul], he exists, after his body is dead, by virtue of the prior corporeal nature, and he is a composite, prior to being an animal, according to his corporeal nature and the soul.[21]

Scripture regularly shifts from one aspect of a human being to another. Sometimes, the term "man" refers principally to a soul (Colossians 3:10), sometimes to a body (2 Corinthians 4:16), and sometimes to the aggregate of the two, which philosophers understand to refer to a rational animal, a composite of body and soul. In a fourth way, scriptures refer to Christ as a man, alternating between the previous senses while still referring to the same God-man.

> [F]or the person or for the substance, which is any of these three natures or things, or indeed all beings contracted [together], which is each of them, and in this way the faith speaks from Scripture that this Man, who created heaven and earth, was born of a virgin, conversed with men, suffered, died, and was buried, descended to hell, and ascended, etc. Not according to the assumed nature did He create the kingdom, nor according to Deity did He suffer, nor according to His soul was He dead and buried, nor according to His body or other integrated nature did He descend to hell, but since the same person was all these, according to one of these He did one, and according to another He did the rest, just as it was best suitable.[22]

One final element from *De Composicione Hominis* aids our understanding of its place in Wyclif's Christology. While discussing the relation of corporeal essence to the human form, Wyclif asks whether Christ's incarnation preceded creation, a question common in many *Sentences* commentaries.[23] The priority of the created human essence, or humanity as such, to all individual human beings means that individual humans are instantiations of a universal by community. By virtue of the corporeal presence of the created human essence in Adam, all men are contained in Adam. In the sense that each being exists in *raciones seminales*, contained within first principles being actualized in the earlier creation, each of us preexists our own existence, but the level of preexistence is extremely weak. Better to say that each person exists as intelligible to God, which does not posit anyone preexisting, only God's knowing eternally.

There are differences between how the human nature becomes instantiated in a particular human being and how the word became man. Humanity is united to its particular, and does not unite itself. It is passive in this sense, and does not come together ahead of time with the soul that will occupy the body, but is active in the sense that it acts upon the individual substance realizing the nature of the species therein. The word, on the other hand, temporally precedes humanity, because the word creates, then assumes humanity. It acts upon humanity and remains the word while also becoming the integrated whole (word + humanity) and each of its parts. The number of parts varies, depending on how you count the elements and the composites that arise from them, which in Wyclif's account, can be dizzying in their complexity. Many of the difficulties that arise in the Christologically oriented study of scripture can be avoided by remembering that "there are three incommunicable natures in Christ: deity, body, and soul. This is clear in this way. Christ is God and perfect man, as supported by the faith: God is wholly deity, and the perfect man is wholly as much body as soul."[24] While any individual member of the species is body, soul, and the aggregate (body + soul), Christ differs through the addition of deity to these three components, although this in no way affects the truly human nature of Christ. The word assumed not *a* human nature, but humanity as such. Perhaps the right approach is to imagine that deity, the universal divine nature shared by the persons of the Trinity, needs something more than *a* human nature to offset its magnitude in the Christ: the balance is achieved by the word's assuming humanity as such.

In the medieval play *Everyman*, Death causes the eponymous character to go from carefree ignorance of his place in creation to an awareness of his need for good deeds and the sacraments. Death says, "Every man I will beset that liveth beastly / Out of God's laws, and dreadeth not folly. . . . Lo, yonder I see Everyman walking; / Full little he thinketh on my coming."[25] Wyclif makes a jump similar to the one Death has just made. He argues that, if every man would be Everyman, then Everyman would only be one man, and if Christ assumes humanity, then Christ, too, would be Everyman.[26] It cannot be that Christ is every man, of course, nor that Christ is more than one man, nor can the universal humanity itself be a man capable of receiving accidents like individual men. What Wyclif means is that Christ has the same kind of body and soul as all other men have. In assuming the universal, he did not become the being of the universal by which all of its particulars have their being. There need be no posited haecceity by which individualization occurs for Wyclif, and there need be no additional individuating element added to the hypostatic union of the word and humanity. In assuming humanity, Christ did not assume every relation that holds between the universal and its particulars.

Wyclif proceeds from the being of Christ into creation by means of the truth he defines. In *De Veritate Sacrae Scripturae*, he describes five gradations, or equivocations, by which we can understand the identity of Christ with scripture. First is the Book of Life, described in Revelation 20:12, which represents the divine mind revealed in glory at the apocalypse as divine legislator and judge. Second are the truths contained within the Book of Life. These are not essentially distinct from the being of the Christ, but formally distinct in that we can consider individual divine ideas apart from the being of the word in which they have eternal being. Third are the truths considered as realized in creation, each defining genus and species by which created being is organized. These are the universals of Wyclif's ontology, which correspond to the divine ideas as created instantiations of the unchanging eternal truths. Fourth are the truths we comprehend when we encounter the world and gain understanding. These are the subject of epistemology, the concepts that reflect created beings that we use to recognize the universals. At this level are the concepts we glean from experience, as when we encounter people and formulate the concept "humanity." This concept refers to the universal humanity, which itself is the created manifestation of God's idea of humanity. Finally, at the lowest level of Christ's truth is scripture, the written signs, manuscripts, and so forth that tell us of the reality of Christ at the center of the universe.[27]

From a philosophical viewpoint, this is an interesting way to unite Christ to the contents of the set of books that describes the Old and New Law, but Wyclif's scope was far broader than incarnational theology. Throughout his adult life, he was engaged in an active program of scripture commentary. While still in Oxford, he completed a *Postilla* of the Bible and had begun writing and preaching a remarkable number of sermons. Further, in his last years, he composed a sustained commentary on Matthew 5–7, *De Sermone Domini in Monte*, and in his final major work, *De Antichristo*, a commentary on Matthew 23–25 and John 13–17, all grouped together under the title *Opus Evangelicum*. Wyclif's scriptural works are remarkable in their combination of traditional medieval hermeneutic method with Wyclif's own unique vision of the church as it was, and as he believed it could be. Readers and scholars interested in Wyclif's vision of the clergy, in his ethical program, his ecclesiology, his eschatology, or his soteriology will find this portion of his work rich with ideas, opinions, and reasoning. Further, Wyclif's theological debt to Augustine, the Victorines, and other important figures in the medieval commentary tradition is particularly evident in these works. Following the theme of scripture as embodying the "logic of Christ," we will follow Wyclif's interpretation of the Beatitudes, which he believed contained the very essence of the Christian life, throughout his biblical works.

Wyclif the Postillator and Exegete

Medieval scripture commentary is a universe unto itself. Readers of the Bible were committed to weaving connections not only between every part of scripture, but also to the vast body of writings of the authoritative commentators who had preceded them. The classic image of the medieval commentary tradition is of a page with a line of text from, say, the prophet Isaiah, surrounded with a selection from a sermon of Ambrose or some other Latin father, itself enclosed in a running commentary composed by a twelfth-century theologian. The term "gloss," earlier used for a continuous commentary on a selection from the Bible, had lost its earlier sense of straightforward theological explication by the later medieval period. The earlier glosses of theologians like Stephen Langton, Peter Comestor, or the Victorines had become so compendious as to require their own system of summaries. The student of the sacred page in the later Middle Ages was also in great need of linguistic advice and terminological explanation, given the respect that had grown for the Hebrew biblical tradition in the preceding centuries. A new species of scriptural tool evolved in the thirteenth century, called the *postilla*, possibly from the phrase "after these words" (*post illa verba*). Twenty-first-century readers may be familiar with *The Jerome Biblical Commentary* or *Harper's Bible Commentary*; a *postilla* is the medieval equivalent. The Dominican Hugh of St. Cher (d. 1263) was the first to compose a *Postilla* on the entire Bible, summarizing biblical scholarship, particularly literal and moral interpretations, for preaching friars and students. The Franciscan Nicholas of Lyra (1270–1349) is perhaps the most famous postillator. His *Postilla Literallis et Moralis in Vetus et Novum Testamentum* is imbued with medieval Jewish scripture scholarship, along with a distinct suspicion that the Jews had rewritten their holy texts to erase evidence of Christ's divinity. The tendency before Lyra was for postillators to use their summaries to further their own positions. Dominicans and Franciscans tended to argue for apostolic poverty, and followers of Joachim of Fiore for an eschatological interpretation of the events described. Lyra eschewed this, preferring the earlier, nonparticularizing approach that had been the hallmark of earlier postillators. His style was to avoid referring to church fathers, Franciscan ideals, or other topics not immediate to his exegesis, which earned him the nickname "clear and plain doctor."[28]

Wyclif had high regard for Lyra, describing him as, "although recent, yet a copious and gifted postillator of Scripture" with sensitivity for historical tradition.[29] It is likely that Wyclif's *Postilla* was presented in lecture format, from 1372 to 1374, later transcribed, and much later, likely during his last years, reedited. In both structure and substance, Wyclif's approach is similar to Lyra's; he avoids the hectoring tone and polemical approach of his sermons and *Opus Evangelicum*, while emphasizing the centrality of scripture to the Christian life and especially to the work of the theologian. Following Peter Aureol, he divides his *Postilla* into eight parts, of which five survive in manuscript. His summaries of the Pentateuch, the historical books, and Proverbs, Wisdom, and Ecclesiasticus are lost, although the flavor of his *postillae* of Genesis and Exodus likely remains in *De Statu Innocencie* and *De Mandatis Divinis*. An emphasis on exploring the senses buried in seemingly simple words begins with the opening verses of Genesis. Wyclif describes a threefold allegorical sense, a sixfold tropological or moral sense, and a twofold analogical sense, all described in Grosseteste's masterful *Hexamaeron*.[30] The fact that Wyclif, a secular, took on the task was itself noteworthy. Since Stephen Langton (d. 1228), only friars had done this sort of thing. In distilling the contents of scripture into lectures and his *Postilla*, Wyclif was demonstrating that preaching was the province not of friars only, but of all clergy. In fact, Wyclif's *Postilla* follows Lyra very closely, although Wyclif is more prone to cite the fathers. Beryl Smalley, the greatest scholar of Wyclif's *Postilla*, distills his postillating formula into a simple recipe: "use Auriol's *Compendium* as a mould, pour in Lyre, flavour with Augustine, and sprinkle with Grosseteste."[31]

Postillating and glossing were serious business for the evangelical doctor. A tendency to elide subjects that might prove tricky for a theologian with extratheological motives had already given rise to the tendency to "gloss over" extraneous details. Wyclif was tireless in decrying this as but the first step to the creation of a private religion. A classic example appears in eucharistic theology:

> If, without scriptural authority, one may stray by calling a sacrament what scripture calls bread, [or] not bread but a quantity, or some other vanity (and there is no end of doing so when glossing), it seems that the whole sacred scripture by equal authority can thus be glossed, and so the whole ancient faith is perverted from scripture and led into something new, to denying the whole history of the deeds of Christ in the letter and asserting the opposite, and likewise of other things grafted into the Bible.[32]

A study of Wyclif's reading of scripture will require analysis of all that remains of Wyclif's *Postilla*, in addition to the extant sermons and *Opus Evangelicum*, which would be a project that would greatly advance our understanding of Wyclif's thought.

Our scope here is restricted to a survey of Wyclif's reading of a brief section from Matthew 5, the Sermon on the Mount, which "most suffices perfectly to regulate the wayfarer without any [extraneous] human tradition."[33] Following Augustine, who produced two books of commentary on it, Wyclif devoted half of the *Opus Evangelicum* and several sermons to the Beatitudes, in addition to references scattered throughout his other works. Gustav Benrath's study surveys the content and scope of Wyclif's *Postilla* and provides a reliable point of departure for any study of his reading of scripture. In his account of Wyclif's treatment of Matthew 5–7, Christ the divine legislator is the central figure, who realizes the distilled truth of the Mosaic law in his perfect life, and Benrath rightly stresses the significance of the Beatitudes as the essence of Christian morality for Wyclif. The Old Law of the Jews is by no means superseded by the coming of the New. Just as we see the type of Christ throughout the Old Testament, and the fulfillment of the prophecies in the New, both laws are means by which God perfects creation, and both are continually present in the integrated whole. This is what makes the Sermon on the Mount the focal point of the Christian life. Its prescription of a life given over to kindness, love, and a spiritual identity with the Christ unites one with the Savior, the fulfillment of the law. It is the perfect expression of Christian morality.

This same young Jesus who began his ministry with the Sermon on the Mount, Wyclif reminds us, is identical to the eternal word who framed the universe. Just as the movement of the celestial firmament does not lose uniformity despite the wobbling of the sublunar sphere, so the soul need not be disturbed by the changing goods of fortune. The conclusion is clear: the moral legislation of the Sermon on the Mount should guide the soul with the same infinite certainty with which the celestial legislator governs the spheres. The antithesis of the Beatitudes is the Pharisaical legalism that is described as characterizing Jesus' critics. We must concentrate on realizing the theological virtues without excessive concern for the details that so easily captivate the mundane mind. The worldly concerns that accompany a life given over to temporal matters are resolved in the life Christ outlines. Simplicity and orderly balance characterize the soul of the Christian

who realizes this ideal, just as they define the Lord's Prayer, which Christ
teaches in Matthew 6:

> The Lord's Prayer excels in authority because it is edited by the Savior, in
> utility because it asks with greater order that for which one ought ask or
> that which is conceded by God to man, in brevity because it only contains
> seven request[s], and finally, in simplicity, first because of brevity, and
> next because of the delectation consequent upon it.[34]

Familiar concerns soon surface. With Matthew 5:13, "You are the salt
of the earth," we see Wyclif returning to the threats facing the church. He
begins by taking Bede's approach, with a discussion of salt's formation from
"sand and water and the heat of the air, compacted by blowing air," and
its properties of desiccating and flavoring food. This signifies good priests,
who at one time may have come from shifting sand, but have been trans-
formed by the waters of baptism and the fires of divine ardor, and whitened
in purity. When this salt is mixed with the earth, the earth becomes sterile.
In the same way, when priests come into contact with mundane evil, their
purity nullifies its powers. As salt desiccates meat, keeping it from putre-
faction, so too the priest can keep his flock from the corrosion of sin, the
stink of defamation, and the corruption of the devouring worm. But if the
salt should lose its taste, if the priest should be caught up in the very temporal desires he is meant to overcome, then he becomes useless and is best
trampled underfoot. The clergymen who turn to avarice or lust hasten the
spread of sin throughout the church. The best course is to fight the threat
by relieving priests and bishops of any source of temptation: "It would be
meritorious for someone to lovingly relieve our clerics from temporal dig-
nities, so that, made spiritual, they could regard the law of God."[35]

The unmistakable form of Aristotelian philosophy gives shape to Wyclif's
account of Christ's teachings throughout. The virtues by which one realizes
happiness both in this life and in the next define the normative commands of
Jesus. Not for Wyclif the mystic elevation from scholastic reason, nor the
ineffable encounter with the godhead, nor even the prospect of a journey of
the mind to God through love of the visible creatures of the world. Despite
being an advocate of the illumination theory of understanding and a devoted
adherent of the connection of every created particular to its divine idea, the
Bonaventuran spiritual approach is foreign to Wyclif. His Beatitudes are the
means by which the virtues are perfectly realized, by which body and soul
are placed into the balance for which they were created, and ultimately by

which the church can best function on earth. Benrath comments that, for Wyclif, the Golden Rule is the rational basis for all Christian morality. Love should be sought not because the loving soul realizes Christ's ongoing relation to creation, but because it best aligns every soul with the purposes for which they were created: "What the Square of Opposition is to logic, thus the Golden Rule is to ethics."[36] For Wyclif, the New Testament does indeed provide a road map for the soul's journey to God, but it is a map defined by justice and reasoned truths for communal use, not one by which the soul necessarily enters into the holy otherness of the divine.

Is this a fair judgment? After all, one rarely finds the spiritual path to mystic union with God from a concise scripture summary, which is only a tool for preachers and scholars. Benrath's assessment is accurate, though, as a reliable guide through Wyclif's exegetical works. A good instance is the brief, later work *De Amore* (1383). Here, in an apparent response to a request for an explanation of the nature of love, Wyclif delivers a terse, reasoned response. True love, he explains, is a movement of the will toward a given subject, the ideal of which is God. Hence, only those for whom God is the object of the will experience true love. Lovingly studying the law of God lies at the base of such a life, and the laws of Christ lie at the base of a loving understanding of the ideal object of the will. All of the teachings of the Old and New Law are summed up in Christ's teachings, interconnected and made into a perfect whole to be realized by diligent study. But which state of life is most proper for a man to love God? This depends on whether one is a priest, a soldier, or a laborer. Ideally, the states most suitable are those of the virgin and of the priest, as was Jesus, but "for some men, one state is right, for others, another is right." The important thing is that every man should study the gospel "in that tongue in which the reasonings of the evangelist are most clear, because all the faithful should follow their Lord Jesus Christ from faith, and insofar as they are able to follow Him in a like manner, thus the more meritoriously will they love Him." Perhaps the best expression of this love is martyrdom, a total giving of the self to God, but for those for whom this is not an option, a communal life in Christ is the best choice.[37]

Opus Evangelicum

While Wyclif believed that the Gospels comprise the perfect clothing for the soul of the Christian, he felt some parts to be more important than others, requiring particularly careful exposition. The final major work of his life, *Opus Evangelicum (OE)*, is devoted to this concerted exegesis. The first part is given to analysis of Matthew 5–7, the second, known as *De Antichristo*, to Matthew 23–25, and the third to John 13–17, although Wyclif never gets beyond John 13. Williell Thomson observes in his catalog entry on *OE* that classifying these works as exegetical is too restrictive. They range over most of the topics that captivated Wyclif throughout his life, with digressions on philosophical conceptions of identity, division within the church, the Eucharist, heresy, and of course, popes and friars. It is not difficult to imagine Wyclif reliving his battles in the isolation of Lutterworth, warmed by memories of academic triumph and burning with frustration at the church's refusal to follow his sage advice. Along with *Trialogus* and the sermons, we have Wyclif at his most personal in the *OE*, at least where he chooses to write in his own voice. More than in any other work, Wyclif adorns his prose with long quotations from his favorite theological authorities, including Augustine, Chrysostom, Jerome, and Grosseteste. This is a feature which, in itself, helps us to assess Wyclif's final view of his place in the church. Throughout his writings, he complains that innovation and infatuation with novelty threaten the integrity of Christianity and the church. The remedy for this, Wyclif believes, lies in a return to scripture and the pure interpretation of the fathers, from antiquity through to the giants of early scholasticism. What better final statement than to embody this in a prolonged study of *lex Christi,* the basis for all just law, for all religious life?

His exegesis of Matthew 5–7, the Sermon on the Mount, takes up the first two books of the *OE*, with Augustine's *De Sermone Domini in Monte* as its theological guide. Wyclif turns to Matthew 23–25 in the third book. This section of Matthew contains the "little apocalypse" (Matthew 24:4–31), the seven "woes" of Christ's indictment of the scribes and Pharisees (Matthew 23:13–39), and the parables of the bridesmaids and of the talents (Matthew 25:1–13, 14–30), lending itself admirably to Wyclif's chosen theme, which is the looming threat of Antichrist. The fourth and final book (Wyclif calls it the third, counting the first two as one), devoted to John 13–15, begins by observing that here, in Christ's farewell message to his disciples, he summarizes all that led to the final sacrifice and victory of Easter. This seems to have been a conscious choice of subject matter, for it and *De Antichristo* are filled with references to his earlier biblical teachings and to his postillating organization, and finally, the work ends with some parting words for theo-logians, perhaps written within a week of his death:

> It is necessary that a theologian be instructed in right logic, philosophy and metaphysics, and that he have these five pieces of armor at hand: first that he know universals apart from things, through which he can know the words Moses spoke of genus and species. . . . Second he should know the teachings of Christ according to right metaphysics of the nature of time and other accidents, how they do not exist unless as formal and accidentally inherent dispositions of their subject. And through this he can under-stand the distinction of the nine kinds of accident and how Augustine rightly teaches that from his youth he had taught that it is not possible for an accident to be without a subject. And this confounds the heresy that consecrated host could be accident without underlying subject, or a nothing. Third that he knows that with God and the creating spirit everything that was or will be are present to Him in the greatness of time. . . . Fourth, that he know that a creature has in God ideal eternal being existing in its kind antecedently. . . . And fifth that he know the natural essence to be perpetual and not composed of quanta, and mate-rial forms to be its dispositions, although they would be quiddities of the species and the genus. And through this it can be known how God sees everything that He [has] made and they [are] very good, how one ele-ment will remain, although substantial form[s] which are material acci-dents would be renewed. Through these five with their appendices the subtle logician can theologically defend the catholic text of Scriptures.[38]

Wyclif's sources are the core of his treatment of the Sermon on the Mount and, given their authors, warrant some attention. Woven into the Beatitudes are the guiding words of Augustine and Chrysostom, two pillars of right exegetical and preaching practice. But aside from Augustine and his *De Sermone Domini in Monte*, Wyclif's sources turn out to be people very different from these models of orthodoxy. Chrysostom's *Opus Imperfectum*, a collection of sermons on Matthew cited at length throughout Wyclif's exposition of the Sermon on the Mount, would seem a logical choice for an exegesis of the Gospel of Matthew. The *Opus Imperfectum* was a widely used source for later medieval exegetes, as is clear by the wealth of manu-scripts remaining, but by the time it was included in Migne's collection of Chrysostom's works in the *Patrologia Graeca*, it was clear that it could not have come from Chrysostom's hand. It has turned out to be a sermon col-lection written by an anonymous Arian cleric of the fifth century, likely from the region of the southern Danube. Its Arianism is negligible in the selections Wyclif cites, and any medievalist knows that spurious sources like these were common. Because Lollards were very glad to make use of sources that Wyclif favored, particularly in *Opus Evangelicum*, citations from the *Opus Imperfectum* were relatively common in their sermons.[39]

Much more interesting is an odd piece that Wyclif attributes to Augustine, entitled *De Duodecem Abusivis Saeculii* (*De XII*), the centerpiece for his handling of the Beatitudes. The bulk of Wyclif's efforts are devoted to correlating the nine groups Christ lists as "blessed" with the twelve threats to the Christian kingdom described in *De XII*. The treatise is a catalog of the moral evils that plague humanity. Six of these affect the lives of every Christian, including clerical hypocrisy, the immoral behavior of social leaders, rebellious youth, widespread avarice, sexual prurience, and incompetent nobles. The remaining abuses target specific evils in the body politic: strife among Christians, rebellious peasants, wicked kings, negligent bishops, schismatic sects, and people who have turned away from religion. The list seems ideally crafted for fourteenth-century England, and Wyclif likely treasured the text for its seemingly perfect intersection of Augustinian authority and the social and ecclesiastical diagnoses at which he himself had arrived. So apposite are its critiques to Wyclif's own thought that one wonders why *De XII* plays no part in his other works. Its hefty authority and pungent phrases might have added just the right force to his critiques of the papacy, the friars, the bishops, and the unraveling social order. However, *De XII* might not have been available to Wyclif until 1383, since its general structure would have fit very nicely with the twelve torments of the church described in *De Blasphemia*, written shortly after the Peasants' Revolt of 1381.

Perhaps Wyclif suspected the truth about the treatise. It is not Augustine's work, as anyone familiar with his polished Latin style would recognize instantly. *De XII* was written by someone with a much more primitive style, and was attributed as much to Cyprian as to Augustine. It was an extremely popular work, mined by preachers throughout the Middle Ages for pithy images and succinct indictments of a failed social order. Manuscripts have been found with the text in Old and Middle English, Castilian Spanish, Latin, and Irish, from Scandinavia to Byzantium. While its author remains anonymous, scholars agree that it likely dates to seventh-century Ireland and is perhaps the work of a Benedictine well read in Isidore of Seville and Jerome, among many others. Its prevalence in Irish manuscripts lent it to be attributed to St. Patrick, but this is very unlikely.[40]

The tone of sustained moral outrage of *De XII* blends smoothly into Wyclif's exposition of *lex Christi* in *Opus Evangelicum*, and the plight of a society that allows itself to stray from an original commitment to the Beatitudes is sharply defined by its catalog of ills. The words of the Sermon on the Mount form the basis for the purest expression of divine law given to man, and here again Wyclif emphasizes the dictum that all just human law, whether civil or ecclesiastical, must be grounded in this infinite wisdom. Christ's injunction to humility in the first Beatitude is directed principally against the sin of pride, and Grosseteste's helpful list of the eight signs of humility, included in the body of the text, includes one's willingness to be rebuked by juniors, indifference to honors, and an unwillingness to return evil for evil. Prelate and pope alike, Wyclif continues, repeatedly demonstrate their unfamiliarity with humility. Correcting the pope invites ecclesiastical remonstrance, while puffing him up with honors is a sure way to advance in the church:

> It is clear in practice how one pope curses the other with the utmost severity, which is a sign that the pope who curses the other more lightly is less cursed by God. Both reveal themselves in doing this, and infinitely many other things, not to be vicars of Christ but chief vicars of antichrist.[41]

While these references to the ongoing schism, as well as to other ecclesiastical problems, run throughout the *Opus Evangelicum*, this is not the substance of the work. In an important sense, Wyclif intends his exegesis of the Sermon on the Mount as a completion of what he began in *De Mandatis Divinis*, almost a decade earlier. The relation of the Old Law to the New is not antithetical, but both are of a piece with God's eternal ordering of creation. Before Christ's coming, the Mosaic code laid the foundation for his life, which is clear throughout the Gospels. In each of Christ's actions, he demonstrates the consonance of Mosaic law with the simple, pure precepts he formulates in the Sermon on the Mount. The first five Beatitudes cancel out the seven deadly sins through their distillation of the virtuous life: "The first virtue excludes pride, the second envy and wrath, the third sloth, the fourth gluttony, lust, and greed, indeed all the virtues are connected, so that any of them excludes any of the seven [sins]; whoever has one of the virtues has all of them, and whoever lacks one, lacks all."[42] In the "Treatise on Love," which is an exegesis on the First Commandment, Wyclif lays out the theoretical basis for his argument in *Opus Evangelicum* that the

Beatitudes express the essence of *lex Christi*: "Since the whole Christian religion is founded in this love, it is clear how it is the work of any believer to learn this art of loving, in which the whole salvation of man rests, and [which is] the reason of every good thing."[43]

"Christ's law would in itself suffice to regulate the entire church militant better than it is ruled through artificed human tradition. . . . the Sermon on the Mount should suffice to rule viators perfectly without any human tradition."[44] While Benrath's assessment is of the *Postilla*, it applies equally to the much more detailed *Opus Evangelicum*. Along with the philosophical reduction of Christ's teachings to the fundamental, rationally self-evident precept of the Golden Rule, to which Wyclif repeatedly reduces the contents of Matthew 5–7, we also find stern injunctions to root out those social evils that keep us from realizing this. Christ gave us a renewed natural dominion through his victory over death, yet his church continues to embrace sin and death, Wyclif declares. Taking the salt that has lost its flavor and trampling it underfoot is not an empty metaphor, it is a call to action. The church must be cleansed of its impurities, divested of the cares that keep it from realizing the ongoing perfection of *lex Christi*, and secular lords are the ones to do the work.

Our brief description of one part of Wyclif's extensive exegesis has borrowed heavily from the tone of all of his exegetical works. The threats that Wyclif devoted himself to uncovering—the unruly cleric, the immoral noble, the dissolute bishop, and the schismatic sect—are never far from his mind as he explicates the reasonableness of Christian morality. Neither is his conviction that no part of scripture is greater than the rest in embodying God's word. A study of Wyclif the exegete, a very welcome addition to scholarship, will involve both the theoretical elements of *De Veritate Sacrae Scripturae* and the applied exegesis of *De Mandatis Divinis,* the (still largely unedited) *Postilla,* and the *Opus Evangelicum.*

Wyclif the Preacher

It is tempting to suppose that there were two kinds of sermons preached in late medieval England: those addressed to the educated, preached in Latin, and those to the uneducated, preached in English. But this is not terribly helpful. Sermons preached in English were likely to have had listeners fluent in Latin, while those preached in Latin were likely to have had non-Latin-speaking listeners sufficiently familiar to make out what was going on, especially if they could talk about the sermon with someone who had a clearer grasp of the language afterward. It is better to divide up medieval English preaching into venues, of which there were generally four. There were the standard, liturgical sermons of ordinary parish life, which could be preached from the pulpit of a humble parish church or a private family chapel, or from the bishop's chair in a cathedral filled with parishioners high born and low. There were the sermons preached by friars, in marketplaces and at public festivals, for the edification and entertainment of audiences hungry for the outdoor spectacle of a stem-winding, stump sermon. There were the sermons preached in universities, both to demonstrate theological competence and for ceremonial occasions, and there were sermons designed specifically to stir up popular spirits, for any number of reasons. While the academic sermons were likely to have been in Latin, it is presumptive to assume that either Latin or English would be the exclusive language of any of the other types. And why assume that the preacher would stick to one language? He might well have moved from a Latin gospel reading, to an English translation, back to Latin quotations from the fathers, and back again to English for the body of the homily.

Academic theologians with a preaching office might have used the pulpit to weave their formal thought into the day's lesson, but the evidence belies this. Generally, learned preaching was understood as a place not for continued disputation, and authority-laden logical disquisition is foreign to medieval English sermons. While most preachers made free use of the usual host of authorities, from the fathers to more contemporary luminaries, it was not in the service of some theological position. The central source was first and always the Bible. Preachers routinely infused every sentence of their sermons with scriptural citations and allusions, confident that their audiences would follow and appreciate their skillful use of its riches. For many, the art was in the deft infusion of extrabiblical sources, including saints' lives, historical tales, and classical literature, into the biblically based mixture. Especially among the friars, anecdotes and verbal pictures lifted from Virgil, Macrobius, and others made listening to their sermons as aesthetically entertaining as it was spiritually edifying. "Classicizing" friars competed with one another for the most ingenious combinations of Virgil and biblical morality, or Ovid and Old Testament history.[45]

One of the best indicators of the potential for integrating classical learning and biblically rich preaching is Robert Holcot's *Commentary* on the

Book of Wisdom. On the face of it, Holcot's work is an exegetical analysis of the apocryphal book of Wisdom, but it functions as one of the greatest handbooks for learned and entertaining preaching of the Middle Ages. If the range and substance of Holcot's sermons are reflected in his Wisdom *Commentary*, his preaching was likely both deeply informed and delightfully entertaining. The popular image of medieval English preaching given by Chaucer's Parson is but a pale shadow of the heights to which it could aspire. Evidence for the widespread appreciation of Holcot's Wisdom *Commentary* and a continuation of his erudite and witty preaching style lies in the significant number of manuscripts of the text. Unfortunately, its content remains obscure, in large part due to the absence of any modern edition.

If Holcot was foremost among fourteenth-century Oxford preachers, the guiding light and definitive force of medieval English preaching as a whole was Robert Grosseteste. While Oxford's theologians may have turned from his Augustinian philosophical approach in enough numbers to warrant Wyclif's anger, its preachers continued to regard his *dicta, De Decem Mandatis, Hexamaeron,* and *De Cessatione Legalium* as models of exegesis and ready sources for their preaching. Wyclif was by no means alone in his willingness to cite whole paragraphs from Grosseteste, whose rhetorical style was as popular as those of Bernard and Augustine. Nor was he the only one to rely on Grosseteste's emphasis on pastoral responsibility, which characterizes his sermons and letters. Well into the fifteenth century, Lincolniensis figured as the pastoral model and preaching master for Oxford preachers. Siegfried Wenzel, whose research in medieval sermons continues to enrich twenty-first-century understanding of the subject, argues that allegiance to Grosseteste defines the English theology of preaching of the later Middle Ages. This frees us from the presumption that Wyclif's regular references to Lincolniensis in his sermons and his theology of preaching was a departure from the norms of his day, and helps to resolve our focus on his theology of preaching.

All that we have of Wyclif's sermons are academic sermons, in Latin, preached to or written for an educated audience. The large body of English sermons that were collected and edited by Thomas Arnold cannot be linked to his hand, and are now known as the English Wycliffite sermons.[46] So, to get a sense of Wyclif the preacher, we must turn to a body of sermons many of which may never be able to be dated with certainty. Edited and published by Johannes Loserth over a century ago, they fill four volumes and are divisible into two distinct groups. The larger collection makes up the first three volumes, which were likely compiled during Wyclif's last years in Lutterworth, perhaps as a homiletic manual for the band of preachers he seems to have been organizing. They certainly do not seem to have the popular appeal one would expect from a preacher sensitive to the needs of ordinary listeners, as they contain arguments for predestination and the true nature of the church, frequent interjections of pastoral theology, and vituperative indictments of academic practices. It is likely that this collection, with 120 sermons on the Gospels and 58 on epistolary readings, was meant as the practical application of Wyclif's pastoral program as described in *De Veritate Sacrae Scripturae, De Officio Pastoralis,* and *Opus Evangelicum.*[47] Wyclif himself described this collection as the product of his last years:

> And so that the teaching of God be more distinct and his servant better exempted from uselessness, it appears that in this quiet in which we are at leisure from scholastic affairs, we are roused, in the end of our days, into the building of a portion for the church, to collecting simple sermons for the people, so that things they might recognize in the right teaching of Christ be better known, and things be avoided by which will have slid away from the catholic truth.[48]

Another, much smaller collection of sermons provides an example of Wyclif's preaching earlier in his career. The forty collected in Loserth's fourth volume of sermons differ from the others by their generally orthodox content, free from the polemical bitterness that flavors the contents of the other three volumes. Dating from January 1375 to September 1379, this collection may have been edited by Wyclif later, but with a different purpose, namely, to apply the formal program of the *Summa Theologie.* William Mallard has described the overall message of the *Forty Sermons* as an exhortation to be strong, a stout hierarchical articulation of the just dominion of the spirit over the flesh. Recognizing the truth of the Gospels demands the right ordering of reason, in which the excellence of the universal determines the value of the particular, which can only occur in a mind free of materialistic desires and anxieties. Only then can the Christian understand how to apply the truths of scripture in life, to articulate the logic of Christ in the sustained proposition of Christian living. Running throughout this collection is the idea that part of the Christian life involves patient suffering, enduring injustice and tyranny on earth to avoid damnation for succumbing to the temptation to return evil for evil. Mallard notes that this injunction to patient acquiescence to temporal evil also entails a willingness to engage in fraternal correction. A good and faithful Christian will not shrink from admonishing a fellow for moral lapses for fear of a reputation for being difficult. If all Christians are equal heirs of a restored natural dominion, no one can shirk in upholding *lex Christi*, whatever their earthly station. It is one thing to suffer the injustice of a powerful temporal lord, but quite another to ignore priestly tyranny.

All of this suggests that Wyclif had the same audience in mind for both sets of sermons. Sprinkled throughout the *Forty Sermons* are reminders that preaching the word lies at the heart of the priest's life. Preaching well requires not simply a sound understanding of scripture, but a sober demeanor, forceful delivery, and awareness of the needs of the audience.[49] Just as in the parable of the sower, seed carelessly strewn onto rocky soil, or to the crows, will fail to grow, no matter its great potential, and so it is with sowing the word of God. This familiar parable from Luke warrants two disparate sermons in this collection. The first, Sermon 30, is a sober consideration of the preacher's need to steer away from sin in his own life and to fearlessly face it down in the lives of his flock. The sin lying at the base of every other is pride, and Wyclif devotes the bulk of his message to warning against its insidious way of sneaking into one's thoughts, slipping in among praiseworthy ideas and emotions and planting the seeds that sprout quickly into thorns that choke out the word of God. Reading it, one cannot help but suspect that Wyclif had some familiarity with this vice. The next sermon is a tour de force of Wyclif's preaching abilities, beginning with a survey of the levels of meaning possible in the parable and fixing quickly on the connection between sowing the divine seed and preaching the gospel. Preachers today, Wyclif exclaims, have taken on the loathsome habits of the vainglorious display of learning, clever rhythmic schemes and metrical novelties, and a tiresome reliance on silly stories. No wonder that the word does not have the force it once had; its preachers have killed it with their worldly sophistication and gross popularizing. What once leaped and danced gracefully as the simple, sweet word of God has become a ponderous beast, or worse, is now like a reanimated cadaver, lurching out of the grave to wreak havoc among the living. Readers who sigh at Wyclif's tendentious and dusty prose in his theological and political works would do well to investigate his sermons. His voice remains the same, but freed of the constraints and formal requirements of the schools, his sermons can be zestful, even entertaining.[50]

In his sermons, he begins exegetically, perhaps introducing a related theological issue familiar to the college classroom, and then moving to the pastoral ramifications of applying the formal analysis to preaching the lesson at hand. Throughout the sermons, Wyclif warns of three impediments to effective preaching: laziness in addressing the needs of the laity, episcopal hegemonic control of preaching authority, and the practice of avoiding preaching to laity served by another priest. Zeal for evangelizing must outstrip worldly caution, and a true minister of the word will not shrink from preaching the gospel truth in the face of social, or even mortal, danger. A good preacher bases his message on biblical texts, eschews literary flourishes that detract from the force of the words of scripture, and places his sermon foremost in the laity's worship experience. The first duty of every Christian is familiarity with the teachings of the wellspring of created truth, the scriptures; salvation rests upon it. So preaching the Bible is, in a real sense, uniting the hearers with the living word of God, "the most dignified work a creature can perform." If one were told that he would sire the next king of England, Wyclif comments, he would "take great pains to accomplish the task." So much more for the preacher, who through his office spiritually begets children of God.[51] One might consecrate a host, and dispense its salvific grace to only a small number, but preaching brings the possibility of salvation to all within earshot. Wyclif never tires of emphasizing that the power of preaching far exceeds that of the sacraments, always condemning any attempt to place the liturgy of the table over that of the word: "Preaching the gospel exceeds prayer and administration of the sacraments to an infinite degree."[52]

So rich a source of authority is the Bible that it perfectly instructs the preacher in his work. All one need do is adopt Jesus' own teachings to strengthen one's homiletical skills. Jesus never indulged in learned stories or rhetorical flourishes, but time and again used the words of the prophets to illustrate *lex Christi*. Simple preaching, lacking the fripperies of classical learning or droll tales, serves the Christian soul best. Indeed, the clergyman who uses his preaching office more to entertain than to sow the word might better serve his flock by allowing the educated laity to preach in the simple words of the people. Metaphor and allegory ought not be emphasized in explicating scripture for this same reason; it is too easy to allow what is novel or entrancing, even if true, to lead the attention of the audience astray. Simple preaching and the moral life are never far from Wyclif's mind: "There are two things that pertain to the status of the pastor: the holiness of the pastor and the wholesomeness of his teaching." Friars who seek money, priests and bishops concerned with temporal status, and prelates enamored of political authority, from priests to popes, are all incapable of perceiving their own *cupiditas*, their own inability to live as shepherds of Christ's flock. A good pastor does not shrink from telling his flock about this danger and should expect his flock to be vigilant accordingly: "The faithful conclude that when a curate is notoriously negligent in his office, they as subjects should, yea ought, to withdraw offerings and tithes from him and whatever might be the occasion for fostering such wickedness."[53] This warning, which recurs throughout Wyclif's writings, lies at the base of the accusations of Donatism against him, which we will consider in the next chapter.

The friars are usually the object of Wyclif's criticism in his homiletic teachings. Time and again, if he inveighs against some bad preaching habit, it's likely to be a hallmark of fraternal preaching. They school their preachers to develop an entertaining delivery and to put minimal emphasis on the need for penitence. They manipulate their preaching venues to garner the largest offerings from their audiences and avoid those where funds are scarce. Such a preacher happily tells his audience what they want to hear, all the while handing around the collection plate, bilking the very souls for whom he pretends to care. Wyclif comments that the friars' habit of using frivolous stories in preaching appears to come from a deliberate refusal to take Christ's sewing advice in Matthew 9:16. They are willing to attach themselves to their sect, which is a patch ready to unravel at the seams from the fabric of the church, and so delight in their "unseemly" stories.[54] While an honest preacher goes no further than scripture for his meter and rhythm, the friars consistently indulge in ornament and deride those who do not as fools:

> And thus with clamor and ornate words they overcome the faithful who would speak the sense of God, and where God wills to have helpers for the simple, and mild speaking, as the Apostle says with "We are God's servants," they regard this with disdain, asking against the rule of love for money, doing the devil's work with frivolous tales and sophistication, rather than the simple truth of the gospel.[55]

During the Despenser crusade, it appears that friars were particularly enthusiastic in their support of the bishop's campaign of sustained pillage and murder, which Wyclif viewed as another, predictable result of the friars' departure from *lex Christi*: "They use their preaching office to incite the people to spill their blood in misguided crusades, like the fiasco led by Bishop Spencer in Flanders, and this more for the money they can hope to gain from the plunder!"[56]

Vernacular Preaching and Scripture

Modern understanding of the relation of Wyclif to Lollardy, and of the further relation of the two to the Protestant reformation, has shifted considerably. A century ago, the long-standing assumption of the legitimacy of both relations began to crumble, until scholars routinely discounted strong connections both between Wyclif and Protestantism and between Wyclif and Lollardy. By the mid-twentieth century, the received opinion was that of K. B. McFarlane, who discounted the significance of both, leading to a sharp distinction between Wyclif and the variegated Lollard advocates of ideas he had voiced. Anne Hudson's landmark study *The Premature Reformation* put an end to the legitimacy of this tendency to draw a distinct line between the academic Wyclif and the lower- and middle-class lay piety movement that had adopted his ideas, pointing to the possibility that Wycliffism might even have had some impact on events in sixteenth-century England, if not on the Continent. More recent studies have encouraged a nuanced understanding of the relation between Wyclif's thought and vernacular literature, in which lay authors and readers are given credit for a greater intellectual sophistication than had been imagined.[57] Our survey of Wyclif's thought cannot address Lollardy as a phenomenon, much less the possible ties between Wyclif and the birth of Protestantism. We must remain within the bounds of his own life, if only because the growing body of literature catalyzed by Hudson's work would demand a survey of a length equal to this.[58]

Two related areas of contention remain, then: did Wyclif organize a band of preachers to evangelize throughout England, and what was his relation to the translation of the Bible into English? The popular image of the exiled reformer translating scripture into the language of the people and disseminating the word by sending forth a small army of educated preachers remains in numerous popular histories. Was Wyclif a theological Robin Hood, taking scripture—the ultimate source of true wealth—from the hands of the privileged and putting it into those of the poor? The way to answer this is by looking at the evidence. Is there reason to believe that he was involved either in the production of the eponymous Bible or with the storied russet-robed preachers? As to Wyclif's having translated the Bible from Jerome's Latin into Middle English, an idea reported as commonly understood by Hus in 1411: this was laid to rest in Margaret Deansley's *The Lollard Bible* in 1920. Wyclif's disciples, chiefly Nicholas Hereford, were given the credit.

The second question has been more controversial. Workman's 1926 biography is dramatic:

> Clad in russet robes of undressed wool reaching to their feet (a garb which Wyclif had assumed at Canterbury), without sandals, purse, or scrip, a long staff in their hand, dependent for food and shelter on the good will of their neighbors, their only possession a few pages of Wyclif's Bible (especially the gospel and the epistles for the day), his tracts and sermons, moving constantly from place to place like the early Methodist preachers on their "circuits"—for Wyclif feared as Wesley feared lest they should become "possessioners," tied to one place like a dog—given not "to frequenting taverns, hunting or to chess," but "to the duties which befit the priesthood, studious acquaintance with God's law, plain preaching of the word of God, and devout thankfulness," Wyclif's poor priests, like the friars before them, soon became a power in the land.[59]

Workman's depiction harks back to Thomas Walsingham's description of Wyclif's Oxford comrades wearing russet robes to demonstrate their superiority, going barefoot to trample popular errors underfoot. But Walsingham's description lacks the approving tone of Workman; the famous chronicler was a monk at St. Alban's, and he thought that Wyclif's teachings were venomous poison seeping into the body of Christ, especially given the violence of the Peasants' Uprising in the summer of 1381. Walsingham's narration of the chaos spreading across the land attributes at least some of the blame to Wyclif, given the reputation of one of the rebellion's leaders, the priest John Ball: "He taught the perverse doctrine of the perfidious John Wiclyf, and the opinions that he held, and the insane lies, and many other things it would take long to recite."[60] Wyclif's horrified reaction to the uprising notwithstanding, the story of the russet-robed poor preachers sent out to promulgate his reforming agenda would stand as long as writers connected Wycliffite ideology with the Peasants' Revolt. Thus, mid-twentieth-century scholars found themselves searching for firmer evidence than the assumptions made in biased contemporary sources and the passing references in English works once thought to be Wyclif's. While several other chroniclers describe educated disciples of Wyclif gathering his teachings of their own volition, they do not constitute reliable evidence for an organized movement actively launched by Wyclif. Scholars have found themselves unable to believe in the reality behind the myth:

> If he had been active in the development of preaching programs, then one would have expected Lutterworth to have been a centre of popular Lollardy. Yet it produced [a] single Lollard in all the record of heresy trials. . . . Wyclif was not the organizer of the heresy: his legacy to his followers lay in the realm of ideas.[61]

The myth had its foundation in more than just the frets of chroniclers, though. Michael Wilks noticed that Wyclif's writings are filled with references to the small number of his associates who saw the awful truth of the church's need for renewal and reform. While Wyclif certainly had the tendency to view himself as a lonely, prophetic figure, his gestures toward "the simple few who speak the truth," the "unknown true priests in the world," as well as the fact that his sermons are unmistakably designed to instruct an educated elite group of preachers, make certain the reality of a small number of "poor preachers." Whether Wyclif hand-picked his disciples during his years at Oxford, preparing them for evangelizing throughout the country, or whether it was a self-selecting group of Oxford scholars, given benefices by their colleges in parishes across England, is beside the point.[62] The fact remains that an educated corps of preachers, likely also responsible for the Wyclif Bible, did champion his ideas throughout England in the 1380s. In one of Wyclif's sermons on the parable of the sower, he devotes considerable attention to the need for preachers to pay close attention to the ground on which their words are cast, and his references to "my brothers" certainly suggest that these earlier sermons could be evidence that Wyclif was consciously organizing a band of educated preachers while still at Oxford. In this sermon, dating to February 1376, Wyclif also refers to "your fraternity," which was an unusual form for him to use. This is a common address for papal rescripts, letters in which the pope answers specific requests with the force of ecclesiastical law.[63] Wyclif also uses this form in Sermons 37 and 38 from the same, earlier collection. Leaving aside, for now, the question of tone in his use of a form of address normally reserved for popes, his audience must have had a degree of internal coherence to deserve being called a fraternity. Whether this was simply because of collegiate ties, or something more, remains open to speculation.

So, answering the second question remains a problem. On the one hand, as Anne Hudson has commented, given that a fair number of educated men set out from Oxford before or shortly after Wyclif's departure in 1381, "it would seem perverse to maintain that Wyclif himself had nothing to do with their activities." On the other hand, as Gillian Evans has observed, we have no texts explicitly outlining plans for organizing a band of poor preachers written by Wyclif himself. All we have is the basis for an inductive conclusion. If Wyclif *had* purposively organized a band of preachers, there are numerous references throughout his works that would apply well to them. For example, embedded in several of his sermons is what appears to be a treatise describing the six yokes that bind people together in the service of Christ. It is reasonable to assume that the sermons are intended for an educated audience preparing to engage in their own homiletics, not least because of the frequent excursions into homiletic theory they contain. Here, Wyclif actually provides a handy outline for the extemporaneous preacher in need of a structure for a series of sermons outlining the Christian life: "Since these six yokes are, by their lightness and smoothness, able to be grounded in Scripture, evangelists animated by God ought preach this order with zest and strength."[64] Still, his antipathy for what he called "private religions," which he viewed as nothing more than sects founded on the charismatic force of a saintly personality, suggests something other than the founding of an order of preachers.[65] A thorough study of the content of *Sermones* will likely provide the best means of tackling this question, which for now must remain unresolved.

PREDESTINATION AND THE CHURCH

Of the four major orders of mendicant friars in the medieval period, the Carmelites laid claim to the earliest origins. The Dominicans, Franciscans, and Augustinians (or "Austyns") originated in the thirteenth century, as do the first records of the Carmelites, but these earliest records point to a community of hermits on Mount Carmel in Israel dating to the time of Elijah. John the Baptist, say the Carmelites, was a member of this ancient and honored community, and St. Anne, mother of the Virgin, had sought their advice. There had been Carmelites at Pentecost, and they had worn their white cloaks with pride, until Muslims conquered the holy lands, when they had to shift to a black-and-white-striped habit. This mythic history seems to have been well received, since the number of Carmelite houses in England increased from six to twenty-seven in the second half of the thirteenth century.[1] Not only were they daring in making historical claims questionable even to sympathetic popes, they were relentless in their criticism of Wyclif's views of the church and its ordering. One of the earliest records of the tempestuous events of Wyclif's career was given the provocative title *Fasciculi Zizianorum Vuiclevi*, or *The Bundle of Wyclif's Weeds*. Following the parable in Matthew 13:36–43, where Jesus likens evildoers to the weeds that will be separated out at the harvest and cast into the fire, the English Carmelite friars began gathering up records of Wyclif's arguments with his contemporaries for the eventual systematic identification of this dangerous new heresy.

The *Fasciculi Zizianorum (FZ)* has long been associated with the famous Carmelite Thomas Netter of Walden, the confessor of Henry V and Henry VI and a tireless foe of Lollardy. While Netter compiled the *Doctrinale Fidei Ecclesiae*, a systematic refutation of Wyclif's theology, internal textual evidence suggests that he may have contributed to *FZ*, but could not have authored it. Netter's grasp of Wyclif's thought was considerable, and his *Doctrinale* is a meticulous dissection of Wyclif's philosophical and theological system, centering on the Eucharist and especially on Wyclif's troubling conception of the church as the eternally foreknown body of the elect. Netter was not the first Carmelite to be deeply concerned with the theological basis for Wyclif's conception of the church, though; a sizable portion of *FZ* is devoted to John Kenningham's earlier critique of Wyclif. Kenningham (d. 1399), later confessor to John of Gaunt, seems to have been a slightly senior contemporary of Wyclif's. Their correspondence, namely, three of Kenningham's criticisms of Wyclif's thought and parts of Wyclif's responses, suggests an ongoing, rather combative relationship between the two theologians.

Most troubling of Wyclif's philosophical doctrines, Kenningham argued, was what Wyclif believed to follow from a phrase that recurs throughout his writings, "Everything that occurs, occurs of necessity."[2] This determinism, a theme running throughout Wyclif's thought, is in itself unremarkable, if understood properly. That God foreknows all that will occur in creation, and that this perfect foreknowledge is necessary, is a commonplace in medieval theology. As we will see, Wyclif has very carefully worked out a philosophical approach whereby the absolute necessity of God's knowledge of all events in creation does not rule out human freedom. In part, this is because he is applying the strongly determinist thought of Thomas Bradwardine to what he perceived as the dangerous misreadings of scripture of the *moderni* doctors. He needs a workable theory of the relation of God's understanding to the revealed truth of scripture to explain cases in which educated readers might question the truth of problematic sections. In parts of the Gospels, Christ's enemies tell lies about him. In what sense are they true, and in what sense does this truth reflect God's immutable, perfect understanding? Obviously, one cannot take the indirect discourse of a statement like "[he] has a demon" in John 10:20 as true, but are the levels of truth in the Jews' accusations sufficiently evident to permit universal agreement with the proposition that "all that is in scripture is truth"?

Kenningham argued, as do most twenty-first-century scripture scholars, that sensitivity to the human hands behind the Gospels is a central part of appreciating biblical truth, while Wyclif stoutly defends the self-evidence of its truth by reason of its divine authorship.[3] Lying behind their debate was Kenningham's great distaste for Wyclif's contention that all that is, was, or will be is immediate to God's understanding. The absolute necessity of God's knowledge of all created events, Wyclif believed, involved everything being immediately present to God's cognition. This rules out the possibility of counterfactuals that lead one to conclude that "it might have been otherwise," objected Kenningham, who pushed for nuance in describing God's understanding. Better to say that things in time are present to God subjectively, as something is present in a mode of time, rather than in the immediate clarity of objective understanding. This prevents us from reasoning that "A is known by God, therefore A is," which, at the least, endangers human freedom. The appeal of the idea for Wyclif, though, lies in the ties possible between eternal divine ideas, the universals to which they correspond in creation, and created particulars, on the one hand, and the Book of Life (another way of referring to the divine ideas), scripture, and truth in creation, on the other. If all created truth is tied directly to scripture, as we noted in chapter 5, and scripture is a particular of the Book of Life, a certain degree of determinism will be unavoidable.

While Kenningham's objections are more to what follows from Wyclif's hard-headed hermeneutic than to the implications of his determinism, he felt that Wyclif's readiness to transcend temporal limitation in interpreting scripture was impracticable in the church. Even more problematic were its implications for understanding sentences like "Now you are the body of Christ and individually members of it" (1 Corinthians 12:27). By Wyclif's reasoning, God knows to whom "you" refers, and to whom it does not, down to the last member. This makes defining the church as the elect, those eternally foreknown to merit salvation, and no one else, a natural conclusion. Wyclif is clear about this: "Although the church is mentioned many times in scripture, I suppose that it can be taken most famously by the proposition, the congregation of the faithful."[4] This definition, with its roots in Augustine's thought, was foundational to the medieval church. Wyclif's position, as it will be articulated in this chapter, turns out to be an attempt at mediating between the fatalistic determinism he perceives in

Bradwardine and the semi-Pelagian position of the *moderni*. The connection between scriptural hermeneutics and the definition of the church will hinge on how we are to understand Christ's prediction that Peter would deny him. If Christ knew with eternal certainty that Peter would deny him, then it follows that God knows the two classes of the elect and the damned from eternity as well. From this, it would appear to follow that Peter had no choice in the matter, which is the first step on the slippery slope to the doctrine of double predestination. The trouble with this is that, if God predestines a group of humans to damnation, it seems that he creates them without any hope of salvation. This would mean that Christ did not die for all men, but only for those whom he eternally foreknew would be saved. This is so opposed to the faith that one wants to find a way for God to know who will be in which group without making that knowledge causal. The philosophical heirs of Ockham, trading on the venerable inceptor's innovations in understanding the truth value of future contingent propositions, argued that Christ's assertion at the Passover feast was a future contingent truth, lacking the ontological certainty of statements about things in creation that had already occurred. As we will see, this line of thinking ignited a fiery debate in fourteenth-century Oxford schools. Wyclif and Kenningham were arguing about hermeneutics, but at stake was more than how the reader understands the sacred page. The nature of salvation and the efficacy of the church hung in the balance.

As with his dominion thought, Wyclif's description of the church provides a certain connection between his earlier, metaphysical analysis of the divine ideas and his later thought. In the late 1360s, when he wrote *De Ydeis*, he argued, "If God understands Peter, it is true that Peter is understood by God. But since this truth cannot depend upon the existence of Peter, it remains that it would be eternal . . . and this truth is the reason or the Idea of Peter, which is called his intelligible being." If this is true for a given individual, and for a species, it must be true for an aggregate like the church, the existence of which is eternally foreknown. This is not something Wyclif was eager to pursue at the time, but he seems to be steeling himself: "I say, along with Luke 14, that he who would not consider a creature save in its proper essence is shaking with fear. Ascend willingly the heights and see how the creature is according to the eternal reason in God as it is known by Him."[5] Wyclif's understanding of the church as the congregation of the elect relies upon his philosophical understanding of necessity, which provides the underpinning for his understanding of the relation of God to human action. In his accounts of God's knowing, understanding, and willing (*De Sciencia Dei, De Intellecione Dei, De Volucione Dei*), his arguments provide firm support for his belief that the church's membership is brought about as much by human agency as by divine willing. Here, we will recount the position formulated in *De Volucione Dei* to illustrate the reciprocity Wyclif envisioned between divine and human willing, which he believed allowed for escape from a fatalistic determinism. The major work that articulates Wyclif's vision of the church, *De Ecclesia,* assumes a general understanding of these theological positions, making his arguments for the church's identification with the elect little more than afterthoughts. Our discussion of this treatise will be somewhat anticlimactic as a result. A significant portion of Wyclif's writing includes treatises, polemical tracts, and responses concerning the state of the church *militans*, particularly of the papacy and the friars. Limits of space will preclude all but the briefest overview of this body of Wyclif's writings, which made him notorious in his day, but are not dissimilar in argument or content from many other fourteenth-century critics of the ecclesiastical status quo.

Determinism and Free Will:
Bradwardine's *De Causa Dei*

The philosophical problem of reconciling the absolute perfection of God's knowledge of created events with the freedom of human willing had been in the forefront of Oxford theological debates for several decades before Wyclif arrived there. William Ockham had argued that statements of the form "X will occur at time N" have a truth value contingent upon what will happen in the future, so knowing them must be a different sort of knowledge than knowing statements about the present or the past, for which the truth value is already clear. Since this is a natural fact about such future contingent statements, God's knowledge, too, must be that "X will occur at time N" is true contingent upon X's occurrence. The difference between our fallible and uncertain knowing and God's infallible and perfect knowledge is that, while for us knowing X or knowing not-X are two very different mental states, for God, knowing X or knowing not-X are the same. "For just as this or that future contingent contingently will be, so God knows that it contingently will be, for if He knows it, He can *not* know that it will be." Ockham was aware that what he was suggesting, while certainly preserving the freedom of human willing and action, could easily be understood to restrict the range of God's knowledge, and he admitted, "it is impossible to express clearly the way in which God knows future contingents; nevertheless, it must be held that He does, but contingently."[6]

Ockham's resolution of the puzzle was not necessarily a departure from earlier thinkers like Grosseteste or Peter Lombard, but in his delicately nuanced treatment of the relation of God's eternal knowledge and the contingency of action in time, it seemed that we might be able to earn salvation on our own merit, without grace. In short, it was possible to interpret Ockham's approach as countenancing elements of Pelagianism. Bradwardine describes it this way:

> When I was applying myself to the study of philosophy, I was foolish and empty of the knowledge of God, and was seduced into error. When I heard theologians discuss this matter, the part of the Pelagians appeared more true to me. In the schools of the philosophers, I rarely heard any talk of grace, unless perchance through equivocation, but all the time I heard that we ourselves are the lords of our actions, and that it is in our power to do good and evil, to have virtue and vices, and many similar things. And if, in church, I ever heard a reading from the Apostle explaining grace, as in Romans 9, "Not on [human] willing or exertion, but on the mercy of God," and such like, it grated on me mightily. With the Manichees I believed the Apostle in his humanity to have deviated from the path of truth, just as anyone might have done.[7]

Bradwardine appears to have come to this realization as he began his theological studies in the late 1320s. His first approach to the question of God's foreknowledge and future contingents can be found in some recently discovered *Sentences* commentaries, dating to 1332–1334, and in the more developed *De Futuris Contingentibus*, which was written several years later. Bradwardine's interest in the subject developed, and after he had become a member of de Bury's circle, he compiled *De Causa Dei*, a labyrinthine refutation of "the Pelagians." This massive work is not constructed along a recognizably scholastic model, but appears instead to be a *summa* encompassing all that Bradwardine understood to be involved in explaining grace, merit, human salvation, and God's knowing and willing. Unlike Aquinas's *Summa*, Bradwardine's does not proceed methodically and logically; instead, each topic Bradwardine addresses finds its way back to God's unmediated causal influence over creation. Topics that do not interest him, particularly metaphysical questions of ontology or epistemology, rarely arise. He appears to have had no interest whatsoever in the question of universals, for example, and questions of how terms or propositions express created or divine truths do not arise. Earlier readers have supposed that Bradwardine's departure from the logico-semantic approach of the Ockhamists represents a reactionary Augustinianism, but this fails to take into consideration his earlier, mathematically oriented thought, including his fully developed theory of signification in his treatise on insolubles of 1324. The more freely flowing theological arguments of *De Causa Dei* suggest a polemicized *summa*, in which the reader is able to recover the nature of more informal—but still extraordinarily complex—arguments in which Bradwardine engaged during his years in Durham.[8]

At the heart of Bradwardine's theology is the fundamental truth that God's causal power over creation is absolute; nothing occurs that is not willed by God. On the face of it, this seems so deterministic as to be fatalistic. If all that happens is in accord with God's will, then the revealed certainty that some will be damned and others saved amounts to double predestination, the ancient heresy in which God has consigned some to hell and others to heaven from eternity. Later theologians with a predilection for determinism, particularly Luther, the Calvinists, and the Jansenists, interpreted Augustine's thought in this manner, and some philosophers like Descartes and Nicolas Malebranche even espoused occasionalism, the position that God directly causes every created occurrence, without created agency playing any role. Bradwardine's position was not so extreme. Even if God is a co-agent in every created action, including the evil that men do, he is neither responsible for evil nor is his foreknowledge the cause of men's damnation. Those who would warn theologians away from the murky depths of this problem for fear of causing despair and abandonment of the faith should know that only the shortsighted will suffer:

> On the basis of such preaching a predestinate person grows in a useful way; for he can know on the basis of it that if he is predestinate he will be saved, and so he has more material for praising God than if he were not to know the eternity of predestination and the eternity of reprobation. . . . But all the same, it can allowably be left out [of preaching] because of the simplicity of most men, since they can easily fall into heresies by thinking a great deal on the difficult subject of whether they are reprobate or elect.[9]

That said, Bradwardine's position that God is a co-agent in all human actions provides the basis for his arguments against Pelagianism, but it also demands an account of how we, not God, are responsible for evil. This is particularly a problem if (a) God necessarily knows all that will occur in creation, (b) necessarily, all that God knows will occur, will occur, and (c) God's will and knowing are identical, so if God knows that a thing will occur, God necessarily wills that it occur. Theologians from Anselm onward had responded to this by exploring the nature of necessity and contingency, and *De Causa Dei* is exhaustive in its analysis of the wide variation that scholastic thinkers found in these apparently basic notions. Modal philosophy is the metaphysical analysis of the possible, or what can or could be; the actual, or what is; the necessary, or what cannot not be; and the impossible, or what cannot be. Medieval philosophers developed a complex body of philosophical literature in this area, primarily because of the difficulties of the problem of God's foreknowledge and human freedom. On the face of it, necessity is a simple notion: if a thing is necessary, it cannot not be. Likewise, if something is contingent, this means that it relies on something outside of it for its being. Complications arise when we try to qualify things within time; if we consider a past event, from our vantage point, its occurrence is necessary, in that we cannot undo the past. But what about the relation of God, who is outside of time, to events in time? If God knows something that occurs in time, and that knowledge is eternal, does this mean that what occurs in time is connected to God's knowledge?

Wyclif's Modal Theory

Augustine had argued that, just as our memory does not force the past to have happened, so God's knowledge does not force the future to happen, at least as far as human sin is concerned. A problem arose with understanding the prophets' foretelling of Christ's coming and his death, though. Was Christ's suffering and death necessary eternally by reason of something that occurred in time, namely, human sin? Anselm explained that "there is a necessity which precedes, being the cause for an actuality's existence, and there is a necessity which is consequent, being caused by an actuality."[10] That is, there is a difference between saying "it is necessary that Socrates sits," meaning that Socrates cannot help but sit, and saying the same thing simply because Socrates has already taken a seat. The first rules out Socrates choosing to sit, while the second simply describes what already is true. Likewise, Anselm believed that God knows our sinning by consequent necessity, the kind that follows from what already is true, and not by the former, compulsive kind, called antecedent necessity.

Peter Lombard popularized a further distinction, between kinds of consequent necessity. If it is necessarily true that "if God knows that man will sin, then man will sin," it follows that "if God knows that man will sin, then man's sinning is necessary" is also necessarily true. Aquinas would argue that the first conditional statement, "if God knows that man will sin, then man sins," is true by "necessity of the consequent" (*necessitas consequentiae*), but the second conditional statement, "if God knows that man will sin, then man's sinning is necessary," is necessary conditionally (*necessitas consequentis*). Human freedom is preserved, Aquinas argued, in the first statement, because man's sinning is not necessitated by God's knowing. In the second, freedom is compromised since the consequence follows necessarily from the antecedent, and so instead of saying that the will of God has a necessary relation to man's sinning, it is better to say that it is necessary by supposition. Aquinas introduced this kind of necessity in distinguishing between the necessity by which a bachelor is an unmarried male, or man is a rational animal, and the necessity by which Socrates sits. In the latter, so long as he is sitting, he must necessarily be sitting, but he certainly needn't be sitting.[11] This makes "if God knows that man will sin, then man sins" true because the necessity in "man sins" is not inescapable, and not brought about by God's knowing, but entirely reliant upon the fact that, so long as he is sinning, he must necessarily be sinning. Another way that Aquinas clarifies the difference between kinds of consequent necessity, one that Wyclif would favor, is by describing the freedom-threatening necessity of "if God knows that man will sin, then man's sinning is necessary" as absolute necessity, and the necessity of the freedom-preserving "if God knows that man will sin, then man sins" as necessity by supposition. So long as man's sinning is not necessitated by God's knowing, but only by man's choice, the consequent necessity by which man sins is necessary by supposition.

Unlike Aquinas, Bradwardine felt that *necessitas consequentis*, or absolute necessity, is commensurate with God's foreknowledge without leading to a fatalistic determinism. Talk of God knowing a thing before it happens, or of a thing being necessary because God knows it ahead of time, is confused. God is eternal, and eternality is not a mode in which "before" or "ahead of time" applies. Hence, if God eternally wills that man act freely in time, the freedom of human action is not limited by the necessity of the divine willing. This is not the fatalism that Stephen Tempier condemned in 1277, because God has ordained that, despite divine co-agency in every act and all good willing, human willing and action be free. Bradwardine managed to have both God's eternal foreknowledge and human freedom by distinguishing between kinds of antecedent necessity. Recall that, for Anselm, antecedent necessity precedes the event, serving as the cause. Bradwardine argued that some antecedent necessity is wholly absolute, but some is relative to an extent. The relative antecedent necessity can describe the secondary cause of an event, or it can describe the first cause. Peter may be free to choose to sin by virtue of an antecedent necessity relative by virtue of his being a member of the human species (a secondary cause of Peter's existence), or by virtue of God's willing (the primary cause of all created acts). Peter's choice may be determined to an extent by being a member of the human species, but his biological form does not compel his choice. God's will, on the other hand, does, by virtue of its being the sufficient cause of every effect in creation, including human willing. Bradwardine believed that he preserved God's eternal foreknowledge by making antecedent relative necessity commensurate with *necessitas consequentis.* The statement "if God knows that man will sin, then man's sinning is necessary" is true, but escapes fatalism by decreeing that man's sinning is free by virtue of God's willing it to be so. The final effect of Bradwardine's exhaustive catalog of arguments in *De Causa Dei* is to strike down any attempt at compromising the necessity of divine knowing and willing. The correspondent robust predestinarian view regarding human willing struck many of his readers, Wyclif included, as heavy-handed.[12]

Wyclif felt that Bradwardine's approach was excessively deterministic, and commented that the doctor profundus dove too deep, leading to questionable conclusions about the divine nature.[13] Bradwardine had strayed too far from the balanced position of Aquinas for Wyclif's taste, largely because of his belief that *necessitas consequentis* did not compromise human freedom. Wyclif's approach was to distinguish between absolute and hypothetical, or suppositional, necessity, but the blizzard of kinds of necessity he generated in his modal thought does not make the distinction immediately clear. In the interests of clarity, we will keep track of the kinds of necessity

Wyclif described, because losing track can too easily lead one to suspect that he obscured the question of determinism with an ink cloud of distinctions. He described necessity in four places: *Logice continuacio* I.11, *De Logica* III.10, *De Actibus Anime* 1, and *De Universalibus* 14. Wyclif was not overly consistent in his terminology in his catalog of types of necessity in these four works, much to the frustration of anyone trying to formulate a coherent Wycliffian modal philosophy. In the chapters in *De Logica*, he began by distinguishing between what cannot not be by virtue of itself, or "primary per se necessity" (i.e., God's being) (A); that which cannot not be by virtue of something outside itself, or "secondary per se necessity" (B); and things that are necessary, but could have been otherwise, or "accidental necessity" (C). In *De Actibus Anime*, he called the necessity of God's being "simple, absolute necessity" (A.1), and seems willing to include the world's being, which by *Logice continuacio*.11 would be secondary per se necessity (B), under the heading "created absolute necessity," suggesting a close tie between A and B. (Here, he described the secondary per se necessity as "a created truth without which God could not be," the meaning of which he does not pursue.) For our purposes, A and B seem to point to the kind of absolute necessity that earlier philosophers had posited as distinct from necessity by supposition. What he described in. *Logice continuacio* 11 as "necessary *secundum quid*" appears to be the same as necessary by supposition in *De Logica* III.10 and in *De Actibus Anime*, and likely would correspond to accidental necessity (C).[14] In this category, Wyclif described antecedent (C.1), consequent (C.2), and concomitant necessity (C.3) by supposition in the two sections of *De Logica* and *De Actibus Anime*. In *De Universalibus*, suppositional necessity is divided into "nonvolitional natural necessity," "volition-dependent natural necessity," "agent compulsive natural necessity," and "free necessity." Where did "natural" necessity come from? It seems to refer to C.1. In *Logice continuacio*.11, Wyclif divided antecedent suppositional necessity into "necessity of volition" (C.1.a), a willing that brings something about by necessity; "necessity of nature" (C.1.b), as with fire burning anything combustible; and "necessity of coercion" (C.1.c), when a force elicits a response that rules out freedom. "Free necessity" (C.1.d) seems to point to an antecedent necessity by supposition that lacks a defining force like a will or a law, "free either in the sense of freedom between alternatives or of freedom from compulsion." Anthony Kenny described nine kinds of necessity in his catalog of Wyclif's modal thought, but Wyclif himself suggested that this could be the tip of the iceberg: "There are many other similar, non-exclusive notional distinctions."[15]

Consider the following argument:

1. If God eternally knows that Peter sins today, then Peter sins today.
2. God eternally knows that Peter sins today.
3. Therefore, Peter sins today.

Statement 1 is eternally true, and would be logically unavoidable, no matter what. This is an instance of absolute necessity because it is connected to the necessity of divine omniscience (A.1). Likewise, the argument formed by combining 1 and 2 leads directly to the conclusion according to *modus ponens*. This argument is both valid and true by absolute necessity from eternity, according to Wyclif's understanding of the nature of logic. All logical, mathematical, and geometric truths are absolutely necessary (A.2).

Suppositional necessity is so called because everything depends on the relation of the truth of one part of a proposition to another. An if-then statement might not be an instance of relative necessity for a host of reasons; both antecedent and consequent might be impossible, or contingent, or even absolutely necessarily true. But the world is structured so that many things that are necessarily true are so because of the truth of something prior. Wyclif envisions a complex modal system to describe the many sorts of necessary truths that derive their necessity from the relation of one truth to another. Any given modal proposition, he explains, must be dissected carefully prior to seeing how the whole statement works. There is a world of difference between the assertion "Peter necessarily sins" and "necessarily, Peter sins," and this realm of suppositional necessity is where this kind of care is needed. With antecedent suppositional necessity (C.1), once the truth of the situation described as antecedent is met, the consequent will necessarily come about; as with "God wills Socrates to exist," the truth of "Socrates exists" will necessarily follow. As just mentioned, there are three species of antecedent necessity by supposition. The first, volitional, involves a willing that brings something about by necessity, as with "God wills Socrates to exist" (C.1.a). Wyclif believes this to be the critical issue in the problem of free will and determinism. That God's willing brings about Socrates' existing is necessary, but that Socrates might not have existed is also a real contingency. Likewise, that God knows that Peter sins today may be necessary, but Peter's sin is not thereby inescapable. The necessity of the truth of statement 2 in our paradigmatic argument, Wyclif thinks, is C.1.a necessity: "And this does not eliminate freedom of choice, merit, demerit, contingency, or fortune, just as the theologians declare."[16]

The second species is the necessity of nature (C.1.b), as when fire comes into contact with something combustible, it will burn it. Third is the necessity of coercion, as when some external force compels somebody to do something against his will, and he does it (C.1.c). This might also be subdivided into cases in which someone is compelled to do something through duress, as in giving over money to a robber (C.1.c.i), and doing something with absolute spontaneity, as when the blessed in heaven adore God (C.1.c.ii). One is not likely to gain merit from actions following from C.1.b or C.1.c.i, Wyclif comments, but one might well suffer demerit, because vice causes people to behave with this species of compulsion, as when an addict cannot help but give in to the addiction.

The next kind of hypothetical necessity, consequent necessity (C.2), simply describes whatever effect follows as the consequent follows from the antecedent. Wyclif does not distinguish between *necessitas consequentis* and *necessitas consequentiae* because the distinction needed to preserve human freedom in the statement "if God knows that Peter sins, then Peter sins" already has been made. If we can say that the antecedent is necessary (C.1), then the consequent, "Peter sins," is only relatively necessary. Human freedom is preserved, so long as "Peter sins" is not absolutely necessary.

The result of Wyclif's analysis is to begin with a relatively orthodox position and then to argue that truths like "God eternally knows that Peter sins today," true by antecedent suppositional necessity, do not thereby lose contingency. Peter's sinning is dependent upon Peter, and God's knowledge follows from Peter's choice. That God eternally knows how Peter will choose does not cause Peter's choice. This allows room for contingency in Peter's action without plunging the eternality of God's knowledge into temporal constraints. While God knows what Peter will choose, it is possible from all eternity that Peter might have chosen differently, thereby admitting contingency into the mix without limiting the necessity of God's knowing:

> Such a relationship depends on each of the terms, since if God is to will that Peter or some other creature should be, it is requisite that it should in fact be. And thus the existence of the creature, even though it is temporal, causes in God an eternal mental relationship, which is always in the process of being caused and yet is always already completely caused.

He departs from the traditional position by positing a two-way relation between eternal knowledge and created action, as contingent created acts bring about divine knowledge. Anthony Kenny comments that earlier condemnations of Wyclif for excessive determinism were very wide of the mark; if anything, Wyclif started from a Thomistic position and erred on the side of allowing contingent created acts a causal power over God's necessary understanding of them. Wyclif admits that he had been convinced by a different position, likely Ockhamist, early on, but that he came to embrace this interpretation of the traditional approach as he learned more:

> Once I had imagined it madness to speak this way, because I was burdened by a young mind, and smitten with the mutability of corporeal fantasmata, not conceiving of the priority and the coexistence of eternity with time. . . . Error in this logic causes many to err in the matter of the necessity of futures. Some suppose that every future is absolutely necessary, perhaps because of foreknowledge, foreordination, or the determination of God. But this does not follow, since it can always be that God did not know it thus; and as it is contingent for the world not to be, or not to have been, it is as contingent for this soul not to be in the future, indicating whatever that soul produces.[17]

Reciprocity in God's Willing:
De Volucione Dei

J. A. Robson rightly points out that Wyclif charted his position on necessity and contingency by tacking between Bradwardine's *De Causa Dei* and Fitzralph's *De Quaestionibus Armenorum*. Fitzralph's antipredestinarian position appears to have been well established by the time he was called upon to summarize the points of disagreement between the Western church and the Armenian church in the early 1340s. Here, he articulates a position akin to Bradwardine's, but emphasizes the infallibility of scripture, which gives him a moderating position between the profound doctor and the *moderni*. In fact, his emphasis on scripture's centrality to theological argument would later inspire the Lollards to list him among their guiding lights. In *De Dominio Divino* I.14–18, Wyclif relates Fitzralph as arguing that Christ's knowledge of futures was imperfect during his time on earth, so that he could have preached inaccurately about the future. In effect, Peter might have gotten through that famous Thursday night without denying Jesus, had he really tried. The temporally oriented Christ might have been wrong about Peter's denial, because otherwise Peter would have been fatally compelled to sin. This nuanced understanding of prophetic statements and Christ's predictions, like the one made about Peter's denial, gave Wyclif a reason to implement the results of his modal theory in describing the relation of God's knowledge and willing to human action.[18] Of the treatises in which Wyclif most fully articulates this position, *De Intellectione Dei*, *De Sciencia Dei*, and *De Volucione Dei (Summa de Ente* II.1–3), only two have been edited and published, and these from the poorer of the two extant manuscripts. In the case of *De Volucione Dei*, the present edition is missing chapter 12 and most of chapter 13. It is easy to get the sense that Wyclif's zeal for explaining it all was beginning to flag by the time he was to weave the elements of his philosophical theology into a coherent picture of God's dominion. As he begins his explanation of how our actions have causal power over divine ideas, he grumbles, "I am certain that nobody may discover another solution of the argument of the necessity of futures, even if he were to study diligently through a life as long as Methuselah's."[19]

If created action has a causative effect on God's knowing, is it true also to say that created willing might affect God's willing? Wyclif is prepared to argue that one can cause God's willing, without imagining that God's will is within human power. The relation of God's knowing and willing is so close as to demand care to avoid both the fatalism of Bradwardine and the voluntarism of the *moderni*. If God eternally knows that Peter denies Jesus, in what sense does he will this? Wyclif explains that God's will is a consequence of Peter's denial in the same way that the divine knowledge is: that God will something about Peter's denial is absolutely necessary, but that he will that Peter denies Jesus is hypothetically necessary, and could have been otherwise, had Peter not denied Jesus. There is a strong reciprocity holding between God and creation, then. The creature has its being through the divine idea that exists eternally. God has this eternal idea by virtue of the temporal being that is realized as the creature lives in time:

> Thus the logician concedes that for the instant of eternity, there is such contingent willing completely caused, since in this measure it lacks the creature's [moving] causing. And this is consonant with the popular and philosophical way of speaking in which it is truly said that God's willing is not satisfied before what He intends occurs.[20]

Is God complicit in sin? If sinners can expect punishment, then either their punishment is to a certain extent unjust, or God created a class of human beings knowing—and willing—that they be damned. Wyclif departs from Aquinas's clear rejection of the possibility that God is the cause, either direct or indirect, of sin in *Summa Theologica* Ia–IIae, q.79, a.1. In *De Intellectione Dei* 5, Wyclif stipulates that God does not cause error in us when we act in error, despite being the cause of all created action, because the error lies in our subjective reception and not in the positive nature of the act. It is as if God had said at our creation:

> Behold, I fortify you from all evil, and suggest that under pain of certain damnation, you shun it, since I have given you assistance through grace by which to avoid Satanic temptation. Yet a condition of your liberty is that you have free power to accomplish whatever you might wish, whether good or evil. I will not incite you nor stir you to something, nor permit anything evil, save the punishment of sin.[21]

While it is madness to imagine that God approves of our sinning, it does not follow that God does not will sin. In fact, the main thrust of *De Volucione Dei* is that God *does* will sin, but that he does not will the sinner to sin. This runs against the scriptural assurance that God wills the salvation of all mankind (1 Timothy 2:4), but there are many ways of construing such a blanket statement. Paul might have meant all *classes* of men, rich and poor alike, or he might have meant that God wills that all men *ought* to be saved. Wyclif thinks the possibility that God wills all men's salvation insofar as each human being wills his or her own salvation is the most likely. It also challenges the assumption that God's will would not be perfectly free if it were in some way caused by something outside it, which is Bradwardine's position. In most cases, it is probably wiser to be quiet about this around most people: "It seems expedient to me to be silent about such things with the ill-educated and the common people, as much because they are not disposed to addressing scripture's subtlety as because of the sense in which they might err heretically by supposing that God unduly or culpably ordains things."[22] Should such questions arise, it is helpful to have Paul's analogy of a potter in mind (Romans 9:21). A pot cannot censure a potter, if it is made to hold urine, even if it is made from the same lump from which a wine jug is made. Likewise, a man cannot censure God, even if created insufficient in his nature, because God created the mass of humanity from nothing.

This analogy appears to oppose Wyclif's argument, perhaps leading to double predestination. But Wyclif reminds us that nobody is so poorly created as to be unable to receive saving grace. If one does what lies within him, God will not fail in directing him to his proper end. And since God wills all humanity's salvation as its proper end, the threat of double predestination is vanquished. The threat to God's freedom is equally illusory, because in giving human beings a free will, God freely obligates himself to what follows:

> Just as the religious, who by choice necessitates himself to the act of observing the rule, does not make himself less free than the secular who does not obligate himself in this way, so God does not give less freely in promise and pledge of reward, than if He did not obligate Himself by promise or foreordination, but is far freer, as Paul says in Hebrews 6.

The confusion arises from conceiving of God's willing as able to begin or cease as do ours in time. God's will is not consequent upon our own in a temporal sense, and precedes ours as prior and perfect. But just as human freedom is preserved in Wyclif's system by the hypothetical necessity of God's knowing, so it is with God's willing: "And although God had made many miraculous things, yet among everything caused by Him, His relative knowledge and will are the most miraculous."[23]

But what of the idea of the group of people foreknown to be damned? Is there an eternal idea of the damned, and another of the elect, and does this mean two kinds of humanity? Wyclif's conception of the divine ideas leaves no space for double predestination. There is no idea for a sin or other defect in a creature, so no creature as producible by God is designed for damnation. We bring that about ourselves. As we have seen, we cause God's eternal understanding of the two ideas, the foreknown and the elect, through our actions in time. As in his modal theory and his understanding of divine volition, Wyclif's conception of the ideas emphasizes a reciprocal relation between eternal knowledge and created action. Contingent created acts bring about divine knowledge, while eternal ideas serve as the basis for all created acts, as described in scripture. This remarkable position depends on Wyclif's earlier account of modality. Given his articulation of how hypothetical necessity functions in the relation of God's knowledge of human action, Wyclif is able to argue that human acts in time have a causal bearing on God's knowledge and willing. If this is so, individual human choice lies at the basis of God's eternal understanding of who among us will be saved or damned. This will allow Wyclif to champion the Augustinian conception of the church as the body of the elect in the face of semi-Pelagian *moderni* theologians, without running afoul of fatalism.

The Church as the Unknowable
Body of the Elect

The centerpiece of Gordon Leff's assessment of Wyclif's thought in his noted study of medieval heresy is his withering indictment of Wyclif's idea of the church.[24] Wyclif's dedication to 1 John 3:9, where it is said that those born of God cannot sin, appears to lead him to a terrible misunderstanding of Augustine's two cities argument. There is the institution that functions as the church in the world, and there is the congregation of the elect, known only to God. The intersection of the two is an unknown, taking away the sacramental office, the teaching authority, and the social structure of the institution that defined medieval society. Earlier heresies, like those of some of the Beguines or the Waldensians, had demanded a new church to replace the tired mechanism of their day, but Wyclif managed one better. With his conviction that the church is nothing other than the body of the elect, he as much as denied any claim that the historical church made to being the body of Christ on earth. Along with the call for civil lords to take control of the church in all matters other than preaching and spiritual guidance, Leff concludes, Wyclif's thought is politically impracticable, given the reality of fourteenth-century Europe. Further, Wyclif's denunciation of the ecclesiastical hierarchy, the very office of the pope, and any hint of immorality among the clergy so decentralized and secularized the church as to destroy it altogether. Small wonder that the official reaction was to condemn him as a heresiarch.

Wyclif does little to help the contemporary reader to garner sympathy for his position, despite his repeated claims of willingness to accept correction for any ideas that might be shown untenable. Sprinkled throughout his indictments of the church hierarchy, the friars, the papacy, and the generally disreputable state of the ecclesiastical status quo, they have a disingenuous cast that only adds to Leff's indictment. Yet the fact remains that Wyclif was never actually excommunicated and that he continued to function as a priest, to celebrate Mass, to preach and pray as a Catholic believer. Is this disconnection between thought and practice evidence of bad faith, or of something else? While it would be an overstatement to claim that Wyclif's many writings on the church, the pope, and the friars constitute a well-conceived ecclesiology, it seems premature to dismiss it as impractical rant and vituperative polemics. Wyclif's conviction that God necessarily eternally knows the elect and the damned leads him to emphasize determinism in all of his definitions of the church. In each case, though, Wyclif emphasizes its traditional threefold division: the church militant (in the world today), the church dormant (those who have already died), and the church triumphant (post-judgment). Augustine had written that the population of the church militant may well fluctuate throughout time, even from day to day. Those who threaten the church from within, he continued, have the chance of redemption. If they give this up, they pass from membership, yet still serve the purpose of training the church: "They train her in benevolence, or even beneficence, so that love may be shown her enemies, whether this takes the form of persuasive teaching or stern discipline."[25] All too often, the evil within the church causes those who want to lead a devout life to suffer. Yet in that suffering arises a love for the persecutor and for one's fellow sufferers.

It is reasonable to imagine that Wyclif saw himself as one of these "persuasive teachers," seeking to enrich the spiritual life of the members of the church militant rather than to redefine the entire structure of the institution. The trick is in recognizing that he slips from the church as we understand it within time to the church as God eternally knows it to be without any explanation, assuming that the reader understands the difference between created instantiation and divine idea. Wyclif envisions his readers or audiences to be university-trained sophisticates, conversant with the distinction between absolute and hypothetical necessity, with Augustine and the other fathers, and with the disputes then occupying the church at its highest intellectual levels. Thus, when he begins *De Ecclesia* with the assertion that the church militant does not have any of the damned in it, he expects the reader to be aware of the nuance behind this statement. Those who would include the damned and the elect under the same rubric completely miss the point. It is one thing to equivocate by speaking of the English church and the Roman one, but it is simply illogical to understand "the church" to mean both the damned and the saved. One might as well think that, when we read of "the church," we are meant to think of the stone building in which we worship.[26]

Christ has remained the head of this church throughout its history, from the beginning down to the present. Sadly, as the church has grown and aged, it has become weaker than it once was:

> Once the Elect so fully filled the Church Militant that few weeds could mix in. . . . but after these, those who followed were much more thinly dispersed, so that you would survey many a wayfarer before you would find one of the Elect, as one after harvest seeking to find a cornstalk, with one here, and another far away. From the blindness of stupidity, they accept wayfarers who are thistles and other poisonous weeds as branches of the Mother Church, when they really deserve to be eradicated as members of the devil.[27]

This sentiment appears repeatedly throughout his writings, usually in equally explicit language. Along those lines, those who would imagine themselves to be safely among the elect do themselves a serious disservice:

> From the faith of the Scripture it is clear that nobody can cease to be a member of the holy mother church, or [cease to] be condemned in perpetuity, and from this, those wayfarers unfamiliar with the revelation of the apostles, who were told that they should not idly anticipate that they are the head of the church or its members, do whatever they would, and thereby contradict [their membership] with their life and presumption.[28]

Acting as if scriptural injunctions against hypocrisy, greed, and selfishness do not apply in every moral decision, even if apparently on behalf of the church, is definitive of sin. The result is that those who do behave this way, whether lay or ordained, are eternally known to be damned—but we cannot lay claim to this kind of knowledge:

> And it is clear how the prayers of the predestinate are infinitely better than the prayers of the foreknown, since God, who cannot err in His judgement, accepts the first to be infinitely better than the second. And this we piously believe to be the reason why God willed the Elect and the damned to be hidden from us in this life, so that we may escape the urge to buy a priest's prayers. If the ministering priest is of the Elect, or this curate, priest or prelate is damned, the prayer and the merit of the ministering priest is infinitely more valid than is the merit or prayer of the other kind of priest. Who is so prudent as to buy with certainty?[29]

This is the kind of statement that led many to identify Wyclif with the Protestantism that would evolve over a century after his death, or even with the ancient Donatist heresy. The very existence of the priestly office appears up for questioning. If we cannot know who is damned, and who is saved, why rely on a clerical class for sacraments? Indeed, why have any sacraments at all, if one's fate is eternally foreknown? And if these are valid questions, then why even go to the trouble of reforming the earthly church, when its true membership is unknowable? Yet for all the seeming ecclesiastical anarchy that results from his criticisms, we also find frequent indictments of any attempts to revolutionize the social structure. At the time, critics invariably connected his ideas with the uproar of the 1381 Peasants' Revolt. His defense of the social status quo, with its division into nobility, clergy, and peasantry, is an important aspect of his ecclesiology. While he did not actively condemn the Peasants' Revolt, his social ideals were far from incendiary:

> It is fitting that in this household [of Christ] there be three kinds of ministers reciprocally helping one another, so that the clergy, who should be the highest and most worthy of God, but not attending to earthly honors or wealth, should expect a whole faith of the retribution to come in the Church triumphant. The second, middle part should be the knights and secular lords; the third, lowest part, defending the house as above should be the community of commoners, as cultivators of fields and other artisans. And from all those three parts come the martyrs and the glorious of the Church triumphant. . . . it is clear that anyone of these three estates will have suffered meritoriously and [be] among those accepted of the Lord.[30]

The storm that was to envelop Western Christianity in the sixteenth century continues to make medieval reformative ideals difficult to envision, and this is certainly so with Wyclif's idea of the church and its ministers. His writings are filled with sentiments that bespeak Lutheran, Calvinist, or Anabaptist ideas: a universal spiritual priesthood of Christians, an emphasis on scripture preaching over sacramental offices, a rejection of ecclesiastical hierarchy, and the absolute revocation of secular political authority for the church—all suggest Protestantism. Yet Wyclif's intent was far from that of the later Reformers, not least because he never seemed to imagine the doctrine of justification by faith. Understanding Wyclif's reformative scheme involves understanding the medieval dispensationalist philosophy of history that he took as part and parcel of the Augustinian world view.

Apocalypse or Reform?

Augustine had divided history into six ages in *De Catechizandi Rudibus*, and Christian thinkers henceforth were to view the church's history in terms of specific periods corresponding to a human life. Michael Wilks described Wyclif's historical vision of the church as a cycle divided into distinct periods, with the incarnation at the apex of the circle. Leading up to the incarnation were the Old Testament ages: the period of innocence, the patriarchal age, and the period of the Levitical priesthood. As society grew more complex, the temple priesthood became more defined by laws and material definitions, until the coming of Christ signaled a radical change, a new covenant. The first age of the church, Wyclif explained, was commensurate with the period before the Fall, an age of apostolic purity and poverty, in which property ownership and civil authority were absolutely foreign to Christians, who enjoyed relatively direct access to Christ through the teachings of the apostles and the early fathers. The first turning point came with the Donation of Constantine, which Wyclif, along with everybody else until the fifteenth century, believed to be associated with the Constantinian legitimation of Christianity in the fourth century. During this period, the church suffered its greatest threats not from Rome, but from heresy within its own body. With the institutionalization of Christianity came a shared, "two-swords" arrangement, in which kings exercised power in the secular sphere, while priests, bishops, and popes exercised spiritual power. From the fourth to the eleventh century, the church needed the cooperation of both secular and spiritual power to ward off the great threats from the non-Christian world, most particularly from Islam. But just as the progress of the ages in the Old Testament steadily rose to the new covenant through Christ, the movement of ages after the incarnation was downward, away from the purity of apostolic times and into the chaos of the time of Antichrist. The coming of the third age, the time of the imperial papacy, was bringing the church to the lowest point of the cycle, to the age of Antichrist. The time of the Gregorian reforms and the attendant rise of the decretals and canon law enabled the papacy to take on the accoutrements of secular power. Now the pope was the most powerful ruler in Europe, and his rule aped the Caesars, the persecutors of the first popes. All that had cropped up in recent centuries, Wyclif argued, gave evidence that sin was in the ascendancy in the church, that Antichrist was building authority and power to previously unimagined heights. The pope's seemingly endless wealth of lands, armies, and secular authority had fostered the expansion of canon law to encompass all worldly affairs. The time was coming for a change, Wyclif concluded, and with it a completion of the cycle of history. If the incarnation were the midpoint, then the end would come at the close of the third age.[31]

But if the end times were at hand, why bother reforming the church? To understand Wyclif's brand of apocalypticism, it is necessary to gain perspective on the range of orthodox and heterodox apocalyptic ideas prevalent in his era. Two figures define later medieval apocalyptic literature, Hildegard of Bingen and Joachim of Fiore. Of the two, Joachim's influence on the Franciscans warrants our attention, especially because of Wyclif's use of Franciscan conceptions of poverty and property. Joachim of Fiore (c. 1135–1222) had founded an offshoot of the Cistercian order and had become one of the great prophetic voices of the period. Joachim's approach to scripture was similar to Wyclif's in that both believed it to contain the whole of created truth. The two differed significantly about what to take out of scriptural study. Joachim read the Bible to understand the whole of human history and devised a complex schema using numerology and prophetic imagery to tease out God's plan for Christendom. The result was that Joachim's thought was taken to endorse a prophetic approach to history, and kings like Richard I of England and Emperor Henry VI came to him for advice about their crusading ventures. By one reading, Joachim's moments of mystic revelation opened the curtains to show the biblical forces at work in contemporary events, and central to this mechanism was the coming new age. The Old Testament was the age of the Father, and the New Testament heralded the age of the Son, but the future was the domain of the Spirit proceeding from Father and Son. The age of the Son replaced law with grace, but the age of the Spirit would replace both with love. Hence, the incarnation was not the completion of God's creation, but only a milestone. By another reading, Joachim believed the incarnation to be the crucial dividing point in created history, and the age of the Spirit was to be understood as arising from the ages of the Father and the Son, just as the Spirit proceeds from the first two persons of the Trinity.[32] The two readings go together for Joachim, but many who would take up his cause were not as subtle in their prophetic understanding.

Of the many who would embrace Joachism, perhaps the most notorious were the spiritual Franciscans, who eagerly placed St. Francis at the inauguration of the age of the Spirit. Most dramatic was Gerard de Borgo

San Donnino, whose innovation it was to proclaim Joachim's works, along with some of his own, to be the "Eternal Evangel," superseding the Old and New Testaments. Gerard and similar enthusiasts were disciplined by their fellows, and Bonaventure was named general of the order with the charge of sobering the Franciscans. Bonaventure himself appears to have adopted Joachite tendencies in the philosophy of history he lays out in *Collationes in Hexamaeron*, and the Franciscan chronicler Salimbene suggests that Bonaventure's refined Joachism represented only the more conservative attitude among the friars. In the later decades of the thirteenth and into the fourteenth century, there was no shortage of Franciscans willing to use Joachim to support their vision of the overthrow of Antichrist and the corrupted, old church and the subsequent triumph of the new spiritual men, the spiritual Franciscans. These would found a new church on the ideals of St. Francis, with communal, apostolic poverty and simple goodness as the hallmarks of the age of spirit. Angelo Clareno, Peter John Olivi, and Ubertino de Casale were among the most notable advocates of a Joachite apocalypticism among the spirituals, while Ockham became involved with their cause in his defense of apostolic poverty, although he did not espouse their prophetic tone.[33] The church's response to this was energetic persecution of Joachite spiritual Franciscans, and after John XXII's 1322 rejection of apostolic poverty, of all spiritual Franciscans. While Joachim himself seems to have done his best to stay within the bounds of orthodoxy, many of his adherents strayed into heresy, poisoning the general ecclesiastical attitude against Joachism.

A long-standing myth has it that England never really felt much of the impact of Joachim and that, for medieval Englishmen, heterodox calls for ecclesiastical reform entailed Wycliffism. Kathryn Kerby-Fulton has shown that not only was there non-Wycliffite heterodoxy in England, but that Joachism had indeed figured importantly in the reformative dialogue there. Dark prophecies, reliant on adroit interpretations of scripture and recent events, loomed behind many worries for Englishmen high born and low. If the structure of ecclesiastical reform within Wycliffism has one notable property, though, it is a rejection of this prophetic element. Wyclif had no patience with Joachite willingness to engage in prophetic foretelling, and ridiculed the Calabrian abbot throughout his writings. In *De Universalibus*, he mocks Joachim's understanding of the Trinity for its lack of comprehension about universals, while in *De Antichristo*, he castigates anyone, particularly Joachim, who claims knowledge about the timing of the day of judgment.[34] Wyclif explains that Christ wisely keeps three things hidden from us, namely, the hour of our death, the nature of our election or damnation, and the exact time of the apocalypse. Preachers who pretend knowledge of such things only confuse the faithful: "preaching to the people of the future should be moderated prudently. . . . By narrating the events of the day of judgement and the future from prognosticating by the constellations they often deceive themselves and others."[35] A presumptuous care to discover things that God means us not to know only detracts from the more important business of saving souls.

While Wyclif had no patience with Joachism, his entire ecclesiology depends on awareness that the end was soon to come. His commentary on the "little apocalypse" in Matthew 24 illustrates this well. Rather than parsing scripture to eke out hints about historical warnings of the end times, we ought to take Jesus at his word and accept that no one knows the day and hour of the coming end. He speaks of those in Judea who flee to the mountains, and of one on the house top, and another in the field (Matthew 24:16–18). These tell us of the three classes of society that will have to face the end times, namely, the priests, who should flee to the example of the early church; the secular lords, who ought to keep to their civic duties and guard society against the depredations of Antichrist; and the common people, whose duty it is to labor for the good of all: "And if these three parts of the Church are constantly instructed in this catholic faith, it would be a sufficient medium for removing the perfidy of Antichrist."[36] The traditional temptations each class will face, whether it be secular authority for priests, a life of ease for lords, or material goods for peasants, are the chief means by which Antichrist will keep the church militant from its end. Any movement from within the church that fosters these temptations can only be meant to forestall the completion of history.

Popes and Friars

Two dark forces swirl through the shadows of the twilight of history, namely, the papacy and the friars. While Wyclif's program for reform of the church is as vague on details as his eucharistic theology, it is quite specific in its rejection of a papal hierarchy and the proliferation of fraternal orders. Before the imperial papacy and the four sects were introduced, the church blossomed, but afterward, its blooms withered and its branches became tangled in diabolical knots. So poisonous has their influence become that it is more fitting to expect an end to the church as it exists today: "Just as a pond that had perchance been formed through the advent of pooled water would be able to be dispelled, so a kingdom is finally ruptured by the build-up of sin, and as with one kingdom, it is the same with the whole of Christianity or the Church Militant."[37] Before we look at his specific concerns, though, we should be careful about the terms Wyclif employs. "Antichrist," for Wyclif, is not one particular, historical personage; rather, it refers to the diabolical forces actively working against Christ and his body on earth. Hence, when Wyclif identifies the pope with Antichrist, he never has specific eschatological intentions. Still, the line of Antichrist is rooted in the priestly class. And just as we are told of sects in the time of Christ, of the Pharisees, the Sadducees, and the Essenes, so in our own time, Wyclif reasons, the monks, canons, and friars comprise another branch of Antichrist's line. These three, along with priests and bishops entranced with secular authority, known as "Caesarian clergy," make up the "four sects" Wyclif constantly attacks. Among the friars are four distinct orders, from whose names Wyclif crafted the name "Caim" (a then common alternative to the Cain from Genesis 4). The acronym stands for Carmelites, Austins (or Augustinians), Jacobites (another name for Dominicans), and Minorites (referring to the whole of the Franciscan order). All receive the name "Antichrist" at one time or another in Wyclif's voluminous polemical attacks on popes and friars.[38]

Wyclif devotes considerable intellectual energy to the papacy throughout his writings, with a major treatise, *De Potestate Pape*, designed to fit into the church-state program outlined in the *Summa Theologie*'s *De Civili Dominio* and *De Officio Regis*, as well as thirty-five minor works either summarizing his antipapal ideas or criticizing specific aspects of the present state of the office. The foundation of Wyclif's description lies in *De Potestate Pape*. Here, he describes the nature of the papacy in terms of the power to which it lays claim. The most well-known division of power was made by Hugh of St. Victor, into power over the body and power over the soul, Wyclif begins. Hugh identified the former with secular authority, and the latter with spiritual. The disagreements that arise over the relation of the two kinds are manifold, with some parties giving pride of place to spiritual power, but in God the power of materially ruling creation precedes spiritual power. Just as the work of sustenance follows upon creation, so too must created power mirror the divine order. God grants all men corporeal and spiritual power, but there is a notable difference in how God wills these to be organized in human affairs. While God gives all a degree of secular power by which they can direct themselves and their goods, civil lords have been ordained to direct more generally. It is similar with spiritual power, a degree of which is entrusted to all, and another degree of which is given to the clerical order. The mistake lies in the clergy's assumption that their power is analogous to that of civil lords. God gives kings authority to make material judgments about subjects, but popes and bishops can never lay claim to a similar spiritual authority over the laity. Further, kings may delegate to lesser lords power over material goods, but spiritual lords have no basis for delegating their power to clerical authority. There is no simple basis for comparing the spiritual to the material in allocating and quantifying power, because the two kinds lack a commonly shared property, other than being itself.

Here, Wyclif's metaphysics provides the ground for his assessment of power. His conviction that the order and structure of created being lies in universals and, even more fundamentally, in the divine ideas, leads him to concentrate more power in God's direct control the higher up the chain of being we inquire. Material goods are lower than spiritual ones and have a lower degree of correspondent being. Hence, while all that occurs materially is directly subject to God, our rational, spiritual power allows us some control over material goods. The same is not true for spiritual goods. Grace, by which God sustains and nurtures the universe, is the basis for all spiritual goods' distribution in creation. While material goods are also distributed by grace, the higher nature of spiritual goods places them more directly under divine control. In the case of spiritual goods in the purview of spiritual lords, which is the term Wyclif frequently uses for the clergy, grace is always the means by which preaching and the sacraments are directly distributed. Priests are only human vehicles for their promulgation and distribution.[39] But Wyclif's theology of the priesthood is so heavily weighted toward preaching as to require attention to the specifics of a priest's role in creation. God ordained the priestly office to protect Christ's body on earth from external evils and to foster its growth and life in *lex Christi*. To that end, priests must instruct the members of the body both by personal example and by the specific duties of their office. The actions and words of the individual priest's life have a more immediate force than do the sacraments, because they are more evident to the faithful. Hence, "preaching the gospel exceeds prayer and administration of the sacraments to an infinite degree."

As is clear following the careful delineation of Wyclif's understanding of the necessity by which God knows and wills our salvation, the individual Christian's will is so actively involved as to demand regular, careful instruction in Christ's teachings. That the instruction and encouragement offered by preaching the gospel must reach the ears of the faithful is critical to salvation, more important in the ordering of the church militant than the sacramental machinery through which the hierarchy maintains its control. Likewise, the personal behavior of the spiritual lord must be exemplary, free from the anxieties and vices to which material concerns subject his flock. A priest who allows himself to use alms entrusted to him for the poor for his own ends, or who engages in greedy or lustful behavior, is guilty of a tyranny more grievous than any civil lord could perpetrate. And while such sins are damnable in a rector, "they are even more damnable in a bishop or abbot, not only because they exceed rectors [in possible material wealth] . . . but because from greater obligation and hypocrisy they do these things more openly in the world."[40]

Given this demand that priests embody the spiritual concerns of *lex Christi* and abandon concern for material affairs, the conclusions at which Wyclif arrived from his observations of the schismatic papacy, the Despenser crusade, and his own prosecution by Archbishop William Courtenay should come as no surprise. The ecclesiastical hierarchy, from popes to cardinals to bishops, he believed, was riddled with disease and ought be cut away just as a surgeon cuts away a tumor, as we will discuss in the next chapter. To many contemporary ears, Wyclif's approach smacked of Donatism, the ancient heresy in which the priest's individual morality has a bearing on the efficacy of the sacraments. Among the propositions listed as heretical at Blackfriars in 1382, and again at Constance in 1415, "If a bishop or a priest exists in a state of mortal sin, he does not ordain, nor consecrate, nor baptize" figures importantly. Wyclif's reputation for Donatism continued, despite his protestations in *De Ecclesia* and in *Sermones*: "It appears to me that the damned in mortal sin might actually minister to the faithful, although damnably." This was almost certainly thanks to his growing impatience with clerical misbehavior; his later writings contained increasingly irate comments regarding the utility of the sacramental ministry of immoral priests.[41]

In a similar manner, as he aged, Wyclif's view of the papacy itself grew increasingly dimmer. At a relatively early stage, he had emphasized the importance of the papacy for the well-being of the church. In *De Ecclesia*

(c. 1379), he argued that the church militant needs a pope, but that the pope ought to be wary of assuming that he is, by the fact of exercising papal office, necessarily among the elect. *De Potestate Pape* followed within the year, and he took up papalist theories with great enthusiasm. What Bradwardine's *De Causa Dei* is to Pelagianism, *De Potestate Pape* is to papal triumphalism, both in structure and approach. Wyclif refuted any and all arguments for any papal responsibility or power beyond continual prayer on behalf of the faithful without reference to contemporary papal theorists like Giles of Rome or Augustinus Triumphus, but also without the structure and reasoned approach of John of Paris. At the center was Wyclif's admission that if the church must have a pope, he should meet the thirty-four rigorous standards that Bernard set in his Letter to Eugenius.[42] Arguments intimating the need for papal rule as a basis for sacraments, bishops, or other ecclesiastical necessities are specious at best, and are evidence of Antichrist's use of clerical weakness in the face of material temptation. Excommunication, a favorite weapon in the pope's bag of dirty tricks, has no theological justification whatever, given the close connection between divine and human will. If someone excommunicates himself from Christ's body on earth, God knows of this eternally, and no papal pronouncement will make the slightest difference one way or the other.[43]

While the friars lacked a treatise of their own, Wyclif's attacks against them appeared throughout his works. His attitude against them was adversarial in Oxford, but developed into real antifraternalism as organized ecclesiastical opposition against him mounted. Wyclif's antifraternalism was of a piece with the attitude of many secular clergy of his age, who resented the friars for a host of reasons. They were accused of hypocrisy; abusing their vow of poverty; slick, crowd-pleasing preaching; and stealing the rights of secular priests and bishops. Any reader of Chaucer or Langland will recall the portraits of nefarious, seedy friars preying on the ignorant laity. As far as Wyclif was concerned, the best that might be expected for these artificial churches within the church would be for them to be dissolved and their members absorbed into Christ's body. But the odds of this happening are as good for the Saracen or the Jew, Wyclif continued, so it would be best simply to cleanse the church of the friars, root and branch.[44] If any among the friars could lay claim to the apostolic ideal of the church, though, it was the Franciscan spirituals. Wyclif noted that Ockham had worked "along with other faithful friars" in an attempt to lift his order from the sorry state to which it had sunk. If only all the Franciscans were like their founder, he commented, they would serve as an ideal for the Christian life, rather than its antithesis.[45] As we will see in the next chapter, Wyclif's opinion on the Franciscan dedication to poverty and his view of the apostolic ideal that had inspired the friars were by no means the same. The friars' claim to poverty is grounded in the rule of St. Francis, a human invention, while the pure apostolic communalism of the early church is a recovered Edenic state.

DOMINIUM AS FOUNDATION OF WYCLIF'S POLITICAL AND ECCLESIOLOGICAL VISION

In 1373, Wyclif's attention turned from expressly philosophical topics to more ecclesiological and political concerns. "It is time for me," he wrote, "to devote the rest of my life to matters that are as much speculative as practical, according to the measure God has given me."[1] While his primary focus shifted from the philosophical theology and metaphysics that had occupied him during the 1360s, his realism continued to undergird his thought at least through the 1370s, when he wrote the first treatises of his *Summa Theologie.* In *De Dominio Divino, De Mandatis Divinis, De Statu Innocencie,* and *De Civili Dominio,* he provides the theological foundation for the radical transformation of the church he prescribes in *De Ecclesia, De Potestate Pape,* and *De Officio Regis.* The *dominium* that defines God's primary relation to creation justifies all human *dominium,* whether it be the mastery of a king, a lesser civil lord, or a priest. But unlike his predecessors who were content to define God's mastery as foundational to human lordship in non-metaphysical terms, Wyclif made ready use of his realist ontology to argue that God's *dominium* functions as a universal by causality for all instances of just human *dominium.* For medieval political theorists, this was not common practice. While a few thinkers, like Aquinas, may have presented unified systems of metaphysics, political thought, and ecclesiology, many others, including Ockham, Marsilius of Padua, John of Paris, and Giles of Rome, cannot be held to the same standard. If, like Ockham or Giles, they had metaphysical positions, it is impossible to argue persuasively that their ontologies affected their politics.[2] This makes Wyclif's political and ecclesiological thought notable, for it is one of the few cases where a distinguished metaphysician used his ontology as a foundation for a detailed examination of the just arrangement of authority in church and state.

Wyclif's vision of the church's renewal involved a thorough reform of clerical hierarchy, a shift in emphasis away from manmade law to scripture as the basis of theology, and a return to the simplicity of the apostolic ideal. He was certainly not the first theologian to make such arguments, nor would he be the last. Indeed, from Wyclif's day to the present, critics have derided his program for ecclesiastical reform as impracticable, with its contention that the king's first duty is to the true church, which is the body of the elect known only to God. How would the king know whom to number among the church's members? The earlier clerical reform of Archbishop Peckam, and the later structural and theological reformation begun by Luther and Calvin both were more practically applicable than Wyclif's program. Wyclif's vision is unique because of the framework he used to articulate its theological and political details. He believed that *dominium*, translated loosely as "lordship," defines God's relation to creation, man's natural place in creation, the central element of political power, and the true nature of ecclesiastical authority. This framework allowed him to construct a social order in which the church is protected from dangers without and within by a civil lord who, as God's steward, governs both church and state through God's law of love (*caritas*). While this vision likely had little direct causal influence on the Tudor Reformation that was to come 150 years in the future, it does suggest a continuity between later medieval and early modern England.

Wyclif's writings on *dominium*, which make up the bulk of the first half of his *Summa Theologie*, contain the essence of his theological vision, uniting his metaphysics to his sociopolitical and ecclesiological thought. The first treatise begins as an outgrowth of his realist philosophical theology, and the final works in which *dominium* figure contain Wyclif's detailed prescription for the revival of the church and the right ordering of society. Wyclif was not the first to use *dominium* to describe God's relation to creation and men's relation to other men. The use of terms referring to mastery runs throughout recorded history, and Wyclif made use of ideas like *proprietas, iurisdictio,* and *ius* that had been mainstays of Roman law for centuries. The theological dialogue on divine and human mastery in which Wyclif participated has its roots in Augustine's *De Civitate Dei*, in the flourishing of the papal monarchy, and in the Franciscan poverty controversy. It will be easier to recognize what is unique to Wyclif's thought by becoming familiar with the disparate voices that influenced him.

The *Dominium* Tradition
preceding Wyclif

While to post-Enlightenment ears, *dominium* and the generally accepted translation "lordship" suggest the sovereignty that one individual exercises over another, necessarily entailing ownership and governmental authority, this is a canard. Roman law allowed for complexity in distinguishing among property ownership, *dominium*'s primary referent, and jurisdiction, governance, and political power. In the twelfth century, when canon lawyers resurrected Roman law to give structure to a legal edifice for the ascendant papal monarchy, it was common to distinguish among jurisdictive authority, secular power, and the use and possession of private property.[3] By the beginning of the fourteenth century, *dominium* had primarily proprietary connotations, although it was an inescapable fact that those who owned the most property tended to have the most jurisdictive authority. Most political theorists agreed with Thomas Aquinas in saying that a civil lord who supposed that his jurisdictive authority arose from his property ownership, and not from a constitution, was a tyrant.[4] Given that the medieval legal use of *dominium* referred to property ownership, and not to the authority to govern, it makes sense to wonder why Wyclif used the term to do so much more. The reasons lie in the connection of Augustinian theology to theories of the justice of property ownership; as the church developed into a political force in Europe, papal theorists like Giles of Rome found it useful to identify all earthly justice—including just property ownership—with the source of justice in creation.

Augustine's *De Civitate Dei* is the primary theological authority to relate property ownership and secular justice to divine authority. Here, the division between two classes of men is clear: some are members of the city of man, motivated by love of self, with wills turned from God and true justice, while others are motivated instead by love of God and a contempt for self, placing them in the city of God: "In the one, the princes and the nations he subdues are ruled by the love of ruling; in the other, the princes and the subjects serve one another in love, the latter obeying while the former take thought for all."[5] There is really only one true lord in creation, God; mastery of one man over another is the result of original sin and is unnatural, save in the case of paternity, which is founded in the parent's love for the child. Among members of the city of God, the relation of prince and subject is not a political one as understood in the city of man, and it does not entail mastery, but rather service and sacrifice, as exemplified in parental relations.

Property ownership has become associated with mastery in the city of man because of original sin, when man turned away from God and mistakenly believed that he could make claims of exclusive ownership of created beings. This is not to say that Augustine thought that all private property relations are wrong; indeed, he is famous for having argued that all things belong to the just.[6] People who own things are not de facto just. Those for whom ownership is not an end in itself but a means by which to do God's will are freed from the bondage of selfishness imposed by the Fall. They easily recognize the truth of the dictum "[o]ne should abstain from the possession of private things, or if one cannot abstain from possession, then from the love of property."[7]

These brief summaries show that Augustine's thought on the relation of ownership to political authority is open to interpretation. One can easily read Augustine as having argued that the church, as the body of Christ and the earthly instantiation of the city of God, can best exemplify love-centered lord-subject relations in its hierarchical clerical structure, thereby justifying a top-down papal monarchy. Likewise, one can interpret him as having so totally separated secular political authority from the rule of love as to rule out all similarity between political and ecclesiastical jurisdictive authority. Again, one can interpret Augustine's "all things belong to the just" as meaning that the church is the arbiter of all property ownership by virtue of its being the body of Christ and the seat of all created justice. Or, one could argue that the church should abandon all claims to property ownership, just as the apostles abstained from the possession of private things. This openness to interpretation was the source of several competing theories that led to Wyclif's position.

In 1301, during the conflict between Philip IV of France and Pope Boniface VIII, an Augustinian friar named Giles of Rome wrote *De Ecclesiastica Potestate*, a treatise designed to establish the absolute secular superiority of the papacy. Earlier, Giles had written a less papally centered,

Aristotelian treatise meant to help Philip IV learn to govern his kingdom, somewhat akin to the political thought of Aquinas, who may have been Giles's teacher. Giles's master, Boniface VIII, was responsible for the two famous bulls *Clericos laicos* (1296), which forbade the clergy to give up property without papal approval, and *Unam sanctam* (1302), which declared that secular power was in the service of, and subject to, papal authority. *De Ecclesiastica Potestate* is an exposition of the theological conception of power underlying these bulls, which is reliant on one of the two possible interpretations of Augustine mentioned earlier. In it, Giles describes all power—spiritual and secular—as rooted in the papacy, likening its structure to a papal river, from which smaller, secular streams snake out. The source of this river, he continues, is the sea, which is God: "God is a kind of fount and a kind of sea of force and power, from which sea all forces and all powers are derived like streams."[8] Secular power is not all that is reliant on papal authority. All property ownership, insofar as it is just, is similarly reliant on an ecclesiastical foundation. The only owner who can make a just claim to ownership is a servant of the church, by whose sacraments man receives the grace necessary to make such a claim. The key element in just secular power and just ownership, he continues, is sacramental grace, without which power and ownership are empty claims, devoid of justice. While Giles does not explicitly call the combination of ownership and temporal power *dominium*, that he unites the two in a consistent, Augustinian-centered argument was sufficient for the next generation of Augustinian theorists.

Twenty years earlier, another movement within the church had taken quite a different approach to property ownership, which they identified as *dominium*. The Franciscans had defined any property ownership, communal or individual, as inimical to the ideals of their order in Bonaventure's *Apologia pauperum* of 1269. The Fall from paradise and the introduction of selfishness into human nature makes property ownership of any type—private or communal—equivalent to a separation from our place in the right ordering of creation. For the Franciscans, all things belong to the just only in the sense that "belonging" entails non-exclusive sharing, not ownership. Within three decades, a distinct division had eroded the order's unity; one party, the spirituals, rigorously demanded that the friars adopt *usus pauper* as the ideal of their spiritual perfection, while the other, the conventuals, argued for a more lenient interpretation of the rule. The spirituals, under the guidance of Peter John Olivi and Ubertino de Casale, outnumbered the conventuals by century's end, and had become sufficiently vocal as to attract the attention of the pope.[9]

In the investigation that followed from 1309 to 1312, Clement V struggled to mediate between the two factions, legitimizing a discussion of the possible harmony of apostolic poverty and ecclesiastical authority. Clement's eventual successor, John XXII, was deeply suspicious of the spiritual Franciscans' arguments, perhaps in part suspecting a reappearance of the communitarian Waldensian heresy, which had plagued the church for over one hundred years. Private ownership, John argued, was not the result of original sin, but a gift from God that Adam had enjoyed in paradise. Grace provides a blessed justification for property ownership, and the righteous property owner can rest secure in the knowledge that his ownership is sanctioned by God's *dominium*. This wrangling between Franciscan factions and the pope had notable consequences; John's eventual controversy with the spirituals' champion William Ockham led to the first important use of the concept of a natural right, but for our purposes what matters is that *iurisdictio* and *proprietas* were united in the concept *dominium*. Wyclif would soon make use of the Franciscans' arguments for apostolic poverty and of John XXII's idea that divine *dominium* provides the basis for all human *dominium* in a way that would certainly have displeased both parties.[10]

By the 1350s, critics of the mendicant ideal had shifted their attention away from the poverty issue and toward the legitimacy of friars' engagement in pastoral work outside of parochial or diocesan supervision. Never mind the aspersions they cast on church ownership, ran the argument; how can they preach and administer the sacraments without the direct supervision of the local bishop? One of Avignon's most incisive critics of the friars' privileges was Richard Fitzralph, who wrote *De Pauperie Salvatoris*, a sustained examination of the Franciscans' place in the church. Fitzralph's approach was not expressly antifraternal, despite appearances. His arguments showed a deep respect for the ideals of apostolic poverty and selfless pastoral work, which Franciscans have always valued highly. The problem, he explained, lies in the Franciscans' assertion that their apostolic poverty has no restrictive bearing on their preaching privileges. Why is it licit for a friar to make use of someone else's property without accepting some of the responsibilities of that ownership being transferred along with the use? If the friars rely on the justice of the owners of what they use, they are bound by the same laws that bind the owners. If the owners of what the friars use are ecclesiastical, it follows that the friars are bound to obey ecclesiastical authority. Thus, friars' claims to be unaffected by ecclesiastical authority—at the papal, diocesan, or parochial level—are unfounded.[11]

For our purposes, Fitzralph's position is important because it argues that grace alone is the justification for any instance of *dominium* in creation, and that all just *dominium* ultimately relies on God's *dominium*; both serve as the cornerstones of Wyclif's position. All species of man's exercising authority involve, at their base, divine *dominium*, he explains. Fitzralph's interest is directed primarily toward ownership, and much less so toward political jurisdiction, but his catalog of the many species of private and communal ownership, possession, and rights of use occasionally lead him to address the legitimacy of political authority and its relation to ecclesiastical authority. God's *dominium* over creation is a natural consequence of the act of creating, and with it comes divine governance and conservation of created being. The rational beings in creation, angels and men, enjoy the loan of elements of God's created universe, but this communicative giving is not a divine abdication of ultimate authority, because everything is still directly subject to divine *dominium*.

When the nature of the *dominium* loaned to Adam changed with the Fall, the peaceful coexistence of Eden and the love embodying the grace of our natural *dominium* was damaged, but not eradicated. Man devised political *dominium* to restrict and regulate the property relations that were no longer guaranteed to be pure by grace. Original sin clouds our eyes, keeping us from naturally recognizing the loaned nature of any *dominium* in creation, but it does not preclude there being grace-justified property ownership. In some cases, God infuses the artificial property relations that we call *dominium* with sufficient grace to make them almost as pure as prelapsarian *dominium*. These grace-favored cases of human *dominium* cannot claim the authority of God's *dominium*, but can be so pure as to exhibit the *caritas*, or love, that characterizes God's *dominium*. Unfortunately, Fitzralph is not particularly clear about determining which of our *dominium* relations are favored by grace, and which are phantoms, thereby restricting the applicability of his argument to theological investigation about the friars' claims to be free from ecclesiastical authority.

Thus, from Augustine's position that all things belong to the just comes Giles's position that all property ownership and all secular lordship are grounded in ecclesiastical authority, as well as Franciscan arguments that expressly reject connections between property ownership and the apostolic ideal. Fitzralph's expression of the Augustinian papal position made grace the deciding factor in ownership relations, and ultimately in political authority, both of which had become nested in the term *dominium*. Wyclif's interpretation of the Augustinian position would stretch past arguments about papal authority and the friars, even past arguments between popes and kings, to stir the very nature of the church as Christ's earthly body. All of this begins, he would argue, with an understanding of God's *dominium* as the causal exemplar of all created lordship.

Dominium's Foundation: *De Dominio Divino*

The relation of universal to particular defines Wyclif's conception of how God's *dominium* causes all instances of *dominium* in creation. Divine *dominium* is "the standard prior to and presupposition of all other *dominium*; if a creature has *dominium* over anything, God already has *dominium* over it, so any created *dominium* follows upon divine *dominium*."[12] This relation is powerful, exceeding mere exemplarity, in which human *dominium* struggles to approximate the perfect ideal of God's *dominium*. An exemplary relation would not necessarily involve God's direct causal influence. One can imagine a lord imitating every aspect of God's *dominium* to the letter for purposes that are quite his own, even going so far as to mold his will to act lovingly in every dominative action. Western literature provides a wealth of examples of characters like Captain Ahab, whose pious imitation of God's loving governance masks a (likely unwitting) tyranny evident only in fleeting glimpses. Wyclif thinks that mere exemplarity is not enough. God's *dominium* has causal efficacy on all instances of human mastery such that no true created *dominium* is possible without direct participation in and constant reliance upon God's *dominium*. Each instance of just, created *dominium* can exemplify the perfection of divine *dominium* only through this causal efficacy; without it, a human lordship relation is only a pantomime, however many characteristics it might have in common with God's *dominium*. The instrument through which divine *dominium* moves is grace, which instills in human lords an essential *caritas* that characterizes their every dominative action. Thus, every case of just human *dominium* entails a constant reliance upon grace as the hallmark of its being an instantiation of God's universal *dominium*.

God's *dominium* has six aspects, three identifiable with lordship's rul-ing element (creation, sustenance, and governance), and three that define lordship's proprietary nature (giving, receiving, and lending).[13] Wyclif argues that the necessary precondition for an act of *dominium* is the first act, creation, of which no created being is capable. This makes God's *domi-nium* the only true instance of *dominium*, the source from which all created instances of *dominium* originate. Because the divine ideas and their created correlates, the universals, are prior in being to particular created beings, God's *dominium* over universals is prior to his *dominium* over particulars. This means that God creates, sustains, and governs the species humanity prior to ruling—and knowing—individual people. Without the carefully crafted modal theory lying at the base of his understanding of how God knows and wills human actions, Wyclif's position could be crippled by fatalism. This is why a significant portion of the first book of *De Dominio Divino* involves his recapitulation of the position described in the previous chapter of this volume.

The second set of acts that defines *dominium*—giving, receiving, and lending—provides the foundation for his arguments that all created *domi-nium* necessarily requires grace. God's act of giving the divine essence in order to realize creation is the truest form of giving because God is giving of himself through himself, which no created being can do. Nor can any created being receive as God receives. God truly receives only from himself through his giving. God gives up nothing in his giving, and acquires noth-ing in his receiving; creation is God's self-expression in which the divine essence is neither decreased nor increased. The crucial act from the created standpoint is God's lending, for here there is real interaction between the Lord and his subjects. What human beings, as rationally aware participants in God's lending relation, can claim as their own is loaned to them by divine authority, and they enjoy it through grace.

People can confuse giving with lending, because a lord who has been "loaned" a gift of God for use during his lifetime appears to have been "given" that gift. God's giving is communicative, not translative. For us, most giv-ing is translative, in that it involves the giver's surrender of every connec-tion to the gift, making it natural for us to suppose that God renounces his authority over what he gives to us. In fact, God's giving is communicative, which does not involve surrender of the gift. His gifts to people are meant to be enjoyed in common, and the more commonly enjoyed, the more the giver is enriched. On the broadest level, God's gift to creatures is being, given through the Holy Spirit, which is differentiated through the divine ideas into created substance. Two aspects of that gift, Wyclif explains, are necessarily connected: *caritas* and *dominium*. Rational creatures are given participation in divine *dominium* through the Holy Spirit, and are thereby responsible to God for that gift, which, when enjoyed commonly, engenders true *caritas*, God's caring love, in creation, thereby enriching both the creature and the Creator.[14]

Because all that God gives to creation will ultimately return to him, it makes more sense to speak of God's giving as lending. With any instance of lending, Wyclif explains, the lender seeks assurance that the borrower truly deserves what is to be loaned. Rational beings' desert of the *dominium* they are loaned is a matter of some complexity involving examination of the relation of deserving to grace, which is particularly clear in the distinction between congruent and condign grace. When a temporal lord lends to his subject according to the subject's worthiness, the subject's merit is on a measurable level to the lord's merit, and the mutual agreement that defines the loan is made according to the respective merit of each party. The merit that allows the subject desert of consideration for the loan is condign, grounded in the *dignitas* shared by lender and subject. Condign merit implies that the meritorious truly deserves the reward, requiring the giver to give the merited as something due, as when an Olympic athlete earns a gold medal by besting all opponents. Such a loan is impossible between the Creator and creature, because there is no way of comparing a creature's merit with God's perfect nature; all that is the creature's, including its worth, is from outside itself, from God, while God's perfection is from within. There is no way in which a creature can be considered to "deserve" anything from God in such a relation. Congruent merit is when the meritorious does not have the power to require of the giver. In instances of congruent merit, the goodness of the act does not require the giver to reward the agent, but it provides sufficient cause for the reward to be given, as when one receives an Academy Award. While many of the audience members may deserve an Oscar, the recipient receives one because something about her performance was somehow pleasing to the academy. Yet Wyclif believes that it must make some sense to talk of deserving grace: "It is the invariable law of God that nobody is awarded blessedness unless they first deserve it."[15] Merit, he says, requires the motion of an object, the deliberation of the mind, and finally voluntary adherence, which does not happen instantaneously. We can move our wills to the good, and from this, Wyclif says, grace may—but need not—follow. Thus, we merit congruently thanks to God's generosity toward a will in accord with his own. In effect, God lends merit.

To understand how grace functions in this divine lending relation, it is important to understand the difference between divine and temporal grace. The former, uncreated grace essentially denotes the divine essence, personally denotes the Holy Spirit, and habitudinally denotes God's good will toward creatures. It is with all creatures intrinsically, and with all things simply coeternal with God, as is said of divine understanding, knowing, and willing. Temporal, or created, grace is supernaturally given to rational creatures as the basis for all theological and moral virtues. All rational creatures ought to have such grace by virtue of their being as caused by God, and this is prevenient to meriting. Uncreated grace and condign merit are roughly complementary, for both correspond to a quality in the subject: condign merit indicates a quality of deserving in the subject, while uncreated grace indicates God's good will toward creation. If we could have a perfect will, we might merit God's gift condignly. Created grace and congruent merit are also roughly complementary, for both are based on something extrinsic to the recipient, namely, the uncreated grace of God's will. In fact, because created grace is what is loaned to creatures who merit congruently, both are corresponding elements of God's lending. So God's lending is the temporal bestowal of created grace on the congruently meritorious, which is based in the uncreated grace that characterizes the Holy Spirit itself.[16]

Wyclif's theology of grace is the key to understanding how his theory of human *dominium* relates to divine *dominium,* its causal paradigm. Man's lordship is at once ownership and jurisdictive mastery, but when a human lord governs, or gives, or receives, or lends, these acts are only just insofar as the lord recognizes that his authority is that of a steward: "Any rational creature is only improperly called a lord, and is rather a minister or steward of the supreme Lord . . . and whatever he has to distribute, he has purely by grace."[17] The necessary characteristic of every instance of human *dominium* is the created grace God lends to the individual lord, which itself is grounded in the uncreated grace of the Holy Spirit. Thus, grace-favored human lordship is causally brought about by God's perfect *dominium* without mediation by some other, created source: any human lord is a steward, or bailiff of God, and grace allows a clear understanding of this relation. The human lord appears to have proprietary and jurisdictive authority by virtue of his own excellence, but is really only an instantiation of divine *dominium,* a grace-realized agent of God's lordship. This makes the human lord both master and servant; from the divine perspective, the lord is God's servant, but from the viewpoint of the subject, he is master. Wyclif is tireless in his emphasis on the illusory nature of this mastery. Grace allows the human lord to recognize that he is, in fact, his subjects' servant, ministering to them as a nurturing steward, not lording over them as would a powerful sovereign.

Natural *Dominium* in Eden

De Civili Dominio begins with the motto "Civil justice presupposes divine justice; civil *dominium* presupposes natural *dominium*." Wyclif means his readers to be aware that his discourse on human *dominium* is already in full swing as he begins his explication of how the grace-favored civil lord is obligated to take control of the church. Critics who have dismissed Wyclif's political thought as an iteration of Marsilius of Padua, as did Pope Gregory XI in 1377, or as written largely as a vehicle for John of Gaunt's anticlerical leanings, as has K. B. McFarlane, should take Wyclif at his word. Man's *dominium* is threefold—natural, civil, and evangelical—but comprehensible only in terms of its instantiation of the justice of God's *dominium*. As he moved into his general analysis of human *dominium*, his thoughts turned to the most fundamental instance of God's loving governance, the scriptural commandments. The foundation of all that is right (*ius*) in creation, he explains, is the justice (*iustitia*) of God's eternal righteousness, which means that we cannot begin to understand right and wrong in creation without understanding God's uncreated right. This is a significant departure from the Aristotelian position that unaided human reason is capable of justice, and Wyclif explicitly rejects any conception of justice that does not rely on uncreated right.[18] The basis for justice in creation is not necessarily evident to human eyes, because the Fall has made humans prone to value natural, material goods above spiritual ones: "Because the human community appreciates greatly these goods, of course it says that this law [founded in material goods] is most useful, and the law of the Gospel which is of the virtues and in general against the vices they call useless."[19]

The laws of scripture are the purest expression of uncreated right available to human eyes, he explains, and are most clearly expressed in the Ten Commandments of Exodus 20 and again in Matthew 22:37–40. Wyclif's analysis of Christ's law of love and of the Ten Commandments proceeds directly from his disquisition on the relation of earthly justice to eternal right in his *De Mandatis Divinis.* That Wyclif uses the same title that Robert Grosseteste had used in his analysis of the Decalogue is no accident; Wyclif's debt to Grosseteste's conceptions of sin, love of God, idolatry, and the substance of true faith is obvious throughout the treatise. In the catalog of sins in the later commandments, Wyclif makes repeated use of the thirteenth-century Dominican William Peraldus, whose treatise *Summa de Vitiis* was influential in disseminating the conception of the traditional seven deadly sins.

Almost as an afterthought, Wyclif reflects that it might be useful to digress for a bit on how man lived in paradise, before the Fall. In *De Statu Innocencie,* the innocence into which we were created, he says, is the optimal state for any rational being. Lacking sin, death would be unknown. As man aged, he would gradually attain an indissoluble spiritual body ultimately destined to worship God in the celestial Jerusalem that now awaits only the elect. In this prelapsarian state, the wills of men would be in perfect concord with the divine will, and all human action would be just, effortlessly aligned with the natural ordering of creation. In this condition, all need for the liberal arts would be met naturally, meaning that quadrivium, trivium, and mechanical arts would be unnecessary, as would any civil or criminal law, since man would understand the right naturally. This denial of the need for human law is of special import, for Wyclif will later argue that the evangelical lord, or priest, as heir of Christ's restoration of the possibility of natural *dominium*, should never be concerned with such matters. Nor, Wyclif argues in a later chapter, would there be any need for the moral virtues, or even the theological virtues, although he admits that it is difficult to imagine our natural state without the theological virtue of *caritas.* This may be one benefit of the Fall: "It is probable that we have now a degree of *caritas* from grace which we would not have had in innocence, for . . . *maiorem caritatem* [*sic*] *nemo habet quam ut animam suam ponat quis pro amicis suis.*"[20]

In such a state, private property ownership would be unknown. The natural *dominium* described in Genesis 1:26 is characterized by lack of selfishness, ownership, and the distinction between "mine" and "thine." Every act of a natural lord epitomizes love and is a direct participation in, and an instantiation of, the perfect *caritas* of God's loving *dominium.* The selfless natural lord's position is his by virtue of grace, of course; an absence of sin does not ensure a connection between uncreated grace and condign merit. The true sense of Augustine's "all things belong to the just" is most fully apparent in the prelapsarian natural disposition to share in the use of creation while acting as a faithful steward to its perfect Lord.[21]

The Fall was brought about by the first sin, which Wyclif characterizes as nothing other than the privation of God's right in man's soul. The result is that man's natural concord is gone, as are his power over the animals and his ability to serve God according to the order of his nature. We are left with wills that are prone to value the physical, material world above spiritual concerns, and the unavoidable result is private property ownership and all the anxieties and cares that attend it. We no longer understand a given created good as a gift on loan from God, but can only see it in terms of our own self-interest and can only comprehend it in the expressly selfish terms mine or thine. The execrable result is civil *dominium*, the odious and endless enslavement to material goods.

After the Fall: The Institution of Civil
Dominium and Christ's Redemption

Wyclif defines civil *dominium* as "proprietary lordship in a wayfarer over the goods of fortune fully according to human law."[22] This definition is centered not on legislative authority, but on the private property ownership enjoyed by "active travelers" (not monks) along life's path of created goods. This is because all civil *dominium* is based on the use of goods owned, which is the basis for all postlapsarian conceptions of justice. Before the Fall, our use of created goods was communal, unencumbered by the complexity that follows from selfishness. Now, Wyclif explains, there are three types of use: that directly consequent on civil ownership, civil use without ownership, and evangelical use. The first two are natural results of the Fall, and the third is the result of Christ's incarnation. Before the incarnation, civil ownership and civil use were grounded in manmade laws designed primarily to regulate property ownership. These legal systems tended to have two general structures; they were either monarchical, as in most cases, or they were aristocratic polities. The harmony of an aristocratic polity is certainly preferable, because it most resembles the state enjoyed before the Fall. A benevolent aristocracy would foster the contemplative life, communalism, and an absence of corruptible governmental apparatus. Wyclif has the time of the judges in mind, and he doubts that this arrangement is attainable now, in an age rife with avarice.

The most common species of civil *dominium* is monarchy, which Wyclif holds to be necessary, given man's fallen nature. In any kind of state, he argues, a chief executive power that holds ultimate legislative authority is necessary, otherwise there would not be order in the implementation of any kind of political act. The possibility that the many are capable of ruling on behalf of the many is negligible, given the prevalence of sin. Wyclif's divergence from a traditionally Aristotelian approach to political theory is clear; the point of civil *dominium* is not, as with Aristotle, the sustenance of individual virtuous activity. Civil *dominium* is a phenomenon that arises from original sin and is not likely to result in justice in itself. The government of Caesar may on occasion be just, but only if it accidentally realizes divine justice. At this point, a tension in Wyclif's general talk of civil *dominium* should be evident. If civil *dominium* that is not grounded directly in divine *dominium* is incapable of sustained just governance, and if natural *dominium* is the instantiation of divine *dominium* for which man was created, how can any talk of just civil *dominium* be possible? To return to the opening dictum of *De Civili Dominio*, if natural *dominium* is free from private property ownership, how can civil *dominium* rely upon it in any way? Before resolving this problem, we will need to address evangelical *dominium* as yet another factor in Wyclif's conception of man's postlapsarian state.

Christ makes possible the attainment of the natural *dominium* that man lost with the Fall, both through the exemplary apostolic poverty and the redemptive sacrifice described in holy scripture. Because of Christ's sinless nature, he was the first man since Adam to be capable of the purity that characterized natural *dominium*. This, Christ shared with the disciples, who were able to renounce all exclusive claims to created goods in a recreation of the communal *caritas* that was lost with the Fall: "Christ was a true pauper, as was prophesied in the Old Testament, in that He came into the world to destroy sin, and above all the customs of human secular conduct that had developed since the state of innocence . . . which He could not have done unless He adopted the opposite state, which is poverty."[23] This poverty is not simply the state of not owning things, though. One can as easily live sinfully in squalor as one can in luxury, if one's attentions are turned toward material goods. The apostolic poverty which characterized Christ's life and the state of the early church is a spiritual state, not an economic one. To view Christ's poverty as a reaction against and a rejection of civil *dominium* is to err by presupposing the potential validity of civil *dominium*. On the contrary, Wyclif argues that Christ's poverty is a realization of the

state we enjoyed prior to the institution of civil *dominium*, before selfishness and private property were even shadowy threats: "Man in a state of
innocence had lordship over every part of the sensible world and by virtue
of Christ's passion the just man is forgiven all sins and restored in lordship;
thus the temporal recipients of grace rightly have the fullness of universal
dominium."[24]

It might appear that Wyclif is making a case similar to the spiritual Franciscans, for certainly the results are the same: Christ's life was
exemplary for all Christians, Christ lived in apostolic poverty, hence, all
Christians ought to follow his example or, at the least, have the option
open to them. Wyclif's consonance with the Franciscan tradition is also
suggested in his use of Bonaventure's definition of apostolic poverty in the
third book of *De Civili Dominio*, but as mentioned at the end of the previous chapter, Wyclif's motives are distinctly different from those of the friars.[25] While the Franciscans argued that their rule allowed them to regain
the ownership-free purity enjoyed by the early apostolic church, Wyclif is
arguing that Christ's redemptive sacrifice enables all Christians to regain
natural *dominium* itself. This as much as made Franciscanism a pale imitation of true Christianity, and Wyclif's Franciscan colleagues were quick
to notice this. One of the first critics of Wyclif's *dominium* thought was
William Woodford, O.F.M., who argued that, among other things, Wyclif
had gone too far in equating apostolic, spiritual poverty with prelapsarian purity. The third book of *De Civili Dominio*, by far the largest of the
three, is Wyclif's prolonged response to Franciscan critics like Woodford
in which lie the seeds of the antifraternalism of his later writings. The
Franciscan rule, despite its goodness and moral reliance on divine justice, is
but the product of human hands and not equal to the evangelical rule given
by Christ. Followers of St. Francis's rule are called "Franciscans"; while
followers of Christ are called "Christians," not "Jesusans." In a manmade
order like Franciscanism, obedience to the rule may or may not be a necessary condition for grace, for one can easily envision Franciscans who live a
life of sinful poverty. A faithful life in Christ, the divinely ordained ideal,
involves more than life according to a rule; it is a spiritual change involving
a redirected will, not just the outward trappings of apostolic purity.[26]

Wyclif describes apostolic poverty as a mode of having with *caritas*, the
degree of which is comprehensible in terms of the use the owner makes of
a created good for the greatest spiritual benefit. The *caritas* that instantiates divine *dominium* is only possible through grace, which makes grace

necessary for apostolic poverty. The church, Christ's body on earth, ought to preserve this apostolic poverty with a purity exceeding any manmade institution, because it is based in the true justice of Christ's evangelical law, not the illusory justice of human law: "For the law of Christ teaches about the glory of tribulations and condemns fame, prosperity, and the riches of the world, advising the relinquishment of proprietary lordship; civil law seems to command the opposites of all these."[27] Because the church is founded not on the materially based laws of man, but on the spiritually grounded *lex Christi*, it must be absolutely free of any property ownership, the better to realize the ideal of spiritual purity required by apostolic poverty. That the church must be characterized by a total absence of ownership is central to Wyclif's understanding of the ecclesiastical implementation of Christ's law. Any material riches that the church comes upon as "goods of fortune" must be distributed as alms for the poor, which was the practice of Christ, the disciples, and the apostolic church. This alms giving must not be motivated by worldly aspirations to appear "charitable," for that is nothing more than the kind of giving common to civil *dominium*. A kindly civil lord may give the use of some good to a poor subject while still retaining ultimate *dominium* over that good, but true giving according to the evangelical law entails recognition that the church—and no man—has the *dominium* necessary to make this kind of gift. Hence, what goods come to the church ought automatically to be bestowed upon those in need as a matter of course, without the church's having anything to do with civil *dominium*.

This is the ideal for which the church was ordered by Christ, and some of the harshest invective in Wyclif's prose is against the church's inability even to desire to return to this apostolic state. For example, in *Dialogus sive Speculum Ecclesie Militantis (The Dialogue; or, A Mirror of the Church Militant*, 1379), he attributes all of the clergy's shortcomings to their captivation with property: "And so as the devil perverts [the church's] priests from Christ's poverty to secular lordship, thus he turns them away from humility, from evangelical preaching and from every other duty for which Christ anointed them."[28] The turning point in church history was the Donation of Constantine, the basis from which the church claims to have the civil *dominium* of a Caesar. Wyclif was vigorous in his condemnation of the Donation and would likely have been pleased, had he lived into the early fifteenth century, when Nicholas of Cusa, Lorenzo Valla, and Reginald Pecock argued persuasively that the document in which Constantine conferred considerable temporal privileges to the papacy was a ninth-century forgery.

Not only was such a gift impossible, according to the right understanding of civil *dominium*—for, as we will see, a just civil lord cannot grant any gift in perpetuity—but the Donation opened wide the floodgates that had been protecting the church from the evils of the world, the flesh, and the devil. Now that the pope and the bishops were allowed to be temporal lords, they were polluted with the same cares and fears that haunt the machinery of secular human *dominium*. The result is not a class of evangelical lords who, through the power of grace, are better able to guide the secular world, for civil *dominium* is an onerous, degrading business that soils anyone involved. The Donation has resulted in a church riddled with tumorous growths of civil *dominium* that strangle its chances of embodying Christ's law of *caritas*.

Given the obviously poisonous influence that civil *dominium* has had on the evangelical *dominium* of Christ's law, it is difficult to imagine how Wyclif would set aside some civil lords as capable of instantiating divine justice. But apostolic poverty is not identical to an absence of property ownership; it is having with *caritas*. While the clergy as spiritual lords ought to follow Christ's example of material poverty, this does not mean that all ownership precludes *caritas*. Recall that Wyclif had argued that all grace-favored human lords who instantiate divine *dominium* are able to recognize their true place as stewards. Those civil lords made able through grace to recognize this truth are as much capable of apostolic poverty, he reasons, as are any of the postlapsarian meritorious. But this does not mean that Wyclif endorses the feudal structure of fourteenth-century Europe. We will see that he rejects hereditary succession and servitude, two practices that defined the lordship of his age.

Wyclif envisions the just civil lord or king as the means by which the church is relieved of its accumulated burden of property ownership. So long as the church exists in postlapsarian society, it must be protected from the avarice of thieves, the errors of heresy, and the depredations of infidels. Certainly, priests ought not to be concerned with such matters, given their higher responsibility for the welfare of Christian souls. As a result, the church needs a worldly protector, a guardian to ward off enemies while caring for the church's physical health and administering its alms on behalf of the poor. This allows Wyclif to describe just, grace-favored civil *dominium* as different in kind from the civil lordship predicated on materialistic human concerns: "It is right for God to have two vicars in His church, namely a king in temporal affairs, and a priest in spiritual. The king should strongly check rebellion, as did God in the Old Testament, while priests ought minister the precepts mildly . . . as did Christ, who was at once priest and king."[29] In saying this, he calls to mind an argument made by an anonymous Norman political theorist in the twelfth century, in which the king is an image of God, the almighty Lord, while the priest is an image of Christ the spiritual counselor. While it is unlikely that Wyclif had access to the writings of "Norman Anonymous," and while Wyclif's conception of kingship was not theocratic, it is interesting to note that both argued for the church's need for the guiding hand of secular rule.

When Wyclif discusses civil *dominium* and kingship, which terms he generally uses synonymously, his interest is in explaining their function in God's *dominium*, especially as paladins of Christ's body on earth:

> Since the king is the minister of God, according to the correspondent eminence of virtue, it is clear that he should rule according to the divine law by which men are ordered. Since it is the part of justice to decline from evil and to do good, the king should coerce rebels against divine law and other authorities, and advance the factors of justice according to the rules of *caritas*. The king should have the power of ruling his subjects as a minister from God, not by human law without divine sanction.[30]

His attention occasionally wanders to conventional topics in political thought, like the particulars of just rule, the responsibilities of royal councilors to their king, the nature of just war, and royal jurisdiction in commerce. When he does mention such subjects, his advice is priestly: "[A] lord ought not treat his subjects in a way other than he would rationally wish to be treated in similar circumstances. . . . the Christian lord should not desire subjects for love of dominating, but . . . for the correction and spiritual improvement of his subjects, and so to[o] the efficacy of the church."[31] He advises the king to provide few and just laws wisely and accurately administered, and to live subject to these laws, since the law is more necessary for the community than is the king. Also, the king should strive to protect the lower classes' claims on temporal goods in the interests of social order, for "nothing is more destructive in a kingdom in its political life than immoderately to deprive the lower classes of the goods of fortune."[32] Occasionally, he hints at the king's need for reliable advisors, generally when discussing the king's need for sacerdotal advice in directing church reform. Wyclif never mentions Parliament as a significant aspect of civil rule, and the only international relations that interest him are those between king and pope.

As a consequence, it is difficult to classify him as a political theorist in the sense that Marsilius of Padua or Ockham are; civil *dominium* is less a political phenomenon than an aspect of divinely guided human *dominium* meant to protect and defend the church in the postlapsarian state.

Certainly, the most immediate concern of a civil lord living in an age in which the church has become bloated on the poison of material wealth should be the radical divestment of all ecclesiastical ownership. Wyclif is tireless in arguing for the king's right to take all land, all goods, indeed even the buildings themselves away from the church to purge it of the virulent infection that impedes its realization of Christ's restored natural *dominium*. Should the clergy protest against royal appropriation, threatening the king with excommunication or interdict, the king should proceed with steely resolve, just as a physician applies his lancet to an infected boil. The threat of excommunication need not bar a king from his duty, Wyclif explains, since no one can be cast out of Christ's body unless he has first cast himself out. Certainly, a king acting on behalf of the health of the church is in no danger of casting himself out of Christ's body, so long as his actions are grace-founded and his motivation is ecclesiastical well-being. In places, Wyclif even argues that the buildings that make up England's mantle of churches are superfluous extravagance, suggesting that in times of national emergency they be razed to construct fortresses or watchtowers. No grace-favored civil lord will be disposed to save up the divested goods of the church for his own enrichment, despite the obvious temptations. He will distribute the church's ill-gotten lands and goods to the people of his kingdom, acting as a beadle to give alms on the church's behalf. This, Wyclif explains, will be his continued responsibility even after the church has been purged, for he is the church's custodian as well as its protector.

The hereditary succession by which civil lordship passes from father to son is a problem for Wyclif. How can someone inherit the grace needed to ensure just ownership and jurisdiction from a parent? The practice of primogeniture has injured the possibility of grace-founded civil lordship, because lords are thereby prone to rule on behalf of their own familial interests rather than in the interests of their subjects. The only means by which Wyclif can envision hereditary succession operating is through spiritual filiation, in which a civil lord instructs a worthy successor, "which is analogously similar to natural filiation, for the seed, the Word of God, is sown in an instructed soul."[33] He suggests adoption as the basis for the spiritual primogeniture by which lordship is passed on, possibly akin to the way

Antoninus Pius adopted Marcus Aurelius. This would be preferable to general election, for Wyclif is clear about the impossibility of the widespread recognition of grace in a potential civil lord: "It does not follow that 'all the people want Peter to be their civil lord, therefore it is just.'"[34] But just as a rejection of hereditary succession and popular election poses a problem for the practical implementation of Wyclif's political theory, it underscores his contention that any instance of human giving based in human convention alone lacks divine justice. Grants in perpetuity, which were commonly employed by civil lords to guarantee the ongoing obligation of liegemen in return for a gift of land or political authority, are as impossible as hereditary inheritance. A lord might reward a liegeman with a grant while acting as God's steward, but he certainly cannot thereby grant that his subject's progeny likewise deserve the gift. If civil lords cannot make such grants to their liegemen, they certainly cannot do so to priests, which provides Wyclif with further ammunition to question the validity of ecclesiastical reliance on the Donation of Constantine to justify the church's secular power.

The grace-favored civil lord, then, must bear the responsibility of material power as a steward or bailiff of God, ever aware of his duty to protect and provide for both his realm and the church within it. History is rich with examples of kings who lost sight of their ministerial positions and wielded secular authority in their own interests, cruelly using the land and the church for their own gain. Such tyrants cause Wyclif problems, because in many cases it is difficult for the subjects to determine whether their lord is acting viciously as a crowned brigand, or sternly, as a physician purging a patient. For the same reason that Wyclif denies the suitability of popular elections and the possibility of excommunication, he is cautious regarding tyranny. It is impossible for human minds to gauge the presence of grace in another. What may be cruel persecution to a subject may in fact be just punishment, while what may appear to be benign, permissive rule may in fact be a poisonous lassitude indicative of malignant misrule. A priest is in no position to assess the justice of a civil lord, given his dedication to apostolic ideals, which are foreign to civil *dominium*. Thus, in some cases, Wyclif advises that one must suffer tyrannical rule as a divine punishment, a scourge cleansing the realm or the church of impurities, particularly in instances where a king deprives subjects of material wealth. In other cases, especially when a civil lord is fostering ecclesiastical decay by not persecuting heretics or regulating the church's goods, Wyclif suggests that resistance to tyranny may be justifiable. Better to focus on the greater danger of priestly tyranny; after all, a tyrannical civil lord can only do damage to one's material well-being, but a tyrannical priest can endanger one's very soul.

The guardian against priestly tyranny must be the civil lord, whose responsibility to the church requires him to monitor the clergy's execution of its spiritual duties. This responsibility is his by virtue of the responsibility he has to God to protect the church from dangers without and within. Those who argue that a civil lord has no business interfering with spiritual concerns overlook the fundamental relation that holds between just civil law and divine law; because the civil lord's responsibility is to God, his first concern must be to ensure that nothing any man may do can block obedience to divine law. The cumbersome apparatus of canon law that has built up over the centuries like barnacles on a ship's hull is held up as the means by which the church regulates spiritual affairs, but this, Wyclif explains, is a superfluous creation of priests, ultimately hindering the church by introducing material structure to what should be a spiritual enterprise. This is not to say that the king should take on the spiritual authority of a pope, for as we will discuss, such a concentration of spiritual authority is antithetical to Wyclif's vision of ecclesiastical structure.

The means by which a king ought to monitor the spiritual offices of priests are bishops, who exist to correct the errant and to reward the excellent clergy. Bishops, he explains, were the early church's means by which its priests were protected from error, and the king should use them as his deputies to protect the church from the dangers of simony, pluralism, absenteeism, and heresy. The bishops ought also to act as royal theological advisors, helping the civil lord to understand how *lex Christi* is best implemented in his own legislation. Post-Reformation readers of Wyclif may be surprised by this apparent reliance on a hierarchy of the spiritual lords, given Wyclif's generally dim view of the church being organized according to the needs of secular society. Yet a bishop's power is analogous to a civil lord's. Just as a civil lord is God's steward and a servant to his subjects, a bishop is not superior to the laity or the priests, but a steward whose responsibility is to God and the divine law, which ordains subservience to the grace-favored civil lord.

Wyclif continued to argue for the centrality of the episcopal office throughout his life, despite his troubles with the bishop of London and the archbishop of Canterbury. While a church untroubled by the material world may need only priests as spiritual shepherds, he argues in *Trialogus*

IV.15 in early 1383, in this age it needs bishops to provide supervisory and regulatory guidance in the service of a just civil lord.

This, then, is Wyclif's conception of how human lords ought to serve as instantiations of God's *dominium* in postlapsarian society. A civil lord must recognize that his jurisdictive and proprietary authority are based not in his own worth, but are founded in grace given for the purpose of serving God's will in human society. Kings must hold all material power as stewards in service of the divine Lord and are bound especially to protect the church, Christ's body on earth, from the world, the flesh, and the devil. While evangelical lords may believe themselves to wield secular authority justly, theirs is a higher, purer sphere of influence, and the civil lord's responsibility is to help them to realize this. Given the ecclesiastical status quo of the late fourteenth century, this would involve the radical divestment of all church property ownership and a strict regulation of clerical behavior. The place of the human lord—whether natural, evangelical, or civil—in Wyclif's thought is ultimately that of a guardian, not a philosopher-king, a means by which creation's true Lord realizes perfect justice.

EPILOGUE

Wyclif's legacy has long been a matter for partisan debate. The theological cataclysm that broke over sixteenth-century Europe dramatically polarized opinions about a thinker whose ideas appeared to presage those of Luther. His monarchism seemed to foresee the Tudor state, his emphasis on scripture as the divine standard of truth evoked Protestant bibliolatry, and his vigorous antipapalism rivaled all but the most vehement of Reformers. It is no wonder that modern assessments of Wyclif's thought have ranged from vigorous Catholic condemnation to adulatory Protestant encomia, with almost nothing in between.

Even before the Reformation, polarization over Wyclif had been common. In England, his Oxford-trained preachers had instigated a program of preaching and teaching according to his ideals, which continued after his death in 1384. The first fruit was the Wyclif Bible, a complete translation of Jerome's Vulgate into English. While parts of scripture had been available in translation as far back as King Alfred the Great, the Wyclif Bible warrants attention as the first complete English Bible in the history of the language. This Bible, and the energetic preaching that became associated with its proponents, gave rise to the Lollard movement, the lay piety phenomenon that, because of Lancastrian politics, would soon be associated with treason. The Lancastrian crusade against Wycliffism brought burning at the stake to England in 1401, and scores would perish in this way for their association with the writings of a man for whom rebellion against the social order was unthinkable. Defining Lollardy became very much a matter of circumstance, though; by the middle of the fifteenth century, an accusation of Lollardy might be made for any number of reasons. Some were accused of questioning the ecclesiastical monopoly on scripture interpretation, others for their complaints about what they perceived as idolatry, while still others were questioned for expressing doubts about the sacraments. Our understanding of the Lollards continues to develop as scholars continue to study fifteenth-century England, and the phenomenon appears to have been much more complex than it was previously understood to be. The absence of the formal organization of the Protestant movements that scholars first used as paradigms to explain Lollardy does not demonstrate a correspondent theological simplicity. Something linked to Wyclif's teachings certainly compelled Bishop Reginald Pecock (c. 1390–1461) to launch a one-man crusade against scripturally founded anticlericalism, using reasoned argument, rather than the more standard threats of imprisonment and burning. The result was what may be the first genuine philosophical literature in the English language. Pecock's unpleasant personality and his willingness to count church doctrine as secondary to reason led to his own conviction for heresy, and rather than face the fate of the Lollards, he recanted. Pecock's campaign ended two decades before the end of medieval England on Bosworth field, suggesting that there were "fellow travelers," if not actual Lollards, into the first decades of the Tudor era. Most scholars agree that Lollardy had little to do with the genesis of Anglicanism. John Foxe (1517–1587), author of the widely read *Actes and Monuments* (1563), introduced Wyclif into the sixteenth-century mix from his encounters with his manuscripts on the Continent, and contributed significantly to the Protestant myth of Wyclif and Lollardy as proto-Protestantism. The same is true of John Bale (1495–1563), an ex-Carmelite who embraced Wyclif's memory, coining the epithet "morning star of the Reformation."

The established church, on the other hand, had long followed the lead of the Earthquake Council and refused to admit that Wyclif or his writings had described Catholic truth. Wyclif's ideas had attracted some attention among the lesser English nobility in the 1380s, prompting Richard II to join forces with Archbishop Courtenay in an active program dedicated to eliminating Wycliffism. A minor uprising against Henry V, led by a Lollard knight, Sir John Oldcastle, in 1414, made Wycliffism synonymous with treason. Henry's confessor, the Carmelite Thomas Netter, penned the most complete denunciation of Wyclif's thought yet to have appeared, the *Doctrinale Fidei Catholicae,* between 1423 and 1430. The *Doctrinale* would remain the standard account of Wyclif's theology for Rome for centuries to come. Netter had been present at Constance, where the orthodoxy of the English church had been impugned by the specter of Wycliffism, and his *Doctrinale* offers an exhaustive, point-by-point refutation of Wyclif's errors. While Wyclif's own writings were scarcely available after Constance, the *Doctrinale* was reprinted three times in the seventeenth century and again in 1757. Before antiquarians began to recover Wyclif from his own writings, Netter's depiction of Wyclif as the Donatistic, antipapalist denier of transubstantiation was the standard portrait accepted by the majority of Western Christians, both Catholic and Protestant.

A minority viewed Wyclif in a different light. Richard II's marriage to Anne of Bohemia in 1382 had opened Oxford to Bohemian scholars, who returned to Charles University in Prague with the latest in English theological innovations. The Bohemian scholars, resentful of the imperial authority exercised over the university, were quick to notice that Wyclif's metaphysics proved particularly irksome to their Ockhamist German superiors. Wyclif's theological works soon garnered Czech attention, and two figures in particular quickly became associated with Wyclif's thought: Jan Hus (c. 1373–1415) and Jerome of Prague (c. 1373–1416). Frustration with the ecclesiastical status quo had smoldered throughout Bohemia before the influx of Wyclif's thought, and the two preachers fanned this into a burning flame during the first decade of the fifteenth century. Both ended up being tried for heresy. Jerome recanted, was released, and then took back his recantation; he was executed, defending Wyclif to the last. Hus was tricked into appearing at Constance in 1415, where his trial and execution were foregone certainties. These two martyrdoms kindled a Czech revolution against the empire and the pope, and led to wars that raged across Bohemia from 1420 to 1434. The Hussite wars saw the first use of massed gunfire against armored cavalry, and the Bohemians invented the mobile fortress, circling their caravan of stout war wagons into impregnable defensive formations. While the Hussite revolution ultimately ended in imperial and papal victory, the figure of Jan Hus and his Wycliffite theology inspired Czech nationalism through the German and Russian occupations of the twentieth century. The largest collection of Wyclif's writings remains at Charles University, and the as-yet little understood phenomenon of fifteenth-century Czech scholasticism suggests an exciting frontier for intellectual historians.

Wyclif's legacy as a late medieval philosopher rests on his contribution to realist metaphysics for three reasons. First, his writings helped to define scholastic thought at Charles University, which remains one of the great universities of Europe. Second, the official response to Wyclif's thought coincided with a general dissatisfaction with nominalism at the beginning of the fifteenth century. Philosophers at Oxford and Paris had begun to shift away from Ockhamism, and the condemnation of Wyclif's approach encouraged a tendency toward Scotism and Thomism among many fifteenth-century thinkers.[1] While Wyclif certainly never intended his thought to serve in this fashion, it functioned as the ontologically opposite pole to Ockhamism, providing a second point by which fifteenth-century metaphysicians could triangulate a more suitable approach. Finally, Wyclif's thought provides a fascinating instance of scholastic philosophy rigorously applied to its foundational commitments to doctrinal truths.

I hope to have shown in this survey that many elements of Wyclif's thought were not original to him, but arose from a complex dialogue that had been ongoing at Oxford from the early decades of the fourteenth century. Wyclif's genius lies in the philosophically consistent approach he constructed from what he believed to be the scripturally defined truth of a scholasticism that had run afoul of newfangled innovation. He more than meets the criteria that William James set forth for the religious innovator, who introduces "one to regions of religious truth, to corners of the universe, which your robust Philistine type of nervous system, forever offering its biceps to be felt, thumping its breast and thanking Heaven that it hasn't a single morbid fibre in its composition, would be sure to hide forever from its self-satisfied possessors."[2]

APPENDIX

Wyclif's Confessio

In late 1380, when a panel of twelve Oxford theologians condemned his eucharistic theology, Wyclif is reported to have been astounded. Soon, John of Gaunt began to pressure him to rethink his rejection of transubstantiation. This led to Wyclif's publication of this document on 10 May 1381. The *Confessio* is a precis of the arguments in *De Eucharistia*, which he had written in 1380, and the manuscripts that exist fall into two groups. The first, larger group contains a relatively shorter version, which was published in the *Fasciculi Zizianorum*, along with an extended refutation by John Tyssington, O.F.M. Wyclif used parts of what follows in *De Apostasia*, although it is not clear whether he borrowed from *De Apostasia* in the composition of the *Confessio*, as Williel Thomson argues, or whether he improved a later version of *De Apostasia* with what he had written to explain himself to the authorities. The Bohemian manuscripts contain a longer version, the additional material of which Wyclif used also in a sermon for Corpus Christi Day, with only slight variations. This additional material was published by I. H. Stein in his "An Unpublished Fragment of Wyclif's *Confessio*," as well as in Sermon 34 in the Wyclif Society edition of the *Sermones*. Parts of this entire document, then, appear in three of Wyclif's works. Aside from its value in articulating Wyclif's eucharistic theology in a relatively brief manner, then, what follows illustrates the problem lying at the base of providing a firm date for any of Wyclif's writings. Since he was actively engaged in reworking earlier works while in Lutterworth, we must conclude that any work we examine, whether a title associated with his earlier days or one written during his final years, has been subjected to his editorial hand.

Text of the *Confessio*

I have often confessed and acknowledge that numerically the same body of Christ that was assumed from the Virgin, that suffered on the cross, that [lay] dead in the tomb during the holy triduum, that rose on the third day, that ascended into heaven after forty days, and that sits forever on the right hand of God the Father, this same, I say, the same body and the same substance is truly and really the sacramental bread or consecrated host that the faithful perceive in the hands of the priest. This was established because Christ, who cannot lie, asserts as much. I do not dare to say, though, that the body of Christ is essentially, substantially, corporeally, or identically this bread. Just as the body of Christ was extended, this bread [is], but the same body is not extensionally or dimensionally this bread.

Indeed, we believe that the way of being of the body of Christ in the consecrated host is threefold, namely, virtually, spiritually, and sacramentally. It is virtual by which He does the good throughout all His kingdom, according to the goodness of nature or of grace. The spiritual mode of being, though, is that by which the body of Christ is in the Eucharist and holy through grace. And the third way of being is sacramental, by which the body of Christ is singularly in the consecrated host. And just as the second way precedes the first, so the third precedes the second, because it is impossible for the foreknown, lacking faith according to the present justice, to obtain. He who believes, either consumes or one does not consume, as one chews as Augustine says in Homily 25 on John.[1] And this mode of spiritual being is more true in the soul. Indeed, it is more true and more real than the first way of being, or according to a part of the second way of being in the consecrated host, since it is a per se cause of this kind (of being in the consecrated host), either efficient or final, and a per se cause is a greater and more true being in its causation.

The mode of being by which the body of Christ is in the consecrated host is a true and real way, since the Author who cannot lie said, "This is my body," and left to his priests the power of doing similarly. This is completely gathered from Scripture. Thus Christ is in a more special way in this sacrament than in the others, since He is at the same time the truth and figured in this; however, He is not this way in the other sacraments.

And so this miraculous way of sacramental being is evident. Worshippers of signs do not know how to establish that their sacrament is really the body of Christ.

But beyond these three ways of being of the body of Christ, three other ways should be given, more real and true, which the body of Christ properly has in heaven, namely the modes of substantial, corporeal, and dimensional being. And many, not understanding other modes of being of material substance beyond these, are greatly indisposed to conceiving the mystery of the Eucharist and the subtlety of Scripture. So I say to them that the two prior ways coincide, unless substantial being is attendant upon the body of Christ insofar as [it is] substance, and corporeal being is attendant upon the body of Christ insofar as [it is] a body. The mode of dimensional being, however, follows upon the two prior, just as a passion [follows upon the being of] a subject. And any of these three ways will be more real, and [are] causes more prior than the earlier ones. The body of Christ is in the sacrament in none of these three modes, but in heaven, because otherwise the body of Christ would be seven feet high in the host. So just as the body of Christ is this host, so it is substantially, corporeally, and dimensionally the same, regarding the host according to its nature, as was said above, and not regarding the body of Christ according to its nature. And so it is conceded that just as the body of Christ is corporeal substance in the consecrated host, so it is in the host in the third way, according to the reason by which it is this host, but not according to the reason by which it is the body of Christ. And so it is conceded that the body of Christ is varied inasmuch as how much it is here, since it is in any quantitative part of this host, and yet it is not quantified by any quantity of this kind, and so it is variably great in the diverse parts of this host, but not formally great in itself, in some other such magnitude.

But many grumble beyond this, that it follows from this reasoning that the body of Christ would not be in the Eucharist in any way other than being a sign, as He is in the image of a crucifix.[2] Here the faithful say that, the body of Christ is not in heaven or in the assumed humanity in a different way than in a sign, because then He would be in a different way here than in some sign, and since either of these are signs, He would be in a different way here than He would be there. Yet they say that although the body of Christ is not otherwise in a sacrament than He is in a sign, He is, nevertheless, here in a different way than the way He is in a sign. For the sacrament, insofar as it is in this way, is a sign, and indeed humanity is a sign, since in Luke 2:34 it is said that "He is given for the falling and rising of many, and in His sign is He opposed."

And the second part of the conclusion is clear because the way of being a sign of the body of Christ is one thing, and the way of true and real being by the power of the words of our Lord Jesus Christ is another. It is conceded that these two ways are conjoined inseparably. Yet this infinite sign is more present than the sign of the body of Christ in the Old Law, or the images in the New Law, since it is at the same time the truth and a figure.

Moreover, I understand what I have said in this matter according to the logic of Scripture, and indeed, according to the logic of the ancient doctors and the decrees of the Roman church, according to which I declare myself prudently to have spoken. It is not right, though, to cause a scandal in the whole Roman church when the bread and wine are said to be, after consecration, the body and blood of Jesus Christ, and, when not impeded by the glossators' error, this faith remains constant in the church, especially among the laity. Since the faithful do not desire corporeally to eat the body of Christ, but spiritually, it is clear that the All-Knowing prepared this spiritual way of the being of His body in the host according to which He should be eaten by the faithful. Any other mode of being, since it would be superfluous, He has excluded.

So those without faith murmur, either with those who have cast [this teaching] away from them, saying "This teaching is hard," when the body of Christ would be corporeally eaten, or with those legal observers of the Old Law, who do not imagine there to be a more immediate degree or mode of being of Christ in the sign of the Eucharist than there was in the Old Law, or than there is in the humanly instituted signs. And they imagine that an accident can be made of the body Christ, and that Christ would better and more plainly have said, "This accident without a subject signifies my body." Both of these sects are, through their faithlessness, the poorer from their ignorance in the gradations of signs.

So we hold that, by the power of Christ's words, the bread becomes miraculously the body of Christ, beyond the possibility of a humanly instituted sign. Nevertheless, this unity, whether a union or a joining, does not achieve the identical, numerical, or hypostatic unity, but it is believed that it would be unmediated after this, and so the corporeal accidents of the body of Christ, such as quantity, the corporeal quality of the body of Christ do not appear to be multiplied concomitantly to the body of Christ in the host, and through this, no other respective accidents which are based in this, because all of these accidents have already gone on to be corporeal with their subject, wherever they were. So that if here is "seven feet tall," or "colour," or "corporeal glory of the Lord," then it is here that the body of Christ is seven feet tall, coloured, and corporeally glorified, and so Christ has corporeal existence here. Since this is false, such a multiplication of accidents concomitant to the body of Christ was denied, according to material conditions in the consecrated host.

The quantitative parts of the body of Christ have a spiritual being in the host, indeed they have the same sacramental being, since, in a certain way, they are any quantitative part of this host. And the soul of Christ is much more greatly multiplied through the host, according to a certain spiritual being, than is that being that the body of Christ has in heaven. And the cause of this multiplication of the soul of Christ is that it is more foundational in the person of the Word than is His body. The immaterial qualities which have the soul of Christ as a subject are multiplied with it in the host, such as knowledge, justice, and the other powers of the soul of Christ, which do not require a preexisting body, wherever they have been. These same powers were with Him, because with His spirit, in Hell. So just as Christ is powerful throughout the entire host, so the power of Christ is throughout it. So the author of *On the Divine Office*[3] believes that because of the spiritual body of Christ in the host, there is a concomitance of the angels. Because this oblation can be complicated by defects in the power of faith, and of the words of the priest, many of the religious adore this host conditionally, and they are unmistakenly at rest in the body of Christ, which is substantially, and ineffably, raised up, and is walking in heaven.

But the ignorant continue to grumble, asking how the body is this holy bread, since it is not [holy] according to substance or nature. But it is right for them to learn about the incarnation, how two substances or natures, very distinct from one another, are the same suppositum, and yet are not the same, because both of them are Christ, and then they can ascend, by a posteriori reasoning, to cognizing this miraculous union; conserving both natures, not made identical, in the Word of God. But it is right that they bear in mind a gradation of signs, and put away the baseless blasphemy of the miraculous coming-into-being of accidents, and believe the power of the words of Christ, and then they can know how this bread is truly, miraculously, really, and powerfully, and sacramentally the body of Christ. But many are not contented by this way, and demand that this bread, or at least through this bread, is substantially and corporeally the body of

Christ. So they want to eat Christ with the zeal of blasphemers, but they cannot.

There is a witness for this in Hugh of St. Victor, *On the Sacraments* II, 8.7, "In whatever way this species is distinguished, the thing or substance of which is not believed to be here; so the thing is believed truly and substantially to be here present, the species of which is not distinct." Regarding this doctor, it is clear what he subtly mixes into the above-said Catholic reasoning. He wants [to argue] that the species are perceived sensibly here, and that these same species are essentially bread and wine, which are distinguished, although through the accidents [alone]. So he often calls them bread and wine, the which are usually foods, and principally the substance of food, as is clear in the chapter mentioned, and in those following. He says that the same bread having the substance by which it is perceived, is not here distinguished, since it is the body of Christ.

But for this adverb, "substantially," it should be known that whenever it is taken simply for the mode of substance, [it is] such that the same thing would be the body of Christ present there substantially, and being there in the substantial way. And this is how Hugh spoke. In due time, he adds "reduplicative" by reason of body, insofar as [it is] such a substance. And so I properly understand this adverb in this way. So in the same chapter it is said that, we take Christ at the altar corporeally, according to the power of the body and blood of Christ. It is fitting that it be understood that we spiritually take the body of Christ at the altar. And this is the true mode of the body, although it is not a mode in which "body" is understood as body, because [in] John 6:63, Christ says, "[It is the spirit that gives life;] the flesh is useless," since He is brought forth neither by corporeal assumption nor by the corporeal eating of the body of the Lord. For it is taken invisibly insofar as the form of His body, as the doctor [Hugh] says in chapter 3 of the same work, but visibly insofar as the substance of the sacrament. So such equivocation was made adverbially, for the declaration of the excellence of the Eucharist beyond the figure of the Old Law. Our words are appropriate because otherwise it would be right to concede that to be substantially would be to be accidentally, and to be corporeally would be to be spiritually, and to be carnally would be to be virtually, and to be dimensively would be to be multiplicatively, and ways of making distinction would cease.

So, then, it is conceded that the body of Christ is held in symbol, or in the host, and it is perceived; and yet it is not moved thus, because [it is] not according to the nature of the body of Christ or insofar as [it is] the same body; thus it is conceded that the body of Christ is in the host in the accidental mode of substance, because the spiritual way and the sacramental presupposing three other ways [are] more real ways for the same body [to] exist causatively. So it was not in the figure of the Old Law, nor [was it] in the sign of our laws humanly instituted. And so before the fact, the ways can be distinguished by which [the body of Christ] is in heaven, and after the fact [the ways] by which it is in the sacrament.

So we differ in three ways from the sect of signs.

First, we hold that the venerable sacrament of the altar is bread and wine in nature, but the body and blood of Christ sacramentally. But the opposing sect imagines the same sacrament to be unknown accidents without substantial subject.

And [second,] from this erroneous root a wide variety of errors grows. For our sect adores the sacrament not as the substance of bread and wine, but as the body and blood of Christ. But the sect of the cult of accidents, as I believe, adores this sacrament not as it is accidents without a subject, but as it is the sacramental sign of the body and blood of Christ. The signs of their cult show that they adore this sacrament, since they adore the cross and other images of the church, which have less a reason for adoration than does this venerable sacrament. For God is more really in any created substance and more substantially, than the body of Christ is in the consecrated host. So unless the same makes His body by power of the words of Christ, there is no reason for such excellence of adoring.

Third, our sect would take up the arguments of our adversaries through the detection of equivocation and of other fallacies, so that some things are said of the sacrament as it is bread, and others speak of it not as identical with the body of Christ, but sacramentally. But the sects of our adversaries introduce useless difficulties, imagining miracles about the operations of accidents.

For our reasoning there is the definition of the Highest Judge [*Summa Judicis* from *Decreta Summi Pontificis* V], our Lord Jesus Christ, who at table on the night he was betrayed, took bread in His hands, blessed it and broke it, and instructed that they eat of it, saying, "This is my body." When the bread had been indicated, which He had referred to with the demonstrative pronoun ["this"], then, according to He who does not lie, the complete rest of the proposition signifies that the same is His body. So it is manifest from the authority and the words of Christ that this bread was and is sacramentally His body.

Seven witnesses are added onto this to testify to the judgment of the church about this reasoning.[4]

The first is the Blessed Ignatius, contemporaneous to the apostles, who from them and with them received the sense from the Lord. And Lincolniensis cites him in *On the Ecclesiastical Hierarchy* 3. "The sacrament," he says, "or the Eucharist is the body of Christ."

The second witness is the Blessed Cyprianus in his letter of the body of Christ. "Taking the cup on the day of the passion, He blessed it and gave it to His disciples, saying, 'Take and drink of this all of you, this is the blood of the new covenant, which is spilled for many for the remission of sins. Verily I say to you, I will not drink again of this fruit of the vine until the day when I drink it new with you in my Father's kingdom.'" "By which in part," says the saint, "we have discovered the mixed chalice to have been what He offered, and the wine to have been what He called His blood."

The third witness is Blessed Ambrose in his book on the sacraments, and he is placed in the canon on *Consecration*, d.2, "The bread is on the altar." "What the bread was," he said, "before the consecration, the same is the body of Christ after the consecration."

The fourth witness is Blessed Augustine in a certain sermon explaining Luke 24:35, "They knew Him in the breaking of the bread." "Not all bread," he said, "but in taking the bread with the blessing of Christ was it the body of Christ." And this is held in the canon mentioned above.

The fifth witness is the Blessed Jerome in the letter to Elvidam. "We understand the bread which the Lord broke and gave to His disciples to be the body of our Lord Saviour, Himself saying to them, 'Take and eat, this is my body.'"

The sixth witness is the decretum of the Roman church in which Nicholas II, with 114 bishops, dictated prudently under right reasoning, which was taken for the entire church, that the bread and wine that are placed on the altar are, after consecration, not only sacramentally but truly the body and blood of our Lord Jesus Christ, as is clear in the canon given above.

The seventh witness is the use of the church, in the canon according to which the Mass is held, [which] says that this oblation becomes for us the body and blood of our Lord Jesus Christ. This oblation the church calls earthly substance, just as is clear in the *secreto mediae* of the mass of the nativity of the Lord.

The glossators poison these witnesses, so that they say tacitly all such words of the saints ought [to] be understood through what is contrary to them, and so [should] in the end be denied, with Scripture. The faithful should consider whether it is sound to make heresy, or to cause scandal, in this way, of these witnesses and many similar. He should consider secondly how he could extend honor to the body of Christ, or [how he could direct] the devotion of the people, with this same most worthy body being accidents without subject, which Augustine says is not able to be, or if it is, it is one nothing or something most abject in its nature. Then, I say, Augustine would be largely consonant with a heretic, when he writes in Epistle XIV to Boniface of the faith of the Church: "If a sacrament did not have a certain similitude to the things of which they are sacraments, there would not be any sacraments. They take their names from these similitudes and from the fullness of strength in these things. Just as according to a certain sacramental way the body of Christ is corporeally Christ, and the sacrament of the blood is Christ's blood."[5] Here it is plain that it is said of the sacrament that the accidents are imagined without a subject. But in what, I ask, is its similitude to the body of Christ? Really the fruit of this madness would be to blaspheme God, to bring scandal to the saints, and to ridicule the church through lies about accidents. To this, certain testimonies of the saints are subverted by glossators, so that by thinking in an equivocal sense, anything that is said, even scripturally, is not shameless to the faith.

Hilary writes, as is repeated in *On Consecration* d.2, "The body of Christ which is taken on the altar is the figure, while it appears bread and wine externally, the truth is believed on the inside, with the body and blood of Christ." See how plainly this sacrament is the bread and wine, as in the decretum *Ego Berengarius*. So for the uncovering of equivocations in this matter, it is written according to Jerome, "Of this particular host, through which a commemoration of Christ is miraculously made, one may eat" [Jerome's commentary *On Leviticus*]. Here it is plain that what is discussed is corporeal eating, and he distinguishes between these two hosts according to their substances or natures; granted that this bread would be according to another reason as sacramentally the same body as Jerome says in his letter to Elvidam, as listed above.

And it is clear how difficult the cultivators of signs are in this matter of heresy, not to say because they impose a heresy upon the faithful when they elucidate this faith; and an accusation of heresy obligates a punishment in retaliation, because they deny and falsify our Lord Jesus Christ. For we ought [to] believe nothing according to faith in the gospel of Jesus Christ if He did not assert that the bread that He held in His hand and broke was

His body, just as Augustine says about Psalm 66, "If I were to have said anything, I do not will that you believe it thereby, but if Christ speaks, woe to he who does not believe." Nor should we believe something to be the sense of the Gospels, if it is not so.

So woe to the adulterous generation, who believes more the testimony of Innocent or Raymond, than the sense of the Gospels taken from the witnesses just given. This would indeed bring scandal to them, and impose the heresy through the perversion of Scripture. Particularly again, woe to the perverse mouth of the apostate accumulating lies about the Roman church, who imagines that the later church has corrected the faith of the early church through opposing it, that this sacrament would be accident without a subject, and not true bread and wine, as the Gospels say with the decretum. For by Augustine's witness, priests cannot confect such accidents without a subject. And yet the priests of Baal prize this above all, lying without a doubt, just as they have been instructed by their father, about the consecration of accidents, so that they count other masses to have been heard unworthily, or those who dissent from their position to be unfit for a position anywhere.

But I believe that, in the end, the truth will overcome them.[6]

From the understanding that every adverb determines its verb in comparison to the subject, with this proposition "The body of Christ is substantially in the sacrament of the altar," this sense should be held, i.e., the body of Christ is in the sacrament of the altar in substantial mode. But it remains that it is not there in an incorporeal, substantial mode, therefore it is there in a corporeal, substantial mode, and hence, dimensively. Again, the body of Christ is not otherwise in the sacrament of the altar than it is [when] eaten by the faithful; but it is not eaten by the faithful substantially, therefore it is not in the sacrament of the altar substantially. The minor is clear from the blessed Augustine and is posited in the decretal, where it says this, "The body of Christ may not be ground down by faithful teeth." Again, Christ is not in the sacrament of the altar in some way other than the way He is there sacramentally. But nothing being Christ is essentially its sacramental being, therefore Christ is not in the sacrament of the altar essentially. The minor is clear, that He is only there sacramentally, just as is clear through the exponents, therefore, etc. Again, thus truly is Christ in the soul of the just in the same way as He is in the sacrament of the altar, but He is not in the soul of the just essentially substantially. Therefore He is not in the sacrament of the altar, and this can be proven as such with Anselm. And the major is proven [in that] where Christ has perfect and real being, there He is perfectly and really, but in the soul of the just He has a being more perfect and real than in the sacrament of the altar, therefore, etc. And many doubt what is denoted by the word "this" when "this is my body" is said.

A certain decretist as ordinary glossator [John of God] holds that nothing is denoted by the name "this" since the same and the whole oration is taken materially just as spoken by Christ; which if it were true in signifying everything the whole oration and the good subject it denotes, it would indicate nothing on the inside. How would these words of Christ be an effective sacrament of the altar in us, or bread miraculously convertible?

Thus others say that through this pronoun is denoted the body absolutely simply, but these fools soil the faith, since according to them Christ would not intend more save that His body is His body, which was true beginning with His birth. Thus the reasoning of the blessed Jerome in his letter to Hedibiam was held, "We should hear the bread which the Lord broke and gave to His disciples to eat to be the body of the Lord Savior, Himself saying, 'This is my body.'" Where it is clear that this saint, who more understood the sense of Scripture than all the lying postillators from the time of Innocent III to today, acknowledges as a certitude of the faith that in this proposition, bread is denoted sacramentally as substance rather than Christ, just as its speaker had accepted it in His hands before, and from this repeatedly the Apostle in this treatise chapters 10 and 11 pronounces this sacrament to be bread. And the same is clear in the four evangelists (Luke 24 and Acts 2). Nor do I doubt but that the authors of Scripture understood the bread to be not a nothing, or unknown accidents, but the true bread which the priest transubstantiates by virtue of the sacramental words into the body of the Lord; and truly this holy doctor [Jerome] with others in the age of Christ clearly and deeply perceives the sense of Scripture, and especially the propositions of the faith, better than every pope or postillator succeeding from the time in which the devil was loosed. This same saint manifestly says that this bread that the priest takes in consecrating hands is the body of the Lord; which proves through this that He who cannot lie says, "This is my body" when without doubt he denotes this bread. But from the time in which the Church was divided through the introduction of apostasy, the faith about the sacrament of the Eucharist was divided, indicating an ulterior division between popes and such and the simple religion of the Christian, since nevertheless the Apostle says that there should be one faith. But all the friars or others from private religions do not know what is denoted by the pronoun, or what in its nature would be the perceptible sacrament discernible to the eye, secondly divided into three parts, and third devoured by chewing teeth. The instant one of the faithful asks this question of the satraps, they flee in ignorance, insanely simulating weight with extensive subterfuge. He cannot convince the faithful that this is the faith before he could disclose this matter of the faith. I often have asked the friars in what sense the sacrament that is frequently called bread should be understood, but they have not dared to express their position, as if they were innocents not knowing the faith.

But these ignorant ones argue against our reasonings and the sense of the Lord first, paralogistically, which they call an expository syllogism, claiming that they prove that the entire body of Christ, united and in each individual part, may cruelly be broken by us, decay, and be devoured by vile beasts, because this bread has been treated thus by many, and this bread according to us is the body of Christ, therefore the body of Christ is thus treated.

But, as I have often said, these ignorant people should first learn by logic and the faith of the Church how this does not follow expositorily if this divine nature is communicated to these three supposits, and thus of a thousand examples in the matter of the Trinity. The second example is in the matter of Incarnation, where it does not follow: This Christ is the assumed humanity, and this Christ is deity, therefore the assumed humanity is deity; indeed, through this same argument they argue and hold with other infidels that deity had been laid open and died, because Christ, who is this deity, underwent this. The third example is in the matter of universals, through which an example of the ignorant faith is brought into service in the matter: if A is the common man [i.e., humanity], it is not right if this A were Socrates and this same A [because] since the common man is every man, that the pope would be Socrates. Therefore, as they say reasoning properly, only when the middle term [i.e., humanity] exists, is this necessitated through the force of an expository syllogism for the extreme terms [i.e., Socrates and the pope], of which one is as such conjoined through the common, because this way, if Socrates dies, and he is as such the human species, then the whole species dies. The minor is false, since Socrates is an individual according to his personal propriety; but a man is the human species according to the commonality that is communicated to any individual of the species, and you will run into such wasteful reasoning whenever such a paralogism is called expository syllogism.

So some ignoramuses, because of fear of similitude, deny the reasoning about the common things [i.e., universals]. But they cannot escape their reasons, and neither can they turn away from the common nature of the three divine persons, nor from the disparate communion in the person of the nature of the Word. So a certain secular scholar was present at a perfidious Council in which his adversary, along with his puppies, decided through Scripture that [the scholar] had damned himself [by saying] that after the consecration the substance of the bread remained, but by arguing thus and not receiving a response, the secular disagreed with their perfidy. The most general genus of substance remains there, he said, and the same genus is in any substance, and thus the substance of the bread, unless everything of the bread were to be destroyed, and so the substance of the bread remains after consecration. If the church were to acknowledge that since Christ is our substance united in heaven, not to say the most general genus but because in species and nature human, with which in His nature He is everyman in common with every individual human being.

Such an innocent would not forsake logic so much as syllogisms and consequences, lest they be seduced by children, and so faithlessly might seduce the Christian people. Just as expository paralogism is absent in the three examples given, thus it is absent in this matter: If one will have had this sacramental bread for himself, and this bread is the body of the Lord, then he has the body of the Lord for himself. The faithful should be far indeed from these heretics who think that in any sacrament of the altar they see the body of the Lord with corporeal eyes, that a mouse eats the body of Christ, or that they might tear apart and break the body of Christ with their fingers, or with the grinding of their teeth. Although such conclusions will have been approved in bulls or letters from the Roman curia, they ought to be denied. And the ignorant who speak in syllogistic manner and figure with right reasoning ought to be taken in the same way: All sacramental bread is round, they say, and has a figure and other such accidents, the whole sacramental bread is the whole body of Christ, therefore the whole body of Christ has such accidents. And the multiplication of the aforesaid inconveniences follows.

But these innocents unknowingly syllogize fraudulently about these three terms: the friar, the liar, and the mendicant think syllogistically in the three matters mentioned. It does not follow: The whole Christ is the divine nature, the whole humanity is in Christ, therefore the whole humanity in Christ is the divine nature, and similarly of other such syllogisms.

But third a certain puppy argues principally in this manner: If the sacrament of the altar were material bread, it follows, that every viator would be thus perfected in his nature, such that the final form of any man would be accidentally more perfect; the final form of this sacrament would be accidental, since the same would be a sacrament accidentally. But the fox has often grumbled about this argument, first about the conclusion of the first proposition, since every dog contrary to the faith of the sacrament perceives that the same would be more imperfect in its nature than what could be allotted to another substance. In this way, then, this puppy holds as unsuitable that a man in whose grace the sacrament is eaten would be more perfect than the sacrament on its own. I am astounded at the form of this dog's argument. For if this argument were to describe the faith, then any created substance would be more imperfect than what might be allotted to another.

Fourth, it is not created substance, although it were informed with accidents. In dismissing these arguments I concede that this sacrament would be in its nature more imperfect than the paschal lamb prefigured in the old testament, but it is sacramentally far more perfect, because [it is the] created body of Christ. And I wish that the faithful, or the heretical if they dare, would place their faith on the quiddity of this venerable sacrament. Nor do I doubt but that everyone pertinaciously opposed to this reasoning are the heretics, whether pope, or bishop, or member of a private religion. For according to the saints in the age of Christ, and especially in the ancient faith preserving the laity, this sacrament is the body of Christ in the form of bread. But these obtusely defend the contrary, so according to the definition of heresy, these are manifestly heretics, which if they will have denied Holy Scripture to assert this, they fall apart through the testimony of the saints and arguments of the watchful about how the words of Truth that cannot lie should be understood: "This is my body." They ought not believe the false fables of the false brothers, that this sacrament is nothing or accidents, but (as the Scripture faith often says) the substance of true bread. Just as Christ is two natures, namely humanity and divinity united in [one] person, such that any of these is the person of Christ, so in the same manner this sacrament is true bread naturally and sacramentally the body of Christ. And in this union of titles the hypostatic union is most fully. It is right, though, for the faithful theologian to know triple predication for detecting sophistic arguments of the devil in this matter, namely formal predication, essential predication, and habitual predication. Whoever is ignorant of these three [should be] securely forewarned against [the sophistic arguments], and he will not know how this bread is truly the body of Christ; not according to predication of identity, or identically, but sacramentally and figuratively is this bread the body of the Lord; just as according to Augustine man truly and really, but figuratively eats the body of Christ.

And through this knowledge of triple predication can the faithful defend the manner in which the truth of this matter should be enclosed in the form of the words, as well follows in the expository syllogisms aforementioned that the body of Christ is that which is broken, that it decays and is chewed by teeth, and yet the body of Christ does not formally have itself so, as in a like manner of speaking it is in the threefold example given above. And in the same way the syllogism in the second conclusion has been formed in the essential predication that follows.

Secondly the faithful should know how it should be conceded that the body is Christ is shown in the sacrament, because the bread is shown, and yet neither He nor any part of Him is shown, but He has spiritual being that is multiplied there as the soul; nor do I dare say that the bread or any part of it is the head of Christ or any other of His parts, although probably it can be said that any quantitative part of this bread is truly the body of Christ and since any part of this host would be spiritually according to the concomitance of any of His parts.

Third the faithful should stop up the cases of the heretics when they argue through place from similitude, and through the same, "the paschal lamb" and any figure or term signifying being should be conceded to be the same as "the body of Christ" in the Eucharist. In doing so, it would be good in so arguing first to establish that the Word which cannot lie will have said such a thing to be His body, as He said of the sacramental bread, that if Christ had conceded this, then I will so concede. It plays no part that our imposition or imagination of signs has as much efficiency as the word of Truth has, who says "this was done for all"; I concede, though that Christ is "a lion," "a worm," and "a calf" with similar figurative predications; and that in predications of this type there are many degrees of which the final evidence is this: the Scriptures say it. And from this I do not wish to be wasteful in terms beyond learned conversation, in defining that this sacrament is material bread, the substance of bread, or any other name that comes up, with which one will be able to cause trouble for the church beyond the faith of Scripture. Many are the truths which can be said scholastically and especially with catholicity. The faith of Scripture, though, says that the same sacrament is the bread that is broken, and it is certain that this bread is not identical to the body of Christ, nor [is it] the accidents obscure to the faithful, nor [is it] nothing. And so I deny that this bread in its nature is prior [to] the bread a horse might eat, nor to any other material substance as poison. So in such arguments I look closely at heretics seeking the way of Christ from these things that they themselves perceive of the quiddity and the passions of this venerable sacrament.

Returning to the text, [which is] often put forth as the reasoning of Christ alluding to our reasoning, where He says, "Do this in remembrance of me." For Christ wished the bread and wine to be sacramentally consumed as a memorial for His faithful. In doing this, the text says the chalice there is "a new testament" in the blood of Christ [which] is fully indicated through predication of *habitus*, since the new testament has been understood to be identical with neither the chalice nor the wine it contains. It is treachery to disbelieve that the Word of God, who is eternal wisdom, alternates with His words indifferently in this, but productively and with comprehensive reasoning. He does not say this wine is my blood, but "this cup is the new testament" in my blood, where it is clear that according to metonymy He understands through this chalice, the wine to be contained in the chalice, and through this is taught that in the prior proposition, "this is my body," is uniformly demonstrated through the pronoun that sacrament, since there would not be an imaginable reason why in the following proposition "this cup is the new testament" the liquor perceptibly contained in the cup is demonstrated, but that through the same in the prior proposition would be demonstrated the bread that He holds in His hands.

Second it is known how Christ through the second word says in different ways "this cup" not "to be" His blood but "a new testament in His blood," so that thus He would teach His church such predication to be habitual, and not identical. Thus the postillators, who say that from the order of words before and after it is clear that this is not figurative locution without foundation, in fact deceive themselves and their followers.

But third it is clear that, just as the sprinkling of the blood of a calf remotely figured the confirmation of the old testament, thus the wine of this cup figures the nearness of the new testament, and it is in accordance with the realization of the testament itself, and is not contradictory. Indeed the Holy Spirit at once says both, although differently and equivocally, that "This is the cup of my blood of the new and eternal testament," and

"This cup is the new testament" in my blood, because on both sides, the same reasoning is thus expressed.

And a grammarian would be ashamed by the baseless rudeness with which they say that this pronoun "this" refers only to an insensible thing. For the Holy Spirit shows in the grammar a thing commonly perceptible, as is clear in this proposition from the end of Ecclesiastes, "Fear God and keep His commandment, this is all man" [Ecclesiastes 12:13]. And this at the end of Mark, "And these signs shall follow them that believe" [Mark 16:17]. "For as often," it says, "as you shall eat this bread and drink this cup, you shall show the death of the Lord, until He comes" [1 Corinthians 11:26]. A certain body is to that end made sacramental and whence to the day of judgment the viator may memorialize the death of the Lord. But from this to arriving at clear knowledge of the presence of the body of Christ in accidents through experience would be a waste of this kind of sacrament. Thus, "Whoever will have eaten the bread and drunk this cup of the Lord unworthily will be answerable for the body and blood of the Lord" [perhaps a variant of 1 Corinthians 11:27], for just as a lying traitor impiously kissing, he simulates the sacramental and fruitful memory, and like another Judas, he lies beneath the cup pointlessly pretending.

For "let a man prove himself" [1 Corinthians 11:28] and thus the world may be saved from crime, and in the right intention to fruitful remembering through these parts of the Lord, as much in the body as in the soul. "He who eats and drinks unworthily, eats and drinks in judgment of himself" [1 Corinthians 11:29] since falsity presents an appearance contrary to the judgment of the truth; in which way, therefore, "he discerns," that is, in distinguishing in his memory the end from which he judges with the reason of which such a corporeal meal is eaten; the end of which God would intend of such thoughtless judgment of a traitor of this kind has been frustrated. If, on the other hand, without such eating a man would drink the fruitful memory from the body and blood of Christ, he spiritually eats the body of Christ and drinks His blood [as] well. And by this quadruple recitation by which the sacrament is said to be "bread" is the faithful awakened to defending the reasoning and words of Paul, even though he had been baselessly dreaming during the words and the extraneous reasoning. What, then, would Saint Paul understand by bread and wine?

But if it is objected that according to this reasoning the sacrament is violated, it may be said to the adversary of the faith that they themselves object even as they are idolatrously raising up perceptible creatures in their faithless worship of God; thus indeed the ignorant carry on, who, unaware of the proper voices, lack understanding of what the sacrament is. But they know, just as they falsely imagine, that it [the sacrament] would be more imperfect than any other material substance signified, and through this they seduce the people that this sacrament is not honorable in its nature, but deserves honor because it is really, if imperceptibly, the body of Christ. We, however, say that this sacrament is honorable in its nature and much less in its nature, but the same really is, as the faithful people believe, the body of Christ. The faithful are stimulated in their faith by this faithless reasoning, for they believe in concord, and they adore in effect, this sensible thing just as they would Christ, and by lifting up some little piece of wood there is in it the blessed Trinity, since necessarily it would be both, and consequently a more perfect body of Christ, in which indeed there is commonly the same body of Christ, since it has itself spiritually in any part of His kingdom. By this the adversary of the faith would dishonor through evil ignorance the body of Christ inasmuch as it is in the sacrament. And thus this little treatise is ended.

NOTES

CHAPTER I

1. William James, *The Varieties of Religious Experience* (Viking Penguin, 1982), "Lecture I: Religion and Neurology," 24.

2. See H. B. Workman, *John Wyclif: A Study of the English Medieval Church* (Oxford, 1926), 2 vols., which remains the fullest biography. More recently, Gillian Evans, *John Wyclif: Myth and Reality* (Lion Hudson, 2005), provides an accurate and useful biographical study. I am indebted to Anne Hudson for providing me with her recent research on Wyclif's early years, which appears in her entry on Wyclif for the *New Dictionary of National Biography*, and to Stella Wilks, for providing me with her late husband's papers, from which I have mined a wealth of information. For an analysis of Wyclif's later years of contention with ecclesiastical authority, see Joseph Dahmus, *The Prosecution of John Wyclyf* (New Haven, Conn., 1952), and Andrew Larsen, "John Wyclif, c.1331–1384," in Levy, 2006; for examination of his Oxford experiences, see J. A. Robson, *Wyclif and the Oxford Schools* (Cambridge, 1966). The fullest contemporary chronicle of Wyclif's later career is *Fasciculi Zizianorum Magistri Johannis Wyclif*, ed. W. W. Shirley (London, 1858) (hereafter *FZ*).

3. Thoresby's Latin catechism and Gaytrick's Middle English versification of it are published in *The Lay Folk's Catechism*, ed. T. F. Simon and H. E. Nolloth, *EETS*, o.s. 118 (London, 1901), along with a later Wycliffite version of the same catechism and corresponding canons from the Lambeth Council of 1281.

4. For Wyclif's Oxford education, see Robson 1966 and Evans 2005. See also William Courtenay, *Schools and Scholars in Fourteenth Century England* (Princeton, N.J., 1987), for a complete overview of the intellectual milieu in which Wyclif participated.

5. For accounts of Wittgenstein's behavior in arguments with Karl Popper, see John Eidinow and David Edmonds, *Wittgenstein's Poker* (New York, 2005).

6. See Anne Hudson, "Cross-Referencing in Wyclif's Latin Works," in *The Medieval Church: University, Heresy, and the Religious Life*, ed. Peter Biller and Barrie Dobson (1999), 193–216; "The Development of Wyclif's *Summa Theologie*," in *John Wyclif: Logica, Politica, Teologia*, ed. Mariateresa Fumagalli and Stefano Simoneta (Florence, 2003), 57–70. I rely on the dating provided by S. H. Thomson and W. R. Thomson in the latter's *The Latin Writings of John Wyclyf* (Toronto, 1983), an indispensable guide to Wyclif's voluminous philosophical, theological, and polemical writings.

7. For a thorough overview of the development of logic from the twelfth century onward, see Norman Kretzman, Anthony Kenny, and Jan Pinborg, eds., *The Cambridge History of Later Medieval Philosophy* (Cambridge, 1982), 99–383 (hereafter *CHLMP*). See also Alexander Broadie, *Introduction to Medieval Logic* (Oxford, 1993).

8. *Tractatus de Logica*, I, 1.2–10. Translation by Norman Kretzman in his "Continua, Indivisibles, and Change," in Anthony Kenny, ed., *Wyclif in His Times* (Oxford, 1986), 42.

9. For Ockham's ideas on the ontological status of concepts, particularly on his progression from concepts having *esse objectiva* to having *esse subjectiva*, see Marilyn McCord Adams, *William Ockham* (Notre Dame, Ind., 1987), 73–107.

10. *On Universals*, trans. A. Kenny (Oxford, 1985), chap. 3, 22.162–165.

11. Robson convincingly argues for this in his study of the *Summa de Ente* (Cambridge, 1966), see 128–135. For an overview of the extant manuscripts of the treatises of this *Summa*, see W. Thomson 1983.

12. *DCH*, chap. 1, esp. 2.20–3.22; see also *De Ente Predicamentali*, chap. 7, 66. 17–67.14; and the causal relation extant between God's *dominium* over universals and created substance and the *dominium* given to mankind as described in *DD, De Statu Innocencie*, and *DCD*.

13. Wyclif makes frequent mention of Aquinas and Scotus in these pre-1372 writings. Amusingly, he complains in *DI* (chap. 4, 51.4) that Scotus's Latin is, as far as he and many of his associates are concerned, far more difficult to understand than Augustine's. Given the inventive and inconsistent nature of Wyclif's own Latin, this is understandable, and reassuring to twenty-first-century readers for whom Latin is more foreign than it was for Wyclif.

14. See J. I. Catto, ed., *The History of the University of Oxford* (Oxford, 1984), vol. 1; Courtenay, *Schools and Scholars*; John M. Fletcher, "Inter-Faculty Disputes in Late Medieval Oxford," in *From Ockham to Wyclif, ed.* Anne Hudson and M. Wilks (Oxford, 1987), 331–342.

15. *FZ* 54–55.

16. See *FZ*. For a history of the manuscript and the identity of its compiler, see James Crompton, "*Fasciculi Zizianorum I* and *II*," *Journal of Ecclesiastical History* 12 (1962): 35–45, 155–166.

17. *DD* I.1, 1.6. W. Thompson estimates that Wyclif had begun work on this treatise in 1373.

18. For development of this tie between Wyclif's metaphysics and his *dominium* treatises, see chapter 4 below, and also my *Philosophy and Politics in the Thought of John Wyclif* (Cambridge, 2003). Earlier scholars have dismissed the possibility that this tie binds the two bodies of work, perhaps because it had been assumed that the only extant manuscripts of *DD* are incomplete.

19. See Eric Doyle, O.F.M., "William Woodford, O.F.M., His Life and Works," *Franciscan Studies* 43 (1983): 17–187; and his "William Woodford's *De Dominio Civili Clericorum* against John Wyclif," *Archivum Franciscanum Historicum* 66 (1973): 49–109. See also Jeremy Catto, "William Woodford, O.F.M. (c. 1330–c. 1397)," D.Phil. thesis, University of Oxford, 1969.

20. Quoted in Joseph Dahmus, *The Persecution of John Wyclyf* (New Haven, Conn., 1952), 46; see also *Chronicon Angliae* 180–181.

21. Wyclif's defense of the duke's actions appears as chapter 7 of *De Ecclesia*. His formal arguments supporting this defense comprise the next nine chapters,

which makes up the middle portion of a treatise otherwise devoted to theological analysis of the proposition that the church is made up of the body of the elect. Shakyl managed to keep his captive until 1383, when Parliament granted him 20,000 gold francs. Hauley's sister sued for a portion, but the suit was not resolved until 1409, after Shakyl had died of old age.

22. *Responsiones ad argumenta Radulfi Strode*, in *Opera Minora* I, 175–200. See also Wyclif's responses to Strode's criticisms of *DCD* I, 398–404, and to Strode's criticisms of Wyclif's antipapalism, 258–312. For Strode's own work, see Wallace K. Seaton, "An Edition and Translation of the Consequentiae of Ralph Strode, Fourteenth Century Logician and Friend of Geoffrey Chaucer," Ph.D. diss., University of California, Berkeley, 1973.

23. See Dahmus 1952, 141–142, for a translation of the 1384 letter.

24. There has been considerable discussion as to the proper referents of the terms "Wycliffite" and "Lollard." Some scholars hold that the former refers to the earlier, academic stage of the movement and the latter to the more widespread, social stage, but Anne Hudson has argued convincingly that the two terms should be viewed as synonymous. See Hudson, *The Premature Reformation: Wycliffite Texts and Lollard History* (Oxford, 1988), 2–4; 1986, 85–86.

25. Simon Forde, "Theological Sources Cited by Two Canons of Repton: Philip Repyngdon and John Eyton," in Wilks and Hudson 419–428, provides a good overview of Repingdon's theology.

26. See M. Jurkowski, "New Light on John Purvey," *English Historical Review* 110 (1995): 1180–1190.

27. For the twelve conclusions, see *FZ* 105–109; for Berton's condemnation and Wyclif's subsequent response, see 110–132.

28. *Confessio; FZ* 131. The references are presumably to Innocent III and Raymond of Penafort, a Dominican canonist.

29. Workman, vol. 2, 148, who quotes John Foxe's *Book of Martyrs*, vol. 3, 20. Several Victorian engravings of this scene exist, the compositions of which are obviously influenced by David's *Death of Socrates*. Wyclif's supposed quote is a reference to Psalm 118.17, "non moriar sed vivam et narrabo opera Domini."

30. Hudson 1986, 228–247.

31. *DCD* III.2, 15.5–23.

32. *De Blasphemia* 13, 190.

33. For Wyclif, the poor preachers, and the Peasants' Revolt, see Michael Wilks, "*Reformatio Regni*: Wyclif and Hus as Leaders of Religious Protest Movements," *Studies in Church History* 9 (1972): 109–130; "Wyclif and the Great Persecution," *Studies in Church History Subsidia* 10 (1994): 39–63 (both reprinted in Wilks 2000, 63–84 and 179–204). See also Hudson 1988, 60–69.

34. *FZ* 272–273; translation by Joseph Dahmus in Dahmus 1952, 93. See also Dahmus, *William Courtenay, Archbishop of Canterbury* (Pennsylvania State University, 1966).

35. *Johannis Wiclif Trialogus cum Supplemento Trialogi*, ed. Gotthard Lechler (Oxford, 1869). I expect to complete a translation of this text soon, which will take into consideration all extant manuscripts of the work.

36. *Opus Evangelicum* III, 107.19–22.

37. See Janet Coleman, *Medieval Writers and Readers, 1350–1400* (Columbia, 1981); Steven Justice, *Writing and Rebellion: England in 1381* (Berkeley, Calif., 1994); Fiona Somerset, *Clerical Discourse and Lay Audience in Late Medieval England* (Cambridge, 1998).

38. *Trialogus* IV, chap. 28. See Hudson, "Wyclif and the English Language," in Kenny 1986.

39. Hudson, *English Wycliffite Sermons*, vol. 1 (Oxford, 1983); Margaret Aston, *Lollards and Reformers* (London, 1984); Hudson, "Contributions to a History of Wycliffite Writings," in her *Lollards and Their Books* (London, 1985). The collection of sermons that Thomas Arnold published in his multivolume *Select English Works of John Wyclif* has since been reedited and published in Anne Hudson's *English Wycliffite Sermons*, vols. 1–5. The collection of writings edited by F. D. Matthew and published as *The English Works of Wyclif* by the Early English Text Society (o.s. 74; 1902) also cannot be ascribed to Wyclif with certainty.

40. *De Blasphemia*, chap. 10, 154.13–155.13. His reflections on mortality are based on Ambrose of Milan's *De Bono Mortis*.

41. David Hume, *The History of England*, vol. 2 (Philadelphia, 185). For a historiography of Wyclif, see Margaret Aston, "Wyclif's Reformation Reputation," in *Lollards and Reformers*, 243–272; also see Workman, vol. 1, 12–20. The premier study of Lollardy remains Anne Hudson's *The Premature Reformation* (Oxford, 1988); for the Hussite phenomenon, see Howard Kaminsky, *The History of the Hussite Revolution* (Berkeley, Calif., 1967). See the bibliography of the Lollard Society at http://lollardsociety.org/bibhome.html for a much more extensive listing of secondary works.

CHAPTER 2

1. See R. L. Poole's introduction to *DD*, xxi. The groundbreaking survey of the philosophy and theology of the period remains *The Cambridge History of Later Medieval Philosophy*, ed. Norman Kretzman, Anthony Kenny, and Jan Pinborg (Cambridge, 1982). Accompanying this is *The Cambridge Translations of Medieval Philosophical Texts*, a set of anthologies exemplifying

the development and breadth of later medieval thought. See volume 1, *Logic and the Philosophy of Language*, ed. Norman Kretzman and Eleonore Stump (1988); volume 2, *Ethics and Politics*, ed. A. S. McGrade, John Kilcullen, and Matthew Kempshall (2001); volume 3, *Mind and Knowledge*, ed. Robert Pasnau (2002). Volume 2 contains Kilcullen's translation of the first ten chapters of Wyclif's *DCD* I.

2. See Marilyn McCord Adams, *William Ockham* (Notre Dame, Ind., 1988), 2 vols.; Paul Vincent Spade, *A Cambridge Companion to Ockham* (Cambridge, 1999). For an overview of Oxford's "golden age," see William Courtenay, *Schools and Scholars in Fourteenth Century England* (Princeton, N.J., 1987).

3. Hester Gelber, *It Could Have Been Otherwise: Contingency and Necessity in Dominican Theology at Oxford 1300–1350* (Leiden, 2004), 313n9; reference is to Scotus's *Ordinatio* I, d.44, in *Opera Omnia*, ed. Charles Balic (Vatican City, 1963), 6, 363.17–364.10.

4. William Ockham, *Quodlibetal Questions*, trans. Alfred Freddosso (New Haven, Conn., 1991), vol. 2, 491.

5. See William Courtenay, *Capacity and Volition* (Bergamo, Italy, 1990).

6. See ibid., 265–266; also Gracia 674–675. The influence of Chatton on Wyclif deserves much fuller consideration than is possible here, where Wyclif's more immediate opponents are of interest. See Girard Etzkorn and Joseph Wey, eds., *Reportatio in I Sent. Dist. 1–9 and Dist. 10–48* (Toronto, 2002), 2 vols.

7. Adam de Wodeham, *Lectura Secunda in Librum Primum Sentatiarum*, ed. Rega Wood and Gedeon Gàl (St. Bonaventure, N.Y., 1990). "Et ideo ad variationem mediorum secundum speciem variatur actus sciendi secundum speciem, et diversae scientiae non probant formaliter eandem conclusionem per idem medium, nisi mendicando" (d.1, q.3.12, 247).

8. Ibid., vol. 2, "Et ideo nisi per fidem nobis innotuisset quod una res est tres res, credidissemus firmiter sophismata praedicta bona fuissa argumenta" (d.2, q.1.13, 25).

9. See Norman Kretzman and Barbara Ensign Kretzman, *The Sophismata of Richard Kilvington* (Cambridge, 1990); Edith Dudley Sylla, "The Oxford Calculators," in Kretzman, Kenny, and Pinborg 1982, 540–563.

10. John E. Murdoch, "*Mathesis in Philosophiam Scholasticam Introducta:* The Rise and Development of the Application of Mathematics in Fourteenth Century Philosophy and Theology," in *Arts Libéraux et Philosophie au Moyen Age* (Montreal and Paris, 1969), 215–254.

11. Curtis Wilson, *William Heytesbury: Medieval Logic and the Rise of Mathematical Physics* (Madison, Wisc., 1956); Marshall Clagett, *The Science of Mechanics in the Middle Ages* (Madison, Wisc., 1959).

12. See *Opus oxoniense* I, d.III, q.4, in *Philosophical Writings*, trans. Allan Wolter (Hackett, 1987), 97–132, esp. 106–115.

13. Philosophically, the term "nominalist" today suggests an ontology generally more sparse than the Aristotelian categories to which Ockham was committed. While Ockham believed that universals have no reality beyond the concepts we use to describe things, he also believed that there are spatiotemporal objects that exist independently of our perceptions, with properties and relations independent of our concepts. The philosophical antirealism that can be associated with contemporary nominalism is foreign to the "nominalism" of the medieval thinkers. For an overview, see D. M. Armstrong, *Universals and Scientific Realism* (Cambridge, 1978), or his *Universals: An Opinionated Introduction* (Boulder, Colo., 1989).

14. See Nicholas of Autrecourt, *The Universal Treatise*, trans. Leonard Kennedy, Richard Arnold, and Arthur Millward (Milwaukee, Wisc., 1971).

15. Leonard Kennedy, "Philosophical Scepticism in England in the Mid-Fourteenth Century," *Vivarium* 21.1 (1983): 43–44. Kennedy's survey of fourteenth-century skeptical tendencies here and in his "Late-Fourteenth-Century Philosophical Scepticism at Oxford," *Vivarium* 23.2 (1985): 124–151, are useful resources, although his *The Philosophy of Robert Holcot: A Fourteenth Century Skeptic* (Lewiston, Maine, 1993) overemphasizes the place that skepticism had in Holcot's thought. See also Paul A. Streveler, "Gregory of Rimini and the Black Monk on Sense and Reference," *Vivarium* 18.1 (1980).

16. L. L. Hammerich, *The Beginning of the Strife between Richard Fitzralph and the Mendicants* (Copenhagen, 1938), 20.74–80. See also Katherine Walsh, *A Fourteenth-Century Scholar and Primate: Richard Fitzralph of Oxford, Avignon, and Armagh* (Oxford, 1981).

17. Augustine, *On the Teacher*, II.38, trans. Peter King (Hackett, 1995), 139. See Gareth Matthews, "Knowledge and Illumination," in *The Cambridge Companion to Augustine*, ed. Eleonore Stump and Norman Kretzman (Cambridge, 2001), 171–185.

18. Gordon Leff, *Richard Fitzralph: Commentator on the Sentences* (Manchester, 1963); see also Katherine Tachau, *Vision and Certitude in the Age of Ockham* (Leiden, 1988), 236–242. I am grateful to Dr. Michael Dunne for his advice about the likelihood of Fitzralph's authoring the question discussed.

19. Kennedy 53. See Joel L. Bender's "Nicholas Aston: A Study in Oxford Thought after the Black Death," Ph.D. diss., University of Wisconsin, 1979, for a well-rounded study of this overlooked figure.

20. See Holcot's denial of the possibility of establishing God's existence through unaided reason, "non habemus ab aliquo philosopho demonstrative probatum quod aliquis angelus est, neque de deo, neque de aliquo incorporeo," 144, in J. T. Muckle, C.S.B., "*Utrum Theologia Sit Scientia:* A Quodlibetal Question of Robert Holcot, O.P.," *Mediaeval Studies* 20 (1958): 127–153.

21. *Quodlibet* 87, *Utrum haec est concedenda: Deus est Pater et Filius et Spiritus Sanctus*, in Hester Gelber, *Exploring the Boundaries of Reason: Three Questions on the Nature of God by Robert Holcot, OP* (Toronto, 1983), 34–36.

22. Robert Holcot, *Super Libros Sapientiae* (Hagenau, 1494; rpt., Frankfurt, 1974), lect. 155, translated by Beryl Smalley in *English Friars and Antiquity in the Early Fourteenth Century* (Oxford, 1960), 185.

23. It is still too soon to declare certain treatises to have been included in Wyclif's *Sentences* commentary. This line of reasoning was introduced by J. A. Robson in *Wyclif and the Oxford Schools* (Cambridge, 1961); I explore it more in "Wyclif's Trinitarian and Christological Theology," in *A Companion to John Wyclif*, ed. Ian Levy (Leiden, 2006), 127–198, but further documentary research is needed.

24. See also *De Trinitate,* chap. 10, 110.

25. See Katherine Tachau, *Vision and Certitude in the Age of Ockham: Optics, Epistemology and the Foundations of Semantics 1250–1345* (Leiden, 1988), for a definitive history of the complexities of early fourteenth-century epistemology. For Peter Aureol, see *Scriptum proem* I, 204–205 (Aureol's *Sentences Commentary* in its second version), in E. Buytaert, ed., *Petri Aureoli Scriptum super primum Sententiarum, prooemium-dist. 8*, 2 vols. (St. Bonaventure, N.Y., 1953–1956); Tachau 85–112. For Scotus on intuitive cognition, see Sebastian Day, *Intuitive Cognition: A Key to the Significance of the Later Scholastics* (St. Bonaventure, N.Y., 1947); Allan Wolter, "Duns Scotus on Intuition, Memory, and Our Knowledge of Individuals," in *The Philosophical Theology of John Duns Scotus*, ed. Marilyn McCord Adams (Ithaca, N.Y., 1990).

26. For Rodington, see Tachau 216–236; for Bacon, Pecham, and Witelo on optics, see David C. Linberg, "Lines of Influence in Thirteenth-Century Optics: Bacon, Witelo, and Pecham," *Speculum* 46: 66–83; for Witelo, see Sabetai Unguru, "*Witelonis Perspectivae Liber Primus*," *Studia Copernicana* 15 (1977).

27. *Trialogus* II.6.

28. See Unguru 12–40.

29. See Eleonore Stump, "The Mechanisms of Cognition: Ockham on Mediating Species," in Spade 1999, 168–203.

30. Translated by Robert Pasnau, in *The Cambridge Translations of Medieval Philosophical Texts:* vol. 3, *Mind and Knowledge* (Cambridge, 2003), 255.

31. For Crathorn, see *Quaestiones super librum sententiarum,* in *Questionen Zum ersten Sentenzenbuch,* ed. F. Hoffmann (Münster, 1988); also *Sent.* I, q.1, trans. Pasnau; Tachau 255–274; Robert Aurélien, "William Crathorn," in *Stanford Encyclopedia of Philosophy*, available at http://plato.stanford.edu/entries/crathorn/#8b.

32. *De Actibus Anime* I, 1.1–10.

33. Pasnau 298–299. See also Adams, *William Ockham,* vol. 1, 552–571, for Henry of Ghent's position, and William Frank and Allan Wolter, *Duns Scotus,*

Metaphysician, 125, 167. See Julius Weinberg, *Nicholas of Autrecourt* (Princeton, N.J., 1948), and Constantin Michalski, *Le Criticisme et le Scepticisme dans la Philosophie du XIVe Siècle* (Cracow, 1926), reprinted in *La Philosophie au XIVe Siècle: Six Etudes* (Frankfurt, 1969), 100. On the differences between Descartes' use of this argument and Augustine's, see Gareth Matthews, "*Si fallor, sum*," in *Augustine: A Collection of Critical Essays*, ed. R. A. Markus (New York, 1972), 151–167.

34. *Insolubilia* literature is extensive in medieval logic. See Paul V. Spade, "Insolubilia," in *CHLMP* 246–253, and also online at *The Stanford Encyclopedia of Philosophy*. See *Johannis Wyclif: Summa Insolubilium*, ed. Paul V. Spade and Gordon Wilson (Binghamton, N.Y., 1986).

35. *De Logica*, vol. 1, 181.

36. *Purgans Errores circa Universalia in Communi, De Ente I, Tractatus IV,* chap. 5, in *Johannis Wyclif De Ente Librorum Duorum* (WS 1909), 47.7–22.

37. See Gordon Leff, *Richard Fitzralph: Commentator on the Sentences* (Manchester, 1963), 52–55. My thanks are due to Michael Dunne, who kindly provided me with a draft of his edition of Fitzralph's discussion in I, q.5, a.6.

38. Zénon Kaluza, "L'ouevre théologique de Richard Brinkley, OFM," *Archives d'Histoire Doctrinale et Littéraire du Moyen Age* 56: 169–273.

39. *Summa de Ente, Libri Primi: Tractatus primus et secundus,* ed. S. Harrison Thomson (Oxford, 1930), xxv (translation by Thomson).

40. *Trialogus* I, i.

41. *DT*, chap. 1, 3: "Hic dicitur communiter, quod nemo potest sine fide prima assentire isti deduccioni, et ideo non est mere naturalis, et sic non demonstratur in lumine naturali."

42. *Trialogus* I.6, 55.

43. *DT*, chap. 2, 19.

CHAPTER 3

1. James McEvoy, *Robert Grosseteste* (Oxford, 2000); and Marilyn McCord Adams, *William Ockham* (Notre Dame, Ind., 1987).

2. See Marilyn McCord Adams, "Universals in the Early Fourteenth Century," in *CHLMP* 411–439.

3. *The Philobiblon of Richard de Bury*, trans. E. C. Thomas (London, 1888), chap. 9. See www.philobiblon.com/philobiblon.htm.

4. See Beryl Smalley, *English Friars and Antiquity in the Early Fourteenth Century* (Oxford, 1960), for development of the idea that Oxford friars were moving toward humanism.

5. Jennifer Ottman and Rega Wood, "Walter of Burley: His Life and Works," *Vivarium* 37.1 (1999): 1–23. This edition of *Vivarium* is devoted entirely to Burley and provides the most up-to-date introduction available.

6. For Aquinas, see *Sententia super Posteriora Analytica* II.20.14. For Burley, see n. 7. See also Alessandro Conti, "Walter Burley," in *The Stanford Encyclopedia of Philosophy*, online at http://plato.stanford.edu/archives/fa112004/entries/burley. Also see his "Ontology in Walter Burley's Last Commentary on the *Ars Vetus*," *Franciscan Studies* 50 (1990): 121–176; and Elizabeth Karger, "Walter Burley's Realism," *Vivarium* 37.1 (1999): 24–40.

7. See Walter Burley, *Super artem veterem Porphirii et Aristotles*, trans. Paul Vincent Spade, in *Readings in Medieval Philosophy*, ed. Andrew Schoedinger (Oxford, 1996), 619–646. Reference here is to *Metaphysics* VII.

8. Stephen F. Brown, "Walter Burley's *Quaestiones in Librum Perihermeneias*," *Franciscan Studies* 34 (1974): 213 (1.82). See Elizabeth Karger's discussion in Karger 1999, 34–36.

9. William Courtenay, *Adam Wodeham* (Leiden, 1978), 59–60.

10. Tachau 269n81. See 255–274 for a more complete discussion than is possible here.

11. Robert Holcot, *Conferentiae*, ed. Fritz Hoffman, in *Die "Conferentiae" des Robert Holcot O.P. und die Akademischen Auseinandersetzungen an der Univerität Oxford 1330–1332* (Münster, 1993), 73–82.

12. Peter Lombard, *Sententiae* I, d.1, chap. 1; reference is to Augustine, *De Doctrina Christiana* I.2.

13. Walter Chatton, *Lectura*, prologue, q.1, translated in Tachau 205.

14. William Ockham, *Exposition super librum Perihermenias*, translated in *Philosophical Writings*, ed. Philotheus Boehner and Stephen Brown, 44.

15. Adam de Wodeham, *Lectura Secunda in Librum Primum Sententiarum*, ed. Rega Wood and Gedeon Gàl (St. Bonaventure, N.Y., 1990), I, d.1, q.1, 180–208; see also Jack Zupko, *John Buridan: Portrait of a Fourteenth-Century Arts Master* (Notre Dame, Ind., 2003), 126; and Gabriel Nuchelmans, "Adam Wodeham on the Meaning of Declarative Sentences," *Historiographia Linguistica* 7 (1980): 177–187.

16. Bertrand Russell, "The Philosophy of Logical Atomism: 1. Facts and Propositions," in *Logic and Knowledge*, ed. Robert Charles Marsh (London, 1956, 1989), 185.

17. See Laurent Cesalli, "Le 'pan-propositionalisme' de Jean Wyclif," *Vivarium* 43.1: 124–155. See also his "Some Fourteenth-Century Realist Theories of the Proposition: A Historical and Speculative Study," in *Signification in Language and Culture*, ed. H. S. Gill (Shimla, 2002), 83–118, and his *Le réalisme propositionnel: Sémantique et ontologie des propositions chez Jean Duns Scot, Gauthier Burley, Richard Brinkley et Jean Wyclif* (Paris, 2007).

18. *De Logica*, vol. 1, chap. 5, 14.1–4. Recall that this first treatise of *De Logica* is Wyclif's primer written for students hungry to understand the logic of scripture through the lens of formal academic logic.

19. Ibid., lines 13–24.

20. *DU,* chap. 1, 5.215–218, trans. Kenny.

21. See Paul V. Spade, "Introduction," in John Wyclif, *On Universals,* trans. Kenny (Oxford, 1985), 31–45; Cesalli 137.

22. "From all this it is clear, I think, that all envy or actual sin is caused by the lack of an ordered love of universals . . . because every such sin consists in a will preferring a lesser good to a greater good, whereas in general the more universal goods are better." *DU,* chap. 3, 11.145–157, trans. Kenny.

23. Wyclif, *Summa de Ente, Libri Primi: Tractatus primus, De Ente in Communi,* ed. S. Harrison Thomson (Oxford, 1930), 2.5–7. Reference is to Aristotle's *Physics* I, chap. 2, esp. 184b25–185b7. For a complete list of the treatises of *Summa de Ente,* see the bibliography.

24. See Bertrand Russell, "On Denoting," in *Logic and Knowledge,* ed. R. C. Marsh (London, 1968). See also Barry Miller, "Existence," in *The Stanford Encyclopedia of Philosophy,* available at http://plato.stanford.edu/entries/existence.

25. See John Wippel, "Metaphysics," in *The Cambridge Companion to Aquinas,* ed. Norman Kretzman and Eleonore Stump (Cambridge, 1993), 85–127, for an introduction to the senses of being as Aquinas described them.

26. Wyclif, *Summa de Ente, Libri Primi,* ed. S. Harrison Thomson, 1.5–9.

27. Thomas Aquinas, *De Esse et Essentia,* par. 3, in Joseph Bobik, *Aquinas on Being and Essence* (Notre Dame, Ind.), 21. For the division of kinds of being, see also 31–43.

28. *De Ente in Communi* 7.23–8.10. A century later, Reginald Pecock would make the same argument in his description of judgment; see my "Reginald Pecock on the Authority of Reason, Scripture, and Tradition," *Journal of Ecclesiastical History* 56.2 (April 2005): 241–242.

29. *De Ente in Communi,* chap. 4, 47.15–20.

30. Wyclif's reference is to Genesis 26–27 and, in Aristotle, to *Metaphysics* V, chap. 11, esp. 1018b30–36.

31. *Purgans Errores circa Veritates in Communi,* chap. 1, 4.22. See also Augustine, *De Trinitate* V, chap. 4: "He cannot be everlastingly lord, or we would be compelled to say that creation is everlasting, because he would only be everlastingly lord if creation were everlastingly serving him" (Edmund Hill, trans., 200).

32. Augustine, *De Diversis Quaestionibus* 83, q.46, PL 40, cols. 29–31.

33. *De Ideis,* chap. 2. In this description, I have made use of the unpublished version of *De Ideis* that was prepared by a transcriber of the Wyclif Society at the beginning of the twentieth century. This was rediscovered in 2005 by Lesley Ann Dyer in Trinity College library, Cambridge, who generously made it available to me. A list of the manuscripts used in this book can be found in

the bibliography. Professor Wilem Herold and Dr. Ivan Mueller are in the finishing stages of a complete edition of *De Ideis*, which will certainly supersede the incomplete version I've used.

34. *De Veritate*, q.3, a.1, ad.5; *Summa Theologica* Ia, q.15, aa.1–2. For a comparison of theories of divine ideas, see M. J. F. M. Hoenen, *Marsilius of Inghen* (Leiden, 1993), 121–156; Alessandro Conti, "Divine Ideas and Exemplar Causality in Auriol," *Vivarium* 38 (2000): 99–116.

35. For Henry of Ghent, see *Quodlibeta* VIII, q.1 and q.8; IX, q.2. For Scotus, see *Lectura* I, d.35. For a discussion of the relation of Henry and Scotus, see William Frank and Allan Wolter, *Duns Scotus, Metaphysician* (West Lafayette, Ind., 1995), 165–166. For Peter Aureol, see *Commentariorum in primum librum Sententiarum Pars prima*, d.35.

36. *Ordinatio* I, d.35, q.5, in *Opera Theologica* IV, 483, ed. Etzkorn and Kelly (St. Bonaventure, N.Y., 1979).

37. See Adams, *William Ockham*, 1033–1063; Thomas Bradwardine, *De Causa Dei* I.xvii, 219; Walter Chatton, *Reportatio super Sententias* I, d.35, q.2, 316–317.

38. *De Ideis,* chap. 3

39. *De Ideis*, chap. 4.

40. See Robson 1961, 141–171. For a recent plea for moderation regarding Wyclif's realism, see Paul V. Spade, "Universals and Wyclif's Alleged 'Ultrarealism,'" *Vivarium* 43.1 (2004): 111–123. See this also for a complete bibliography of recent scholarly assessments of Wyclif's thought on universals.

41. *DU*, trans. Kenny, chap. 9, 402–405.

42. For Boethius, see *Second Commentary on Porphyry's Isagoge*, in P. V. Spade, ed., *Five Texts on the Mediaeval Problem of Universals* (Hackett, 1994), 20–26; for Abelard, see "Glosses on Porphyry," in *Logica "ingredientibus,"* ibid., 26–56.

43. This explanation of Wyclif's types of universals is more fully presented in Paul V. Spade's "Introduction" to Kenny's *DU* translation. For an excellent introduction to the medieval discourse on universals, see Spade's *Five Texts on the Mediaeval Problem of Universals*.

44. This is more fully discussed in my *Philosophy and Politics in the Thought of John Wyclif* (Cambridge, 2003), 73–75. See also *De Logica* III, chap. 2, 35. 11–33; *Purgans Errores*, chap. 4, 41.14–30; *DU,* chap. 4, 28.

45. *De Ente Predicamentali*, chap. 5, 43.9–27. For a more complete discussion of Wyclif's conception of essence and being, see A. D. Conti, "Logica intensionale e metafisica dell'essenza in John Wyclif," *Bullettino dell'Instituto Storico Italiano per il Medioevo e Archivio Muratoriano* 99.1 (1993): 159–219; Conti, "Wyclif's Logic and Metaphysics," in Levy 2006; Conti, "Wyclif," in *The Stanford Encyclopedia of Philosophy*, available at http://plato.stanford.

edu/entries/wyclif/#3, which this outline follows closely. For Henry of Ghent's assertion that the being of a thing is not something other besides its essence, see *Summa Quaestionum Ordinarium*, q.21, a.3, in *Henry of Ghent's Summa*, trans. Jos Decorte and Roland J. Teske (Leuven, Belgium, 2005), 69. The consonance of *De Ente in Communi* with Henry of Ghent's metaphysics is worth much further analysis.

46. *DU,* chap. 7, 1.55, trans. Kenny, 49. In *Trialogus* II.3, Wyclif's list leaves the fourth kind, accidental being, off the list.

47. Ibid., 11.114–119, trans. Kenny, 50.

48. D. P. Henry, "Wyclif's Deviant Mereology," in *Die Philosophie im 14. Und 15. Jahrhundert,* ed. Olaf Pluta (Amsterdam, 1988), 1–17.

49. See *DU*, chap. 9. For a brief, accessible discussion, see *Trialogus* II, chap. 1.

50. Joachim's *De Unitate seu Essentia Trinitatis* has not been found, and given Wyclif's apparently loose formulation of Joachim's errors, it appears not to have been available to him at Oxford. Joachim's problem lies in his reading of *Sententiae* I, d.25, chap. 2. See Giles Emery, *Trinity in Aquinas* (Ypsilanti, Mich., 2003), 12–13.

CHAPTER 4

1. H. von der Hardt, *Magnum oecumenicum Constantiense concilium*, 6 vols. (Frankfurt and Leipzig, 1696–1700), vol. 4, 406. See John Murdoch, "Infinity and Continuity," in *CHLMP* 576n36. For a translation of much of the council's condemnation of Wyclif, see http://www.dailycatholic.org/history/16ecume1.htm.

2. Augustine, *De Sacramentis* IV, 14–15; *Tractatus in Iohannis Evangelium* XXVI, 11; *De Doctrina Christiana* 55.

3. Levy 135; Gary Macy, *The Theologies of the Eucharist in Early Medieval Europe* (Oxford, 1984). See Paschasius Radbertus, *De Corpore et Sanguine Domini*; Ratramnus Corbie, *De Corpore et Sanguine Domini*.

4. Quoted in Levy 140. Cited in Lanfranc of Bec, *Liber de Corpore et Sanguine Domini*. For Berengar, see *De Sacra Coena Adversus Lanfrancum*.

5. Lotario de Segni, *De Sacro Altaris Mysterio*.

6. See *Summa Theologica* IIIa, q.77, a.1–7.

7. See David Burr, "Scotus and Transubstantiation," *Mediaeval Studies* 34 (1972): 336–360. See Duns Scotus, *Quaestiones in Librum Sententiarum* IV, d.10–11; *Ordinatio Liber Primus*, d.11.

8. William Ockham, *Reportatio* IV, 8; *Tractatus de Quantitate; Tractatus de Corpore Christi*. An edition of the latter two, entitled *De Sacramento Altaris*, ed. T. Bruce Birch (Burlington, Iowa, 1930), has been superseded by the *Opera*

Theologica published by the Franciscan Institute. See also *Quodlibeta* II, 19; IV, 13.

9. Bartolme Maria Xiberta y Roqueta, *De Scriptoribus Scholasticis Saeculis XIV ex Ordine Carmelitarum* (Louvain, 1931).

10. I am indebted to Rega Wood, who provided me with a draft of a translation of *Ordinatio Liber Primus* IV, q.5, which is being prepared by Professor Wood and Father Gedeon Gàl. See also Adam de Wodeham, *Tractatus de Indivisibilibus*, ed. Rega Wood (Dordrecht, 1988).

11. See Levy 280–281; Dallas G. Denery II, "From Sacred Mystery to Divine Deception: Robert Holkot, John Wyclif and the Transformation of Fourteenth-Century Eucharistic Discourse," *Journal of Religious History* 29.2 (June 2005): 129–144. All quotations from Holcot are from *In Quatuor Libros Sententiarum Quaestiones* IV, q.3.

12. See John Murdoch, "Infinity and Continuity," in *CHLMP* 564–591.

13. This translation is from Murdoch's edition published in *CHLMP* 576n36. Note Bradwardine's willingness to include Grosseteste among the atomists. For a lucid survey of Bradwardine's theory of time and rejection of atomism, see Edith Wilks Dolnikowski, *Thomas Bradwardine: A View of Time and a Vision of Eternity in Fourteenth-Century Thought* (Leiden, 1995).

14. Norman Kretzman, "Continua, Indivisibles, and Change in Wyclif's Logic of Scripture," in Kenny 1986, 31–65; here, see n. 78. I am very grateful to the late Professor Kretzman for having given me his extensive notes and the translations of *De Logica* that he used in preparing this article.

15. See Calvin Normore, "Walter Burley on Continuity," in *Infinity and Continuity,* ed. Norman Kretzman (Ithaca, N.Y., 1982), 258–269.

16. Kretzman, 57–58, translating *Logice continuatio*, chap. 14, 194.36–195.2. Note that the Oxford schools were well aware of Zeno's arguments thanks to Aristotle's records of them. Wyclif refers once in passing to Zeno in *De Logica,* but Wodeham explores his arguments in *Tractatus de Indivisibilibus*, q.3.

17. Kretzman, 61–62, translation of *Logice continuatio* 197.3–6.

18. Kretzman, 63, translation of *Logice continuatio* III, 132.25–32.

19. *Trialogus* II, chap. 3.

20. See Robson's (1966) discussion at 156–161. *De Tempore* has been made available to me in the version prepared under the supervision of M. H. Dzwiecki for the Wyclif Society a century ago, thanks to its discovery by Lesley Ann Dyer in the spring of 2005. The text is being prepared in a critical edition by Wlodzimierz Zega.

21. See Simo Knutilla, *Modalities in Medieval Philosophy* (London, 1993), 138–150. For critique of Knutilla's position, see Nicole Wyatt, "Did Duns Scotus Invent Possible Worlds Semantics?" *Australasian Journal of Philosophy* 78.2 (June 2000): 196–212.

22. *DT*, chap. 4.

23. See *Trialogus* II.2 for a discussion of *duracio* as the genus in which time, aevity, and eternity exist.

24. Neil Ward Lewis, "Space and Time," in *The Cambridge Companion to Duns Scotus*, ed. Thomas Williams (Cambridge, 2003), 69–99.

25. *DT*, chap. 1.

26. *De Logica* III, chap. 9, 32.9: "Similarly are given indivisible movements insofar as duration [is] unmediatedly succeeding; therefore also measuring instances, measuring them."

27. *DT*, chap. 6: "nec repugnat eadem personam communicari multis naturis ut patet de Cristo, qui est tam natura humana quam natura divina, sed repugnat ipsam communicari multis suppositis eiusdem nature ut patet alibi." See Thomson 25.

28. *De Logica* III, chap. 8, 192.8; see also chap. 9, 137. It is possible that Wyclif is writing in response to Holcot's advocacy of annihilation, which is discussed in Joseph Incandela, "Robert Holcot, O.P., on Prophecy, the Contingency of Revelation, and the Freedom of God," *Medieval Philosophy and Theology* 4 (1994): 165–188.

29. See *De Ente Librorum Duorum*, ed. M. H. Dziewicki (WS 1909), 287–312, entitled *Tractatus Sexti Fragmentorum*, because Dziewicki included only chapters 12–14 of the otherwise unedited treatise.

30. *De Potentia Productiva*, chap. 12, 289.24.

31. Ibid., 290.30–34; see also *DU,* chap. 13, 307–308, and Levy 2003, 224–226.

32. *Trialogus* IV, chap. 10

33. *Logice continuacio* II.10, 137.12–23 (vol. 3 of WS edition).

34. Heather Phillips, "John Wyclif and the Optics of the Eucharist," in Hudson and Wilks 245–258.

35. *De Eucharistia*, chap. 5, 83, trans. Phillips 254.

36. Gustav Benrath, *Wyclif's Bibelkommentar* (Berlin, 1966), 370, cited in Levy 2003, 229n19 (my translation).

37. *Trialogus* IV, chap. 9.

38. Sermon XLII, 350–351, in *Sermones*, vol. 4 (London, 1890).

39. Ibid., 352.34–353.8. See Peter Lombard, *Sententiae* IV, d.8, c.7; see also Philipp Rosemann, *Peter Lombard* (Oxford, 2004), 152–153.

40. *Summa Theologica* IIIa, q.73, a.6.

41. Henri de Lubac, *Corpus Mysticum: The Eucharist and the Church in the Middle Ages*, trans. Gemma Simmonds, C.J. (1944; rpt., Notre Dame, Ind., 2007).

42. *De Eucharistia*, chap. 8, 242–243.

43. *De Eucharistia* 253.8.

44. See Levy 265.

45. See Dahmus 133–134; based on an aside in *Trialogus* 375.

46. *De Simonia* 1; see John Wyclif, *On Simony*, trans. Terrence A. McVeigh (New York, 1992), 29.

47. *De Apostasia*, chap. 5, 67.1–4. Wyclif likely has Ockham in mind; see *Reportatio* III, q.xi; *Quodlibet* I, q.20; also Lucan Freppert, *The Basis of Morality according to William Ockham* (Chicago, 1988).

48. *De Apostasia*, chap. 15, 205.10–22.

49. *De Blasphemia,* chap. 4, 34.11–14.

50. See S. H. Thomson, "John Wyclif's 'Lost' *De Fide Sacramentorum*," *Journal of Theological Studies* 33 (1932): 359–365; Anne Hudson, ed., *Selections from English Wycliffite Writings* (Toronto, 1997), 17–18; *Trialogus* IV, chaps. 1–10.

51. *Opus Evangelicum* III, chap. 39, 149.

52. Ian Levy's *John Wyclif: Scriptural Logic, Real Presence, and the Parameters of Orthodoxy* (Milwaukee, Wisc., 2003) typifies this approach of avoiding arguments about the preeminence of either theology or philosophy in Wyclif's thought. See also Stephen Penn, "Wyclif and the Sacraments," in *A Companion to John Wyclif*, ed. Ian Levy (Leiden, 2006), 241–272.

CHAPTER 5

1. These honorific titles lack the imprimatur of official sanction, despite their widespread use. In fact, the Catholic designation "doctor of the church," which has been bestowed upon Aquinas, Bonaventure, and Albertus Magnus, each of whom have his own medieval "doctor" cognomen, was first instituted by Boniface VIII in 1925. Hence, Anthony of Padua (1195–1231, proclaimed doctor of the church in 1946) is officially known as doctor evangelicus, while Wyclif's name is not included among the officially celebrated doctors.

2. See Beryl Smalley, *The Study of the Bible in the Middle Ages* (Notre Dame, Ind., 1964), for the classic narrative of the development of this tradition. For theological analysis, as well as a sustained argument for its continued relevance, see Henri de Lubac, *Scripture in the Tradition* (New York, 1968). This work is compiled from his four-volume *Exégèse Médiévale*, which is being published in translation by Eerdmans.

3. See Heiko Oberman, "*Facientibus Quod in se est Deus non Denegat Gratiam*: Robert Holcot, O.P., and the Beginnings of Luther's Theology," in Oberman, *The Dawn of the Reformation* (Grand Rapids, Mich., 1992), 84–103. For a fuller treatment of this in the context of the development of late medieval theology, see Oberman, *The Harvest of Late Medieval Theology* (Harvard, 1963).

4. *De Veritate Sacrae Scripturae* (hereafter *DVSS*) I.vi; translation from Ian Christopher Levy, *On the Truth of Holy Scripture* (Kalamazoo, Mich., 2001), 98. Hereafter, all citations from *DVSS* not otherwise noted will be from Levy's translation.

5. *DVSS* 54, 65.

6. See Hester Gelber, ed., *Exploring the Bounds of Reason: Three Questions on the Nature of God by Robert Holcot, OP* (Toronto, 1983), 23–28. See also *Quodlibet* 86, ed. J. T. Muckle.

7. *DVSS* 60.

8. *DVSS* 62.

9. *DVSS* 264.

10. *DI*, chap. 5, 73. See Levy 2003, 87.

11. Robert Grosseteste, *De Decem Mandatis*, in *Auctores Britannici Medii Aevi VI(2)*, ed. Richard C. Dales and Edward B. King (Oxford, 1987), prologue, chap. 2, 2.18–22.

12. Robert Grosseteste, *De Cessatione Legalium*, in *Auctores Britannici Medii Aevi VI(2)*, ed. Richard C. Dales and Edward B. King (Oxford, 1986), IV, viii, 21, 191.7–11.

13. Robert Grosseteste, *On the Six Days of Creation*, trans. C. F. J. Martin, in *Auctores Britannici Medii Aevi VI(2)*, ed. Richard C. Dales and Edward B. King (Oxford, 1996), 282. See R. W. Southern, *Robert Grosseteste: The Growth of an English Mind in Medieval Europe* (Oxford 1986), 222–225. In contrast, see Thomas Aquinas, *Summa Theologica* IIIa, q.1, a.3.

14. *DMD*, chap. 11, 96.22–27.

15. *DMD*, chap. 11, 102.28–103.2. See Augustine, *Confessions* VIII, chap. 12.

16. *De Amore* in *Opera Minora*, ed. J. Loserth (WS 1913), 9.19–27.

17. *DMD*, chap. 7, 50.

18. Richard Cross, *The Metaphysics of the Incarnation: Thomas Aquinas to Duns Scotus* (Oxford, 2002), 1–26. See also Philipp Rosemann, *Peter Lombard* (Oxford, 2004), 118–143.

19. For the historical evidence of Ockham's struggles against the label of Nestorianism, see Oberman 249–261. For a philosophical analysis of Ockham's Christology, see Marilyn McCord Adams, "Relations, Inherence and Subsistence; or, Was Ockham a Nestorian in Christology?" *Nous* 16 (1982): 62–75.

20. See Gillian Evans, *Mediaeval Commentaries on the Sentences of Peter Lombard* (Leiden, 2002).

21. *DCH*, chap. 3, 48.10–22. See also Emily Michael, "Wyclif on Body and Soul," *Journal of the History of Ideas* (2003): 343–360.

22. *DCH*, chap. 1, 18.3–22. The reference is in fact to 2 Corinthians 12:3. See also *Trialogus* II, chap. 7.

23. This question is the subject of *Sentences* III, d.12, c.1, and it appears that what follows here is Wyclif's discussion of Lombard's position.

24. *DI*, chap. 1, 3.6–11.

25. *Everyman in Medieval English Literature*, ed. J. B. Trapp (Oxford, 1973), 390–391.

26. *DI*, 216.13–16. For a more developed analysis of Wyclif's Christology, see my "Wyclif's Trinitarian and Christological Theology," in *Wyclif Handbook*, ed. Ian C. Levy (Leiden, 2006).

27. *DVSS* I, 6; see Levy 2001, 97–112. By 1382, Wyclif had reduced the number of levels to three; see *Trialogus* III, 31.

28. See Beryl Smalley, *The Study of the Bible in the Middle Ages* (Notre Dame, Ind., 1964); Philip Krey and Lesley Smith, *Nicholas of Lyra: The Senses of Scripture* (Leiden, 2000).

29. *DVSS* I, 12, 276.1–4.

30. Alistair Minnis, "'Authorial Intention' and 'Literal Sense' in the Exegetical Theories of Richard Fitzralph and John Wyclif: An Essay in the Medieval History of Biblical Hermeneutics," *Proceedings of the Royal Irish Academy* (Section C) 75.1 (1975): 1–30.

31. Beryl Smalley, "John Wyclif's *Postilla Super Totam Bibliam*," *Bodleian Library Record* 4.3 (April 1953): 186–205; Smalley, "Wyclif's *Postilla* on the Old Testament and His *Principium*," in *Oxford Studies Presented to Daniel Callus, O.P.* (Oxford, 1964), 256.

32. *De Apostasia,* chap. 3, 49.17–25.

33. *Opus Evangelicum* II, 368.22–24.

34. Benrath 115n3.

35. Benrath 353. Benrath's study contains twelve edited sections from Wyclif's *Postilla*.

36. Benrath 119.

37. *De Amore (ad Quinque Questiones),* in *Opera Minora*, ed. J. Loserth (WS 1913), 8–10.

38. *Opus Evangelicum* IV, chap. 12, 325.17–326.30. W. Thomson suggests that the passage's appearance at the end of the manuscript may give evidence of its composition on the last day of Wyclif's life. While the possibility exists that he had written it earlier and that it was inserted by a later hand, it is satisfying to imagine Wyclif seeing his coming end and attempting one last summation of his guiding principles. See W. Thomson 1983, 221.

39. See J. van Banning, S.J., ed., *Opus Imperfectum in Matthaeum (Praefatio)* (Turnhout, Belgium, 1988), 87B, esp. 276–277. The complete edition has yet to appear, and the reader must be content with Migne's 1859 *PG,* vol. 56, 611–916.

40. Siegmund Hellman, ed., *De Duodecem Abusivis Saeculi: Texte und Untersuchungen zur Geschichte der Altchristlichen Literatur* (Leipzig, 1910). See Aidan Breen, "Pseudo-Cyprian *De Duodecim Abusivis Saeculi* and the Bible," in *Irland und die Christenheit* (1987); and his "*De XII Abusivis*: Text and Transmission," in *Ireland and Europe in the Early Middle Ages: Texts and Transmission*, ed. Próinséas Ní Chatháin and Michael Richter (Four Courts, 2002), 78–94. I am grateful to Dr. Breen for having kindly provided me with his edition and translation of this text.

41. *Opus Evangelicum* I, chap. 6, 18.19–25.

42. *Postilla Matt.* 5:8; *DMD,* chap. 12, 115.32; cited in Benrath 114n102.

43. *De Mandatis Divinis*, chap. 12, 93.8–11. See chapters 11–15 for the entire "Treatise on Love."

44. *Opus Evangelicum* II, chap. 33, 367.30–368.24. See Benrath, esp. 110–122, "Das Gesetz Christi."

45. See Siegfried Wenzel, *Latin Sermon Collections from Later Medieval England: Orthodox Preaching in the Age of Wyclif* (Cambridge, 2005); Smalley 1960.

46. See *English Wycliffite Sermons*, ed. Anne Hudson and Pamela Gradon (Oxford, 1983–1996), 5 vols.

47. Edith Wilks Dolnikowski, "Preaching at Oxford: Academic and Pastoral Themes in Wyclif's Latin Sermon Cycle," in *Medieval Sermons and Society*, ed. J. Hamesse et al. (Louvain-la-Neuve, 1998), 371–386.

48. *Praefatio*, in *Sermones*, vol. 1, 1.7–14.

49. See William Mallard, "Clarity and Dilemma: The *Forty Sermons* of John Wyclif," in *Contemporary Reflections on the Medieval Christian Tradition*, ed. G. H. Shriver et al. (Durham, N.C., 1974), 19–38.

50. See *Sermones,* vol. 4, 256–275.

51. *DVSS* II, 21, trans. Levy 287. For Wyclif on preaching, see Ian Levy, "Wyclif and the Christian Life," in *A Companion to John Wyclif*, ed. Ian Levy (Leiden, 2006), 302–316.

52. *De Officio Pastoralis*, ed. G. Lechler (Leipzig, 1863), II.1, 32. Abridged translation by Ford Lewis Battles in *Advocates of Reform*, ed. M. Spinka (Philadelphia, 1953), 32–60. See also *Sermones* I, 110, 377.

53. *De Officio Pastoralis* I.1, ed. Spinka 32; I.8, ed. Spinka 38. See also *Sermones* I, 244; *DVSS* III.25; Levy 306–310; *DOR*, chap. 7, 165–166.

54. *De Ordinatione Fratrum*, in *Polemical Works in Latin*, ed. R. Buddensieg (WS 1883), vol. 1, 96.15–20. The Latin has *panni rudis* for the untreated patch, and Wyclif also uses *rudis* to refer to their crude stories.

55. *De Diabolo et Membrus Eius*, in *OP*, vol. 1, 372. Reference is to 1 Corinthians 3:9.

56. *De Fundatione Sectarum*, in *Polemical Works,* vol. 1, 20.1–2. See also *De Fide Catholica*, chap. 8; *Opera Minora* 128.

57. See Fiona Somerset, *Clerical Discourse and Lay Audience in Late Medieval England* (Cambridge, 1998).

58. See K. B. McFarlane, *John Wycliffe and the Beginnings of English Non-conformity* (London, 1952), 100–101; following McFarlane, see Gordon Leff, *Heresy in the Later Middle Ages* (Manchester, 1967), 559; Malcolm Lambert, *Medieval Heresy* (Oxford, 1977), 241. See Anne Hudson, *The Premature Reformation* (Oxford, 1988). In Richard Rex, *The Lollards* (London, 2002), we see a useful, if provocative, narrative taking into account the great scholarly advances that have been made since McFarlane's work.

59. H. B. Workman, *John Wyclif* (Oxford, 1926), vol. 2, 203–204; this is reliant on H. L. Cannon, "The Poor Priests: A Study in the Rise of English Lollardy," in *Annual Report of the American Historical Association for 1899* (Washington, D.C., 1900), vol. 1, 451–482.

60. Thomas Walsingham, *Hist. Angl.* II, 32; see also I, 324. For Wyclif's reaction, see *De Blasphemia*, chap. 13, 190–202.

61. Lambert, *Medieval Heresy*, 241.

62. Michael Wilks, "*Reformatio Regni*: Wyclif and Hus as Leaders of Religious Protest Movements," *Studies in Church History* 9 (1972): 109–130; reprinted in Wilks 2000, 63–84. For the argument that Wyclif's preachers were part of an Oxford network of benefices, see A. K. McHardy, "The Dissemination of Wyclif's Ideas," in Hudson and Wilks 361–363.

63. See Sermon XVI, in *Sermones*, vol. 1, ed. J. Loserth (WS 1886), 107–114; W. Thomson 1983, 179; J. I. Catto, "Wyclif and Wycliffism at Oxford: 1356–1430," in *The History of the University of Oxford*, vol. 2, ed. J. I. Catto and R. Evans (Oxford, 1984), 208.

64. *De Sex Iugis* appears serially in Sermons 27, 28, 31, 32, and 33 in *Sermones*, vol. 2. Gotthard Lechler published this as an independent piece in *Johann von Wiclif und die Vorgeschichte der Reformation* (Leipzig, 1873), vol. 2, 591–605.

65. Hudson 1988, 81; see also G. R. Evans, *John Wyclif: Myth and Reality* (Lion Hudson, 2005), 250–254.

CHAPTER 6

1. Richard Copsey, O.C., *The Hermits from Mount Carmel*, vol. 3 of *Carmel in Britain* (Kent, 2004).

2. See *De Volucione Dei* 117.20–21; *Sermones* I, 12; see also W. Thomson 1983, 100n8, citing at least fourteen other instances

3. See Ian Levy, "Defining the Responsibility of the Late Medieval Theologian: The Debate between John Kynnyngham and John Wyclif," *Carmelus* 19

(2002): fasc. 1, 5–29; Martin Hoenen, "Theology and Metaphysics: The Debate between John Wyclif and John Kenningham on the Principles of Reading the Scriptures," in *John Wyclif: Logica, Politica, Teologia*, ed. Fumagalli and Simonetta (Florence, 2003), 23–56.

4. *De Ecclesia,* chap. 1, 2.25. See Augustine, *De Civitate Dei* XVIII, 49; *De Praedestinatione Sanctorum*, chap. 11.

5. *De Ideis*, chap. 3, see n. 21.

6. William Ockham, *Predestination, God's Foreknowledge, and Future Contingents*, ed. Marilyn McCord Adams and Norman Kretzman (Hackett, 1983), q.2, art. 4, pt. 1, 67. See also *Tractatus de Principiis Theologiae* I.5, and Calvin Normore, "Future Contingents," in *CHLMP*.

7. *De Causa Dei* I.35, 308c–d.

8. A complete study of Bradwardine would take both his mathematically grounded physics and his theology into consideration, across the whole of his career. The nearest to this is Edith Wilks Dolnikowski, *Thomas Bradwardine: A View of Time and a Vision of Eternity* (Leiden, 1995). For his earlier theological works, see Jean-Francois Genest, ed., "Le *De futuris contingentibus* de Thomas Bradwardine," *Recherches Augustiniennes* 14 (1979): 249–336; "Les premiers écrits théologiques de Bradwardine: Textes inédits et découvertes récentes," in G. R. Evans, *Mediaeval Commentaries on the Sentences of Peter Lombard* (Leiden, 2002), vol. 1, 395–421.

9. *De Futuris Contingentibus*, trans. Norman Kretzman, unpublished draft, 1981; also see Genest 317.

10. Anselm, *Cur Deus Homo* II.17.

11. *Summa Contra Gentiles* I.67; *Summa Theologica* Ia, q.19, a.3. For Bradwardine's deviation from Aquinas, see Oberman 1957, 71–76.

12. See Calvin Normore, "Future Contingents," in *CHLMP* 374–377; see also Bartolomew De La Torre, *Thomas Buckingham and the Contingency of Futures* (Notre Dame, Ind., 1987).

13. *De Ente Libri II, Tractatus iii (De Volucione Dei)*, 2, in *De Ente Librorum Duorum*, ed. M. H. Dziewicki (WS 1909), 136.16–24.

14. Kenny translates this as "hypothetical" necessity; Conti refers to it as "relational" necessity; to show Wyclif's ties to Aquinas in this discussion, I will use necessity "by supposition."

15. *DU*, chap. 14, 64–68. See Kenny 1985, 31–41; Kenny, "Realism and Determinism in the Early Wyclif," in Hudson and Wilks 165–178; Alessandro Conti, "Wyclif's Logic and Metaphysics," in Levy 2006, 67–126. See also *Logice continuacio* I, xi, 157–161; *De Logica* III, x, 179.17–196.32; *De Actibus Anime* I, 71.23–76.20; *DU,* chap. 14.

16. *De Actibus Anime* I, 72.20.

17. *DU*, chap. 14, 162.336–339; *De Logica* III, x, 181.10–25.

18. See Robson 88–96; Walsh 1981, 129–181; K. Walsh, "Die Rezeption der Schriften des Richard FitzRalph (Armachanus) in lollardisch-hussitischen Kreisen," in *Das Publikum politischer Theorie im 14. Jahrhundert*, ed. J. Miethke (1992), 237–253. An edition of the *Summa de Quaestionibus Armenorum* is sorely needed; the only extant edition is that of Johannis Sudoris (Paris, 1511).

19. *De Dominio Divino* (*DD*) I, 14, 130.23–25. See Ian Levy, "Grace and Freedom in the Soteriology of John Wyclif," *Traditio* 60 (2005): 279–337, for a thorough analysis of the extent of Wyclif's theological determinism.

20. *DD* I, 18, 165.

21. An abridgment of *DD* I, 16, 121.17–30.

22. *De Volucione Dei*, chap. 2, 131.18–24.

23. *De Volucione Dei*, chap. 6, 176.33–35 (see Hebrews 6:13), 180.28–30.

24. Gordon Leff, *Heresy in the Later Middle Ages* (Manchester, 1967), 516–545.

25. *De Civitate Dei* XVIII, chap. 51, for a complete overview of recent literature.

26. *De Ecclesia*, chap. 1, 1–5; *Sermones* 50, vol. 3, 434.

27. *Sermones* 50, vol. 3, 435.8–436.3.

28. *Sermones* 5, vol. 4, 45.7–12.

29. *Sermones* 9, vol. 4, 76.3–14.

30. *Sermones* 49, vol. 2, 354.24.

31. Michael Wilks, "Wyclif and the Wheel of Time," reprinted in *Wyclif: Political Ideas and Practice*, ed. Anne Hudson (Oxbow, 2000), 205–221. I am grateful to Professor Wilks for providing me with his thoughts on Wyclif's understanding of the church in additional correspondence.

32. See Marjorie Reeves, *The Influence of Prophecy in the Later Middle Ages* (Oxford, 1969), 16–27; Reeves, *Joachim of Fiore and the Prophetic Future* (London, 1976), 1–58; E. Randolph Daniel, "The Double Procession of the Holy Spirit in Joachim of Fiore's Understanding of History," *Speculum* 53 (1980): 469–483.

33. See Malcolm Lambert, *Franciscan Poverty* (St. Bonaventure, N.Y., 1998); Christopher Cullen, *Bonaventure* (Oxford, 2006), 177–187; G. C. Coulton, *From St. Francis to Dante: Translations from the Chronicle of the Franciscan Salimbene* (Philadelphia, 1907).

34. Kathryn Kerby-Fulton, *Books under Suspicion: Censorship and Tolerance of Revelatory Writing in Late Medieval England* (Notre Dame, Ind., 2006), 45–188. See *Tractatus de Universalibus,* chap. 11, 108, 119; *Opus Evangelicum* III, chap. 58, 216.35–38. For more of Wyclif's derisory comments about Joachim, see Thomson's list in W. Thomson 1983, 14n4.

35. *De Antichristo*, chap. 28, 102.18–25, which is contained in *Opus Evangelicum* II.

36. *De Antichristo*, chap. 49, 181.6.

37. *De Antichristo*, chap. 24, 125.36. For the ties between Wyclif's eschatology and his antifraternalism, see Penn Szittya, *The Antifraternal Tradition in Medieval Literature* (Princeton, N.J., 1986), 152–182.

38. See Margaret Aston, "'Caim's Castles': Poverty, Politics, and Disendowment," in *The Church, Politics, and Patronage in the Fifteenth Century*, ed. Barrie Dobson (Gloucester, 1984), 45–81.

39. *De Potestate Pape*, chap. 1, 10–17; *DD* II.

40. *De Officio Pastoralis*, ed. G. Lechler (Leipzig, 1863); see a translation by Ford Lewis Battles in *Advocates of Reform*, ed. Matthew Spinka (Philadelphia, 1953), 32–60.

41. *De Ecclesia*, chap. 19, 448–449; *De Antichristo*, chap. 48, 175–176. For a full discussion, see Ian Levy, "Was John Wyclif's Theology of the Eucharist Donatistic?" *Scottish Journal of Theology* 53 (2000): 137–153; Levy 2003, 305–307.

42. *De Potestate Pape*, chap. 11; see Gillian Evans, *Bernard of Clairvaux* (Oxford, 2000), 158–165.

43. *DCD* I, chap. 38, 275.3; *DOR*, chap. 7, 166–175; *De Blasphemia*, chap. 7, 97–110.

44. *De Oratione et Ecclesiae Purgatione*, in *OP* I, 343–354; *De Fundacione Sectarum* (*OP* I), 13–80.

45. *De Ordinatione Fratrum* (*OP* I), 92.2.

CHAPTER 7

1. *DD* I, 1, 1.6.

2. Earlier scholars of medieval political theory expended a lot of energy to establish overarching theories that would predict a philosopher's political position given his metaphysics. The most famous instance of this is Martin Grabmann's *Studien über den Einfluss der aristotelischen Philosophie auf die mittelalterlichen Theorien über das Verhältniss von Kirche und Staat* (Munich, 1934). Much of the scholarship of the past fifty years has demonstrated that such theorizing is premature; particularly influential has been A. S. McGrade's *The Political Thought of William Ockham* (Cambridge, 1974), which demonstrated that Ockham's political thought cannot be connected to his conceptualist ontology.

3. See Janet Coleman, "Property and Poverty," in *The Cambridge History of Medieval Political Thought c. 350–c. 1450*, ed. J. H. Burns (Cambridge 1988), 607–648.

4. *Summa Theologica* Ia–IIae, q.56, a.5; q.58, a.2. See also J. H. Burns, *Lordship, Kingship, and Empire* (Oxford, 1992).

5. Augustine, *On the City of God*, bk. 14, chap. 28; *Basic Writings of St. Augustine*, ed. Whitney Oates (New York, 1948), vol. 2, 451.

6. Augustine, *Epistola* 93, chap. 12; *Nicene and Post-Nicene Fathers*, 1st ser., vol. 1, 400.

7. *Enarratio in Psalmam* 132.4; *Nicene and Post-Nicene Fathers*, 1st ser., vol. 8, 617.

8. Giles of Rome, *On Ecclesiastical Power: The De Ecclesiastica Potestate of Aegidius Romanus*, ed. and trans. R. W. Dyson (Drew, N.H., 1986), III, 2, 4.

9. D. L. Burr, *Olivi and Franciscan Poverty* (Philadelphia, 1989), and M. D. Lambert, *Franciscan Poverty* (St. Bonaventure, N.Y., 1998).

10. For details of the controversy between John XXII and Ockham, see William Ockham, *A Letter to the Friars Minor and Other Writings*, ed. and trans. A. S. McGrade and John Kilcullen (Cambridge, 1995). See also McGrade 1974.

11. Fitzralph's arguments concerning the Franciscans await a thorough scholarly study. The first four books of *De Pauperie Salvatoris* were included in the Wyclif Society's 1890 edition of Wyclif's *DD*, while Richard Brock edited the latter books of the treatise in "An Edition of Richard Fitzralph's 'De Pauperie Salvatoris' Books V, VI, and VII," Ph.D. diss., University of Colorado, 1954. See Katherine Walsh, *A Fourteenth-Century Scholar and Primate: Richard Fitzralph of Oxford, Avignon, and Armagh* (Oxford, 1981); and James Doyne Dawson, "Richard Fitzralph and the Fourteenth Century Poverty Controversies," *Journal of Ecclesiastical History* 34 (1983).

12. *DD* I, 3, 16.18–22.

13. *DD* III, 1, 198.9. Although Wyclif gives a list of sixteen characteristics, he proceeds to discuss only these six. This has prompted some scholars to suppose that his discussion of the remaining ten has been lost, leaving us with only a fragment of the original treatise. I suspect that Wyclif recognized these six acts to be sufficient for his argument and abandoned the remaining ten as superfluous.

14. *DD* III, 2, 207–210. See also my discussion of God's giving and receiving in *Metaphysics and Politics in John Wyclif* (Cambridge, 2003), 97–105.

15. *DD* III, 4, 229.18.

16. This is the sense of *DD* III, 5–7, which corresponds to *Trialogus* III, 7, written in 1383.

17. *DD* III, 6, 250.25–29.

18. Compare Wyclif's discussion of justice and right in *DMD*, chap. 3, to Aquinas's in *Summa Theologica* IIa–IIae, q.57, aa.1–4, and q.58, aa.1–12. Aquinas argues that, while right is the object of justice, natural reason is capable of ascertaining justice without an understanding of God's uncreated right. See also my "Wyclif on Rights," *Journal of the History of Ideas* 58 (1997): 1–20.

19. *DMD*, chap. 4, 32.24–27.

20. *De Statu Innocencie* 8, 34–37. Note that Wyclif uses *caritatem* for the standard *dilectionem* in John 15:13; this is likely because Wyclif is quoting from

memory. Ian Levy has kindly pointed out to me that Wyclif makes this same substitution in *DCD* I, 24, 175; *DVSS* II, 40; and *De Antichristo* 289.

21. *De Statu Innocencie* 6, 508.7–9. For Wyclif's conception of the nature of original sin as an ongoing inherited separation from justice, see *Trialogus* III, 26.

22. *DCD* III, 11, 178.9–17. For a translation of *DCD* I, 1–10, see A. S. McGrade, John Kilcullen, and Matthew Kempshall, eds., *The Cambridge Translations of Medieval Philosophical Texts*: vol. 2, *Ethics and Politics* (Cambridge, 2001), 587–654.

23. *DCD* III, 4, 51.17–24.

24. *DCD* I, 9, 62.9.

25. *DCD* III, 8, 119–120.

26. *DCD* III, 2, 15.5–23. For Woodford's criticism, see Eric Doyle, O.F.M., "William Woodford, O.F.M., His Life and Works," *Franciscan Studies* 43 (1983): 17–187; Doyle, "William Woodford's *De Dominio Civili Clericorum* against John Wyclif," *Archivum Franciscanum Historicum* 66 (1973): 49–109.

27. *DCD* II, 16, 209.13–18.

28. *Dialogus* 35, 83.25–29. See also Michael Wilks, "*Thesaurus Ecclesiae*," reprinted in *Wyclif: Political Ideas and Practice*, ed. Anne Hudson (Oxbow, 2000), 147–177.

29. *DOR*, chap. 1, 13.4–8.

30. *DCD* I, 26, 188.14–24.

31. *DCD* I, 22, 231.18–30.

32. *DOR*, chap. 5, 96.9–27. For a fuller discussion of Wyclif's conceptions of royal responsibility to the realm, see chap. 6 of Lahey 2003. See also William Farr, *Wyclif as Legal Reformer* (Leiden, 1974), for a consideration of Wyclif's use of English law in his vision of the reform of the church.

33. *DCD* I, 30, 215.10–12.

34. *DCD* I, 18, 130.6.

EPILOGUE

1. See Zénon Kaluza, "Late Medieval Philosophy 1350–1500," in *Routledge History of Philosophy*: vol. 3, *Late Medieval Philosophy*, ed. John Marenbon (New York, 1998), 426–451.

2. William James, *The Varieties of Religious Experience* (Viking Penguin, 1982), 25.

APPENDIX

1. Wyclif cites Augustine, *Tractatus in Johannem* 25, "Why preparest thou the teeth and the belly? Believe and thou hast eaten."

2. The text beginning with "But many grumble" through to the paragraph ending "as this same saint says in the letter to Elbidiam" is reproduced without substantial alteration in *De Apostasia*, chap. 16, 222.40–229.37.

3. William Durandus (1237–1296), *Rationale divinorum officiorum* IV, chap. 1, who probably took the remark from Gregory, in whose "Paschal Homily" it occurs.

4. Wyclif appears to have Gratian's *Decretum III De Consecratione* open before him as he writes; aside from Ignatius, which he likely took from Grosseteste, *Super Ecclesiastica Hierarchia,* chap. 3, the sources are all cited in Gratian. See Cyprianus Carthaginensis, *Epistulae*, ep. 63, c.9 (*Corpus Christianorum Series Latina Clavis [CCSLC]* 0050); Ambrosius (*dubia*), *De Sacramentis (CCSLC* 0154); Augustinus, *Sermones* 234 (*CCSLC* 0284); Hieronymus, *Epistulae* 120 (*CCSLC* 0620); Augustinus, *Epistulae* 98 (*CCSLC* 0262).

5. The completion of the text in Augustine's letter is ", thus the sacrament of the faith is the faith." This is not included in Wyclif's citation.

6. Here, the *FZ* version ends; what follows appears in the Bohemian manuscripts. After the first paragraph, this is also the text of Sermon 34 in vol. 3 of *Sermones*, with only minor variants.

BIBLIOGRAPHY

Note: Publications of the Wyclif Society are denoted as WS.

PRIMARY SOURCES

Unpublished Works

De Ydeis, unpublished WS edition of: Praha, UK, IV.H.9 (773) ff. 114r–130v; Praha, UK, VIII.F.1 (1955) ff. 73va–87rb; Stockholm Lat.A.164, ff. 244ra–258va; Trinity B.16.2, ff. 131ra–137va.

De Tempore, unpublished WS edition.

Works by John Wyclif

De Actibus Anime, in *Miscellanea Philosophica*, vol. 1. Ed. M. H. Dziewicki. WS 1902.
De Antichristo, in *Opus Evangelicum*, vol. 2. Ed. J. Loserth. WS 1896.
De Apostasia. Ed. Michael H. Dziewicki. WS 1883.
De Blasphemia. Ed. Michael H. Dziewicki. WS 1893.
De Civili Dominio, Liber I. Ed. R. L. Poole. WS 1885.
De Civili Dominio, Libri II et III. 3 vols. Ed. J. Loserth. WS 1900, 1902, 1904.
De Compositione Hominis. Ed. Rudolf Beer. WS 1884.
De Confessione. Ed. J. Loserth. WS 1892.
De Dominio Divino. Ed. Reginald Lane Poole. WS 1890.
De Ecclesia. Ed. J. Loserth. WS 1885.

De Ente Librorum Duorum. Excerpta: Libri I Tractatus III & IV; Libri II Tractatus I & III; et Fragmentum de Annihilatione. Ed. M. H. Dziewicki. WS 1909.

De Ente Praedicamentali, Quaestiones XIII Logicae et Philosophiae. Ed. Rudolf Beer. WS 1891.

De Eucharistia Tractatus Maior: Accedit Tractatus de Eucharistia et Poenitentia sive De Confessione. Ed. J. Loserth. WS 1892.

De Logica. 3 vols. Ed. M. H. Dziewicki. WS 1893–1899.

De Mandatis Divinis. Ed. Johann Loserth and F. D. Matthew. WS 1922.

De Officio Pastoralis. Ed. G. V. Lechler. Leipzig, 1863.

De Officio Regis. Ed. Alfred W. Pollard and Charles Sayle. WS 1887.

De Potestate Pape. Ed. J. Loserth. WS 1907.

De Simonia. Ed. Herzberg-Frankel and M. H. Dziewicki. WS 1898.

De Statu Innocencie, published in *De Mandatis Divinis.* WS 1922.

De Trinitate. Ed. Allen duPont Breck. Boulder: University of Colorado Press, 1962.

De Veritate Sacrae Scripturae. 3 vols. Ed. Rudolf Buddensieg. WS 1905, 1906, 1907.

Dialogus sive Speculum Ecclesie Militantis. Ed. Alfred W. Pollard. WS 1886.

Johannis Wyclif: Summa Insolubilium. Ed. P. V. Spade and G. A. Wilson. Binghamton, N.Y., 1986.

"A 'Lost' Chapter of Wyclif's *Summa de Ente.*" Ed. S. Harrison Thomson. *Speculum* 4 (1929): 339–346.

Miscellanea Philosophica. 2 vols. Ed. M. H. Dziewicki. WS 1902–1905.

Opera Minora. Ed. J. Loserth. WS 1913.

Opus Evangelicum. 2 vols. Ed. Johann Loserth. WS 1895, 1896.

Polemical Works in Latin. 2 vols. Ed. R. Buddenseig. WS 1883.

Sermones. 4 vols. Ed. J. Loserth. WS 1886–1889.

Tractatus de Benedicta Incarnacione. Ed. Edward Harris. WS 1886.

Tractatus de Universalibus. Ed. Ivan J. Mueller. Oxford: Oxford University Press, 1985.

Trialogus. Published as *Io. Wiclefi viri undiquaque piis. dialogorum libri quattuor.* Ed. Johann Froben. Basel, 1525.

———. Published as *Ioannis Wiclefi viri undiquaque piissimi Dialogorum Libri Quatuor.* Ed. L. P. Wirth. Leipzig, 1753.

———. Published as *Johannis Wiclif Trialogus cum Supplemento Trialogi.* Ed. Gotthard Lechler. Oxford: Oxford University Press, 1869.

"An Unpublished Fragment of Wyclif's *Confessio.*" Ed. I. H. Stein. *Speculum* 8 (1933): 503–510.

Works by Wyclif: English Translations

All translations in the text are from the works listed below. Translations from texts not listed below are my own.

On Civil Lordship: Selections (Book I). Trans. John Kilcullen. In A. S. McGrade, John Kilcullen, and Matthew Kempshall, eds., *The Cambridge Translations of Medieval Philosophical Texts:* vol. 2, *Ethics and Politics*. Cambridge: Cambridge University Press, 2001.

On the Pastoral Office. Ed. and trans. F. L. Battles. In M. Spinka, ed., *Advocates of Reform from Wyclif to Erasmus*. Philadelphia: Westminster, 1953.

On Simony. Trans. Terence A. McVeigh. New York: Fordham University Press, 1992.

On the Truth of Holy Scripture. Trans. Ian Levy. Kalamazoo, Mich.: Medieval Institute, 2001.

On Universals (Tractatus de Universalibus). Trans. Anthony Kenny. Oxford: Oxford University Press, 1985.

Other Primary Sources

Adam de Wodeham, *Lectura Secunda in Librum Primum Sentatiarum*. Ed. Rega Wood and Gedeon Gàl. St. Bonaventure, N.Y.: Franciscan Institute, 1990.

———, *Tractatus de Indivisibilibus*. Ed. Rega Wood. Dordrecht: Kluwer Academic, 1988.

Anselm of Canterbury, *The Major Works*. Ed. Brian Davies and Gillian Evans. Oxford: Oxford University Press, 1998.

———, *Opera Omnia*. Ed. F. S. Schmitt. Stuttgart: Fromann, 1968.

Augustine, *On the City of God*. Ed. R. W. Dyson. Cambridge: Cambridge University Press, 2005.

Giles of Rome, *On Ecclesiastical Power: The De Ecclesiastica Potestate of Aegidius Romanus*. Ed. and trans. R. W. Dyson. Drew, N.H.: 1986.

Henry of Ghent, *Henry of Ghent's Summa*. Trans. Jos Decorte and Roland J. Teske. Leuven, Belgium, 2005.

John Duns Scotus, *God and Creatures: The Quodlibetal Questions*. Trans. F. Alluntis and A. B. Wolter. Princeton, N.J.: Princeton University Press, 1975.

———, *Philosophical Writings: A Selection*. Trans. A. B. Wolter. Indianapolis, Ind.: Hackett, 1987.

Nicholas Aston, *In Sententiae*. Ed. Joel Bender. In Bender, "Nicholas Aston: A Study in Oxford Thought after the Black Death." Ph.D. diss., University of Wisconsin, 1979.

Nicholas of Autrecourt, *Nicholas of Autrecourt: His Correspondence with Master Giles and Bernard of Arezzo*. Trans. L. M. De Rijk. Leiden: Brill, 1994.

———, *The Universal Treatise*. Trans. Leonard Kennedy, Richard Arnold, and Arthur Millward. Milwaukee, Wis.: Marquette University Press, 1971.

Richard Brinkley, *De Significato Propositionis*. Ed. and Trans. Michael J. Fitzgerald. In *Richard Brinkley's Theory of Sentential Reference*. Leiden: Brill, 1987.

Richard Fitzralph, *De Pauperie Salvatoris*. In R. L. Poole, ed., *De Dominio Divino*. WS 1890.

Robert Grosseteste, *De Cessatione Legalium*. In Richard C. Dales and Edward B. King, eds., *Auctores Britannici Medii Aevi VI(2)*. Oxford: Oxford University Press, 1986.

————, *De Decem Mandatis*. In Richard C. Dales and Edward B. King, eds., *Auctores Britannici Medii Aevi VI(2)*. Oxford: Oxford University Press, 1987.

————, *On the Six Days of Creation*. Trans. C. F. J. Martin. In Richard C. Dales and Edward B. King, eds., *Auctores Britannici Medii Aevi VI(2)*. Oxford: Oxford University Press, 1996.

Robert Holcot, *Conferentiae*. In Fritz Hoffmann, ed., *Die "Conferentiae" des Robert Holcot O.P. und die Akademischen Auseinandersetzungen an der Universität Oxford 1330–1332*. Münster: Aschendorff, 1993.

————, *Quaestiones de Quodlibet*. In Hester Gelber, ed., *Exploring the Bounds of Reason: Three Questions on the Nature of God*. Toronto: Pontifical Institute, 1983.

————, *Quaestiones quodlibetales*. In Paul Streveler and Katherine Tachau with William J. Courtenay and Hester Goodenough Gelber, eds., *Seeing the Future Clearly: Questions on Future Contingents*. Toronto: University of Toronto Press, 1995.

————, *Super Libros Sapientiae*. Hagenau, 1494. Rpt., Frankfurt: Minerva, 1974.

————, *Utrum Theologia sit Scientia*. Ed. J. T. Muckle. *Mediaeval Studies* 20 (1958): 127–153.

Thomas Aquinas, *Summa Theologica*. Ed. Petrus Caramello. Turin and Rome, 1948.

Thomas Bradwardine, *De Causa Dei contra Pelagium*. Ed. H. Savile. London, 1618. Rpt., Frankfurt: Minerva, 1964.

————, *De Futuris Contingentibus*. In J.-F. Genest, ed., "Le *De futuris contingentibus* de Thomas Bradwardine." *Recherches Augustiniennes* 14 (1979): 249–336.

————, *Tractatus de Proportionibus*. Ed. H. Lamar Crosby. Madison: University of Wisconsin Press, 1955.

Walter Burley, *De Puritate Artis Logicae Tractatus Longior*. Ed. Philotheus Boehner. St. Bonaventure, N.Y.: Franciscan Institute, 1955.

Walter Chatton, *Questio utrum quantum et continuum componantur ex indivisibilibus sicut ex partibus integrantibus*. Ed. J. Murdoch and E. Synan. *Franciscan Studies* 26 (1966): 234–266.

————, *Reportatio super Sententias*. 4 vols. Ed. Joseph Wey and Girard Etzkorn. Toronto: Pontifical Institute, 2002–2005.

William Crathorn, *Quaestiones super librum sententiarum*. In F. Hoffmann, ed., *Questionen Zum ersten Sentenzenbuch*. Münster: Aschendorff, 1988.

William Ockham, *A Letter to the Friars Minor and Other Writings*. Ed. and Trans. A. S. McGrade and John Kilcullen. Cambridge: Cambridge University Press, 1995.

————, *Opera Philosophica*. 7 vols. Ed. Philotheus Boehner, Gedeon Gàl, et al. St. Bonaventure, N.Y.: Franciscan Institute, 1974–1988.

————, *Predestination, God's Foreknowledge, and Future Contingents*. Ed. Marilyn McCord Adams and Norman Kretzman. Indianapolis, Ind.: Hackett, 1983.

————, *Tractatus de Principiis Theologiae*. Trans. Julian Davies. Published as *A Compendium of Ockham's Teachings*. St. Bonaventure, N.Y.: Franciscan Institute, 1998.

SECONDARY SOURCES

Adams, Marilyn McCord, *William Ockham*. 2 vols. Notre Dame, Ind.: University of Notre Dame Press, 1988.

Aston, Margaret, "'Caim's Castles': Poverty, Politics, and Disendowment." In Barrie Dobson, ed., *The Church, Politics, and Patronage in the Fifteenth Century* (Gloucester, 1984), 45–81. Reprinted in Aston, *Faith and Fire*, 95–132.

————, *Lollards and Reformers: Images and Literacy in Late Medieval Religion*. London: Hambledon, 1984.

Benrath, Gustav, *Wyclif's Bibelkommentar*. Berlin: de Gruyter, 1966.

Beonio-Brocchieri Fumigalli, M. T., and M. Parodi, *Storia della Filosophia Medievale: Da Boezio a Wyclif*. Rome: Editori Laterza, 1988.

Biller, Peter, and Anne Hudson, eds., *Heresy and Literacy, 1000–1530*. Cambridge: Cambridge University Press, 1994.

Breck, Allan DuPont, "John Wyclyf on Time." In W. Yourgrau and Allen d. Breck, eds., *Cosmology, History, and Theology*, 211–218. New York: Plenum, 1977.

————, "The Manuscripts of Wyclif's *De Trinitate*." *Medievalia et Humanistica*, o.s. 7 (1952): 56–70.

Breen, Aidan, "Pseudo-Cyprian *De Duodecim Abusivis Saeculi* and the Bible." In *Irland und die Christenheit*, 1987.

Burns, J. H., ed., *The Cambridge History of Medieval Political Thought c. 350–c. 1450*. Cambridge: Cambridge University Press, 1988.

Burr, David, *Olivi and Franciscan Poverty*. Philadelphia: University of Pennsylvania Press, 1989.

———, "Scotus and Transubstantiation." *Mediaeval Studies* 34 (1972): 336–360.

Catto, J. I., and Ralph Evans, eds., *The History of the University of Oxford*: vol. 2, *Late Medieval Oxford*. Oxford: Oxford University Press, 1992.

———, "John Wyclif and the Cult of the Eucharist." In Walsh and Wood 269–286.

Cesalli, Laurent, "Le 'pan-propositionalisme' de Jean Wyclif." *Vivarium* 43.1: 124–155.

———, *Le réalisme propositionnel: Sémantique et ontologie des propositions chez Jean Duns Scot, Gauthier Burley, Richard Brinkley et Jean Wyclif*. Paris: Vrin, 2007.

———, "Some Fourteenth-Century Realist Theories of the Proposition: A Historical and Speculative Study." In H. S. Gill, ed., *Signification in Language and Culture*, 83–118. Shimla: Indian Institute of Advanced Studies, 2002.

Conti, Alessandro, "Analogy and Formal Distinction: On the Logical Basis of Wyclif's Metaphysics." *Medieval Philosophy and Theology* 6.2 (September 1997): 133–165.

———, "Divine Ideas and Exemplar Causality in Auriol." *Vivarium* 38 (2000): 99–116.

———, "Logica intensionale e metafisica dell'essenza in John Wyclif." *Bullettino dell'Instituto Storico Italiano per il Medioevo e Archivio Muratoriano* 99.1 (1993): 159–219.

———, "Wyclif's Logic and Metaphysics." In Levy 67–126.

Courtenay, William J., *Adam Wodeham*. Leiden: Brill, 1978.

———, "*Antiqui* and *Moderni* in Late Medieval Thought." *Journal of the History of Ideas* 48.1 (1987): 3–10.

———, "Augustinianism at Oxford in the Fourteenth Century." *Augustiniana* 30 (1980): 58–70.

———, *Capacity and Volition*. Bergamo: Pierluigi Lubrina, 1990.

———, "The Dialectic of Divine Omnipotence." In *Covenant and Causality in Medieval Thought*, 1–37. London, 1984.

———, "The Effect of the Black Death on English Higher Education." *Speculum* 55.4 (1980): 696–714.

———, "Force of Words and Figures of Speech: The Crisis over *Virtus Sermonis* in the Fourteenth Century." *Franciscan Studies* 44 (1984): 107–128.

———, "The Reception of Ockham's Thought in Fourteenth-Century England." In Hudson and Wilks 89–107.

———, *Schools and Scholars in Fourteenth-Century England*. Princeton, N.J.: Princeton University Press, 1987.

Crompton, James J., "*Fasciculi Zizaniorum*." *Journal of Ecclesiastical History* 12 (1961): 35–45, 155–165.

Dahmus, Joseph, *The Prosecution of John Wyclyf.* New Haven, Conn.: Yale University Press, 1952.

Daly, Lowrie J., *The Political Theory of John Wyclif.* Chicago: Loyola University Press, 1962.

Dawson, James Doyne, "Richard Fitzralph and the Fourteenth-Century Poverty Controversies." *Journal of Ecclesiastical History* 34 (1983).

Deanesly, Margaret, *The Lollard Bible and Other Medieval Biblical Versions.* Cambridge: Cambridge University Press, 1920. Rpt., Eugene, Ore.: Wipf and Stock, 2002.

Denery, Dallas, "From Sacred Mystery to Divine Deception: Robert Holkot, John Wyclif and the Transformation of Fourteenth-Century Eucharistic Discourse." *Journal of Religious History* 29.2 (June 2005): 129–144.

Dipple, Geoffrey L., "Uthred and the Friars: Apostolic Poverty and Clerical Dominion between Fitzralph and Wyclif." *Traditio* 49 (1994): 235–358.

Dolnikowski, Edith, "The Encouragement of Lay Preaching as an Ecclesiastical Critique in Wyclif's Latin Sermons." In Beverly M. Kinzie et al., eds., *Models of Holiness in Medieval Sermons*, 193–209. Louvain-la-Neuve: Fédération Internationale des Institutes d'Etudes Médiévales, 1996.

———, "Preaching at Oxford: Academic and Pastoral Themes in Wyclif's Latin Sermon Cycle." In J. Hamesse et al., eds., *Medieval Sermons and Society: Cloister, City, University*, 371–386. Louvain-la-Neuve: Fédération Internationale des Institutes d'Etudes Médiévales, 1998.

Doyle, Eric, O.F.M., "William Woodford, O.F.M., His Life and Works." *Franciscan Studies* 43 (1983): 17–187.

———, "William Woodford's *De Dominio Civili Clericorum* against John Wyclif." *Archivum Franciscanum Historicum* 66 (1973): 49–109.

Evans, G. R., *John Wyclif: Myth and Reality.* Lion Hudson, 2005.

———, *Mediaeval Commentaries on the Sentences of Peter Lombard*, vol. 1. Leiden: Brill, 2002.

———, "Wyclif on Literal and Metaphorical." In Hudson and Wilks 259–266.

Farr, William, *Wyclif as Legal Reformer.* Leiden: Brill, 1974.

Fletcher, John M., "Inter-Faculty Disputes in Late Medieval Oxford." In Hudson and Wilks 331–342.

Fumigalli, Maria Theresa, and Stefano Simonetta, eds., *John Wyclif: Logica, Politica, Teologia.* Florence: Sismel, 2003.

Gelber, Hester, *Exploring the Boundaries of Reason: Three Questions on the Nature of God by Robert Holcot, OP.* Toronto: University of Toronto Press, 1983.

———, *It Could Have Been Otherwise: Contingency and Necessity in Dominican Theology at Oxford 1300–1350.* Leiden: Brill, 2004.

Ghosh, Kantik, *The Wycliffite Heresy: Authority and the Interpretation of Texts.* Cambridge: Cambridge University Press, 2002.

Grabmann, Martin, *Studien über den Einfluss der aristotelischen Philosophie auf die mittelalterlichen Theorien über das Verhältniss von Kirche und Staat.* Munich, 1934.

Gwynn, Aubrey, *The English Austin Friars in the Time of Wyclif.* Oxford: Oxford University Press, 1940.

Harvey, Margaret, "Adam Easton and the Condemnation of John Wyclif." *English Historical Review* 113 (April 1998): 321–335.

Henry, Desmond P., *Medieval Mereology.* Amsterdam: Grüner, 1991.

———, "Wyclif's Deviant Mereology." In Olaf Pluta, ed., *Die Philosophie im 14. Und 15. Jahrhundert*, 1–17. Amsterdam, 1988.

Herold, Vilém, "Platonic Ideas and 'Hussite' Philosophy." In David R. Holeton, ed., *The Bohemian Reformation and Religious Practice*: vol. 1, *Papers from the 17th World Congress of the Czechoslovak Society of Arts and* Sciences, 13–18. Prague: Academy of Sciences of the Czech Republic, Main Library, 1994.

Hoenen, Martin, "Theology and Metaphysics: The Debate between John Wyclif and John Kenningham on the Principles of Reading the Scriptures." In Fumagalli and Simonetta 23–56.

Hoffmann, Fritz, *Die "Conferentiae" des Robert Holcot O.P. und die Akademischen Auseinandersetzungen an der Univerität Oxford 1330–1332.* Münster, 1993.

Hudson, Anne, *"Accessus ad auctorem:* The Case of John Wyclif." *Viator* 30 (1999): 323–344.

———, "Aspects of the 'Publication' of Wyclif's Latin Sermons." In Minnis, *Late Medieval Religious Texts*, 121–129.

———, "Cross-Referencing in Wyclif's Latin Works." In Peter Biller and Barrie Dobson, eds., *The Medieval Church: University, Heresy, and the Religious Life* (1999), 193–216.

———, "From Oxford to Prague: The Writings of John Wyclif and His English Followers in Bohemia." *Slavonic and East European Review* 75 (October 1997): 642–658.

———, *Lollards and Their Books.* London: Hambledon, 1985.

———, "The Mouse in the Pyx: Popular Heresy and the Eucharist." *Trivium* 26 (1991): 40–53.

———, "Poor Preachers, Poor Men: Views of Poverty in Wyclif and His Followers." In Šmahel and Müller-Luckner 41–54.

———, *The Premature Reformation: Wycliffite Texts and Lollard History.* Oxford: Clarendon, 1988.

———, "Wyclif and the English Language." In Kenny 85–103.

———, "Wycliffism in Oxford 1381–1411." In Kenny 67–84.

———, "Wyclif's Latin Sermons: Questions of Form, Date and Audience." *Archives d'Histoire Doctrinale et Littéraire du Moyen Âge* 68 (2001): 223–248.

Hudson, Anne, and M. Wilks, eds., *From Ockham to Wyclif*. Oxford: Blackwell, 1987.

Hurley, Michael, "'Scriptura Sola': Wyclif and His Critics." *Traditio* 16 (1960): 275–352.

Jurkowski, Maureen, "Heresy and Factionalism at Merton College in the Early Fifteenth Century." *Journal of Ecclesiastical History* 48 (October 1997): 658–681.

Justice, Steven, *Writing and Rebellion: England in 1381*. Berkeley: University of California Press, 1994.

Kaluza, Zénon, "Late Medieval Philosophy, 1350–1500." In John Marenbon, ed., *Routledge History of Philosophy*: vol. 3, *Late Medieval Philosophy*, 426–451. New York: Routledge, 1998.

————, "L'ouevre théologique de Richard Brinkley, OFM." *Archives d'Histoire Doctrinale et Littéraire du Moyen Age* 56:169–273.

Kaminsky, Howard, "Wyclifism as Ideology of Revolution." *Church History* 32 (1963): 57–74.

Keen, Maurice, *England in the Later Middle Ages: A Political History*. London: Methuen, 1973.

————, "The Influence of Wyclif." In Kenny 127–145.

————, "Wyclif, the Bible, and Transubstantiation." In Kenny 1–17.

Kennedy, Leonard A., "Late-Fourteenth-Century Philosophical Scepticism at Oxford." *Vivarium* 23.2 (1985): 124–151.

————, "Philosophical Scepticism in England in the Mid-Fourteenth Century." *Vivarium* 21.1 (1983): 43–44.

————, *The Philosophy of Robert Holcot: A Fourteenth-Century Skeptic*. Lewiston, Maine: Mellen, 1993.

Kenny, Anthony, "Realism and Determinism in the Early Wyclif." In Hudson and Wilks 165–178.

————, *Wyclif*. Oxford: Oxford University Press, 1985.

Kenny, Anthony, ed., *Wyclif in His Times*. Oxford: Clarendon, 1986.

Kerby-Fulton, Kathryn, *Books under Suspicion: Censorship and Tolerance of Revelatory Writing in Late Medieval England*. Notre Dame, Ind.: Notre Dame University Press, 2006.

Knowles, David, "The Censured Opinions of Uthred of Boldon." In D. Knowles, ed., *The Historian and Character and Other* Essays, 129–170. Cambridge: University of Cambridge Press, 1963.

————, *The Religious Orders in England*. 3 vols. Cambridge: Cambridge University Press, 1961.

Kretzman, Norman, "Continua, Indivisibles, and Change in Wyclif's Logic of Scripture." In Kenny 31–65.

Kretzman, Norman, and Barbara Ensign Kretzman, *The Sophismata of Richard Kilvington*. Cambridge: Cambridge University Press, 1990.

Kretzman, Norman, Anthony Kenny, and Jan Pinborg, eds., *The Cambridge History of Later Medieval Philosophy*. Cambridge: Cambridge University Press, 1982.

Lahey, Stephen, *Philosophy and Politics in the Thought of John Wyclif*. Cambridge: Cambridge University Press, 2003.

————, "Wyclif on Rights." *Journal of the History of Ideas* 58 (1997): 1–20.

————, "Wyclif's Formal Theology." In Ian Levy, ed., *The Companion to John Wyclif*. Leiden: Brill, 2006.

Lambert, M. D., *Franciscan Poverty*. St. Bonaventure, N.Y.: Franciscan Institute, 1998.

Larsen, Andrew E., "The Oxford 'School of Heretics': The Unexamined Case of Friar John." *Vivarium* 37.2 (1999): 168–177.

Lechler, Gotthard, *Johann von Wiclif und die Vorgeschichte der Reformation*. 2 vols. Leipzig, 1873. Published as *John Wycliffe and His English Precursors*, trans. Peter Lorimer. 2 vols. London: Religious Tract Society, 1884.

Leff, Gordon, *Bradwardine and the Pelagians*. Cambridge: Cambridge University Press, 1957.

————, *Heresy in the Later Middle Ages: The Relation of Heterodoxy to Dissent, c. 1250–c. 1450*. 2 vols. Manchester: Manchester University Press, 1967.

————, "Ockham and Wyclif on the Eucharist." *Reading Medieval Studies* 2 (1976): 1–13.

————, "The Place of Metaphysics in Wyclif's Theology." In Hudson and Wilks 217–232.

————, *Richard Fitzralph: Commentator on the Sentences*. Manchester: Manchester University Press, 1963.

————, "Wyclif and the Augustinian Tradition, with Special Reference to His *De Trinitate.*" *Medievalia et Humanistica*, n.s. 1 (1970): 29–39.

————, "Wyclif and Hus: A Doctrinal Comparison." *Bulletin of the John Ryland's Library* 50 (1967): 387–410. Revised version in Kenny 105–125.

Levy, Ian, "*Christus Qui Mentiri Non Potest*: John Wyclif's Rejection of Transubstantiation." *Recherches de Theologie et Philosophie Medievales* (1999): 316–334.

————, "Defining the Responsibility of the Late Medieval Theologian: The Debate between John Kynnyngham and John Wyclif." *Carmelus* 19 (2002): fasc. 1:5–29.

————, "The Fight for the Sacred Sense in Late Medieval England." *Anglican Theological Review* 85 (2003): 165–176.

————, "Grace and Freedom in the Soteriology of John Wyclif." *Traditio* 60 (2005): 279–337.

————, "John Wyclif and Augustinian Realism." *Augustiniana* (1998): fasc. 1–2:87–106.

————, *John Wyclif: Scriptural Logic, Real Presence, and the Parameters of Orthodoxy*. Milwaukee, Wis.: Marquette University Press, 2003.

————, "John Wyclif's Neoplatonic View of Scripture in Its Christological Context." *Medieval Philosophy and Theology* 2 (2003):. 227–240.

————, "Texts for a Poor Church: John Wyclif and the Decretals." *Essays in Medieval Studies* 20.1 (February 2004): 94–107.

————, "Was John Wyclif's Theology of the Eucharist Donatistic?" *Scottish Journal of Theology* 53 (2000): 137–153.

Levy, Ian, ed., *A Companion to John Wyclif, Late Medieval Theologian*. Leiden: Brill, 2006.

Lewis, John, *The History of the Life and Sufferings of the Reverend and Learned John Wiclif, D.D.* London, 1720. Rpt., New York: AMS, 1973.

Loserth, Johann, *Wycliffe and Huss*. Trans. M. J. Evans. London, 1884.

Luscombe, David, "Wyclif and Hierarchy." In Hudson and Wilks 233–244.

Mallard, William, "Clarity and Dilemma: The *Forty Sermons* of John Wyclif." In G. H. Shriver et al., eds., *Contemporary Reflections on the Medieval Christian Tradition: Essays in Honor of Ray C. Petry*, 19–38. Durham, N.C.: Duke University Press, 1974.

————, "Dating the *Sermones Quadraginta* of John Wyclif." *Medievalia et Humanistica*, o.s. 17 (1966): 86–104.

————, "John Wyclif and the Tradition of Biblical Authority." *Church History* 30 (1961): 50–60.

McFarlane, K. B., *John Wycliffe and the Beginnings of English Nonconformity*. London: English Universities Press, 1953.

McGrade, A. S., *The Political Thought of William Ockham*. Cambridge: Cambridge University Press, 1974.

————, "Somersaulting Sovereignty: A Note on Reciprocal Lordship and Servitude in Wyclif." In Wood 261–278.

Michael, Emily, "Wyclif on Body and Soul." *Journal of the History of Ideas* (2003): 343–360.

Michalski, Constantin, *Le Criticisme et le Scepticisme dans la Philosophie du XIVe Siècle*. Cracow, 1926. Reprinted in *La Philosophie au XIVe Siècle: Six Etudes*. Frankfurt, 1969.

Minnis, Alastair J., "'Authorial Intention' and 'Literal Sense' in the Exegetical Theories of Richard Fitzralph and John Wyclif: An Essay in the Medieval Theories of Biblical Hermeneutics." *Proceedings of the Royal Irish Academy* (Section C) 75.1 (1975): 1–30.

————, *Medieval Theory of Authorship*. 2nd ed. Aldershot, England: Wildwood House, 1988.

Muckle, J. T., "*Utrum Theologia Sit Scientia:* A Quodlibetal Question of Robert Holcot, O.P." *Mediaeval Studies* 20 (1958): 127–153.

Mueller, Ivan J., "A 'Lost' Summa of John Wyclif." In Hudson and Wilks 179–183.

Nuchelmans, Gabriel, "Adam Wodeham on the Meaning of Declarative Sentences." *Historiographia Linguistica* 7 (1980): 177–187.

Oberman, Heiko A., *Archbishop Thomas Bradwardine, a Fourteenth-Century Augustinian: A Study of His Theology in Its Historical Context.* Utrecht: Kemink and Zoon, 1958.

———, "*Facientibus Quod in se est Deus non Denegat Gratiam*: Robert Holcot, O. P., and the Beginnings of Luther's Theology." In Oberman, *The Dawn of the Reformation*, 84–103. Grand Rapids, Mich., 1992.

———, *The Harvest of Late Medieval Theology: Gabriel Biel and Late Medieval Nominalism.* 3rd ed. Durham: Labyrinth, 1983.

Owst, G. R., *Literature and Pulpit in Medieval England.* 2nd ed. Oxford: Oxford University Press, 1961.

———, *Preaching in Medieval England.* Cambridge: Cambridge University Press, 1926.

Pantin, William A., "A Benedictine Opponent of John Wyclif." *English Historical Review* 43 (1928): 73–77.

———, "The *Defensorium* of Adam Easton." *English Historical Review* 51 (1936): 675–680.

———, *The English Church in the Fourteenth Century.* Cambridge: Cambridge University Press, 1955.

Penn, Stephen, "Antiquity, Eternity, and the Foundations of Authority: Reflections on a Debate between John Wyclif and John Kenningham, O.Carm." *Trivium* 32 (2000): 107–119.

Phillips, Heather, "John Wyclif and the Optics of the Eucharist." In Hudson and Wilks 245–258.

Pyper, Rachel, "An Abridgement of Wyclif's *De Mandatis Divinis.*" *Medium Aevum* 52.2 (1983): 306–310.

Read, Stephen, "'I Promise a Penny That I Do Not Promise': The Realist/ Nominalist Debate over Intentional Propositions in Fourteenth-Century British Logic and Its Contemporary Relevance." In P. O. Lewry, ed., *The Rise of British Logic*, 335–359. Toronto: Pontifical Institute, 1985.

Rex, Richard, *The Lollards.* London: Palgrave, 2002.

Robson, J. A., *Wyclif and the Oxford Schools: The Relation of the "Summa de Ente" to Scholastic Debates at Oxford in the Later Fourteenth Century.* Cambridge: Cambridge University Press, 1961.

Rubin, Miri, *Corpus Christi: The Eucharist in Late Medieval Culture.* Cambridge: Cambridge University Press, 1991.

Sergeant, Lewis, *John Wyclif: Last of the Schoolmen and First of the English Reformers*. New York, 1893. Rpt., New York: AMS, 1978.

Shogimen, Takashi, "Wyclif's Ecclesiology and Political Thought" In Levy 199–240.

Simonetta, Stefano, "The Concept of Two Churches in the Religious Philosophy of the English Reformer, John Wyclif." *Studi Medievali* 40 (1999): 119–137.

———, "John Wyclif between Utopia and Plan." In Sophie Wlodek, ed., *Société et Église: Textes et discussions dans les universités de l'Europe centrale pendant le moyen âge tardif*, 65–86. Turnhout, Belgium: Brepols, 1995.

———, "La maturazione del progetto riformatore di Giovanni Wyclif: Dal *De Civili Dominio* al *De Officio Regis*." *Medioevo* 22 (1996): 225–258.

———, "Una riforma prematura? Realizzabilita del progetto di Wyclif." *Pensiero Politico: Rivista di Storia della Idee Politiche e Sociali* 29.3 (1996): 343–373.

———, "Una singolare alleanza: Wyclif e Lancaster [A Singular Alliance: John Wyclif and the Duke of Lancaster: A Study of Ecclesial Politics in the Fourteenth-Century English Church]." *Studi Medievali* 36.2 (1995): 797–837.

———, "Two Parallel Trains of Anti-Hierocratic Thought in the Fourteenth Century: Marsilius of Padua and John Wyclif." *Rivista Di Storia Della Philosophia* 52.1 (1997): 91–110.

Smalley, Beryl, "The Bible and Eternity: John Wyclif's Dilemma." *Journal of the Warburg and Courtauld Institutes* 27 (1964): 73–89. Reprinted in Beryl Smalley, ed., *Studies in Medieval Thought and Learning from Abelard to Wyclif*, 399–415. London: Hambledon, 1981.

———, *English Friars and Antiquity in the Early Fourteenth Century*. Oxford: Blackwell, 1960.

———, "John Wyclif's *Postilla Super Totam Bibliam*." *Bodleian Library Record* 5 (1953): 186–205.

———, "Problems of Exegesis in the Fourteenth Century." In Paul Wilpert, ed., *Antike und Orient im Mittelalter*, 266–274. Berlin: de Gruyter, 1962.

———, *The Study of the Bible in the Middle Ages*. Notre Dame, Ind.: University of Notre Dame Press, 1964.

Somerset, Fiona, *Clerical Discourse and Lay Audience in Late Medieval England*. Cambridge: Cambridge University Press, 1998.

Spade, Paul V., *A Cambridge Companion to Ockham*. Cambridge: Cambridge University Press, 1999.

———, "Universals and Wyclif's Alleged 'Ultrarealism.' " *Vivarium* 43.1 (2004): 111–123.

Stein, I. H., "Another 'Lost' Chapter of Wyclif's *Summa de Ente*." *Speculum* 3 (1928): 254–255.

————, "Two Notes on Wyclif." *Speculum* 6 (1931): 465–468.

————, "The Wyclif Manuscript in Florence." *Speculum* 5 (1930): 95–97.

Streveler, Paul A., "Gregory of Rimini and the Black Monk on Sense and Reference." *Vivarium* 18.1 (1980).

Sylla, Edith Dudley, "The Oxford Calculators." In Kretzman, Kenny, and Pinborg 540–563.

Szittya, Penn, *The Antifraternal Tradition in Medieval Literature*. Princeton, N.J.: Princeton University Press, 1986.

Tachau, Katherine, *Vision and Certitude in the Age of Ockham*. Leiden: Brill, 1988.

Tatnall, Edith Comfort, "The Condemnation of John Wyclif at the Council of Constance." In G. J. Cuming and D. Baker, eds., *Councils and Assemblies*, 209–218. Oxford: Blackwell, 1977.

————, "John Wyclif and Ecclesia Anglicana." *Journal of Ecclesiastical History* 30 (1969): 19–43.

Thomson, S. Harrison, "A Gonville and Caius Wyclif Manuscript." *Speculum* 8 (1933): 197–204.

————, "John Wyclif's 'Lost' *De Fide Sacramentorum*." *Journal of Theological Studies* 33 (1932): 359–365.

————, "The Order of Writing of Wyclif's Philosophical Works." In O. Odlozilík et al., eds., *Ceskou Minulostí*, 146–165. Prague, 1929.

————, "The Philosophical Basis of Wyclif's Theology." *Journal of Religion* 11.2 (January 1931): 86–116.

————, "Some Latin Works Erroneously Ascribed to Wyclif." *Speculum* 3 (1928): 382–391.

————, "Three Unprinted *Opuscula* of John Wyclif." *Speculum* 3 (1928): 248–253.

————, "Unnoticed Manuscripts and Works of Wyclif." *Journal of Theological Studies* 38 (1937): 24–36, 139–148.

————, "Unnoticed Manuscripts of Wyclyf's *De Veritate Sacre Scripture*." *Medium Aevum* 12 (1943): 68–70.

————, "Wyclif or Wyclyf?" *English Historical Review* 53 (1938): 675–678.

Thomson, Williell R., *The Latin Writings of John Wyclyf*. Toronto: Pontifical Institute, 1983.

————, "*Manuscripta Wycliffiana Desiderata*: The Potential Contribution of Missing Latin Texts to Our Image of Wyclif's Life and Works." In Hudson and Wilks 343–351.

————, "An Unknown Letter by John Wyclyf in Manchester, John Rylands University Library MS. Eng. 86." *Mediaeval Studies* 43 (1981): 531–537.

Treschow, Michael, "On Aristotle and the Cross at the Center of Creation: John Wyclif's *De Benedicta Incarnacione*, Chapter Seven." *Crux* 33 (1977): 28–37.

Tresko, Michael, "John Wyclif's Metaphysics of Scriptural Integrity in the *De Veritate Sacrae Scripturae*." *Dionysius* 13 (December 1989): 153–196.

Unguru, Sabetai, *"Witelonis Perspectivae Liber Primus."* Studia Copernicana 15 (1977).

van Nolcken, Christina, "Another Kind of Saint: A Lollard Perception of John Wyclif." In Hudson and Wilks 429–443.

Vaughan, Robert, *The Life and Opinions of John De Wycliffe, D.D.* 2 vols. 2nd ed. London: Holdsworth and Ball, 1831.

Walsh, Katherine, *A Fourteenth-Century Scholar and Primate: Richard Fitzralph of Oxford, Avignon, and Armagh.* Oxford: Oxford University Press, 1981.

Walsh, Katherine, and Diana Wood, eds., *The Bible in the Medieval World: Essays in Memory of Beryl Smalley.* Oxford: Blackwell, 1985.

Weinberg, Julius, *Nicholas of Autrecourt.* Princeton, N.J.: Princeton University Press, 1948.

Wenzel, Siegfried, "Academic Sermons at Oxford in the Early Fifteenth Century." *Speculum* 70.2 (April 1995): 305–329.

———, *Latin Sermon Collections from Later Medieval England: Orthodox Preaching in the Age of Wyclif.* Cambridge: Cambridge University Press, 2005.

———, "A New Version of Wyclif's 'Sermones Quadraginta.'" *Journal of Theological Studies* 49 (April 1998): 154–160.

Wilks, Michael, "The Early Oxford Wyclif: Papalist or Nominalist?" *Studies in Church History* 5 (1969): 69–98.

———, "Predestination, Property and Power: Wyclif's Theory of Dominion and Grace." *Studies in Church History* 2 (1965): 220–236.

———, *"Reformatio Regni:* Wyclif and Hus as Leaders of Religious Protest Movements." *Studies in Church History* 9 (1972): 109–130.

———, "Royal Patronage and Anti-Papalism: From Ockham to Wyclif." *Studies in Church History Subsidia* 5 (1987): 135–163.

———, "Royal Priesthood: The Origins of Lollardy." In *The Church in a Changing Society: CIHEC Conference in Uppsala 1977*, 135–163. Uppsala, 1978.

———, *"Thesaurus Ecclesiae."* Studies in Church History 24 (1987): xv–xlv.

———, "Wyclif and the Great Persecution." *Studies in Church History Subsidia* 10 (1994): 39–63.

———, *Wyclif: Political Ideas and Practice.* Ed. Anne Hudson. Oxford: Oxbow, 2000.

———, "Wyclif and the Wheel of Time." *Studies in Church History* 33 (1997): 177–193.

Wilson, Curtis, *William Heytesbury: Medieval Logic and the Rise of Mathematical Physics.* Madison: University of Wisconsin Press, 1956.

Wood, Diana, ed., *The Church and Sovereignty c. 590–1918: Essays in Honour of Michael Wilks.* Oxford: Blackwell, 1991.

Wood, Rega, and Gedeon Gàl, "Richard Brinkley and His Summa Logica." *Franciscan Studies* 40 (1980): 59–102.

Workman, Herbert B., *John Wyclif: A Study of the English Medieval Church.* 2 vols. Oxford: Clarendon, 1926.

INTERNET RESOURCES

Aurélien, Robert, "William Crathorn." *Stanford Encyclopedia of Philosophy.* Available at http://plato.stanford.edu/entries/crathorn/#Oth.

Gelber, Hester, "Robert Holcot." *Stanford Encyclopedia of Philosophy.* Available at http://plato.stanford.edu/entries/holkot.

INDEX